The Rough Guide to
Elvis

Paul Simpson

Credits

Text editors: Greg Ward and Mark Ellingham
Design: Henry Iles Lay-out: Helen Prior
Proofreading: Nikky Twyman Production: Michelle Draycott

Thanks

For taking care of business: Richard Pendleton, Steven Morewood, Juliette Wills,
John Aizlewood, Jo Berry, Uli Hesse-Lichtenberger, Steve Ellerhoff, Peter Nazareth,
Trevor Cajiao, Arjan Deelen, Greg Howell, Simon Kanter, and every fan who picked
their 12 favourite Elvis songs. For interviews: Hal Blaine, Ed Bonja, Estelle Brown,
Bill Burk, Michael Bertrand, Richard Davis, Mike Freeman, Larry Geller, George
Klein, Bernard Lansky, Greil Marcus, Charlie McCoy, Scotty Moore, Donna Presley,
Norbert Putnam, Boots Randolph, Jerry Schilling, Myrna Smith. And a special
thanks to Ernst Jorgensen. Thanks also to the members of the Special Merit
Department: Greg Ward, Mark Ellingham, Henry Iles, Helen Prior, Michelle
Draycott, Nikky Twyman, and Lesley Simpson. And thanks above all to Valerie
Simpson, for introducing the author to Elvis Presley and for everything else.

Publishing Information

This first edition published July 2002 by Rough Guides Ltd,
62-70 Shorts Gardens, London WC2H 9AH
Printed in Spain by Graphy Cems

Distributed by the Penguin Group

Penguin Books Ltd, 80 Strand, London WC2R ORL
Penguin Putnam, Inc., 345 Hudson Street, NY 10014, USA
Penguin Books Australia Ltd, 487 Maroondah Highway, PO Box 257,
Ringwood, Victoria 3134, Australia
Penguin Books Canada Ltd, 10 Alcorn Avenue, Toronto, Ontario, Canada M4V 1E4
Penguin Books (NZ) Ltd, 182–190 Wairau Road, Auckland 10, New Zealand

© Paul Simpson, 2002
480pp, includes index
A catalogue record for this book is available from the British Library
ISBN 1-84353-119-4

Contents

*'Hearing Elvis for the first time
was like busting out of jail'*

Bob Dylan

It might seem the world needs a new book about Elvis Presley about as much as it needs another Elvis impersonator – and at the present rate of expansion there will be more fake Elvises than Belgians by the end of the decade. But the man who maybe changed more lives in the Western world in the second half of the twentieth century than anyone is not – to this fan, at least – given due respect. Too many books, too many articles, seem to see the King as a pharmaceutical or psychological curiosity. Too many writers and critics who should know better spin the fable of a musician who had a brief glory at Sun Studios ... then got his haircut, joined the army, made bad movies, and went to Vegas.

This book, by contrast, is primarily about the Elvis who inspired Dylan and countless others: the King of Rock'n'Roll, the man who sung "Baby Let's Play House" and "Long Black Limousine", "That's Alright Mama' and "Hound Dog", "Promised Land" and "In The Ghetto." The man who defined rock'n'roll culture in the 1950s and, in so doing, shaped the present. The singer who, more than anyone, *is* America.

To this end, the *Rough Guide* charts a course through the Presley career, with its many peaks and plentiful troughs, and attempts along the way to track his life and personality. In this quest, we range through the whole panoply of Elvis: his life (and curious afterlife), his music (with reviews of every major album released in his lifetime and the best of the posthumous releases), his movie career (which could have meant so much to him but ended in ignominy), his most essential songs and the stories behind them, the genres that he influenced and the artists who influenced him. Then there's a guide to Elvis country – with a full tour of Graceland and Memphis, Tupelo and Las Vegas – and a look at the power of Elvis as an icon, because he always had (and still has) that other mythic dimension. We take a look, too, at the Elvis industry, from the best books and websites, to the memorabilia that has engulfed the King, both in life and death.

Critic Nick Tosches famously observed that 'Elvis Presley is a mystery that may never be solved' and although that's likely the case, we hope you'll get something new from this book, however long and however much you've loved Elvis. The background to a song, maybe, which means you never hear it the same way again; the fun of a movie you'd never considered; or the style and wit of a man who was sharper than most players in the rock'n'roll hall of fame. Above all, we hope it turns you back to the real treasure: the songs, the voice which, twenty-five years after its death, continues to astonish even those of us who have spent most of our lives lustening to it with its power, range, and subtlety but, above all, with its very believability.

Elvisly yours
Paul Simpson

Photo Credits

The Life

"Every dream I ever dreamed has come
true a hundred times" *Elvis Presley*

'You have to understand that Elvis was a true chameleon. I promise you, they couldn't put up a maze in a castle like what was in his mind'

Lamar Fike

Elvis Presley may be both the most famous, misunderstood, figure of the twentieth century. The story of his life and death can be seen as a cautionary tale, in the vein of "Long Black Limousine", in which an innocent country boy is fatally tempted by the lights of the big city. It can be seen as a tragic commentary on the American dream, in which the dream becomes a terrible nightmare. Or, if you let Albert Goldman be your guide, you can see it as a tale told by an idiot, full of sound and fury, and signifying not very much at all.

The avalanche of Presley biographies doesn't always help. The best – Peter Guralnick's excellent two-volume set, *Last Train To Memphis* and *Careless Love*, are complemented by Elaine Dundy's near-definitive account of the early years, and Alanna Nash's oral biography. Unfortunately, while reading one Elvis biography can give you a wonderfully clear view of his life, read a second and you might feel as though you're watching one of those movies where every character tells the same basic story to devastatingly different effect.

The multiracial Elvis

While Elvis Presley may seem as American as Coca-Cola, his roots are far more complex than his public image of a God-fearing white Southerner might suggest. The Presley name has been traced to 1745, when a Scots blacksmith called **Andrew Presley** emigrated to North America, while his maternal line can be plotted back to the Scots-Irish **Mansell** family, and, as that means 'of Le Mans', eventually to France.

Elvis the Scot

The family trees of both Elvis's mother and his father point back to **Scotland**. **Richard Mansell**, Elvis's great-great-great-great-grandfather, was part of the Scots-Irish emigration from Ulster to America. Having fought in the War of Independence, he made his home in South Carolina. **Andrew Presley** – Elvis's great-great-great-great-great-grandfather, moved to North Carolina from Scotland. A clergyman's description of a typical Scots-Irish settler, quoted by Elaine Dundy, sounds remarkably like Elvis: He had the will to dare and the power to execute; there was something in his look which bespoke a disdain of control, and an absence of all constraint in all his movements.'

Elvis Schmelvis

The idea that **Jewish** blood flowed in Elvis's veins is still controversial; his cousin Billy Smith flatly denies it. But Dundy says that his great-great-grandmother **Nancy Burdine**, whose daughter **Martha Tacket** married White Mansell, Elvis's great-grandfather, was Jewish. Elvis himself joked about the *chi*, a Jewish symbol of life, that he wore around his neck: 'I don't want to miss out on heaven on a technicality.' He also had Star of David watches made for his close friends, four of whom – Alan Fortas, Larry Geller, George Klein and Marty Lacker – were Jewish. Klein says, 'When Gladys died, when they buried her in Memphis, on the foot stone he put a Star of David on one side and a crucifixion on the other ... I said, "Elvis that's great but why

Elvis school graduation shot in June 1953 – the lip's ready to curl

would you do that?" And he just smiled.'

Elvis the Native American

Elvis's great-great-great-grandmother, on his mother's side of the family, was a Cherokee Indian called **Morning Dove White**, who married **William Mansell**, one of Andrew Jackson's soldiers, in 1818. Elaine Dundy speculates that he owed his promiscuity to their eldest son, **John Mansell**, his great-great-grandfather. Billy Smith says, 'Elvis knew he had Indian blood in him. He liked that. He said that's where he got his high cheekbones.'

Elvis the Southerner

Elvis, says his sometime piano player **David Briggs** was 'a cultured Southern gentleman who knew the name of every Confederate general in the Civil War'. His Southern identity was central to both his personality and his image. **Michael Bertrand**, author of *Race, Rock And Elvis*, says, 'A lot of the hostility he attracted early on was thinly disguised regional hostility and he would often send himself up in interviews, making his Southern accent even thicker, as a means of disarming critics or taking the mickey out of them.' Cousin Gene Smith states that he didn't like to hear his music called **rockabilly**, seeing it as a regional slur, too close to 'hillbilly' for comfort. Elvis's diet, fear of God, love of gospel music, sentimentality and prescription drugs have all been seen, not entirely innaccurately, as Southern traits. Yet, like the region, his roots were racially and politically complex: two of his maternal ancestors were named after **Lafayette** and **Grant**, not names typically revered in the Deep South.

Many basic and crucial aspects of Elvis's life are in dispute. No one can definitively name the day on which he slipped into Sun Studios to make his first record. The official story that he teamed up with guitarist Scotty Moore and bassist Bill Black at the behest of Sun's owner Sam Phillips is challenged by witnesses who insist Elvis knew his bass player long before they started rehearsing.

And so it goes on. Further disputes surround Elvis's attitude to his marriage, and its collapse; the importance of his stillborn twin Jesse Garon; and the reason he never toured outside North America. Friends such as Lamar Fike have a point when they insist Elvis was one of the most elusive characters ever to walk this earth. As Marion Keisker, Sam Phillips' assistant at Sun, observed, 'He was like a mirror: whatever you were looking for, you were going to find in him. He had all the intricacy of the very simple.'

The strength to dream

Elvis Aron Presley was born in Tupelo, Mississippi, on 8 January 1935. He was the second of twins: the first, Jesse Garon, was still-born, and is almost certainly buried in an unmarked grave in Priceville Cemetery. The birth almost killed Elvis's mother, Gladys. Elvis remained an only child, although a nurse at the local hospital claims Gladys had a miscarriage when Elvis was 7.

Elvis's father, Vernon, later recalled seeing a blue light in the sky above the two-room shack that the Presleys called home. Suggestions of a Nativity-like aura are marred by reports that Vernon's father, JD, was too drunk to realize the first baby was dead. Anyone looking for omens in Elvis's early years is better served by the tornado that swept through Tupelo on 5 April 1936. Despite killing 235, and demolishing the church across the street, it left the Presley shack untouched.

The Presleys were poor. Gladys picked cotton, while Vernon drifted from job to job. In 1937, having made less money than expected from the sale of a hog, Vernon was misguided enough to try and forge the cheque. He was, inevitably, arrested. After six months in custody – hoping to teach his son a lesson, J D refused to pay bail – Vernon served a further nine months in Parchman Farm prison. This sudden, if temporary, destruction of the Presley family unit reinforced the already intense relationship between

7

The most famous Presley family snap; Vernon is soon to go to jail

mother and son. At the age of just 3, Elvis began to behave as a surrogate father, patting his mother on the head and saying, 'There, there, my little baby.' It was the start of the transformation that saw him replace his father as the effective head of the family.

While Elvis's relationship with his mother is unquestionably pivotal to his life, it was not as claustrophobic as many have suggested. Only his aggrieved stepmother, Dee Stanley, has seriously suggested incest. They slept in the same bed for one simple reason: for much of Elvis's childhood, the family had only one bed.

Much discussion has centred on Gladys's habit of walking Elvis to school. Some of his Memphis friends don't remember her doing so at all, others say that she did until he got his own car, but partly to make sure that he didn't skip classes.

The controversial twin

The most controversial posthumous 'revelation' about Elvis has been his relationship with his still-born twin, **Jesse Garon**. While Elvis was still alive, Jesse was at most a footnote. So what has changed?

Albert Goldman was the first biographer to emphasise Jesse's role, though many of his revelations have since been disputed. **Billy Smith** insists that the idea that Elvis heard Jesse Garon's voice from the time he was 4 is a 'crock of bull', while other friends say they'd known Elvis for years before he even mentioned his twin.

On the other hand, childhood friend **James Ausborn** told Elaine Dundy that, as a boy in Tupelo, Elvis would often say to him, 'I want to see my brother.' They would then go to Priceville cemetery and 'look at the grave and talk a little to Jesse and after the visit he was always lifted in his spirits'.

Larry Geller says Presley used to think he heard Jesse's voice urging him to 'take care of other people', although he adds, 'He didn't talk about his twin that much, and he didn't talk to him.'

Psychologists agree that the loss of a twin can leave the survivor feeling incomplete, lost and survivor guilt. Could this be why Sam Phillips described Elvis as 'more scared of being hurt than anyone I ever met'? It may, too, explain what Sidney Lumet saw as Elvis's 'unhuman' restless spirit.

The most dramatic effect of Jesse Garon's death might have been in tightening Elvis's already strong bond with his mother, but throughout his life he would acquire surrogate brothers, such as Red West, Scotty Moore, and his cousins Gene and Billy Smith. Geller remembers a dream that Elvis had about his twin. 'He said that they were both up on stage in front of thousands of people, they were both dressed the same and they were both playing guitar. And Elvis said, "You know what? He had a better voice than me".'

9

Gladys protected, cosseted and, as far as their income allowed, even spoiled her son but he was not a typical momma's boy. The stereotype has been useful to those who like to suggest that he stumbled into fame, as casually as most of us step into a puddle. But it is not the whole truth.

When Elvis was as young as 8, he regularly hitched a ride to the studios of local radio station WELO, where he'd watch his first idol, the country singer Mississippi Slim. His childish persistence eventually persuaded the star to accompany him on the Saturday-afternoon amateur show. Although Gladys sometimes came along, both the locals who took him and the station personnel remember that as a rule he was on his own. That hardly squares with the myth that Gladys never let Elvis out of her sight.

There is, though, no denying that Gladys and Elvis had an exceptionally close bond. Psychologically and emotionally, she may never have recovered from the death of his twin. Elvis's great-aunt Christine Robert Presley, who minded him, told Gladys once: 'I lost a baby too and you know what? That will kill you quicker than anything.' Vernon's trial and imprisonment wouldn't have helped, especially as it led to the repossessession of their home.

The Presleys moved frequently thereafter, once even getting as far as Biloxi, and spending a while near the black section of east Tupelo known as Shakerag. Elvis may well have heard black music there for the first time, and certainly ran errands for the local black grocer in return for food. Poverty kept him skinny – as did his habit – in contrast to the gargantuan binges of his later life, of leaving his food for his parents.

Elvis used the guitar he was given for his ninth or tenth birthday to good effect, coming fifth in a talent contest at the 1945 Mississippi–Alabama Fair. 'I didn't have any music or anything, and I couldn't get anybody to play for me, and I couldn't play for myself because I didn't know how, so I just went out there and started singing,' he recalled in 1956. 'I'd set my heart on singing and nothing in the world could have stopped me from entering the talent contest. I did it all by my own.'

A date with Elvis

This unpublished account of a double date which almost went wrong was written by Elvis's cousin Gene Smith for the sequel to his book *Elvis's Man Friday* (Light Of Day Books).

Elvis and I were 16 years old. Elvis was driving Uncle Vernon's 1941 Lincoln Cosmopolitan. Elvis and I had a date with two black girls who lived close to the Courts [Lauderdale Courts, where Elvis lived then], Debra and Joyce. They were first cousins. Joyce was visiting from Chicago. We picked up Debra and Joyce one evening and drove to a deserted industrial area. We didn't drive there because it was a make-out spot, but just to be left alone and so I could entertain with my impersonations of radio celebrities.

On the way back, Elvis was laughing so hard at my animal imitations, he went off the road and the Lincoln got mired in mud. He tried to drive it out and we tried to throw wood and rags under the wheels but just went deeper into the ditch.

All of a sudden, a Memphis police department prowl car pulled up and Elvis and I piled back into the Lincoln. Two big white cops put a spotlight on us and the officer on the driver's side asked, 'What the fuck are you doing out here?'

Elvis said, 'Just riding around after choir practice, sir.' They got out of the squad car and one of the cops said, 'What are you doing riding around with them in your car?' Elvis said, 'We were just practicing gospel together, sir. We're not bothering anybody.'

I kept quiet as one of the officers put the beam of his flashlight in my face, then on Joyce, who was in the back with me, squeezing my hand so hard I thought she would mash it into mush. She and Debra were both crying quietly; they'd heard all the horror stories. Elvis and I thought we were going to get beat up real bad.

The tallest cop thrust his face toward Elvis and said, 'I don't want to ask for your driver's license. And I don't ever want to

11

see your pimply face around here boy – because If I do – your mama won't recognise you.' Then his partner said, 'You boys better get them gals outta here.' Elvis said that was what we were trying to do but our back wheel was stuck. The taller cop took a length of heavy duty chain from the trunk and stood there staring at us. I thought we were going to be beaten with chains and killed. To our relief, he made a show of tying one end to our front bumper and the other to the rear of the prowl car. The cops told Elvis to pull his car out of gear and then they pulled us out of the ditch. Then they unfastened the chain and drove away. Joyce whispered, 'Thank you Jesus.' Elvis said, 'Amen.'

That was no small debut, hard perhaps to reconcile with the stereotypical image, but in character for the boy who'd take his guitar to school, and told his schoolmates with all the certainty of youth that one day he would play the Grand Ole Opry. It was also in character for the boy who'd sit on the porch, with no money to do anything, and (his father recalled) tell himself, 'One day things will be different.'

Even so, things in Tupelo remained stubbornly and unsatisfactorily the same, until the autumn of 1948. Then, prompted partly by sheer poverty and partly (if you believe the rumours) by the horrific murder-by-decapitation of a neighbour, the Presleys piled into their truck and left for Memphis. 'We were broke man, broke,' Elvis said later, as though the journey were an overnight flit, though in fact Gladys's brother Travis and family went with them, and Elvis gave a farewell thirty-minute performance to his schoolmates.

A lonely teenage broncing buck

The Presleys' first years in Memphis were a case of same story, different location, as Gladys, Vernon, and sometimes Elvis, all sought work to make ends meet. Their jobs were as interchangeable as their homes: their one true fixed abode before Graceland was Winchester Avenue, Lauderdale Courts, from 1949 to 1953.

Elvis made few friends at his new school, Humes High, although two of his fellow pupils, Red West and George Klein, became lifelong companions. Never one to suffer isolation quietly, he compensated for a vicious case of acne with a ducktail haircut; Red prevented bullies cutting it off. Even after the acne disappeared, he never lost his taste for flashy clothes or sideburns. His guitar was

13

Sun rise: Elvis, Bill Black, Scotty Moore and Sam Phillips

also ever-present. Johnny Burnette recalled seeing Elvis perform at the local fire station, and he sang to the girls in his life, especially to first love Dixie Locke.

Around this point, rock'n'roll history gets a bit muddy. Received wisdom has Elvis first meeting Scotty Moore and Bill Black in ⁻⁻⁴ when Sun owner Sam Phillips brought them together. son Louis insists that Elvis met Bill in 1951. That's hardly ly: Bill's mother lived in Lauderdale Courts, and his younger

14

Elvis's date with destiny

Astonishingly, no one can quite agree on the seminal date, in the summer of **1953**, when Elvis first walked into Sun Studios to record **My Happiness** and **That's When Your Heartaches Begin**.

It definitely happened after Elvis graduated from Humes High, on 3 June. According to his cousin, Billy Smith, he made the record on **Saturday 13 June**, as a 'Christmas present' for Gladys. **Marion Keisker**, who taped Elvis so Sam Phillips could hear him, told **Bill Burk** that it must have been June, because Sun's logbooks were missing for that month, and they otherwise failed to mention Elvis. Everyone agrees it was a Saturday, so Burk plumps for either 13 June, which he reckons was the first Saturday after Elvis was paid for his temporary job at MB Parker's Machinists' Shop, or **27 June**. Keisker remembers that Elvis wore coveralls, and had grease under his fingernails.

Other sources say Elvis worked for Parker until July, so both **Lee** Cotten and **Elaine Dundy** opt for July instead. Cotton says **18 July**, as Elvis got an advance on his salary from MB Parker, ostensibly to 'make a car payment' for a car that had in fact already been paid off.

Guralnick, in *Last Train To Memphis*, doesn't specify a date, suggesting simply 'mid to late summer, two to three months after graduation', which would make it **August** or **September**. He argues that Elvis was alerted to Sun's recording service by a story in the *Memphis Press Scimitar* on 15 July, about the **Prisonaires** cutting **Just Walking In The Rain** – though of course he could have read the story and walked into Sun on 18 July.

If it was August, it would probably have been early on, as Elvis's stint at M B Parker ended on 29 July. Given his family's financial circumstances, the $3.98 plus tax it cost to cut a record would not have stayed in his pocket for long, and he didn't work again until late September.

brother Johnny used to jam with the 16-year-old Elvis in the laundry room beneath the Presley apartment. The only surviving member of the trio, Scotty Moore says, 'He might have met Bill, because Bill's mother and brother were still living in the Lauderdale Courts. Bill had already married and moved away, but he might have met him if he had gone there visiting. But not in a musical context.'

Another boy, Jesse Lee Denson, was supposed to give Elvis guitar lessons; his father James says he remembers Elvis, his son, Johnny and Dorsey Burnette and Johnny and Bill Black performing outside the Black apartment. Unfortunately, the date he gives was before the Presleys had arrived in Memphis, but he also recalls Presley 'crying like a baby' because Gladys wouldn't let him go with the Burnettes to a concert at Millington naval base. There is also considerable, if not conclusive, evidence that Presley performed with the Burnettes before he walked into Sun in the summer of 1953 to cut My Happiness.

While the divergence might not seem to amount to a hill of beans, it does matter. The 'official' story serves to confirm the view of Presley as an idiot savant, a man whose innate genius was as much of a genetic accident as premature hair loss. Dundy's account gives a sense of a more ambitious, determined Elvis, practising all he can before that all-important first record. Louis Black says his dad had been urging Elvis to go to Sun for at least a year before he finally took his destiny into his hands. We know, also, from Sam Phillips, that Presley used to park his truck outside the studio, as though steeling himself to go in.

Something gave Elvis his final shove. The key may be the Humes school talent show in April 1953. Elvis sang Cold Cold Icy Fingers, and was asked to do an encore. After hearing the thunderous applause of his peers – one girl actually fainted – Elvis came off stage and blurted out to his teacher: 'They really liked me, Mrs Scrivener, they really liked me.' The next month, he hitch-hiked 240 miles to enter a talent contest at the Jimmie Rodgers country festival in Meridian, Mississippi, and won second prize – a guitar.

16

It took Elvis Presley two and a half years to become an overnight success. And the hardest time was the eleven months that it took Sam Phillips to find a song he thought suited the 'kid with the sideburns'. After an abortive first attempt, Phillips put him in touch with guitar player Scotty Moore: 'He came to my house for like a pre-audition. I was very impressed … It seemed like he knew every song in the world. He didn't know all the chords, couldn't play them all on the guitar, but he knew them. He went in the studio the next night for an audition … The thing that some people don't realize, they think that we went in to record. We didn't, we went in for Sam to hear his voice. But during the audition, that song happened. He knew the song – I hadn't never heard it.'

A star is born

The song was That's All Right. The date: 5 July 1954. Although the record went down a storm on the radio show of Dewey Phillips, the Memphis DJ who became Elvis's friend, and Presley became famous in his home town, true stardom still seemed a long way away. Elvis, Scotty and Bill got their first official fan club in September 1954, the same month their second single – A side, Good Rocking Tonight – was released. The very next month, they were snubbed by the Grand Ole Opry, then embraced by the audience at the Louisiana Hayride. The Hayride success was crucial: with a signal that reached 28 states, and CBS radio broadcasting it every third Saturday, the show helped make Presley. His touring grew more ambitious, and as 1955 opened he became a regional (Southern) star, a status made official by a riot at his concert in Jacksonville, Florida.

This was the point at which the most controversial figure in the Elvis Presley story, Colonel Thomas Parker, entered the picture. As described on p.21, he had by the end of the year effectively become Elvis's manager.

17

The Louisiana Hayride

Broadcast live each Saturday night over radio station KWKH, the **Louisiana Hayride** ranked second only to the Grand Ole Opry as a radio forum for country music. Established in 1948, it drew audiences from all over the South to Shreveport's 3800-seat Municipal Auditorium. In what's often called Elvis Presley's **biggest break**, he made his Hayride debut on **16 October 1954**. As he recalled, 'I went down there as just a try-out more or less', but he made enough of an impression to be swiftly signed to a one-year contract, later extended to eighteen months.

Just weeks earlier, Sam Phillips had pulled strings to earn Elvis a disastrous appearance on the Opry. The Hayride was more open to new talent, and had already launched **Hank Williams**, **Webb Pierce** and **Jim Reeves**. It also, unlike the Opry, allowed the use of drums, which were often played (hidden behind curtains) by staff drummer **DJ Fontana**.

Horace 'Hoss' Logan, the programme director, dates Elvis's Hayride at just a week after the Opry debacle, on **9 October 1954**. But a reel capturing Elvis's first night performance owned by Joey Kent, owner of what remains of the Hayride archives, and a diary kept by Joyce Nichols, a teenager who regularly listened to Hayride broadcasts, both put the debut on **16 October**. Who gets the credit for Elvis's appearance is the subject of a complex disputes, with the honour claimed by (and for) promoter **Tillman Franks**, local DJ **Tommy Cutrer**, record shop owner **Sam Lewis** and **Sam Phillips**.

However Elvis got onto the Hayride, what took place on the night in question is not in dispute. Veteran country artist **Floyd Tillman** finished his set just after 9pm. After a Lucky Strike commercial, Page introduced Elvis, seeking to calm his nerves with a warm welcome and an exaggerated build-up. Just as nervous as he'd been on the Opry, Elvis launched uncertainly into **That's All Right**. Hayride acts normally wore Western attire; Elvis, with

The Hayride was Elvis's first big break, making him a regional star

his bow tie and sports coat, and
his hair slicked back, stood out a
mile. The standard Hayride format
required acts to do two numbers;
those who made enough impact
would then return in the second

half for up to five more. At first,
the reaction to Elvis's weird music
was muted, and the engineer had
to turn up the audience microphone to pick up a reasonable
response. Gradually, the several

hundred teenagers present created such a clamour that one performer, **Jimmy C Newton**, was virtually booed off stage. Second time around, Elvis blew them away.

The Hayride was never the same again. Teenagers from across the South soon dominated the audience. As no one could follow Elvis, he became the closing act, on the radio and on the Hayride's package tours and one-off dates.

In Jacksonville, **Hank Snow**, whom Elvis revered, was booed off stage by Presley fans; this was the moment **Colonel Parker** came on the scene. By the time Elvis's Hayride contract was renewed in November 1955, his fee had risen from $18 to $200. That same month, he was signed to RCA Victor. Looking to break him in the North, the Colonel bought out the final seven months of Elvis's Hayride contract, so his last regular appearance was on 31 March 1956. He returned for a final fling on 15 December 1956, with proceeds going to the Shreveport *YMCA*. There was mass hysteria as Elvis took to the stage with the Jordanaires, but the management had forgotten that no one could follow him. As a result, Horace Logan uttered what would become famous words: 'Ladies and Gentlemen, **Elvis has left the building.**'

In November 1955, Sun's interest in Elvis was bought out by RCA Records – already home to Parker's other most famous acts, Eddy Arnold and Hank Snow – for an unprecedented $35,000 (and a $5000 bonus for Elvis). The deal suited Parker, RCA (once the hits started rolling in), and Phillips, who had wrestled with the tough choice of hitching his whole label to this one rising star, or cashing him in and investing the money. RCA A&R man Steve Sholes put his career on the line with the deal; for a few anxious months, everyone was telling him he'd made a mistake. Then the reissue of Elvis's last Sun single, Mystery Train/I Forgot To Remember To Forget, became a country number one, and Heartbreak Hotel soared to number one, after Elvis made his TV debut on the *Dorsey Brothers Stage Show*. By the end of 1956, he had outraged

Elvis and the Colonel

The virtual impossibility of reaching any conclusive verdict about **Colonel Tom Parker** is summed up by two of Elvis's finest biographers. **Peter Guralnick**'s obituary called him 'a brilliant tactician, a promoter of genius, a man of enormous resourcefulness intelligence and wit'. **Dave Marsh** has this to say: 'Parker never, for one minute, grasped what Elvis and his music meant to people. To stand that close to the centre of such a phenomenon and miss altogether its most important, long-lasting qualities, requires a genius that is truly rare.' The debate still rages, a slight majority echoing the Louisiana Hayride's **Horace Logan**: 'The son of a bitch ought to be hung up by his balls. He practically destroyed one of the greatest talents that ever lived.'

Elvis's relationship with Colonel Parker permeates his whole life story, and is discussed throughout this chapter; this box is intended simply to summarize the essentials.

The Colonel was, of course,

neither a Colonel, nor a Parker, nor even an American. Born **Andreas Cornelius van Kuijk** in Breda, Holland, in 1909, he arrived in the US as an illegal immigrant in 1929. He served for three years in the 64th Coast Artillery in Hawaii, and probably took his new name from Thomas R Parker, his commanding officer. After years as a 'carny' in Florida – during which he persuaded Louisiana governor Jimmie Davis to make him an honorary 'Colonel' – he acquired such clients as **Eddy Arnold** and **Hank Snow**. Until 1955, Elvis was managed first by **Scotty Moore** and then by DJ **Bob Neal**. Parker started arranging his concerts that August, and became his manager months later. They remained a team until Elvis's death.

Nobody has ever accused Parker of being a class act. As **Ed Bonja**, the nephew of his right-hand man Tom Diskin, admits, 'That carny background kept coming through.' It would be churlish, however, to deny his

21

brilliance during Elvis's rise to fame. Critics say any manager might have done the same, a point impossible to prove. He certainly made things happen quickly, shifting Elvis to a major label, **RCA**, then breaking him nationally on TV. The move to **Hollywood** was not, in itself, a blunder. Parker's initial commission – around 25 percent – was high but not outlandish. It is from 1960 onwards, as Parker's pursuit of the almighty dollar exposed his

Colonel Parker types in a new commission while Elvis is distracted

client to ridicule, that he looks less sure-footed.

From the start, he had deliberately **isolated** Elvis from alternative sources of advice and support. First, Scotty Moore and Bill Black were told they could only talk to Presley on stage; then, in Hollywood, Leiber and Stoller were inched out of the picture (Stoller was ordered out of Elvis's hotel suite); and later still, in Memphis, Chips Moman was squeezed out. Staff who worked for Parker say the easiest way to get fired was to say hello to Elvis. **Jerry Schilling** says, 'I always felt that as far as the management were concerned, the dumber you were the longer you lasted around Elvis.'

Elvis's role was restricted to making three films a year, recording soundtracks that used as many songs from his own publishing companies as possible, and generally not misbehaving in public. In 1967, when this policy had almost wrecked Presley's career, Parker negotiated a new deal giving him 25 percent of Elvis's basic payments from movies and records, plus half of any additional profits or royalties. In 1973, he secured half of Elvis's recording income and a third of the money from tours, and sold Presley's back catalogue to RCA in a deal which enriched Parker more than Elvis. And in 1976 the deal was revised again, to split the income from touring half and half. It must be noted that each of those renegotiations coincided with a particularly vulnerable moment in Elvis's life.

So what was in it for Presley? Ed Bonja sees Elvis's reliance on Parker as '**psychological dependency**'. Others say he saw Parker as his talisman, fearing that if he broke with him his fame would run out. Schilling says they had a genuine emotional bond.

Both parties had their own painful realities to hide. Just as Elvis retreated into a twilight world following the disintegration of his family, Parker took solace in **gambling** – see p.47 – and, apart from one visit from his brother, only acknowledged his own family by mailing them the occasional Elvis souvenir.

While Parker masterminded Elvis's return to live performance, the artistic **comeback** that made this possible (the 1968 TV special and the 1969 Memphis recording sessions) happened despite, not because of, him. His failure to follow up with a **world tour** remains controversial; see p.39. Instead, Elvis's energy was frittered away, with an average of 150 concerts each year between 1970 and his death in 1977. The people who surrounded Elvis insist that, whatever the autopsy said, **boredom** killed him; and Parker's unimaginative management contributed to that boredom.

For many fans, clinching proof of Parker's disregard came at Presley's funeral, when he turned up wearing seersucker pants and a baseball cap and the answering machine message he made immediately after Elvis's death: 'Elvis didn't die. The body did. We're keeping Elvis alive. I talked to him this morning and he told me to carry on.' At an Elvis conference in 1978, however, Parker told a journalist, as if in answer to an unspoken question, 'Yes, I loved him.'

and inspired millions, sold ten million records – 69 percent of his new label's turnover – and made his first critically panned *movie*, *Love Me Tender*.

Elvis's bump'n'grind rendition of *Hound Dog* on the *Milton Berle Show* made him public enemy number one, a status with which neither he nor his mother was entirely comfortable. They distracted themselves by buying a new house on Audobon Drive,

A gold lamé Elvis bumps and grinds his way to more controversy

only to have to move again to Graceland in 1957, under pressure from neighbours annoyed by the crowds of fans. Having chickens out the back of the new family mansion was, for Gladys, no sub-stitute for the community of family and friends she remembered from Tupelo, nor did it compensate for her son's prolonged absences from home. She soon took to drink, although she did her best to hide it both from her husband – himself no mean drinker and an ex-bootlegger – and from Elvis, whose experiences with drunken relatives such as his grandmother Minnie Mae, his aunt Delta, his father, and his grandfather gave him a lifelong aversion to booze and boozers.

Some members of the Memphis mafia claim that Vernon was by now physically abusing his wife; Lamar Fike says that was the real reason Elvis called her every night. Neither Guralnick nor Dundy, however, discusses the possibility, while Memphis journalist Bill Burk flatly denies it. He does, though, recall seeing Vernon at Memphis's Last Chance liquor store, 'with holes burnt in his trousers where he'd fallen asleep drunk while still smoking'.

In any case, by 1957 Elvis was starting to realise the pitfalls of his new life. His first girlfriend, Dixie Locke, had married someone else, and his first fiancée, June Juanico, had regretfully left too. He found a new long-term girlfriend, Anita Wood, but that Easter he told a local pastor, 'I am the most miserable young man you have ever seen. I have more money than I can ever spend. I have thousands of fans out there, and I have a lot of people who call themselves my friends, but I am miserable. I am not doing a lot of things that you have taught me and I am doing some things that you taught me not to do.'

Alienated by their paltry wages, and by what they saw as Parker's attempts to isolate them from their old friend, Scotty and Bill quit. By now, Elvis was almost too famous to perform live, each concert raising fears of a civil disturbance. In Ottawa, where Elvis played a rare concert outside the US, convent students were asked to sign a declaration, 'I promise that I shall not take part in the reception accorded Elvis Presley and I shall not be present at the programme presented by him.' Eight girls who defied the ruling were expelled.

25

The shoe-shine story

In 1957, **Louie Robinson**, a reporter from the black magazine *Jet*, visited the set of *Jailhouse Rock* to investigate a rumour that Elvis had said, 'The only thing negroes can do for me is to buy my records and shine my shoes.' The remark was alleged to have been made either in Boston, where Elvis had never been, or on the Edward R Murrow TV show, on which he'd never appeared.

Presley told Robinson, 'I never said anything like that, and people who know me know I wouldn't have said it.' The reporter talked to several black people who knew or worked with Presley, including Ivory Joe Hunter and pianist Dudley Brooks who all admitted their surprise at the story. Presley reiterated his debt to black culture, saying he could never hope to match singers like Bill Kenny and Fats Domino, and Robinson concluded that there was nothing in the rumour.

The idea that Presley was a **racist** – as Goldman put it, a closet Klan supporter – is still alive today, although it gets short shrift

from black people who knew him. **James Brown** says, 'There's no way Elvis was a racist', while Estelle Brown of the Sweet Inspirations states flatly, 'Elvis was not a racist. I can tell you that, we can all tell you that and we're black, ain't we? We should know.'

Vernon's often portrayed as racist, something he vehemently denied in a 1979 interview: 'We weren't trash, we weren't prejudiced.' In Tupelo, the young Elvis ran errands for a black grocer, went around with black gospel quartets, and attended a black church. In Memphis, he went to a white school, but it was the black world of **Beale Street** that fascinated him. He didn't just like the music: the clothes and the look also inspired him. Memphis was not, by Southern standards, that rigidly segregated, but Elvis broke several colour bars as a young man. Later, black entertainers like James Brown, Jackie Wilson and Sammy Davis Jr were among his closer showbiz friends.

The case for Elvis the racist rests, largely, on the shoe-shine legend, and a conversation in which Marty Lacker recalls Elvis saying he didn't want Lisa to marry a black man. Billy Smith says, 'Elvis tried hard not to be prejudiced, but at times he came off that way. It's really hard to get that out of your system when you're brought up that way.' Biographer **Peter Guralnick** argues, 'Elvis was like many of our great musicians whether Robert Johnson or Ray Charles. He saw no distinctions between class and race. He saw people as people. He's not what you'd expect from his time and place. Within the world of entrenched racism it's unusual to find someone so altogether open.'

The professional triumphs piled up. All Shook Up became Elvis's first number one single in the US and UK, and the movie and single Jailhouse Rock were smashes. Gladys, though, grew sicker and unhappier, her morale shattered by the news that her son was to be drafted. Her nephew Junior had suffered a nervous breakdown in the Army, and she feared Elvis would be killed – not so very paranoid, just four years after the Korean War had ended.

'Everything I have is gone'

All sorts of conspiracy theories have been advanced about Elvis's draft into the Army, ranging from the odd – Parker arranged it to tame his star and avoid overexposure – to the unproveable – the government arranged it to neutralize the threat Elvis posed to society. Stories also conflict as to whether it was Elvis who decided he would serve as a regular GI, or Parker, who didn't like the idea of his boy giving the merchandise away free serving in the Special Services. Presley's draft, and his public shearing, certainly represented a triumph for the generation that saw his act as being too close to an 'aborigine's mating dance'. That it was deferred to let him finish King Creole failed to placate one outraged fan, who

27

berated the local draft board chairman, 'You didn't put Beethoven in the Army did you?'

Elvis's concern for his career was exacerbated by fears for his mother's declining health. Having been inducted into the Army on 24 March 1958, he was on basic training in Texas when Gladys became so ill that she was shipped back to Memphis. She died of a heart attack on August 14, brought on by hepatitis due in part to her use of alcohol and diet pills. As far as Elvis and the world knew, she was just 42, but she was in fact 46.

Gladys's death came close to unhinging Elvis. When he said at her funeral, an event he described as a circus, 'Everything I have is gone', he wasn't being melodramatic. Lamar Fike says, 'he probably needed grief counselling, though nobody knew about it at the time. Four weeks later, he was shipped overseas. Her death was the most devastating thing that happened to him.' Many friends and family say that Elvis was never the same again; everything he had achieved was thrown into question. His first epitaph for her gravestone sums up his feelings: 'Thy will not mine be done'.

Shipped to Germany, where Elvis lived off base with 'dependents' including his father and grandmother in Bad Nauheim, life seemed meaningless. Elvis's womanizing took on a frenzied, almost herculean, quality. Vernon, meanwhile, turned to drink but soon met Dee Stanley, his second wife. Despite all the mayhem at the house, which was constantly besieged by fans, and Elvis's first experiments with amphetamines – given by fellow GIs who struggled to stay awake on manoeuvres – he impressed colleagues and officers with his dedication, being promoted to sergeant.

Partly in response to Gladys's death, the so-called Memphis mafia expanded, with Joe Esposito, Lamar Fike and Charlie Hodge joining such early recruits as Red West, Marty Lacker, Gene Smith, Billy Smith and George Klein. Elvis's most important new acquaintance while he was in the Army was a 14-year-old Air

29

'Lawd almighty I feel my temperature rising'. But only slightly.

Force brat called Priscilla Beaulieu. Quite how that came about, and how deep their relationship became, has been the subject of various rumours and at least one libel action. All that's certain is that they met in August 1959, and repeatedly thereafter. Some Memphis mafiosi say the special quality of this relationship was immediately obvious, while others disagree. Even Priscilla admits that when he returned to the US in March 1960, she wasn't sure they'd ever meet again. Her fears could hardly have been calmed by his comments at his homecoming press conference, that theirs was 'no big romance'.

Elvis is back!

A civilian once more, as of 5 March 1960, the erstwhile Sergeant Elvis Presley set out to reconquer the world, being welcomed back into the showbiz establishment on Frank Sinatra's TV show. The stream of number ones soon resumed – Stuck On You, It's Now Or Never, Are You Lonesome Tonight? – and Elvis fulfilled his desire to produce a gospel album, *His Hand In Mine*. But his image, his music and, soon, his movies, had all changed. His new respectability was underlined by the April 1961 benefit concert for a memorial to the USS *Arizona*, the chief casualty of Pearl Harbor. This was his last public performance for seven years.

The aura of infinite possibility that surrounded Elvis's return swiftly passed. By 1963, the year the Beatles made their name, he was already seen as something of a recluse, his diary filled by commitments to increasingly dodgy movies. In the spring, following protracted negotiations between Elvis and her stepfather, Priscilla moved into Graceland. But that summer Elvis had an intense affair with Ann Margret while filming *Viva Las Vegas*. In April 1964, Elvis met his hairdresser and on-off spiritual guru Larry Geller, a friendship that sparked his unending quest to find meaning in life in general, and his own life in particular. Neither Parker,

Elvis is back – in a tux on Frank Sinatra's TV show

Priscilla and the women

Priscilla – Mrs Presley

While there were many women in Elvis's life, there was only one **wife**. **Priscilla Beaulieu Presley** was born in Brooklyn in 1945, then whisked around the world by her mom and adoptive dad. She first met Elvis in Germany, when she was 14. She lived with him at Graceland for years before they wed in 1967, and finally left for the West Coast in 1971.

Elvis moulded Priscilla: their desperate desire to look like each other was never more obvious than at their **wedding** in Las Vegas, on 1 May 1967. The new-lyweds escaped, for a while, to a ranch that Elvis had bought in Mississippi, which came to be called the **Circle G**. What started as an idyllic getaway, however, soon soured, partly because spectators began to turn up and partly because both Vernon and, to a lesser extent, Priscilla, were worried about the money Elvis was spending on trailers and pick-up trucks.

Elvis and Priscilla were blissfully happy in the aftermath of Lisa Marie's birth in February 1968, but even before Elvis went on tour Priscilla had probably tired of being his creation. In their home movies, she often looks like a woman trying to convince every-one (including herself) she's hav-ing a good time. She may never have felt as comfortable at Graceland as she obviously did in LA. After finding fame as an actress in *Dallas* and in *The Naked Gun* – a far bigger box-office smash than any of her hubby's movies – she has become the guardian of Elvis's image and estate.

Significant others

Elvis's relationship with his first real love, **Dixie Locke**, died during his prolonged absences on the concert circuit in 1954 and 1955. Next came **June Juanico**, whose *In The Twilight Of Memory* is rec-ommended reading. Memphis DJ **Anita Wood** met Elvis in 1957, but their relationship was undermined first by Parker's insistence that his boy stay single, and then by Priscilla's arrival. Presley actually proposed to **Debra Paget**, his co-star in *Love Me Tender*; when he later persuaded Priscilla to dye her hair black, it was to make her resemble Paget.

From the way **Ann-Margret** wept at Elvis's funeral it was obvi-ous her relationship with the King ran far deeper than the usual movie-star romance. They fell in love and even discussed marriage on the set of *Viva Las Vegas* in 1963, then broke up after reports, denied by Ann-Margret, that she

Elvis and Natalie, before he tired of her attention-seeking ways

had said they were engaged. She and Elvis did something he seldom did with Priscilla: ditch the mafia and just go off together, one on one. At his closing show in Las Vegas in 1973, he introduced her from the stage and told the lighting engineer, 'Just leave the light on her man, let me look at her.'

Linda Thompson met Elvis soon after Priscilla departed, and lived with him for four years, even going on tour with him (which Priscilla had rarely done), while the 20-year-old **Ginger Alden** was his last fiancée. She gets a bad press, but Bill Burk probably hit the nail on the head: 'she just got in way over her head'.

Flings

Among those Elvis also dated or had affairs with were dancer **Dottie Harmony** ('we read the Bible aloud together'), stripper **Tempest Storm**, **Juliet Prowse**, **Joan Blackman**, **Anne Helm**, **Tuesday Weld**, **Joanne Moore**, and backing singer **Kathy Westmoreland**.

Natalie Wood, whom he took to Memphis to meet Gladys, later downplayed the affair, telling her sister that he was just a voice. Presley may have tired of her attention-seeking ways: when she threatened to throw herself out of a hotel window, Elvis told everyone to ignore her, and she soon crawled back off the ledge.

Cybill Shepherd had a much-publicized (by her) fling with Elvis in 1972. 'He was a really nice, gentle guy,' she says. 'Unfortunately, his life had become horribly limited by his fame … That level of fame can be almost a tragedy. It isolates you as a human being.'

Rumour has it

It's often said that Elvis slept with all but one of his leading ladies, but he almost certainly didn't sleep with Lizabeth Scott, Hope Lange, Stella Stevens, Shelley Fabares, Donna Douglas, Deborah Walley, Marlyn Mason and Mary Tyler Moore.

These women may also have had affairs with Elvis: **Bobbie Gentry**, **Barbra Streisand** (James De Spada's Babs biography says they had a one-night stand), **Mamie van Doren** (she insists, and who are we to argue?), **Diana Dors** (ditto), and mobster Sam Giancana's lover, **Phyllis McGuire**.

nor many Memphis mafiosi, showed any great sympathy. Indeed, Parker enraged his client by telling him to get off his 'religious kick'. Elvis complained to friends, 'My life is not a kick.'

Geller insists that by 1965 Elvis was finding his career so unsatisfying that he considered jacking it all in. Driving back from Hollywood to Memphis, he had a vision of a face in a cloud that started out as Joseph Stalin and turned into Jesus. True, Elvis was now experimenting with drugs of all kinds, but Geller says the shaken star told him: 'How can I go back to making those teenybopper movies after what I just went through? After seeing the face of God I've got to go back and do things that have no meaning and are no help to humanity. Maybe I should just become a monk.' Geller says he persuaded Elvis not to quit but to use his influence for good, which led to his return to Nashville in 1966 to make the gospel album *How Great Thou Art*.

That may just be a nice story, but the gospel songs must certainly struck a spiritual chord with a man searching so painfully for meaning. The search was interrupted in March 1967, when Parker

35

Priscilla and Elvis celebrate their nuptial gig, in May 1967 in Vegas

I Just Can't Help Believing

'You know Elvis was basically a **Christian** – philosophically, intellectually and spiritually. He investigated many different religions, but basically he was a Christian,' says Larry Geller. That might seem like a masterpiece of simplification. Elvis was, after all, a student of **numerology**, **astrology** and **cosmology**, who became a member of the **Self-Realization Fellowship** – founded by Indian holy man Paramahansa Yogananda – and encouraged his entourage to read Timothy Leary's *Psychedelic Experience*. Yet he remained, officially, a member of the Pentecostal church of his childhood, the First Assembly of God.

As Geller and Jo Smith, Billy Smith's wife, testify, he never left the Bible behind. 'I had been brought up with all that fire and brimstone but Elvis didn't like religion to be scary,' says Jo Smith, 'but he knew the Bible better than anyone'.

Mary Ann Thornton, a fan who met him in the 1970s, says, 'He giggled when we got into discussions about the scriptures. He wanted to know what he knew that was right and what was in error from the influx of other teachings. "OK, OK," he'd hurriedly say with great impatience, "then what does this mean really?" and he'd quote part of a verse from the Bible.'

By the end of his life, Elvis seldom went on tour without a couple of suitcases of spiritual books. The two he read most voraciously were Kahlil Gibran's *The Prophet* and Joseph Brenner's *The Impersonal Life*. This aspect of his life has been misinterpreted – he did not, for example, see himself as a messenger of God. But he never stopped wondering about the world and his place in it, and in his very reclusiveness it's possible to see the influence of the sermons he had heard as a child, especially the preacher's exhortation, 'Separate yourself from the world! Get to where nothing matters but God.'

banished Geller. Two months later, Elvis married Priscilla in Las Vegas, and the new Mrs Presley celebrated by persuading hubbie to burn the books Geller had given him.

Lisa Marie Presley was born on 1 February 1968; Priscilla recalls in her memoirs that Elvis leaned over and said, 'Nungen [his pet name for her], us has a baby girl.' Though the parents often disagreed as to the best way to raise Lisa Marie, there was no doubting his feelings for her. Another love of his life, Linda Thompson, says, 'Lisa knew unequivocally that her daddy absolutely adored her.'

The original comeback kid

While Elvis's comeback, much like his original climb to fame, seemed to happen overnight, it can be traced back years. The process probably began in May 1966, with the sessions for *How Great Thou Art*. Then, in September 1967, he cut Guitar Man, his first really classy uptempo single since 1962's Return To Sender. Ultimately, television enabled him to remake his image and fashion a second career, just as it had made it all happen back in 1956.

In June 1968, Elvis saved himself from any threat of obscurity with his astonishing TV special. An awestruck Joe Esposito could barely believe that the performer who prowled the stage of NBC's Burbank studios was the man he knew as a friend. 'Afterwards Elvis told me that if he ever lost his voice he'd rather not be on this earth,' he recalled.

It has often been said that the TV special lengthened Elvis's career but shortened his life. Between 1968 and 1971, however, he was slimmed down, fired up and ready to dazzle the world. As the movie contracts ended, he set the seal on his musical resurrection with the 1969 Memphis sessions, the twin peaks of which were the million-selling singles In The Ghetto and Suspicious Minds.

In July 1969, Presley made a triumphant return to live perform-

ance in Las Vegas. As he put together his stage band, almost every musician he had ever worked with was contacted. The personnel was to change over the years, but the core line-up was James Burton on lead guitar; Jerry Scheff on bass; Ronnie Tutt on drums; John Wilkinson on rhythm guitar; Kathy Westmoreland, the Sweet Inspirations, the Imperials, and later JD Sumner and the Stamps, on backing vocals; and Joe Guercio conducting the orchestra. This was, Tutt says, Elvis's vision: he wanted his concerts to embrace all the musics he had loved over the years. What no one foresaw at this point was that they would spend most of the next eight years on the road together.

Elvis, live and unplugged, resurrecting his career in 1968

The world tour controversy

After Elvis's triumphant return to live performance culminated in the *Madison Square Garden* and *Aloha From Hawaii* concerts, the logical next move was a **world tour** but, mysteriously, it never happened.

As early as 1961, Elvis had told a Memphis press conference, 'I know that eventually we've got to do a European tour … but I don't know exactly.' When Parker jumped in with 'We're waiting for a good offer', Elvis added, 'He said that, I didn't.' Similarly, **Scotty Moore** recalls that when he met Elvis for the 1968 TV special, 'He talked to DJ and I about it, he was very enthusiastic. He wanted to do a world tour or a European tour.'

Parker may have been against any such tour right from the start. Elvis's movies, his two concert documentaries, and *Aloha From Hawaii* may have been attempts to make a world tour redundant (Parker's right-hand man Tom Diskin virtully admitted that movies were a world tour substitute in *Billboard* in 1964). By that

reckoning, the Colonel's motivation seems simple. He was, after all, an **illegal alien** (see p.000); he feared that he might be exposed, and, at worst, not allowed back into the US. **Joe Esposito**, however, insists that it was Presley whom Parker worried would fail to get through customs, with his pills and his guns, and that Elvis didn't seriously want to tour abroad. He points out that Parker had passed through customs when Elvis played in Canada in 1957, and that a world tour could have been organized by cohorts like Tom Diskin or Tom Hulett. It's also well-known that Presley often used Parker as his excuse for not doing things.

Ed Bonja says, 'The Colonel would get these offers, of millions of dollars, and he'd ask how much they would have to charge per seat and they'd say "well maybe $175" … The Colonel would say most Elvis fans didn't have that kind of money. He always wanted to keep prices down and Elvis influenced him on that.' Many Elvis associates call such talk a smoke-screen: Parker seemed to have a different objection to every scheme. London's **Wembley Stadium** was supposedly ruled out because Elvis didn't like to play outside, though that didn't stop him grossing $800,000 at Pontiac's Silverdome in 1975. Lamar Fike and Billy Smith still wonder how Parker wriggled out of **Adan Khashoggi**'s $10m offer for Elvis to play in front of the **Pyramids** at Giza; Smith said, 'You could almost see the blood run out of Elvis's face when the deal fell through.' NBC's post-Aloha suggestions of Elvis specials from **Moscow** or the Ginza district of **Tokyo** also came to nought.

As everyone who knew Elvis said, he was magnificent at rising to challenges; it was the ordinary he found hard. A world tour might have been just the challenge he needed. According to Jerry Schilling, 'Elvis was so serious about touring the world he bought those planes … The two of them had an argument about it. Parker told him, "If you do it, you'll do it without me" and Elvis shouted back, "All right, I will."' During his last year, Presley often insisted that he'd be going over-seas in 1978 with or without Parker; sadly, however, he never did. Eventually touring the world only on a **giant video screen** with his 1970s stage line-up in the late 1990s.

A major difficulty in writing about Elvis is that it's hard for mere words to capture how his presence affected people. So many friends, family and musicians use the phrase 'You sensed him before he was actually there' that it's obviously more than a cliché. **Estelle Brown**, a Sweet Inspiration, recalls her first meeting with him: 'Now I liked the man's music, but some of us – y'all know who you are – had the hots for him too. And one of 'em was me! I'm not kidding, when he walked in that room he looked like somebody had kinda moulded him, you know what I mean? Man, he looked like a living Greek god!'

Ed Bonja, who photographed Presley for years, says, 'I under-stand what Jerry Reed meant when he said that after meeting Elvis he'd wished he was a woman. The Colonel and I would go down to his dressing room before a concert and everytime you'd think, "How can a guy look that great?" You'd think after a while you'd get used to it. But you never did. I don't know if I've ever seen anyone, man or woman, who was that striking, looked that good, for so much of the time.'

Beyond Elvis's physical allure was the mystery of his personality. Whatever the muckraking books say, he had an immense capacity to inspire love. His cousin Billy Smith puts it very simply: 'You could not truly know him and not love him'. It can be hard to discern his true personality from the list of overused adjectives – generous, shy, narcissistic, paranoid, charming, childish, sensitive, self-destructive, perverted, loyal, reclusive, exhibitionist – but of all the assessments that have been made over the years, two seem particularly telling.

Sam Phillips told reporter Bill Burk, 'You have to keep in mind that Elvis probably had the greatest inferiority complex of any person, black or white, that I had worked with. He was a total loner. He kind of felt locked out'. Film director Sidney Lumet only had a passing acquaintance with Presley, but was reminded of the mythical bird in Tennessee Williams's play *Orpheus Descending*, condemned to hover in the sky until it dies: 'It evoked such a memory of what I felt of Presley when I watched him work: something otherworldly, unhuman (not inhuman), a kind of restless spirit that could never rest anywhere … yet unaware of his separation from the rest of us.'

Separate ways

Elvis was certainly restless, if not yet that isolated, in 1970. In that year alone, he found time to play two seasons in Las Vegas, one of which was filmed for the MGM documentary *That's The Way It Is* (see p.144); perform in front of record crowds at the Houston Astrodome; make his first US tour since the 1950s; record two fine

Elvis and Nixon

The most requested document from US government archives is not the Constitution, but a picture of two middle-aged men doing a PR handshake. It was taken on **21 December 1970**, when **Richard Milhous Nixon** was engaged in the conspiracy that was to force him to become the first president ever to resign. **Elvis Presley**, whose smile is less obvious but seems more genuine, has just been promised a badge that makes him an agent of the federal narcotics bureau.

With each passing year, the meeting seems more miraculous, as though the Loch Ness monster and Bigfoot had met up to chew the fat. It might never have happened, had Elvis not stormed out of Graceland after a row over his spending habits and caught the first available flight out of Memphis, which happened to be to Washington DC. The destination gave him an idea. After a sweep through LA and Dallas to pick up friends **Jerry Schilling** and **Sonny West**, Presley returned to the capital in his pursuit of a narcotics badge. After the narcotics bureau turned him down, he wrote to the White House, offering to help influence young people against drugs if he could meet the President and get the coveted badge.

Presley's request startled the White House. Nixon's Chief of Staff **Bob Haldeman** thought it must be a joke but approved the meeting. The King and the President came face to face at 1.30pm. After agreeing how tough it was to play Las Vegas, and discussing whether the Beatles were un-American, Presley finally got his badge. According to White House aide Bud Krogh, 'Elvis was so happy, he goes over and he grabs him [Nixon]. One of my abiding memories is Elvis Presley hugging Nixon who's sort of looking up, thinking, "Oh my god."'

West and Schilling had been told by their escort that they wouldn't get to meet Nixon, but Schilling says, 'We told him, "You don't know Elvis". And sure enough we were invited in. Elvis was running things, he was drawing Nixon out, he had that way about him that made him impossible to say no to.'. When Nixon commented on Presley's sartorial splendour, Elvis replied simply, 'Hey you got your show, Mr President, I got mine.' Nixon then presented West and Schilling with some goodies from his desk drawer. Presley was not satisfied, turning to Nixon and saying,

'They've got wives, Mr President.' Shamed, the President dived back into the drawer.

It's not a meeting Schilling will ever forget. 'What strikes me now is that they did kind of bond, they were both probably slightly past their professional prime, although at the top of their fields, and they seemed to share a certain loneliness.'

The Prez and Pres. Note Nixon's taste in office ornaments

studio albums in Nashville; and call on President Nixon. He also tried to go on holiday to Europe with Priscilla and friends, a move Parker vetoed on the grounds that he would offend fans if he visited Europe as a tourist and not a performer. The Presleys eventually settled for the Bahamas, the change an indication that although Elvis was at his most regal he was, in many ways, a constitutional monarch,

Yet this era, from 1968 to 1971, represents the golden age of Elvisness. Whether he was slaving over 23 takes of "In The Ghetto", mesmerizing audiences with his rambling self-mocking autobiographies, or hugging Nixon, there was a beguiling sense that some part of Presley's personality was being exposed, that this was more than mere showmanship, a sense heightened by the speech he gave in January 1971, to accept an award as one of the ten outstanding young men of America. He spoke of his ambitions, of his dreams that had come true, and of the importance of singing a song, 'without a song, the day will never end ...'

If Elvis Presley's life had been written for a classic Hollywood showbiz biopic, this story would end here, with him murmuring, 'So I'll just keep on that singing that song.' Sadly, this was real life, and the story still had six more years to run. If those years make hard reading, they must have been harder to live – for Elvis and for the many people who loved him but could not help him.

Priscilla was the first, but far from the last, to leave, departing Graceland on 30 December 1971. The tours, the rumours – often accurate – of his womanizing and his sheer remoteness had finally driven her away. Her departure and affair with karate instructor Mike Stone unhinged Presley almost as badly as his mother's death, although the effects were not obvious until after the 1973 *Aloha From Hawaii* concert.

While some friends insist that the biggest blow was to Elvis's pride, others report that he was heartbroken. Bass player Jerry Scheff recalls being on the *Lisa Marie* jet with Elvis in 1975, when it was met by Priscilla in LA: 'When she got on the plane, his whole demeanour changed. My wife Diane said, "He knows he's blown it

Generous to a fault

Elvis's lavish, almost irrational, generosity started young: Bill Burk recalls that one Christmas, he gave one of his own toys to a schoolmate, because he couldn't afford to buy a gift. That munificence was echoed when he became rich and famous by his annual presentation of thousands of dollars to Memphis **charities**; his habit of presenting friends, strangers, or even newscasters with **cars**; and his **impulse buys**, like the time he bought an entire truckload of melons off a local boy.

Whereas Vernon never stopped fearing that one day the family would all be poor again, Elvis wanted to give something back. He told Geller: 'My Mom, she slaved her whole life away just to keep food on the table. And she always said, "Honey, remember your roots, the suffering and the pain we all went through." Man, I'll never forget. It's branded on my soul. I know what it's like when you don't have any money, you don't have any food, you

don't have any clothes. I like to help people and that's why God put me in the position I'm in.' Thus when **Lamar Fike** needed an intestinal bypass, Elvis paid his bill, leaving a phone line to the operating theatre open to ensure there were no complications. And he bought the stunned **Jerry Schilling** a house, because 'your mother died when you were one and you never had a home and I wanted to be the one to give you one'.

On the other hand, Elvis's sprees in the 1970s were often, if not drug-induced, intended to cheer himself up or to get him out of a jam. After an on-stage contretemps with the Sweet Inspirations, his need to placate the group saw him spend $85,000 on jewellery. Not that he was naïve enough to think giving could somehow right every wrong. As producer Felton Jarvis recalls, 'Elvis told me he gave people things to show them that their lives would be just the same after they got it as before.'

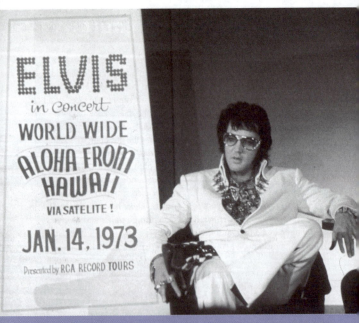

More people watched *Aloha From Hawaii* than the moon landings

with losing her". When Elvis asked JD Sumner why Priscilla had left, he replied, 'When you give 99 per cent of your life to the business, there's not enough left for your family.' And Schilling says on the day Priscilla left, 'Elvis shut himself in his bedroom. Joe or I would sneak up to see how he was. Once I heard him cursing, another time screaming but mostly sobbing. That was the beginning of the end for the Elvis I had known and loved.'

Elvis and Priscilla remained in touch, possibly even in love. Priscilla wrote in *Elvis and Me* that Elvis asked her to come back.

Schilling says, 'They could have got back together in 1974, but Elvis got into his self-destructive mode and that was that.' Priscilla's stepfather told Bill Burk that the sticking point was her demand that he kick the Memphis mafia out of Graceland.

Presley's first live appearances in New York – four sold-out concerts in Madison Square Garden – and Burning Love, a number two single in the US, helped disguise the troubles in his private life. And he kicked off 1973 with *Aloha From Hawaii*, beamed via satellite to over one billion people around the world. He had lost weight, and, say some friends, cut down on pills. But after that high, he was back to Las Vegas, bored and depressed. Ronnie Tutt says, 'The first year in Vegas was great and then he became very bored. He was like a caged animal. He was too much of a free spirit to be hung in one place and having to do two shows a night.'

Elvis's drug use began to spiral out of control in 1973, which his medics called 'the year of the drugs'. When Priscilla suggested that Lisa Marie's visits to see Elvis in Las Vegas be limited, Elvis ordered Red West to put a contract out on her lover, Mike Stone. He backed off days later, saying, 'Aw, hell, that's a bit heavy.'

The expensive impending divorce, coupled with Elvis's generally high spending, led to a financial crisis. That March, Colonel Parker pushed through the controversial sale of Presley's back catalogue to RCA, and the signing of a new seven-year contract with the label. Presley needed the money too, although Parker pocketed $6 million compared to Presley's $4.5 million, but it's hard not to suspect that given Parker's gambling losses he had his own reasons to negotiate a short-term deal which struck many of his colleagues as short-sighted. Nor did Parker seem able or willing to make Elvis's Las Vegas fees reflect his status as the biggest draw the resort had ever known.

Parker and Presley almost split in the autumn of 1973, after Presley berated the *Hilton* management for sacking an employee. Parker's multi-million-dollar estimate of what Elvis owed him terrified Vernon, who didn't have the nous to realize that another manager might pay Parker off just to represent Elvis.

47

The Colonel's addiction

Just how much money Colonel Parker lost in the casinos of Las Vegas will never be known. According to **Alex Shoofey**, president of the *International/Hilton*, Parker was good for losses of $1 million a year. The real figure was probably much higher. Larry Geller remembers: 'The last time we were in Vegas, it was December 1976, there was a crowd in the casino watching Colonel Parker playing the ultimate sucker's game, the Wheel of Fortune. And that night he lost $1.4 million. Elvis heard about it and said, "A lot of people don't make that kind of money in their whole lives. And how's he going to pay it off? **I'm his ransom**."' As Geller is about as neutral about Parker as Leon Trotsky was about Joe Stalin, this might be taken with a bucket of salt but Lamar Fike recalls a similar conversation, in which Elvis said, 'I'll play this town till I die. That old son of a bitch owes so much money **they own him**.'

Presley's shock was shared by Parker's business partners, music publishers Julian and Jean Aberbach and Freddie Bienstock, and right-hand man, Tom Diskin. As a *Hilton* executive told Bill Burk in December 1976, 'What you don't understand is that while we lose money on Elvis on stage, we make up for it by having the Colonel at the tables.'

But **Ed Bonja** dismisses the charge that Parker's gambling influenced his handling of his star as 'far fetched … The Colonel paid off his gambling debts as he went. When he would lose several million dollars, the following week he would bring cash with him. Rather than pay them $5 million he would bring briefcases full of cash, go into the office with the casino manager and he would say, "What kind of discount you gonna give me for cash?" He would usually walk out with a million dollars. I know because I carried the money.'

Whenever Parker tried to confront Presley about his spending sprees or drug habits, the singer would turn the spotlight back, saying, 'This is my thing, you've got yours.' In the last few years, Parker and Presley were like an old married couple, knowing enough about each other's weak spots to make any argument potentially deadly.

Six days after the divorce was finalized, in October 1973, Elvis was rushed into Baptist Memorial Hospital in Memphis with suspected heart failure, and in a near-comatose state. Even he realized that he could have died and, for several months he tried to be a model patient. The immediate cause of the emergency was, his doctor George Nichopoulos decided, probably a six-week course of massive doses of Demerol, cortisone, steroids and Novocaine given to him by a doctor in LA, who was unaware of his other medication. Toxicologists have since said that this experience alone left Elvis 'biologically dependent' on opiates.

Although Dr Nichopoulos decided that Elvis would have to be treated as an addict, once the hospital team had got their famous patient down to one sleeping pill a night he felt Presley might still recover. Returning to Graceland with his new girlfriend Linda Thompson, Elvis recuperated emotionally and physically. His second Stax sessions, in December 1973, were his most productive and challenging since Nashville in June 1970, with Promised Land just one of the highlights.

Under Nichopoulos's orders, Elvis's January 1974 Las Vegas season was cut from four weeks to two. Sadly, such restraint was not shown for the rest of the year. Presley did four tours, as well as the notorious summer season in Las Vegas, when he tried to add more blues and blue ballads to his act, and then switched back to his usual format, disappointed by the audience's lack of response. In an astonishing medication-fuelled performance (known to fans as 'Desert Storm') on 2 September, he attacked rumours of his drug taking. WA Harbinson, an Elvis biographer who was in the audience, captured the experience best: 'Elvis, when not singing pure rock'n'roll, still sang from the soul. Nevertheless, he was strung out and alternating between great singing and rambling drunken

'I had a wife and I had children, I threw them all away.'

Sleep, drugs and rock'n'roll

One of the few major aspects of Elvis's life on which all the Memphis mafia agree is his acute problem with **sleep**. As Joe Esposito wrote, his drugs problem 'originated in his lifelong struggle with insomnia. Even when I first knew him in the Army, he had trouble sleeping. He would snatch a few hours and then wake up.'

The trouble may have started when Elvis was just 5. Gladys's cousin Leona recalls all three Presleys having 'action nightmares' after Vernon returned from prison; they'd get up, take the clothes off the bed, make it up on the floor and go back to sleep, then remember nothing the next morning. As a teenager, he'd sleepwalk the Memphis streets in his underwear. Later on, the fame and the touring, which inverted day and night, didn't help. Elvis told both Esposito and Lamar Fike of his recurring **nightmare** that he was no longer famous. He often dreamed that people were

trying to **stab** him. Fike and others slept either in the same bed or on the floor, sometimes getting punched as he lashed out at imaginary opponents. Billy Smith says, 'When he was making *Loving You*, he almost walked out the eleventh floor of the *Beverly Wilshire*, the window was open, Gene just caught him in time.' *Elvis: What Happened?* describes similar vigils in Las Vegas in the 1970s.

If you're suffering from a sleep disorder, the last thing you need is to discover **amphetamines**. But that's just what Elvis did, probably to stay awake on scouting missions in the Army; they'd been widely used in World War II, to keep bomber crews and soldiers going past the point of normal endurance. When his military service ended, a supply of 'little white pills' followed him across the Atlantic.

Powerful stimulants and irregular hours make a dangerous combination. 'If you take stimulants during the day you're dependent on chemicals to control your sleep/wake rhythm,' says sleep expert **Dr Cosmo Hallstrom**. 'Your brain loses its natural rhythms and by this time you need to be awake or asleep at a certain time, fighting the body's own rhythms.'

But the real problems with amphetamines begin when the user tries to stop. 'You can get quite depressed,' observes psychiatrist **Dr Philip Timms**, 'and if you then carry on taking them to stop you feeling depressed, you get into a vicious cycle.' No one knows whether Elvis did try to stop, but the pills helped him cope with depression after his marriage broke up. He told his stepbrother David Stanley that it was better to be unconscious than to be miserable.

Elvis's vampire-like **nocturnal existence** didn't help. While almost all his pre-Army recording sessions took place in 'normal' hours, afterwards he seemed to feel more comfortable at night. The 1969 sessions at American responsible for *From Elvis In Memphis* took place either side of midnight.

JD Sumner spent many nights either singing with Elvis or talking until he was exhausted. Not that the problems were all chemical: 'In Vegas, he wouldn't come off stage from the second show until one o'clock and it would take anyone hours to come down.' As Elvis put it, 'I stay up all night, and I have my friends with me, and I feel comfortable. In the morning when everybody else is up and going to work, I feel safe because it's daytime – and then I can go to sleep.'

Despite worsening health, Elvis kept touring. 'If the one thing that makes you feel good is being out on stage and getting that wave of love, then of course you're going to do it,' says Dr Timms, 'but the very act of standing up and trying to convince people that you have something to offer them is personally dangerous, because so much of what you do depends on feedback from other people.'

By the end of Elvis's life, his sleep disorder had become submerged by other problems. His spending sprees, erratic behaviour and apparent need to perform all suggest **bipolar depression**, in which moods alternate between euphoria and despair.

Elvis began to dread, says Guralnick, the sleep that came and the sleep that did not come.

The stigma that surrounds the word '**addict**' has led many fans to suggest Elvis only took drugs for his health. In later life, his colon wasn't working, which might explain his **puffiness**; the treatment led to occasional failure to control his bowels. The **steroids** he took for a deficiency in his adrenal gland, and for constipation, caused **weight gain**, which he fought with **diet pills**. He also suffered from **glaucoma**, worsened by stage lights and his hair dye, which ran into his eyes during concerts.

But the hard, undeniable, fact is that Elvis also took drugs because he liked them. He seldom took street drugs, like LSD or cocaine, but he still ingested some very powerful ones – such as dilaudid, a painkiller normally prescribed to cancer patients. Ultimately, the responsibility for Elvis's drug addiction, and its contribution to his untimely death, lies with Elvis. This was a man, after all, who studied the *Physician's Desk Reference*. Like many other victims, he rationalized that he controlled the drugs, they didn't control him, though Geller says he belatedly realised the dangers the summer he died.

monologues so bizarre they made me, in my exhausted, condition, believe that I really was hallucinating. He was funny, threatening, distracted, charming, paranoid, and absolutely irresistible. Listening to him ramble on between songs was like listening to a voice in your own head when you're losing your mind.'

Elvis missed two other great opportunities to break out of his cage. His obsession with karate had deepened through the years, and in 1974 he began to plan his own karate movie, either a documentary with him as a narrator, or a martial arts variation on the gunslinger-coming-out-of-retirement angle. Schilling says, 'He never got the respect that he deserved on this issue, and his health problems got in the way. But the damn thing would have made a lot of money and it would have been just the kind of challenge Elvis needed.' Another movie offer, from Barbra Streisand to play opposite her in *A Star Is Born*, fell through because, Schilling says, 'the Colonel demanded a superstar salary for Elvis and he didn't care about the money, he knew that a supporting role in a dramatic picture might just have been his ticket back.'

For Elvis, the highlight of 1974 came in July, when he arrived to watch the Memphis Grizzlies play the Portland Storm in the new World Football League, and received a standing ovation. Elvis was a regular attendee, says Mike Freeman, co-author of *Memphis Elvis Style*. Hardly the behaviour you'd expect of a man who had, according to one associate, become so reclusive he made Howard Hughes look like an extrovert.

A world troubled with pain

By the time Elvis celebrated his fortieth birthday in January 1975, he was, says his stepbrother David Stanley, 'like a caged animal. We would just get in a car and go, it didn't matter much where, except it was never anywhere new and he was never alone. We would just go back and forth to places he was familiar with, like he was looking for something he'd lost and if he could find it, he'd be happy.'

The last two years of his life passed in a recurring cycle of exertion, exhaustion, collapse and recovery. Though he needed the tours financially and emotionally as much as Parker, both Linda Thompson and Dr Nichopoulos were alarmed to see how the demands they placed on him exacerbated his pill taking. A life once punctuated by professional highlights was now punctuated by admissions to hospital: January 1975, June 1975, August 1975. The tours ground on, but his behaviour was often erratic and even uncharacteristically mean. In July 1975, he insulted the Sweet Inspirations on stage, and had to apologize during the next show.

And yet, as Tutt remembers, 'He was one of the most resilient men I have ever known. There were times he'd be out of shape and we were rehearsing, and he'd show up the first night and look just great. It was like he'd jumped in a convenient telephone booth and put on his Elvis Presley uniform like Superman.'

With hindsight, the outcome seems inevitable, but it didn't appear so at the time. There were days when Elvis would go to a football match almost like anyone else, tours when he sounded and looked back to his best. Bill Porter, the sound engineer who recorded most of Elvis's concerts, says that 'In 1975, he took time off to really get himself together. Everybody commented about it. He looked slim, he looked trim. He looked tanned. Why he didn't keep doing that I don't know.' By 1976, however, when Porter asked Nichopoulos what it would take to get Elvis off the pills, the doctor told him, 'Six feet of dirt.' Guralnick's suggestion that Elvis was clinically depressed, possibly as far back as 1973, is quite plausible; certainly he exhibited many of the classic symptoms.

Elvis kicked off 1976 with some difficult recording sessions in Graceland's Jungle Room. The rest of the year was full of tours and, given Elvis's spending habits, financial worries. In April, John O'Grady, an investigator who worked for Elvis, and lawyer Ed Hookstraten tried to get him into a drug treatment plan, but he ignored them. 'He was avoiding reality,' says David Stanley, 'and as with a lot of other things he did, he was world class at it.'

Jerry Schilling left Elvis in February 1976, because he felt working for him was killing their friendship. Vernon used the financial worries to fire Elvis's friends and bodyguards, Red and Sonny West. As ever, Elvis's intentions are unclear. The Wests' muscular approach to security work had sparked some expensive lawsuits, but their habit of confronting Presley about his pills might have also been a factor. Elvis may just have wanted to teach them a lesson; he had, after all, fired and rehired them all many times. Their dismissal might have seemed a smart financial move to Vernon, but when they began to write the book that became *Elvis: What Happened?*, the worry added enormously to his son's stress. Elvis called Red in October, hoping – although he didn't quite ask – to persuade them not to go ahead.

The Wests were soon followed by Linda Thompson, who

Elvis at Graceland in 1976, with flares as wide as the Mississippi

couldn't bear to watch Elvis destroy himself. Her defection contributed to the regretful mood of his last proper recording session in October 1976. She was replaced by the young local girl Ginger Alden, who became his fiancée, although no one agrees whether he really intended to marry her. A panicking Colonel Parker brought Dr Nichopoulos back into the fold to regulate Elvis's drug taking, and even allowed Larry Geller to return. He was stunned to see what had become of his old friend: 'No-one saw the hard fact that Elvis was on a track toward death. No-one wanted to see it. They were just blind, and they were in denial. Everybody was in denial.'

Bill Burk saw the hard facts when he caught a Presley performance in Las Vegas in December 1976. He was struck by the star's loneliness – 'his sadness jumped out at you' – and felt the only reason fans came was, as he wrote in his column, 'Maybe they think this will be the last time around'. In his hotel room, Elvis wrote a note that seemed to prove Burk's point, ending, 'I have no need for all of this / Help me lord'. Even so, the singer was sufficiently inspired by Alden's presence to wrap up 1976 with some above-average concerts, the stand-out being a ninety-minute performance on New Year's Eve in Pittsburgh.

Elvis's final year began with more tours, more inconsistent performances and, in April, another admission to hospital. Porter, who remembered Presley telling him he wouldn't outlive his mother, began to wonder if Elvis would survive, 'We used to all kind of say, "Well, what show is he gonna freak out on this time? Is he gonna quit? Is he gonna pass out on stage?"'.

In March 1977, Elvis spent $100,000 on a vacation in Hawaii. That seemed excessive to Vernon, but as Elvis told Geller, 'What does it profit a man if he gain the whole world and lose his soul?' The threat of the bodyguards' book loomed even larger, with Elvis alternately philosophical and furious; David Stanley describes him as 'like a 747 with a wing cut off'. Bill Burk met him at a Dunkin Donuts near Graceland, after he'd read Burk's piece about his Vegas concerts: 'I asked him why he couldn't take a year off, and he said he felt he owed it to the fans to be there as long as they wanted him, and he had so many people depending on him.'

In April, Colonel Parker, who had contemplated selling Elvis's contract (he even admitted, 'My artist is out of control': signed a deal with CBS for a TV special. His motivation may not have been exclusively financial), he probably desperately wanted to believe that the cameras would shake Presley out of his torpor.

In May, Larry Geller had a memorable confrontation with Parker in Elvis's hotel room, while on tour in Louisville, Kentucky. Presley was ill, Geller recalls, when Parker barged in. 'When he opened the door, I saw Elvis in a semi-conscious state, almost comatose. The doctor was kneeling at his bed holding his body up and ducking his head into a bucket of ice water to revive him because Elvis was moaning and groaning. My initial thought was

57

"I'm glad the Colonel is here to see this." I thought Parker was going to stay with Elvis for awhile, make sure he was okay, and there'd be an end to the tour and Elvis would go into a hospital. To my dismay, within ninety seconds, the door opened, the Colonel walks up to me, and he shakes his cane and he looks at me right in the eyes and he said, "The only thing that's important is that that man is on the stage tonight. Do you hear me?" To Parker, Elvis was a commodity. The almighty dollar.'

In the Midwest for the last tour he'd ever complete, Elvis stopped outside a gas station to help an attendant who was being set upon by two hoods. Stunned when they realized the identity of this would-be rescuer, everyone stopped fighting to have their pictures taken with him. Elvis gave his last concert at Indianapolis on 26 June 1977, and then returned to an unusually empty Graceland. With the mafia all but broken up, his only frequent companions were his cousin Billy Smith and his wife.

It's possible that even Elvis had begun to realize things had to change. Both Geller and cousin Donna Presley recall him contemplating a decisive break with Parker and the endless touring. Geller says Elvis told him, 'I've got to get off these drugs. I want to get rid of Colonel Parker and I want Tom Hulett to be my manager. I want to take a year off, go to Hawaii, rejuvenate, charge my batteries, and get into movies again.' When Billy Smith asked Elvis that summer about the Wests' book, and what would happen if someone heckled him, 'He said he would say, "I know you've read a lot about me over the years and after this tour, I'm going to take time to get myself straightened out." That was a giant step to say he needed treatment, to face reality.'

That recognition became sadly irrelevant when Elvis died on 16 August 1977. August was seldom kind to Elvis: his mother Gladys had died on 14 August 1958 and his divorce settlement was agreed in a Santa Monica court on 18 August 1972. Other smaller catastrophes to strike in the eighth month were the most serious death threats (in August 1970), an admission to hospital (in August 1975) and the death of an uncle (Travis Smith, in August 1973).

No wonder it was a month he often dreaded.

How (and why) exactly Elvis died remains a matter for acrimonious debate, but on one point there's a surprising consensus. The analysis of many of Elvis's musicians, friends and family is summarized by Jerry Schilling: 'What happened to Elvis is what happens to any creative person when short-term thinking takes over. This is not to entirely blame the Colonel, but the biggest failure of Elvis's partnership with the Colonel is that Elvis is not still with us today. He didn't die because of the drugs, he died because he couldn't find the challenges that would have kept him motivated'.

Afterlife

' Wise men know, when it's time to go'

Elvis Presley, in concert, 30 March 1977

Elvis Presley's death stunned fans and media alike. What was astonishing, as British DJ Paul Gambaccini put it, was not so much that Elvis had died, 'it was that Elvis Presley could die'.

His family and friends, however, were not so shocked. Neither were concert-business insiders, who had felt for some time that Elvis 'was a walking dead man'. He had almost died before, perhaps as often as four times in 1973. The make-up artist on the CBS TV special, filmed in June 1977, told Todd Slaughter, head of the British Elvis Presley Fan Club, that Presley had six months to live. She was half right: in fact he died in six weeks, not six months.

Immediately after Elvis died, David Stanley and others cleaned up the bathroom at Graceland, to conceal the scale of his use of (mainly prescription) drugs, and erected a wall of silence. Although, as they saw it, they were just taking care of business, protecting the boss, their actions – coupled with the abrupt announcement that Presley had died of an irregular heartbeat – fuelled a sense in the watching world that the whole truth was not being told.

Some speculated that Elvis had died of a drug overdose, whether accidental or deliberate. A surprising number of his own family members, including Vernon, and his cousins Donna Presley and Gene Smith, suspected he had been murdered. A few thought he had faked his own death, and was in hiding. This was, after all, a man who in his final years had told his record producer Felton Jarvis and cousin Billy Smith, 'I'm so tired of being Elvis Presley.'

The causes of death

For most, the controversy was not whether Elvis had died but how he had died. The bottom line is that he was last seen between 8am and 9am on the morning of 16 August 1977, by his fiancée Ginger Alden, and was discovered dead by her at around 2pm that afternoon. Despite all the speculation and obfuscation, there are only four basic scenarios.

Suicide

Although even Elvis had admitted 'I am self-destructive', no one suggested that he had deliberately killed himself until Albert Goldman's book *Elvis The Last 24 Hours* was published in 1990. Goldman theorized that, depressed by the forthcoming exposé by old friends Red and Sonny West, Elvis downed in one go the three envelopes of sleep medication that he normally took in stages, and then didn't eat to ensure that the drugs killed him. In support, Goldman cited statements from Elvis's stepbrother David Stanley that the singer had told him, 'David take care of yourself, I'll never see you again on this earth', and also the likelihood that Elvis was, in his last few years, clinically depressed. Like much of Goldman's first book on Elvis, however, the story may owe as much to his need to be sensational as it does to the actual facts.

Stanley's claim should be treated with caution. He didn't mention it in *Elvis We Love You Tender*, the Stanley family's first book, ghostwritten by Martin Torgoff. Nor does it feature in his *The Elvis Encyclopaedia* (1994), which presents Presley's death as a straightforward drug overdose. Dee Stanley, on the other hand, supports her son's story, saying (about the time she also accused Elvis of incest) that a suicide note was destroyed.

61

Elvis may have sensed that his own death was near. Larry Geller, Kathy Westmoreland and Rick Stanley all recall him saying on his last tour words to the effect, 'I may not look good tonight but I'll look good in my coffin.' Bill Burk, who met him in early 1977, remembers, 'He didn't look like a man who was suicidal as much as a man who was going through the motions of life, who wouldn't welcome death but for whom it wouldn't be exactly unwelcome either.'

Billy Smith states categorically that Elvis took the first two packets of drugs at 6am and 7.45am. Smith left after that, so he's not sure when (or if) Elvis took the third, but all three were definitely not ingested at once. His medication packets usually contained varying amounts of Seconal, Placidyl, Valmid, Tuinal and Demerol, with the third packet consisting of two Valmids and a placebo. According to Graceland staff, Elvis was on a liquid diet to lose weight, but he ate some ice cream and cookies. As David Stanley says he saw syringes on the floor – witnesses disagree how many – Presley may also have taken other drugs.

Most of Presley's friends argue that if he had wanted to kill himself, the world would have been left in no doubt as to his intentions; as Lamar Fike puts it, 'he would have written a book'. The crucial objection is that he wouldn't have done it while Lisa Marie was at Graceland: she was due to leave on 16 August.

Drug overdose

Given that Elvis had fourteen drugs in his system – ten in significant quantities, codeine at ten times the therapeutic level, qualudes in a possibly toxic amount, and three other drugs taken in sufficient quantity to be on the borderline of toxicity – it's hard to see how anyone could dispute the conclusion that he was killed by the interaction of drugs in his body, known as polypharmacy.

Some, especially Vernon, believe that Elvis was allergic to codeine, so its presence could have led to his death. Others say, however, that the allergy was mild; according to Goldman, he'd been taking it for years.

The verdict of polypharmacy is, though, disputed by several leading American pathologists, including Dr Joseph Davis, past president of the National Association of Medical Examiners. The position of the body, suggesting that Presley had fallen forward from the toilet into the carpet – the medical investigator initially suspected that Presley may have crawled a few feet before he died – was consistent with a sudden violent heart attack rather than a drug-related death. Overdose victims are usually found in positions of comfort.

Davis argues that Elvis died too quickly to have suffered an overdose: 'The only way drugs could have killed Elvis Presley that fast was if he were shooting up a lethal amount of heroin.' Accounts conflict as to when rigor mortis set in, varying from noon, about two hours before he was discovered, to 2.55pm, when his body was admitted to the Baptist Memorial Hospital. But it is clear that he had been dead some time before Alden found him.

The fourteen drugs were not necessarily present in sufficient quantities to cause an overdose. Medical technology in 1977 could not differentiate between drugs that had entered his metabolism and those that were active. As Presley had a high level of metabolized chemicals, the active drugs might have been well below a combined poisonous level. And, while drug deaths are normally accompanied by a pulmonary oedema in the lungs, there was no evidence of any fluid forced into the lungs.

Murder

The idea that Elvis was murdered might seem even more sensational than suicide, but members of the Presley family on both sides suspected exactly that. Elvis's father was convinced enough to accuse his stepson David, and to ask everyone at Graceland that day whether an intruder could have got into Elvis's bedroom. He even told Elvis's cousin Donna that he knew who had done it, and would sort it out his way, but died before he could do so. Graceland's head of security, Dick Grob, was also troubled by the fact that someone tipped off a *National Enquirer* stringer two hours before Alden found the body.

The curse of the Smiths

Once you pore over his family tree, the death of Elvis Presley at the age of **42** does not seem quite so exceptional or unexpected. Although his paternal side usually exceeded their three score years and ten, his mother's – **the Smiths** – seem predisposed to die young.

Elvis's mother **Gladys** died when she was **46**. Her **heart attack** was brought upon by hepatitis, itself exacerbated by drinking and diet pills. Her younger brother, **Johnny**, who had taught Elvis to play guitar, and was badly beaten in a fight as a young man, also died at **46**, in 1968. Another brother, **Travis**, died at **51** in 1966, suffering from cirrhosis of the liver.

Three of Elvis's maternal **cousins** also died young. **Junior**, who went mad fighting in Korea, died at just **28**, in 1961 – according to Billy Smith, from 'a cerebral haemorrhage or an alcoholic seizure'. **Bobby Smith**, who had been run over by a drunk driver outside Graceland, killed himself at **27** in 1968, by taking rat poison. And **Bobbie Jane Wren**, the daughter of Gladys's sister Lilian, committed suicide at **38**, in December 1976.

Vernon's suspicions focused on the presence of codeine in Elvis's system, while Gene Smith thought Elvis had been attacked. Although this sounds fanciful, Vernon and Elvis were to be witnesses in a trial of mob-related villains who had conned Elvis out of $950,000 in a scam over his Jetstar. The major biographies hardly mention the case, but the FBI files are available, and it's easy to see how the financial loss and worry added to the pressure on Elvis during his final year. Both Presleys died before things came to court.

The FBI, typically, didn't tell Memphis police about the Presleys' role in what was a much bigger investigation into billions of dollars of fake securities. So local police had no reason to conduct more than a cursory examination of the death scene, which had in any case been cleaned up. They probably wouldn't have found anything, but a methodical examination might at least have disproved Vernon's fears.

Heart attack

According to Dr Joseph Davis, a heart attack is the most likely explanation for Elvis's sudden death. Arrhythmia, which literally means an irregular heartbeat, was after all the original official cause of death. It can be fatal if it originates in the ventricular part of the heart, or if the victim is suffering from heart disease.

Davis's certainty stems from the position of the body, the speed of death, and Presley's weight. By his estimate, Elvis weighed 350 pounds when he died. Many of those pounds had recently been acquired as Elvis sat in his room, eating comfort food: Southern-fried goodies, cheeseburgers, ice cream, pizzas, and deep-fried peanut butter and banana sandwiches. Dr Nichopoulos had tried, unsuccessfully, to change his diet as far back as 1974.

Many members of Presley's entourage have tried to explain the pain he suffered in the final years, and the way he looked. Red West told Elvis on the phone in 1976, 'You ate a lot but you weren't fat, like people that are fat.' Billy Smith described how Elvis's stomach would suddenly puff up, while according to tour photographer Ed Bonja, 'Some days he would come out like he'd been pumped full of air.'

Talking to West, Elvis blamed his appearance on his lower intestine. There was certainly something wrong with his colon, which was full of matter on the autopsy. And his liver had been damaged, probably by drugs. His heart, too, was enlarged, possibly by as much as fifty percent – sufficient, anyway, for one of the specialists to hold it up to show colleagues how big it was.

An enlarged heart is a classic symptom of the chronic condition known as heart failure, which simply means the heart is not as good at pumping blood as it ought to be. Other symptoms sound familiar to those who saw or knew Elvis in the final years: shortness of breath, even while lying flat; feelings of dizziness; weight gain, which may cause swelling of the abdomen, feet and ankles;

decreased alertness; difficulty sleeping; narrowing of the arteries; and high blood pressure. Heart failure can be caused by, and contribute to, arrhythmia.

Could Elvis have had heart failure without knowing? Possibly. Shortness of breath had become a semi-constant concern, and he was taking medicine for high blood pressure. Two years before his death, doctors had fretted about his cholesterol. One specialist said his arteries were only starting to harden when he died, but a hospital worker told *Rolling Stone* that 'Elvis had the arteries of an eighty-year-old man'. Recent research suggests that people with a low birthweight and low weight in childhood are more likely to suffer heart disease in later life. By his own admission, Elvis put on 35 pounds in his first year of national fame, which may have been the first year he felt he could afford to eat.

Some fans grasp at any hint of a medical condition – such as the stories, not confirmed by any doctor, or by the autopsy, that he had bone cancer –in order to absolve Elvis of responsibility for his fate. However, one key cause of heart failure is abuse of toxic substances. In other words, drugs may not have killed him there and then, but, along with his eating habits and his incredible levels of of stress, they may have underlain the attack that ended his life.

Long live the King!

The confused explanations of Presley's sudden death, and the conflicting stories of the Memphis mafia, led, in a roundabout way, to the most bizarre twist on the Elvis Presley story of all – the kind of madcap nonsense that even the Colonel in his heyday would never have dared to dream up. Gail Giorgio's 1978 novel *Orion*, about a rock'n'roll singer who fakes his own death, signalled the start of the 'Is Elvis alive?' farrago. This strange book seemed weirder still in 1979, when an Elvis soundalike released an album called *Reborn* on Sun Records. But, of course, 'Orion' was not Elvis but Ellis – Jimmy Ellis, an American country singer, who had just the previous year recorded a song called I'm Not Trying To Be Like Elvis. Ellis/Orion had some country hits before the dual identities split for good in 1983.

For the Presley family, the final acts of the tragedy were the deaths of Vernon Presley in 1979, from a heart attack, and Elvis's grandmother Minnie Mae in 1980. Control of the estate passed with Vernon's death to Priscilla. With the publication of Goldman's biography in 1981, it didn't seem a very promising inheritance. But, after Graceland opened its gates to the public in 1982 and recouped its costs in days, it was clear the King had not lost all his subjects.

The big story of the early 1980s in Elvis world was the split between the Presley family and Colonel Parker. The case was settled in 1983, after a Tennessee judge declared Parker should receive no more money from the estate, by which time Parker had confirmed the rumours that he was an illegal Dutch immigrant.

Giorgio returned to the fray at the end of the decade with Is Elvis Alive? and The Elvis Files, which came complete with a tape that purported to be a phone conversation with the once and future King, but sounded as much like Reg Presley as Elvis Presley. The spelling of 'Aron' as 'Aaron' on Elvis's gravestone was seen as his coded hint that he wasn't really in there. By now, the suggestion was that Elvis had faked his own death either to escape the confines of stardom, or to flee some sinister organization – a cross between the mob and the sinister consortium that's always foiling Elvis fan Fox Mulder in The X-Files – that was after him because he'd helped government agencies in the war on crime.

Giorgio's novels and exposés sold a total of three million copies, and by the early 1990s sixteen percent of Americans believed Elvis was still alive. There hadn't been this much furore about the resurrection of a dead rock star since Jim Morrison had 'died', also of a heart attack, in 1971. Where Morrison's 'resurrection' had been a small cult affair, Elvis's was a national obsession. Sightings abounded. Some were ludicrous – why would he change his

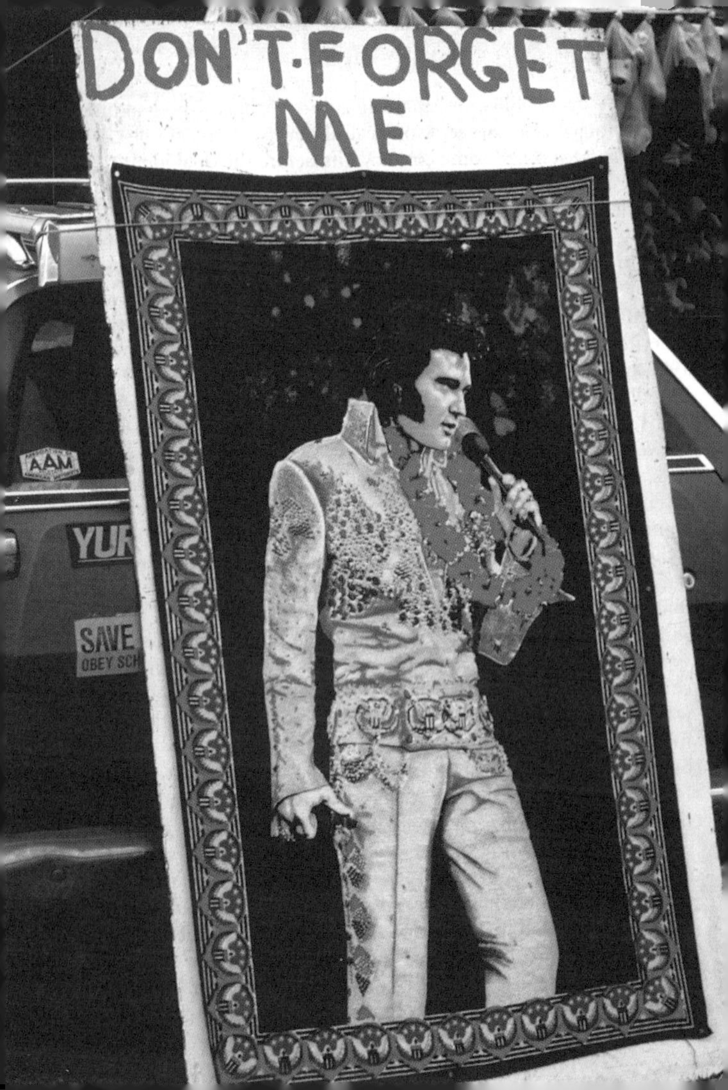
DON'T·FORGET
ME
AAM
YUR
SAVE
OBEY SCH

identity, only to drop into a local supermarket in one of his old jumpsuits singing 'Hunka hunka burning love'? A disproportionate number involved Kalamazoo, Michigan. Others, while absurd, were more intriguing, if only because of what they said about the way Elvis was perceived.

When fans told of meeting Presley in life, he always came across as a humble, humorous hero. The Elvis whom people now 'saw' in death was still humble and heroic, but as melancholy as the tearful 'velvet Elvis' paintings. One sighting will make the point. A quiet stranger called John pulls up at a dairy farm in Wisconsin and buys a quart of milk, which he says he hasn't tasted in years. He seems so visibly moved by the peace, and so obviously nursing a secret sadness, that the farmer and his wife invite him to stay at first for supper, and then for longer. He pays his board in advance and takes the King James Bible to bed. Next morning, at breakfast, a farm hand tells the farmer his guest's true identity. The astonished farmer goes up to John's room, but finds him vanished. This sighting concludes with the farmer's wife praying, 'Wherever he's gone, I hope he finds some place he can stay for a while, some place to rest his heart. It's a long, lonesome road he's on. He may never get to the end of it.'

In most sightings, the Elvis figure was called John because he'd used the aliases John Burrows and John Carpenter – the character he played in *Change Of Habit* – when alive. Besides, John Carpenter shared his initials with a more famous carpenter.

The last hope of those who believed the King would return came and went in 2001. Two mathematical equations convinced the deluded he might return that year. First, if you add the year of his death (1977) to the day he died (16) and the number of the month he died (8), you get 2001, which was, of course, Elvis's theme tune. Similarly – very similarly indeed – if you add the year he was born (1935), the day he was born (8), the day he died (16) and his age

◀ Fans needn't have worried, the King is dead but he's not forgotten

when he died (42), you get, hey presto, 2001. The good news for most Elvis fans is that even the *Weekly World News*, the demented stepchild of the *National Enquirer*, now accepts that Elvis A(a)ron Presley did indeed die – when he was 58.

Sightings

1 A white rat named **Elvis** sparked an interest in the field of psychology for Janet Duchek, PhD. As a high-school senior, she and her classmates used conditioning to train a rat to jump up on a tiny stage and slap his front paws on a miniature guitar to mimic playing. The rat would only perform when he heard the song **Hound Dog** by **Elvis Presley** – *Washington People*, Washington University, December 1988

2 Image of Elvis Presley appears in a grass pattern on the side of a Scottish hillside. '**It's Elvis**', shouted mum-of-three Linda, 37, when she saw it – *BBC News*, August 2000

3 "'Hey, Elvis, sing something for us!'" This is what 18-year-old **Narek Magarian** hears walking along Yerevan streets. For three years, Magarian has dressed as Elvis, behaved as Elvis, lived as Elvis, Armenian-style. "It started as fanaticism but now it's more than that. This is the philosophy of my life," Magarian says' – *Armenia Week*, January 2002

4 **Robbie Williams** has revealed that the secret to his continued abstinence from drink and drugs is regular **prayer**, to Elvis. Robbie has been off the booze and drugs for seven months. 'Before the gig we get in a huddle and pray to Elvis to look after us' – *dotmusic.com*, July 2001

5 After facing down the tanks outside the Russian parliament building, Russian leader **Boris Yeltsin** returned to his official residence and sang **Are You Lonesome Tonight?**, his favourite Elvis song – *CNN*, August 1991

6 A bust of **Elvis Presley** in a southeastern Dutch town reportedly is '**weeping**' salty tears for his fans. The white statuette, decked out in a fur-trimmed cloak and framed by two pink candles, started weeping last week, owner Toon Nieuwenhuisen said – *Associated Press*, August 1997

7 '*Nig-na-me si-ib-ak-ke-en, e-sir kus-za-gin-gu ba-ra-tag-ge-en.*' The words may not seem familiar to most Elvis fans, possibly because they are ancient Sumerian, which was spoken in **Mesopotamia** between 4000BC and 1800 BC. But they are, say Finnish academics Jukka Ammondt and Professor Simo Parpola, how the Sumerians would have sung, 'Do anything that you want to do, but uh, uh, honey lay off my blue suede shoes.' As the Sumerians didn't have shoes or suede, the closest Ammondt could get to Carl Perkins's original line was 'But my sandals of sky-blue leather do not touch' – *Irish Times*, July 2001

8 A jailed Elvis Presley fan is in heartbreak hotel after a judge ordered his vast collection of the King's records to be destroyed. Leung Kwok-hung, 53, known as **Jailhouse Kwok** had spent 40 years collecting 5000 records. Leung admitted some discs were pirated but told officers his Elvis collection was genuine – *Ananova*, August 2000

9 Elvis – A new concept in cell culture and viral diagnostics. Dr Olivo coined the phrase '**Enzyme-Linked Virus Inducible System**' to describe this technology and the term **ELVIS®** has since been used as a popular way to refer to his invention – *DHIUSA.com*, July 2001

10 Question: 'Elvis, are you in this room?' Answer: 'Yes.' Question: 'Do you approve of drug abuse?' Answer: 'No.' Interpretation: Having had the last seventeen years to ponder his last years with us on Earth, it seems Elvis has learned from his own mistakes – *The Elvis Séance*, January 1994

The King and the stamps

Amid all the sightings, America had the excitement of the Elvis elections of 1992. In the first, a million US citizens voted by a massive majority for the 1950s Elvis, as opposed to the 1970s Las Vegas Elvis, to appear on a postage stamp. In the other, the candidate who most resembled the 1970s Elvis – a Southern charmer with a weight problem and a reputation as a womanizer – was elected President of the United States. The big break in Bill Clinton's campaign may have come when he played Heartbreak Hotel on sax on the Arsenio Hall show – perhaps the best sax solo on an Elvis record since Boots Randolph's on I Feel So Bad in 1961.

Meanwhile, the discovery of the very first recording Elvis ever made, My Happiness, an utterly pivotal moment in rock'n'roll history, had passed almost unnoticed in 1990. US schoolchildren, asked who Elvis was, said things like, 'He lived in a big house in Memphis and only came out at night.' It was the release of the 1950s box set, The King Of Rock'n'Roll, complete with that historic debut, that began to remind everyone why Elvis was famous in the first place.

The twentieth anniversary of Presley's demise saw the death of his manager. Which meant, ironically, that Colonel Parker missed out on Elvis's world tour, in 1999, in which he appeared on a giant video screen in front of his old band, playing live – of all Elvis's

The Little Princess

When Lisa Marie Presley was born on 1 February 1968, her father was over the moon, calling her his 'Little Princess' (or 'Buttonhead', or 'Yisa'). As a 5-year-old, she'd swan around her parents' estate wearing mink coats and enough jewellery to sink a ship. When her parents separated, Lisa blamed her mother's affair with karate instructor Mike Stone, rather than her father's numerous liaisons.

Aged 9, Lisa was at Graceland when Elvis died. She heard a commotion in the bathroom, and rushed in to find Ginger Alden standing over her daddy's body. As Elvis's heiress, she was soon the target of kidnapping threats; Priscilla became understandably overprotective, while Lisa rejected her mother. By the time she was 16 she had already suffered from depression, drug addiction and eating disorders – very much her father's child. When John Travolta introduced Priscilla to Scientology, Lisa was sent to a church rehabilitation centre, where she beat drugs and met

her first husband, **Danny Keogh**. They married in 1988, when Lisa was 20 years old, and had **two children**.

They were divorced in the early 1990s, Keogh complaining that Lisa was distant. Pop psychology had it that she was afraid to fall in love lest she lost another man, like she lost her father. She didn't date for a while, then embarked on one of the weirdest adventures the world can offer – she married **Michael Jackson**.

Lisa and Michael became close friends after meeting at a dinner party in 1993. Not long afterwards, Jackson faced **child abuse** allegations, and media reports that he was addicted to **prescription drugs**. Although Lisa got him into rehab, the marriage lasted just twenty months.

The ups and downs have continued. In 1998, when Lisa turned 30, she began taking care of business for Elvis Presley Enterprises, and fell in love with musician John Oszajca. Their engagement ended after sixteen months. Meeting actor **Nicolas**

Cage at a party seemed to have changed her luck. At first, the two didn't get on; Lisa gave Nic a hard time after he talked too much about her father, but he eventually took her to see her dad's old mate Tom Jones in Las Vegas. The pair swiftly announced they were to marry, but then almost as abruptly split.

Lisa has since spent over a year finishing her first album. Some might say that's a brave move, to compete with Dad; others argue that she's mad to try. Lamar Fike says, 'She has talent – like an anvil,' but Myrna Smith of the Sweet Inspirations, who feature on the album, insists: 'Man, she can sing. It'd be bad if she couldn't.'

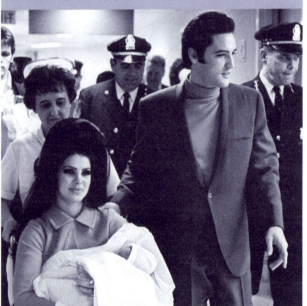

The birth of a princess: the new expanded Presley family in 1968

firsts, this was probably the oddest. In 1969, he'd famously hailed his first Las Vegas concert as his first live appearance in nine years, adding 'I've appeared dead before but this is my first live one.' Now, the joke was reversed. It seemed weird, and yet, to thousands of fans who'd never seen him in concert, it was in its way a strangely moving experience.

The most publicized academic conference ever – the International Conference on Elvis Presley – took place at the University of Mississippi in August 1997. It was guaranteed to unleash the cultural snobbery, as typified by Goldman, which had always refused to concede that Presley exemplified anything, let alone something as grandiose as 'American culture'. In some ways, the sneering worked – subsequent conferences have been less ambitious affairs. But then the furore didn't mark any real change: Elvis had never been respectable in life either.

The very fact the conference took place, coupled with the publication of Peter Guralnick's two-volume biography, suggested that Elvis the king of rock'n'roll was becoming more intriguing than Elvis the burger king. The process of re-evaluation was spurred by the fine work of BMG, which now owns RCA, in producing assorted critically acclaimed box sets, and setting up the collectors' label Follow That Dream. At some point, RCA's release schedule will come to seem less like the opening of a record company's vaults and more like the scraping of a once-profitable barrel, but this campaign has already repositioned Elvis, making his brilliance more accessible and his claims to genius more credible.

After 11 September 2001, an Elvis single of America The Beautiful hit the *Billboard* US top ten of records sold – not the main *Billboard* chart, which gives more priority to radio plays than copies shifted in shops – and raised thousands of dollars for victims of the attack.

Why Elvis Presley's fame has already endured beyond reason may be because, as Lamar Fike says, 'he is both a hero and a joke, an artistic genius and the premier symbol of wretched excess'. Fike admits to having so many dreams in which Elvis talked to him that he saw a psychiatrist. 'And the doctor said, "You're going to have these dreams for the rest of your life". And he's right.' In a much milder form, that applies to millions more of us.

Ten songs that tell the story

Although Elvis only wrote two songs in his life, he often chose material that reflected his own experience – a habit that grew more pronounced as the 1970s wore on. If you were to devise an album of such performances, it might look something like this.

Don't Cry Daddy

Elvis wanted to record two songs during the Memphis 1969 sessions because they reminded him of his parents. The beautifully sung, brilliantly phrased **Don't Cry Daddy**, an obvious tribute to his dad, sold a million. The other, **Mama Liked The Roses**, with its kitsch chimes, was originally buried on a budget Christmas album, but was later issued as the B-side to "The Wonder Of You".

Good Time Charlie's Got The Blues

'Play around you'll lose your wife, play it too long you'll lose your life.' Between 1971 and 1977, Elvis did both. And in 1973 he recorded **Good Time Charlie's Got The Blues** at Stax.

Hurt

The melodramatic, charismatic **Hurt** was recorded at Graceland in 1976. JD Sumner said Elvis extracted every nuance out of Roy Hamilton's classic, pointing out how the surprising stress on the 'so' in 'I'm so hurt' makes the anguish even more powerful.

It's Easy For You

The Lloyd Webber/Rice collaboration **It's Easy For You**, about a man who threw his wife and children away, produced a genuinely heart-wrenching performance from Elvis, and some subtle drumming from Ronnie Tutt.

It's Midnight

The B side of **Promised Land**, available on the eponymous album, was **It's Midnight**, a wonderfully desolate ballad in which Elvis chastises himself for wanting his lost love, and for failing to be the man he'd like to be.

Memphis Tennessee

When Elvis recorded **Memphis Tennessee** in 1963, Chuck Berry's song suited him because it was about his hometown. The happy home that was torn apart, because Mom did not agree, was to come later.

My Way

Perhaps presciently, Elvis sang **My Way** most often when the end was indeed very near. His later readings were far darker than the smugness of the Sinatra/Anka original. His rendition of Marty Robbins's **You Gave Me A Mountain**, which he always denied was autobiographical, is in a similar grand but tortured vein.

Pieces Of My Life

Troy Seals' **Pieces Of My Life**, a ballad about a singer who can't find the best part of his life that  was one of the highlights of *Elvis Today*, fitted Presley a whole lot better than some of his 1970s jumpsuits.

Separate Ways

That Red West wrote **Separate Ways** may explain why it cuts so close to the bone – especially in the second verse, when Elvis sings about the tears his daughter will cry. The emphasis on 'only' in 'only friends' is wonderful.

That's Someone You Never Forget

Red West also crafted this – a lyric which could have been a love song but might, equally, have been about Elvis's yearning for Gladys. She could just as easily have been the 'one who waits for you', presumably in heaven.

'We'll meet again. God bless you. Adios.'

The Music

The highs, the lows,
and the bits in between

The music

So Elvis Presley told Sun office manager Marion Keisker, when she asked what type of song he sang. He was just about to make his first recording, as a present for his mother and for himself. Finding his reply less than informative, she tried again: 'Who do you sound like?' The response was just as enigmatic: 'I don't sound like nobody.' Over the next twenty-four years, Elvis was to prove both statements true, singing country, blues, rock'n'roll, pop, ballads (some semi-operatic) gospel, soul, contemporary Christian, folk, Hawaiian, Mexican, bluegrass, jazz-blues, and downright schmaltz.

Most evaluations of Elvis's musical career are based on the idea that he followed a linear trajectory, from rock'n'roll in the 1950s to the ballads that almost monopolized his studio time in the 1970s. As the shift loosely coincides with his rise to commercial success, as well as his move to Las Vegas as a professional base, it's all too easily assumed that Elvis sold out somewhere, and lost control of

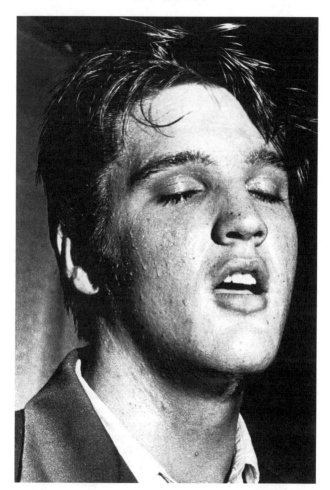

his artistic destiny. The *Penguin Encyclopaedia of Popular Music*, for example, commenting on his 1970s cover of My Way, concludes: 'The irony is he had hardly ever done anything his way.'

For some, Elvis sold out when he let RCA put drums on his records. John Lennon famously charged that he died, musically, when he was drafted. Others, like his most dismissive biographer Albert Goldman, say Elvis never had anything to sell out to begin with. The consensus view tends to interpret his musical career as a Faustian myth. Having begun his musical life in the state of pure innocence epitomized by That's All Right, it runs, Elvis sold his creative birthright for fame, stardom, and the right to sing songs like Do The Clam in drippy movies.

For every Faust, you need at least one Mephistopheles – which is where Colonel Parker comes in so useful. Parker may have had Mephistophelean tendencies but that doesn't necessarily mean Elvis sold his musical soul. Rock writer Stanley Booth once characterized Elvis's Sun records (and, by extension, that kind of music) as 'his thing', while those he made later were 'their thing', but Elvis himself would not have recognized that distinction.

The legendary backstage confrontation in 1955, between Elvis and Ira Louvin, underlines the point. Elvis was sharing a bill with the Louvin Brothers, one of the finest country-gospel acts around and one of his favourite groups. After laying another audience to waste, Elvis sat down at the piano and began to sing an old gospel hymn. According to Ira's less volcanic brother Charlie, as reported in Nicholas Dawidoff's *In The Country Of Country*, the dialogue went as follows:

Elvis: *Here's what I like.*
Ira Louvin: *You fuckin' white nigger, if that's the kind of music you like why don't you do that out there instead of that shit you do?*

◀ 'I don't sound like nobody' – Elvis proved it to the world in 1956

Elvis: *When I'm out there, I do what they want to hear, when I'm back here I do what I want to do.*

Though Elvis was being somewhat disingenuous, gospel, not rock, was always his first musical love. His tastes were in any case wider, as he made clear when asked to name his favourite singer in March 1956:

Elvis: *It's a pretty hard question to answer … I've never really … oh yeah … Frank Sinatra, I like.*
Interviewer: *Did you ever listen to any opera or concert soloists perform?*
Elvis: *No, I like Mario Lanza. I like the way … I like anything he records.*

The music Elvis saw as 'his thing' is incredibly varied. At different times, asked to name his favourite singers and musicians, he cited Lanza, Fats Domino, Dean Martin, Pat Boone, Patti Page, Kay Starr, Pat Boone, Sonny James (before the country singer had his first hit), Roy Orbison, LaVern Baker, Clyde McPhatter, Roy Hamilton, Arthur Crudup, and the Boston Pops Orchestra (one of the names on that list is a joke). In 1972, he told the makers of *Elvis On Tour* : 'At high school, I had Metropolitan opera records … the Spanish … I liked the Mexican-flavored songs.' And in August 1970, he startled the classically trained Kathy Westmoreland, when she joined him as a backing singer, by quizzing her about the great tenors of the past, Enrico Caruso and the Swede Jussi Bjoerling.

All this is not to downplay the importance of the music created by Elvis, Scotty, Bill and Sam Phillips at Sun; merely to suggest that it did not exclusively define Elvis's musical 'soul'. Those first five singles, plus the other Sun tapes RCA bought with Elvis's contract, may be the most revolutionary music he ever made, but that's not to say that he never recorded anything significant or authentic again. It's possible to thrill to the eerie magic of Mystery

84

Train while still loving the indignant drama of Long Black Limousine, recorded, back in Memphis, a full fourteen years later.

Sam Phillips recognized his protégé's unusual gift when he recalled, 'He had the most intuitive ability to hear songs without ever having to classify them, or himself, or anyone I've ever known outside of Jerry Lee Lewis and myself. The songwriters most associated with his post-Sun career, Jerry Leiber and Mike Stoller, were just as astonished . Leiber admits, 'We thought he was just an idiot savant, but he knew all our records, he knew Eddy "Cleanhead" Vinson. He loved Ray Charles' early records.'

There were almost as many musical Elvises as there were flying Elvises in *Honeymoon In Vegas* (34, for anyone who lost count). At Sun in September 1954, he could dredge up a song from a Jerry Lewis/Dean Martin movie, I Don't Care If the Sun Don't Shine, and then record Good Rocking Tonight, as frank an invitation to an orgy as the 1950s would allow. Nor, whatever the myth may say, did Elvis completely forget how to rock. Just listen to his attack on his old rival Jerry Lee Lewis's Whole Lotta Shakin' Goin On, as released in 1971; to his affectionate take on Chuck Berry's Promised Land, recorded in 1973; or to Way Down, a disco-fuelled rocker that was the last single released in his lifetime.

It is true, though, that the songs that moved Elvis most during his last eight years – as his marriage collapsed, his self-destructive drug abuse accelerated, and his health worsened – were ballads, often country-tinged, which seemed to say something about his life. He took It's Midnight, for example – recorded at Stax Studios in Memphis in December 1973 – and conveyed real emotion, getting inside it with a feeling that he knew from the blues. You may not like it, but it was just as expressive of where Elvis was when he sang it as That's All Right had been in 1954.

In a sense, the multiplicity of Elvis's musical personalities, and his very versatility, have worked against him. As Guralnick said in the sleeve notes to *Sunrise*, a seminal collection of his work for Sun, 'If Elvis Presley had never made another record after his last Sun session, there seems little question that his music would have achieved the same mythic status as Robert Johnson's blues.' Elvis would record seven hundred more songs, some as good as Suspicious Minds, others as dire as Yoga Is As Yoga Does. That one man could record both numbers within a single career, let alone in the space of three years, is frankly bizarre, and suggests the scale of the problem in trying to assess his musical legacy.

There are other complicating factors. Elvis, unlike the artists he had inspired, such as Bob Dylan, seldom wrote a song. And soon after Elvis became globally famous, he became a virtual mute. So, it's harder confidently to identify personal significance in many of his songs and many of the crucial questions about his musical career – for example, why he never returned to Chips Moman's studios after the 1969 sessions that produced Suspicious Minds and In The Ghetto – are a matter of conjecture, with almost no insight from the man himself.

As with any artist of his calibre and broad appeal, commercial pressure was a fact of life from the start. Thus each of his Sun singles followed an unvarying formula, with a blues song on one side and a country number on the other; an innocent ploy to secure maximum airplay and sales.

As he changed management and record companies, the pressures changed in unexpected ways. Oddly, Elvis had far more artistic freedom at RCA than at Sun, because nobody at his new label quite knew what to make of him at first. But he lost the focus Phillips had brought to his music. Elvis diversified, as he had always wanted, into pop, ballads and gospel, but his very versatility became harnessed to a marketing plan. By the 1960s his studio albums had eager-to-please titles like Something For Everybody and Elvis For Everyone. In twenty years in the studio after Sun, the only producers to challenge him creatively as Sam had done were Leiber and Stoller, on the sessions for Jailhouse Rock and King Creole, and Chips Moman in American Studios in Memphis in 1969.

When Elvis first signed for RCA, the need was simple and urgent: to cut a hit record. Though Heartbreak Hotel did the trick, the issue of music publishing soon reared its head. Colonel Parker and the publishers Hill & Range set up deals so Elvis would make royalties as a singer and, in partnership with Hill & Range, a publisher. Not such an unreasonable idea, it enriched Presley considerably, but it created a conflict of interest at the heart of the machine. RCA simply wanted hit records but Parker, Hill & Range, and Elvis had, to varying extents, vested interests in those hits being published by their companies. In the 1950s, a writer like Otis Blackwell was happy to give up rights on All Shook Up in the confident expectation that the single would sell two million copies. A decade later, rows over royalties would threaten two of Presley's best singles – Guitar Man and Suspicious Minds.

As early as 1957, Leiber and Stoller were reprimanded for not using proper channels when, at Elvis's request, they wrote Don't. Even though it sold 1.3 million copies and was a US number one, the duo were told that if they did it again, they were out. And after refusing to give up rights on songs for GI Blues, they were exiled. That departure set the pattern for the 1960s, with genuinely gifted songwriters like Pomus and Shuman supplying an ever-decreasing proportion of the King's repertoire.

A row within Hill & Range ultimately led to a split that made the publishing wing of the Elvis empire even less effective in the 1970s. Although Elvis's comeback had stunned the world, all his own publishing company could come up with as the decade wore on seemed to be British songs, already turned down by the likes of Tom Jones. It was an odd, unsatisfactory state of affairs for a singer of Presley's stature and he increasingly turned to songs that he'd heard on the radio, or favourites he'd lived with for years.

While music publishing exerted its behind-the-scenes influence, the most visible force to affect the quality of his music was Hollywood. His first screen test came just days after the release of his self-titled album, the fastest-selling album in RCA's history. Elvis had always wanted to be an actor, so it made sense creatively, and probably helped prolong his career. As Parker said: 'Overexposure is like sunburn, it can hurt.' Beatles manager Brian Epstein later admitted he had considered a similar strategy.

In the studio

The single most dramatic fact about Elvis in the studio, especially as his myth grew after he left Sun, was his sheer physical presence. 'There was something different about him,' says Boots Randolph, 'sounds funny to call it an aura but it's hard to know what else to call it.'

Bass player Norbert Putnam vividly recalls his first session with Presley in June 1970. 'He had an amazing, almost feminine, physical beauty, far greater than you see in any of the films or the photographs. And he entered wearing a cape and a lion's head cane with red ruby eyes, looking more than a little like Dracula.' Later, his presence could be just as disconcerting for different reasons. In those last Graceland sessions in 1976, he would often be an incredible hulking form in pyjamas and dressing gown.

Presley's impact in the studio would be felt even before he made his Dracula-like appearances. 'Put' (as Elvis called him) says, 'The first time I was going to be playing in the same studio, I remember thinking beforehand, "Oh God, don't let me be the one to make the mistake that ruins an Elvis Presley session."' Wood had an even more intense feeling before the 1969 Memphis sessions. 'I knew he was in the back parking lot. I just felt his presence, it was almost like Christ was out there.'

David Briggs, who played on his first Elvis session in 1966, recalls: 'I was scared to death. I had done a Beatles tour with Tommy Roe, but Elvis was something else.' Briggs' nerves worsened when he was called in to play piano on *Love Letters*, 'he had the piano moved up so he could be right on top of it, man, it was a pretty tense situation.'

Fortunately, says Putnam, 'Elvis knew all of us were worrying like that and he had a marvellous way of bringing everybody together at the beginning of the session and telling us some story about

RCA sessions in New York, 1956; the drummer is DJ Fontana ▶

something that happened to him which would have us laughing out loud.'

Although some of Presley's wilder behaviour in the studio (karate demos at the July 1973 Stax session, guns brandished at Graceland) have entered into popular mythology, Charlie McCoy's abiding memory of Elvis in the studio is of his deep courtesy. 'He would always, at the beginning off a session, whether you had played with him or not before, come up to you and make sure you knew how glad he was to have you there.'

Typically, Presley would warm up with a few gospel numbers or, later, by listening to the stack of demos his publishers had sent. Boots Randolph recalls, 'You never quite knew what to expect. Because we weren't on the standard three-hour sessions, you felt anything could happen. I wouldn't have been surprised if he'd ridden a motorbike through the studio but then, suddenly it would be down to business and you'd be on, you'd feel you wanted to get in there quick to show him that you were on top of your game.'

The studio was Elvis's domain

and his effect on how music was made was almost as revolutionary as what music was made. As recording engineer Bones told Elvis's biographer Jerry Hopkins: 'Elvis produced his own records. He came to the session, picked the songs, and if something in the arrangement was changed, he was the one to change it. Everything was worked out spontaneously. Many of the important decisions normally made previous to a recording session were made during the session. He was the forerunner of everything that's record production these days.'

In one respect Presley remained unique. 'He wouldn't just stand by the mike and sing. He would do the full Elvis Presley performance and he'd really be sweating by the end of the song. And every so often he would go the toilet – the toilets would be barred off – with his valet and do a costume change and he would come back in something completely different,' recalls Putnam. 'It was kind of camp in a way but he was just being this creature that he created called Elvis Presley. He could turn that on and off in an instant. I remember once, he and I were having a sandwich, one of the few times I was one-on-one with him, and he said to me, "Put, what time is it?" I told him it was about 1am and he tapped me and said, "Put, it's time for me to go and be Elvis Presley." And then he walked across the studio, picked up the mike and his voice changed and he became Elvis Presley.'

A similar 'live' performance, in his very first RCA session in January 1956, astonished the normally phlegmatic Chet Atkins so much he rang his wife and told her to hotfoot it to the studio ('I didn't want her to miss it,' he explained later). Elvis would use theatrics to get in the mood, turning the lights down to record *Love Letters* and sticking candles on the piano so he could see the lyrics or writhing on the floor as he sang 'If I Can Dream'. JD Sumner said later, 'You always knew with Elvis, at his best, that whatever he was singing, that would be the only thing in his mind.'

He had a perfect ear and could learn a song from a demo in an instant. And he was at ease with musicians in a way that, perhaps, he never was with the rest of the human race apart from his family. Mike Stoller would recall, 'He was completely open. Elvis loved to work. He would do thirty takes and still want to do another. Jerry and I were used to being in a studio for three hours to cut four sides … we were always watching the clock. Elvis would just take over the studio for the whole day and send out for lunch, and stay until he got what he wanted.'

Later, when he began to lose his appetite for studio work, his musicians often relied on his generosity to get another take. Putnam says one of them would go up and ask Elvis to do another, saying one of the musicians had screwed up and Presley would happily oblige. His studio tantrums, although famous, were comparatively rare and often, Ronnie Tutt says, sparked not by his colleagues (he would usually take the blame for a goof himself, whoever's fault it was) but by poor material or technology.

Tutt would say later, 'These are my own words, but he believed the art of recording is an art of recording a live performance, not an art of a recording studio. He was a purist about that.' But this, coupled with the kind of performance Putnam described, didn't make the job of capturing Elvis on record any easier.

As Elvis appearances in the studio grew rarer and, perhaps, as he lost what his faith in his voice, he did what he had done in Hollywood as the films deteriorated and retreated behind his entourage or, as the musicians called them, 'gofers'. He would also hide behind a protective phalanx of backing singers, which didn't help. It is probably no coincidence that three of the best performances on his 1973 studio album feature Elvis by himself at the piano.

Putnam often felt that the trappings, the sycophantic laughter and the cries of 'King!' made it harder for Presley to work as a singer. He had stopped playing bass on sessions in the early 1970s to become a producer but never turned down the chance to work with Presley. 'I'd be in LA, completely booked up and somebody would call and I'd try to say I was busy but I'd always give in. How could you not find the time to work with the King?' For all the tales of guns, karate and tantrums, it's a sentiment most of the musicians who worked with Elvis in his 22 years in the studio would echo.

But Elvis's new career meant that in 1957, his most productive year in the studio, he actually spent less time recording non-movie songs than he had in 1956. RCA A&R man Steve Sholes was soon complaining, 'we are getting consumer mail criticizing us for infrequent releases of Elvis singles and albums'. Hollywood set the musical agenda. When movies and songs were as good as *Jailhouse Rock*, that seemed fine. It was when they fell to the standards of *Paradise, Hawaiian Style* that fans and singer complained.

Yet Presley was not a helpless martyr to the forces of commerce, and can't be absolved from responsibility for his own career. He undoubtedly enjoyed his pre-eminence in the 1950s, and was depressed, disturbed, and even embittered by his slide into near-obscurity in the late 1960s. But after he regained the initiative in 1968-69, he tragically let it slip once more.

Elvis's artistic triumphs were in any case not necessarily commercial successes. Although the interests of art and commerce briefly coincided in the glory that was 1956, thereafter they did so only sporadically, as with Suspicious Minds and Burning Love. The album he was proudest of, *Elvis Is Back!*, sold less than half as many copies as the soundtrack to *Girls! Girls! Girls!* His finest, most coherent, RCA album, *From Elvis In Memphis*, peaked at number twelve on the US charts, while *Roustabout* was a US number one. As 'the King', Elvis may have had a status to which countless stars have aspired, but the interests of King and singer were not always the same.

Good rocking tonight: the 1950s

The Big Bang theory, which dates the origins of rock'n'roll to a single record, has now largely been discredited, partly because nobody can quite agree on which record that might be. Jackie Brenston's Rocket 88, released on Sun in 1951, is the most likely candidate, but the roots of the new genre stretch back into the 1940s. Some musicologists see its first glimmers in the frenetic, humorous output of Fats Waller and Louis Jordan, which was authentically black but appealed to a white audience, possessing a kind of directness, a relevance to the real world, that Tin Pan Alley just wasn't offering.

The style of rhythmic fast blues known as jump blues, as practised by Big Joe Turner and Aaron 'T-Bone' Walker, was a more immediate precursor of rock'n'roll. Turner, whose Shake, Rattle And Roll Elvis covered in 1956, influenced Wynonie Harris, whose

1949 release Good Rocking Tonight would be Elvis's second single. Walker's guitar work was a particular inspiration to Chuck Berry; he was also famous for his sheer sartorial flash, and especially his gold lamé jacket.

Meanwhile, in Chicago, on the Atlantic record label, Ahmet Ertegun was producing what he called 'watered-down versions of the real blues', as sung by the likes of Ruth Brown. They might have dismayed purists, but they had an energy found in few white pop records of the time. Elvis, who owned several of Brown's singles (and discs by other black Atlantic artists like the Drifters) was just one of millions of white teenagers listening to music from what Sam Phillips called 'the other side of the racial Maginot line'.

In 1951 the concept of Top 40 radio was devised by two executives at KOWH in Omaha, in a desperate bid to increase their paltry audience share. The format soon became incredibly popular. Although it has since become synonymous with dumbing down, initially it freed DJs to play the music their listeners wanted to hear, rather than the music the guardians of public decency thought they ought to hear. Elvis was one of the first major acts to really benefit from the new format; for all his talent, he could not have achieved such dominance without it.

Prominent among what white radio listeners wanted to hear were artists like Johnnie Ray and Patti Page. Elvis himself probably bought Page's Tennessee Waltz, a six-million-seller that was among the first records to exploit the invention of magnetic tape. A huge advance on direct-to-disc acetates, this gave artists and studios much greater flexibility to experiment and edit (it allowed Page to sing four-part harmony with herself). The lip-quivering Ray topped the pop and R&B charts in 1951 with the sob-athon Cry, and later covered both the Drifters' Such A Night (which Elvis recorded in 1960), and Just Walking In The Rain, a moody ballad first released by the Prisonaires on Sun.

The white artist who really played John the Baptist to Elvis's Jesus was Bill Haley, whose first national hit was a jive novelty called Crazy Man Crazy. Haley had been emulating the jump blues acts since 1952's Rock The Joint, but didn't really make it big until his Rock Around The Clock – a landmark single that on its first release failed to make the *Billboard Top* 20 – became the theme to the movie *Blackboard Jungle* in 1955. Appropriately enough, one of the songs drawn on by Haley was Around The Clock Blues, by Wynonie Harris.

Elvis's exposure to all these influences was greatly increased by his family's move to Memphis in 1948. From then on all he had to do was tune in the radio, to Dewey Phillips on WHBQ; to Rufus Thomas on WDIA, which called itself 'the mother station of all Negroes'; or to broadcasts by Howlin' Wolf from West Memphis. Nor was there any shortage of country or gospel music on the airwaves.

Elvis did more than just listen. Although the controversy as to whether Elvis stalked Beale Street before he became famous is too involved to resolve here – see 'Elvis and Beale' on p.417 – he certainly bought R&B records at the Home of the Blues store on Beale in the early 1950s. He hung around the WMPS studio on Saturdays, questioning his gospel idols Jake Hess and James Blackwood, and became a regular at local all-night gospel singing sessions. At the same time, in a characteristic combination of the sacred and secular, he joined the throng of young Memphians who poured across the Mississippi bridge at weekends to watch Willie Mitchell play what one of Elvis's school friends called 'beat blues' at *Danny's* club in West Memphis, Arkansas.

All of which is a long-winded way of saying that if you wanted to create a teen idol who could synthesize all these different musical strands, you couldn't have picked a better time and place to put him than Memphis in the early 1950s.

The mystery of Elvis

To return to that summer of 1953, the question that begs to be answered is: What made Sun's office manager Marion Keisker decide to record Elvis? In one of the most often quoted remarks in music history, Sam Phillips had allegedly said that if he could find

Elvis (and Jordanaires) on *Ed Sullivan*, before they cut him off at the waist

a white man who could sing like a black man, he would make a billion dollars. This statement has often been used to support the charge that Elvis, and other white rock'n'rollers, ripped off black music. Phillips, who denies Keisker's claim that he said this, would admit later that he felt, 'If I could just find a white person who would not try to mimic a black artist but had that innate natural feeling, maybe we could break down a few barriers.' The sense that this particular weird-looking white teenager might have that natural feel prompted Keisker to tape him singing My Happiness.

What made Elvis stand out wasn't as simple as being white and

96

sounding black. Stan Kesler, who wrote I'm Left You're Right She's Gone for Elvis, recalled: 'When I first heard Elvis's record, I was flabbergasted. The disc jockeys were thinking "I'm playing Webb Pierce and Faron Young and he don't sound like them. Is he black?" And the black disc jockeys were thinking, "He's got to be white but he don't sound it. Where does he fit?"' As Professor Nat D. Williams, a DJ on Memphis' black radio station WDIA said, after seeing Elvis perform in Beale Street, 'He had a way of singing the blues that was distinctive. He could sing 'em not necessarily like a negro but he didn't sing 'em altogether like a typical white musician. He had something in between that made the blues sort of different … always he had that certain humanness about him that negroes like to put in their songs.'

Incredible as it seems now, both Frankie Laine and Johnnie Ray, two white singers who sang with more emotion than Tin Pan thought was strictly necessary, were initially accused of sounding black and enjoyed brief success on the R&B charts. An echo of their emotion may have been part of what Keisker heard that day, though years later she would call it 'Soul, this negro sound, I taped it, I wanted Sam to know.'

Soul – although in the summer of 1953 it was just a word and not a genre – may come close to explaining the mystery of what, musically, Elvis had to offer. Analysing his most famous pupil's gift, with Peter Guralnick, his best biographer, Sam Phillips waxed mystical: 'the elements of the soil, the sky, the water, even the wind, the quiet nights, people living on plantations, never out of debt, hoping to eat, lights up the river – that's what they used to call Memphis. That was where it all came together. And Elvis Presley may not have been able to verbalize all that – but he damn sure wasn't dumb and he damn sure was intuitive and he damn sure had an appreciation for the total spirituality of the human existence, even if he would never have thought of the term. That was what he cared about.'

'I knew this about him,' Phillips told Bill Burk, 'he had something distinctive in the way he said his words. I didn't want too much of a pretty voice, although he did have a pretty voice. I wanted somebody with that instinctive rhythm feel about him who could switch to a ballad and sing it with some conviction.'

That human-ness, soul, spirituality, conviction, whatever you call it, never completely deserted Elvis. You can hear it in his version of How Great Thou Art, recorded live in Memphis in 1974, and in songs as diverse as Mystery Train, Suspicious Minds and I Really Don't Want To Know. Fans say there is something in Elvis's voice that makes you feel he is singing just to you. Maybe Marion Keisker felt that too.

Sam Phillips

Although the coming together of Sam Phillips and Elvis Presley might seem like a miraculous piece of kismet, in the small community that was downtown Memphis in the early 1950s, it would have been even more miraculous if they had never met. Mentor and pupil had more in common than perhaps even they realised. Both had grown up listening to black music, secular and sacred; Phillips in 1920s Alabama and Presley in the black section of Tupelo. That must in part explain why both instinctively rejected the racial divide that ran through their society. Both were drawn to the world of Beale Street. And both

were inordinately concerned about their appearance in general, and their hair in particular. When Sun's Marion Keisker said, 'He was a beautiful young man … slim and had those incredible eyes; he was … beautifully groomed, terrible about his hair,' she was talking about the young Sam Phillips, not the young Elvis Presley.

Phillips was born in Florence, Alabama, on 5 January 1923. Reared on tales of Beale Street by one of his father's farmhands, and soaked in the rhythm of the cotton fields, he moved to Memphis in 1945. His first break came as a radio announcer and engineer on WREC, while his career as the most influential independent record producer in rock history began on 1 October 1949, when he signed a lease on a storefront on Union Avenue. By the next year, he had launched the Memphis Recording Service, and was working with blues artists like BB King and Howlin' Wolf.

It was Elvis's immense good fortune that when he finally interested a recording company in his talents, his discoverer was not some cash-in merchant, but Phillips, who in his own words 'could play with sound forever', and was on a personal mission not just to make music but to further 'the great association between country music and black blues'.

Presley enabled him to do just that. The two years they spent together are often cited as the most significant in both careers. After selling Elvis to RCA for $35,000, Phillips went on to enjoy real commercial success, selling a million of Carl Perkins's "Blue Suede Shoes" and hitting number one with Jerry Lee Lewis's "Breathless". Sun's hot streak ran out just as Presley was being drafted; in 1969, when Elvis was reborn musically at another

Memphis studios, Phillips sold the label to Shelby Singleton. Phillips' influence on rock in general, and Elvis in particular, runs much deeper than the five singles and half-dozen other tracks he cut with Presley. His informal approach in the studio, and his refusal to watch the clock, set the pattern for Presley's later recording sessions, and thus too for the industry as a whole. Elvis never forgot Sam's insistence that 'feel' mattered above all else, certainly above technical perfection. For the rest of his career, he was in a state of semi-permanent dissatisfaction that his records didn't sound like Sam's. His voice, often brought to the front at RCA, seldom seemed as integral to the song. Presley's tragedy was not that Phillips sold his contract to RCA, but that in the ensuing twenty years few producers ever pushed him as hard again. Individuals such as Chips Moman, Leiber and Stoller, Jerry Reed and (briefly) Felton Jarvis were to make inspirational cameo appearances, but as a rule, on those rare occasions when Elvis did derive artistic satisfaction from recording, he had to provide much of the creative impetus himself.

The Sun years

Whatever the nature of Presley's gift, it was raw and needed guidance. And he was lucky to find a mentor like Sam Phillips, who said his own gift, if he had one, was drawing people out, freeing them to express themselves. He certainly did that with Presley; but he also, to be honest, manipulated his most famous discovery, albeit with Presley's willing consent, and to wondrous effect.

While Phillips gave Elvis some freedom, and let him, against his own judgment, sing too many ballads in studio hours, there were limits. Sam had a pretty broad taste in music, but he was not, as Johnny Cash and Roy Orbison later discovered, that interested in recording gospel or soaring romantic ballads. It wasn't the type of music with which barriers could be brought down.

It was Phillips' idea to bring in Scotty Moore and Bill Black, just as it was his idea not to bring in any other members of Moore's band, Doug Poindexter's Starlite Wranglers. Even though he might not have been able to put what he wanted into words, he was already focusing on the interplay of voice, guitars and bass. What he got in June 1954 was, as Elvis inelegantly put it, a 'goosed up' version of That's All Right.

That first single, backed by Blue Moon Of Kentucky, was unprecedented, but it's remarkable quite how quickly certain people – not just local DJ Dewey Phillips, and the teenagers of Memphis – got the message. On its strength alone, *Billboard*, the bible of the music industry, hailed Presley as a 'potent new chanter'.

B B King, already a legend on Beale Street, began to pay attention: 'When I first met Elvis, I thought he was a handsome young man but he wasn't singing as he started to sing later. Finally I heard him do Arthur Big Boy Crudup. And I started to turn my head a little bit. And he went from there doing some things that sounded black to me. That's when I started having respect, respect, respect. Elvis was doing Crudup's tunes and they were calling that rock'n'roll. And I thought it was a way of saying he's not black.' Elvis made the same point: 'the coloured folks been singing it and playing it just like I'm doing now man, for more years than I know.'

Elvis, Scotty and Bill began to get regular gigs, but record sales didn't take off for a year. In hard sales terms, the next two releases, Good Rocking Tonight and Milkcow Blues Boogie, were a step backwards, the latter saved from oblivion by its country B side, You're A Heartbreaker. The fourth single, coupling Baby Let's Play House with I'm Left You're Right She's Gone, marked Elvis's debut on the national charts when it entered the country charts in July 1955. By then, Colonel Parker and RCA were already circling, attracted by the havoc Elvis was wreaking in his live performances. The final Sun single, Mystery Train and I Forgot To Remember To Forget, built on that success, becoming his first national (albeit country) number one.

The Sun sides could almost form a concept album in their own right. Even the oddest, Blue Moon, still belongs with the rest. All seem to exist in their own musical space, independent of genre, and while Elvis's voice is changing it's already a very subtle instrument. On Good Rocking Tonight and Baby Let's Play House he sounds like the Elvis whose mannerisms would soon astonish the world. Elsewhere, he just sounds different, unclassifiable, as hard to pin down as the sound that emerges from the simple combination of guitars, voice and Bill Black slapping his bass. If it wasn't full-on blues, the absence of steel guitars and fiddles meant it didn't sound like country either.

This was the point when Phillips chose to cash Presley in, and sold his contract to RCA, although new manager Colonel Parker was also agitating for the move. Not for the last time, Elvis's own views are open to debate. Though he was attracted to the fame that Parker promised, both for his own sake and for his family, Phillips later said that 'Elvis wanted to stay.' Elvis himself, in a 1956 interview, simply commented that 'I had no say so about it.' In the light of Phillips' subsequent run of hits with Carl Perkins, Johnny Cash and Jerry Lee Lewis, it's hard to say that the Sun owner was

101

wrong. In a sense, though, his decision sealed Sun's fate. It never did become a major label, and Phillips never again made music quite as mysteriously alive as that he made with Elvis.

Much of Phillips' legacy to Presley lay in his method of working in the studio. Unlike in most studios, there was no clock at Sun, nor would there be at Elvis's subsequent sessions. In Phillips' absence, Presley gradually assumed the role of artist and producer, working in a similarly informal style to his mentor. He was also influenced by Phillips' insistence on 'feel' as being the essence, a view that was not always to serve him well. Phillips had placed Elvis's voice well back into the mix, and Presley always preferred it that way. Over the next twenty years, he had a running debate with RCA and Parker over the proper positioning of his vocals, Parker being firmly of the opinion that people bought records to hear his boy.

For a minority of fans, the real story ends here. Their view was summed up by Mark Knopfler: 'Elvis Presley was a beautiful young person, right, whose recordings were just colossally great. But basically the best stuff he ever did was on the Sun record label. And then he got involved with Colonel Parker and went to RCA and the Hollywood way. The whole thing became completely ruined.'

The King of rock

The one thing that Heartbreak Hotel, Elvis's first RCA single, had in common with any of his Sun sides was that it didn't sound like anything else you had ever heard. Plugged rather haphazardly on TV – Elvis didn't sing it until his third appearance on the Dorsey Brothers' show – it soared after a relatively slow start to number one on *Billboard*'s Top 100, a position Elvis singles occupied for an amazing 25 weeks in 1956. It also became a country number one, and a number three R&B hit. It may be a cliché to say that things would never be the same again, but in this instance it's perfectly true: not for Elvis, Parker, RCA, nor anyone else.

The anti-climax of his next single I Want You I Need You I Love You, was soon forgotten in the excitement and controversy generated by the double A side Hound Dog and Don't Be Cruel. Presley's bump-and-grind performance of the latter on the Milton Berle show remains a pivotal moment in the history of our culture. Watching at home, the young Quincy Jones saw what he called 'an emotional revolution … the first time I had seen a white singer singing black music on national television'. In England, where Elvis's bumping and grinding was invisible, "Hound Dog" still struck a chord. In south London, the boy who would become David Bowie played it hundreds of times, and said it was the first time he realised that music had the power to move people. (Among the single's other later to be famous devotees were Jeff Beck and Elton John.) "Hound Dog" was more than just a piece of music; it was, in its way, as much of an act of naked aggression as the Sex Pistols God Save The Queen would be twenty years later.

The other A side, "Don't Be Cruel", was a much gentler accomplishment, as alive in its way as anything Elvis had cut at Sun yet pointing to a softer future. That future became official when he released Love Me Tender, the favourite single of the 14-year-old Jimi Hendrix, who caught a glimpse of his idol in concert the following year. Even so, there were tracks on Elvis's first two albums such as My Baby Left Me which more than lived up to the promise he had shown at Sun.

By the end of 1956, Presley had sold fourteen million records in the US alone, delighted and outraged millions, inspired a crop of imitators, and made his first movie. And he was already being shrouded in myth. As Nik Cohn said in *Awopbopaloobopalopbamboom*, 'The difference between British and American rock is that Tommy Steele made it to the London Palladium and Elvis Presley made it to God.'

While 1957 was in some respects business as usual, it would hint at problems to come. With the needs of Hollywood paramount, Elvis did not release a studio album of completely new material. Fans were forced to settle instead for the *Loving You* soundtrack

◀ The gold lamé jacket gets a late outing before Elvis joined the army

and the first Christmas album, a colossal commercial success yet also, as exemplified by Santa Claus Is Back In Town and the precocious gospel of Peace In The Valley, a work of real inspiration. Singles varied from the manufactured lurching of Too Much to the magnificence of All Shook Up and the raw aggression of Jailhouse Rock.

For Elvis, let alone for Scotty and Bill, the worst moment of the year was the break-up of the trio. Already feeling, rightly, that they weren't getting paid enough, Scotty and Bill were aggrieved when Presley failed to stick up for them over the promise of studio time to record an instrumental album, and sent him a letter of resignation. RCA's Steve Sholes, on the other hand, was not impressed by their ability as musicians. Even if Bill's repertoire barely extended beyond his brilliance slapping the bass, Moore was integral to Elvis's sound. When the Memphis press got hold of the story, Elvis was dismayed to see his old friends' grievances aired in public. A

Scotty Moore

Winfield 'Scotty' Moore III ranks among the most influential of Elvis's 'big brothers'. For Scotty, who had three brothers himself – 'they played guitar, banjo, fiddle … I was the youngest and there was fourteen years between me and the next' – having someone look up to him made a pleasant change.

Born on 27 December 1931, Moore formed the Starlite Wranglers, with Bill Black on bass, after leaving the Navy in 1952. They described themselves as 'country and western … if you called yourself country you got better jobs, though we'd play country, R&B and pop.' Scotty kept up his day job as a hatter.

Like Elvis, he was attracted to Sun by the recording service. He befriended Sam Phillips when the Wranglers cut a record in May 1954. 'I'd go in maybe two or three times a week, have coffee, talk about the business in general, Elvis's name came up in conversation.'

That Scotty had served as Elvis's first manager meant that the Colonel saw him as a threat: 'He wanted to fire the band the first thing out when he took over, because we were friends with Elvis and he thought that we'd have some kind of influence over him.' Even so, Scotty helped Presley make the transition from Sun to RCA: 'He was having a little growing pains by then.' The speed of his success took them all by surprise: 'I knew for sure he was going to be big after that first TV show, but even then I figured it would be a "pay your dues" situation.'

Parker finally got his way when Scotty and Bill left Elvis following squabbles over money. Moore built up a second career, running his own record label and studio

Scotty (centre) with Elvis and Bill Black – the definitive rock'n'roll trio

while still playing sessions, but returned to Elvis in the 1960s, playing until 1968 on some of the best, and worst, music he ever made. 'The music they were supplying for the movies was the worst part. He'd have to sing gospel numbers with the Jordanaires so he could work himself up to do them. That was one of Parker's big mistakes. He went straight from one movie to the next as fast as possible. If he'd let him do other stuff in between each one, he would have been so much happier. Because he didn't like the music, he liked the money, that was about it.'

The 1968 TV special was Moore's last appearance with his old friend. He turned down the chance to go to Las Vegas: 'They wanted all the Nashville musicians, but they were offering us per week what we were making per day in Nashville and it was peak recording time. They strictly a bottom-line situation. They didn't say, "After this we're going on tour".' He never saw Elvis again. 'It was much easier for him to get in touch with me because of the barriers he'd built around him. You never knew if he'd get your phone call. It was disappointing.'

Although he didn't like Elvis's live medleys of old hits ('they were the songs that put him there'), or much of his 1970s work ('it was all showbiz and glitz'), Scotty is no rock'n'roll purist. Asked to pick his own favourites, he says "Mystery Train", "It's Now Or Never", "Such A Night" … I loved "Don't"'.

What is amazing, perhaps, is his utter lack of rancour. He remembers, especially, jamming with Elvis and Lowell Fulson in a club in Houston. 'There was segregation, but not among musicians. If you were black, white or green, it didn't make no difference. Elvis knew all of Lowell's songs, I think Lowell was surprised.' He also recalls one tantalizing possibility: 'At the 1968 TV special, he asked me, "Do you still have your studio?" I said. "Yeah" and he wanted to know the chances of going in and locking in for a couple of weeks. I said, "Just let me know". He wanted to go in without RCA or any publishing people there. But it never happened. He had something in mind. Don't know what. Never will.'

deal was patched up, but relations were never as warm. Moore saw the Colonel's hand in it all, believing Parker didn't want anyone else around who could influence Elvis, a suspicion echoed by Jerry Leiber and Mike Stoller, who took over the sessions for Jailhouse Rock, inspiring Elvis but upsetting the status quo.

Soldier boy

Although 1958 was a tumultuous year, dominated by Hollywood, the draft and the death of Elvis's mother, Presley somehow managed to make some half-decent music before donning his uniform. While RCA issued the first of the gold records series, *King Creole* was the only album of all-new songs; Elvis initially insisted the soundtrack didn't hold enough good songs, but RCA's shortage of material ensured it was released anyway, and in truth half of it was superlative. Elvis's singles showed him unafraid to rock in charts now dominated by the softer sounds of Ricky Nelson and the Everly Brothers. Wear My Ring had a certain conveyor-belt quality – Elvis wasn't that happy with it – but Don't, One Night and its flip, the infectious I Got Stung, were in a different league.

In the whole of 1959, RCA made do with a second gold record collection, more famous for its gold lamé suit cover than the music, and repackages such as *A Date With Elvis*, which simply assembled the first dozen songs not already released on album. The singles were excellent. A Fool Such As I swung with a verve rarely found on a staid country standard, while B side I Need Your Love Tonight punched above its weight, a light song given a fantastic treatment by Elvis and his new all-star backing band (Chet Atkins and Hank Garland on guitars, Floyd Cramer on piano and Buddy Harman on bongos). This was followed by Big Hunk Of Love – apart from Lloyd Price's Stagger Lee, the only rocking US number one of the year.

Elvis's induction into the Army marks the point when, as Lennon says, he 'officially' died. If a death did take place, it was broader than the 'death' of Elvis as a rock'n'roller. Jerry Lee Lewis's career had collapsed in the scandal of his marriage to a 13-year-old girl; Little Richard had given up rock for religion; Carl Perkins' last two singles had peaked in the 90s in *Billboard*'s hot 100; Fats Domino hadn't had a gold record for a single in more than a year; and Chuck Berry hadn't had a Top 10 hit since 1956. Rock'n'roll was reeling from the payola scandal, exposing DJs who took money or gifts to play records, that ruined rock's most influential DJ Alan Freed. Even if a few of the new teen idols proved to have talent, notably Bobby Darin, most, like Fabian, were exactly what you'd expect to get if you had Elvis Presley redesigned by a marketing department.

1950s albums

Elvis in the 1950s is probably best sampled on compilations: *Sunrise* – a truly essential purchase – gathers all the tracks from his time at Sun Studio, while the five-CD box set *The King Of Rock'n'Roll* is a completist's dream, featuring every original Elvis track from the decade and some genuine rarities. Of the original album releases, the crowning classic is the King's debut, *Elvis Presley* (1956), an icon of both music and design. Every home should have a copy.

Unless specified, the reviews which follow are of the original releases (all of which have been re-released by RCA on CD, often with extra tracks). For the key compilation albums, see the section beginning on p.154.

ELVIS PRESLEY; 1956

Famous for its pink-and-green lettering, the *Elvis Presley* album was originally available in a slightly different form in the UK as *Rock'n'Roll*. It has now been reissued on CD, featuring six bonus songs, and that's the edition reviewed here. It's at its most effective when Elvis pays tribute to his black

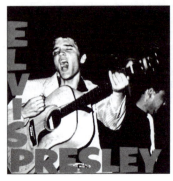

heroes – to Ray Charles (**I Got A Woman**), Roy Hamilton (**I'm Gonna Sit Right Down And Cry**), Joe Turner (**Shake, Rattle And Roll**), Arthur Crudup (**My Baby Left Me**) and Clyde McPhatter/Jesse Stone (**Money Honey**). El's own favourite **I Was The One** is the stand-out of the RCA ballads.

Those who maintain that Elvis's musical talent had diminished or died after he stopped working with Phillips should just listen to this again. A world without Elvis's version of **Lawdy Miss Clawdy** is not a world that many of us would care to contemplate. If you want to show a friend what all the fuss is about, this album or *From Elvis In Memphis* are the ideal present. ✷✷✷✷✷

ELVIS; 1956

If you can still find it, the *Elvis '56* album holds all 22 non-movie tracks he recorded in that historic year. Buying that would save you the hassle of buying his two 1956 albums separately. This album *Elvis* (known as *Rock and Roll No. 2* in the UK) is slightly less effective than its predecessor, but still some has great moments (**How's The World Treating You?** is the acceptable face of **Old Shep**). **Anyplace is Paradise** sounds like a good performance of a good song badly recorded, and too much of the album is marooned in an aural fog that swamps decent songs like **First In Line**. ✷✷✷✷

LOVE ME TENDER EP; 1956

Four songs for his first movie. You can tell the amount of thought which went into three of them by the fact that Scotty and Bill were told they couldn't play on these sessions, by the movie people, because they weren't hillbilly enough. The songs themselves were as close to hillbilly music as the Harem Holiday soundtrack would be to the music of the Middle East. The title track is still a beaut, though. All tracks are available on the 1950s box set. **

LOVING YOU; 1957

Elvis's second film, *Loving You*, was craftily engineered as a vehicle for him to perform lots of rock'n'roll. Songs like Got A Lot Of Livin To Do, Mean Woman Blues, and Party – with its mysterious boast that the singer could shake a chicken in the middle of the room – echoed the freewheeling feel of Sun, while Teddy Bear was catchy don't-take-me-too-seriously pop. Even Loving You itself, Leiber and Stoller's recast of Love Me Tender, works, though it took forty takes before Elvis was happy. Only Lonesome Cowboy and Hot Dog (too short at 72 seconds) disappoint. The seven movie songs were originally released in the US with five bonus numbers: Blueberry Hill, I Need You So, Have I Told You Lately That I Love You, Don't Leave Me Now and Cole Porter's True Love. All are now available on the reissued CD, complete with four other rarities – Is It So Strange, One Night Of Sin, Tell Me Why and When It Rains It Really Pours – and an uptempo version of the title song. ****

ELVIS' CHRISTMAS ALBUM; 1957

Is *Elvis' Christmas Album* the finest rock'n'roll Christmas album of all time? Only Phil Spector's work comes close. Poor old Irving Berlin was so enraged by Elvis's Drifters-influenced performance of White Christmas that he wrote to radio stations asking them not to play the album. Saner critics might just applaud El for having the guts to do something different with a song that, even then, was in danger of becoming over-familiar. Blue Christmas and Santa Bring My Baby Back (To Me) are appealing, but the truly towering performance is Leiber and Stoller's raucous Santa Claus Is Back In Town, so subversive it's a wonder Senator McCarthy didn't demand a Congressional hearing to have them all arrested. On the original album,

111

as on the reissued CD, the eight festive tracks were topped up by the contents of the *Peace In The Valley* EP. All are also available, combined with Elvis's later Christmas songs, on *If Every Day Was Like Christmas*. ✶✶✶✶✶

JAILHOUSE ROCK EP; 1958

Only four new songs for El's third movie but, perhaps because the emphasis was on quality not quantity, not a dud among them. The title song is justly famous but all have their merits, especially **Baby I Don't Care**, which **Bryan Ferry** would later duplicate for his first 1970s covers album. All tracks are now available on *The King Of Rock'n'Roll* box set.

KING CREOLE; 1958

Merely to say that *King Creole* was Elvis's **best soundtrack album** is to damn it with faint praise. Half of it – the rawer half – is immense. **Trouble** – 'If you're looking for trouble, just look right in my face' – is full-on, but it's almost matched by **King Creole**, with surly vocal and an astonishing guitar break by Scotty Moore. **New Orleans** is a stuttering, howling, blues, while **Hard Headed Woman** and **Dixieland Rock** move with a magnificent momentum. Even if the ballads aren't up to the same standard, you can tell that Elvis relished **As Long As I Have You**. And **Crawfish** is weird but beautifully done, vastly preferable to its only rival in the Presley canon, **Song Of The Shrimp**. The whole soundtrack, complete with outtakes and the unconvincing **Danny**, is now available on CD, but all the masters also feature on the 1950s box set. ✱✱✱

FOR LP FANS ONLY; 1959

Known as *Elvis* in the UK (not the last of his albums to be graced by that imaginative title) *For LP Fans Only* was an odd collection of Sun tracks, reissues, B sides like the excellent, plaintive **Playing For Keeps**, and the odd movie tune. Everything is now available elsewhere, notably on the 1950s box set. ✱✱✱

A DATE WITH ELVIS; 1959

A Date With Elvis was another barrel-scraping, vault-raiding exercise, designed to overcome RCA's GI blues. Its few points of interest include the original gatefold packaging on the vinyl version; three songs from *Jailhouse Rock*, among them **Baby I Don't Care**, an album track that's head and shoulders above most of his rivals' hits; and a moody version of Faron Young's **Is It So Strange?** All those tracks are now available elsewhere. ✱✱✱

◀ 'You don't stop playing till the guitar breaks': Elvis in *King Creole*

The fall and rise: the 1960s

When Elvis returned from the Army and sang Stuck On You, backed by a gently rocking beat, some fans took it as a declaration of intent. It wasn't (he didn't like the song, calling it 'Stuck in you'). In Germany, he'd been rehearsing ballads. Even at Sun, he had pestered Sam Phillips to record more ballads and now, with pop music changed so radically, he got his chance. On songs like It's Now Or Never and Are You Lonesome Tonight?, he threw himself into the challenge with all his old determination. Even so, while he was being marketed, through movies like GI Blues and his guest spot on Sinatra's TV show, as a wholesome all-round entertainer, his own choice of music was far from straitjacketed.

The first album of the decade, Elvis Is Back!, may have seemed like a cynical cover-all-the-bases exercise, but it contained strong elements of genuine blues. Sadly, its indifferent sales reinforced the commercial logic of Parker's repositioning of Presley as a more charismatic Pat Boone. So most of the singles were romantic ballads, often derived from Italian sources like It's Now Or Never and Surrender. Those that did move to a beat, as on the gorgeous coupling of His Latest Flame and Little Sister, didn't sell as well.

Throughout the early 1960s, the work with which Elvis was least satisfied with – the movie soundtracks, above all – outsold the albums to which he was personally committed, like Elvis Is Back! and His Hand In Mine. In terms of pure hard cash, Parker's policy of keeping hit singles off the studio albums to save them for gold-record compilation is hard to fault, but it helped ensure that Elvis's best work was increasingly bought only by diehard fans.

The finest of his studio performances in this period benefit from the rich 'Nashville sound'. Chet Atkins lined up some stellar musicians: Scotty Moore returned on guitar, DJ Fontana was still on drums, and Boots Randolph joined on saxophone, with support from guitarist Hank Garland, pianist Floyd Cramer, and drummers Buddy Harman and Hal Blaine. However, while they worked up a storm on songs like the Chuck Willis blues I Feel So Bad, they seemed more comfortable with ballads than with rock.

This was partly down to the quality of the faster numbers, which weren't a patch on most of Elvis's pre-Army rockers. Royalty disputes with the Colonel meant that Leiber and Stoller were all but eased out of the picture; they only wrote one more new Elvis song, She's Not You. In their absence, less gifted writers produced weak imitations of Elvis's earlier hits. The shift also reflected Nashville's production values, which emphasized smoothness over the rough edges that had marked Elvis's best pre-Army work.

Still, between 1960 and the end of 1962, Elvis produced some fine work. His first full gospel album, His Hand In Mine, came as a bit of a shock to rock fans, but it was far better than the GI Blues soundtrack. The best of the ballads – both the singles, and album tracks like Gently and That's Someone You Never Forget – had real class, while His Latest Flame, Little Sister and Return To Sender were pop-rock performances of a calibre seldom matched by Presley's peers, and the smooth rocker Suspicion was a wonderful piece of pop paranoia.

The King in exile

At the start of 1963, One Broken Heart For Sale became the first Elvis single not to reach the US Top 10 since 1956. It was a sign of indignities, commercial and creative, to come. In a minor panic, Elvis rushed back into the studio to cut Devil In Disguise – a rare show of concern, in an organization that had grown ever more complacent.

The only surprise was that fans took so long to stop buying these increasingly indifferent records. Not all the soundtracks were bad, but by 1965 the degeneration was obvious. Charlie McCoy, who played on the Harum Scarum album, says, 'I'd be stretching it to say Elvis was enthused by the material, he was a professional and he did his best. But I felt disappointed at the material he was given,

115

I mean, here was the greatest recording artist in the world.' Many have condemned his 'employee mentality', his apparent acquiescence to his own near-destruction. The artist who made Bob Dylan feel like he was busting out of jail was consenting to his own imprisonment.

The picture isn't quite that simple. Elvis did rebel, but not in a particularly constructive way, throwing tantrums but always turning up for the next soundtrack album. Only once did he take on Parker – over the songs for *GI Blues* – but thereafter 'he would go with the flow', as Scotty Moore says. Out of misguided professionalism, or consideration for his fellow musicians, he plugged away.

The need to record three movie soundtracks per year stretched even Hill & Range's stable of writers to breaking point, and left Elvis with little surplus time. Between 1962 and May 1966, he spent a grand total of five days recording songs not written for movies. He still managed a couple of gems – It Hurts Me and Memphis Tennessee – but his only decent non-movie single in this period was Crying In The Chapel, which had been buried in the vaults since the *His Hand In Mine* sessions. As for the movie songs, the best were two Leiber and Stoller imports, Bossa Nova Baby and Little Egypt, and two Pomus and Shuman songs for Viva Las Vegas, the title track and I Need Somebody To Lean On.

It was the ballads – exquisite gems like In My Way, Suppose and Sand Castles – that kept him going. He did all he could to hone his craft on them, and the results were apparent when he stepped back into the studio in May 1966 to record his second gospel album. Finally, he was in control again. Inspired perhaps by the arrival of new producer Felton Jarvis, he cut the Grammy-award-winning album *How Great Thou Art* as well as Love Letters, Down In the Alley and his first ever Dylan cover, Tomorrow Is A Long Time.

116

Ten years after Elvis had signed for RCA, he was preparing the ground for his comeback. Because the soundtrack albums were still as frequent, and irrelevant, as ever, the world barely noticed. The soundtrack to *Clambake*, astonishingly, contained half a

Leathered up, Gene Vincent-style, for the 1968 comeback *TV Special*

decent album, including the Ray Charles ballad You Don't Know Me, and bonus songs Guitar Man and Big Boss Man, both of which were recorded in September 1967, four months after Elvis's wedding to Priscilla, and owed a great deal to the inspiring presence in the studio of Jerry Reed.

As a single, "Big Boss Man" barely crawled into the US Top 40, and Elvis's powerful, haunting rendition of You'll Never Walk Alone failed to emulate the Top-five success of "Crying In The Chapel". Within nine months, however, the comeback went public, when the movie assembly line halted long enough for Elvis to make what was originally envisaged as a Christmas TV special for NBC.

Elvis in person

After years of watching Hollywood's cartoon version of Elvis, the *NBC TV Special* gave viewers the

117

chance to see Elvis's version of himself. Funnily enough, he didn't play a toy guitar, sing his way to victory in a racing car, or invite bystanders to join his clambake. This Elvis was clad in black leather, thin as a rake, almost oppressively handsome, and funny. Best of all, as he reminded the world of his own roots and of the roots of rock'n'roll, he was singing with a passion not heard for years. The sense of a man breaking free from his chains was only strengthened when, switching to an angelic white suit, he closed the show with If I Can Dream, his first single to sound current since the advent of the Beatles.

For once, Presley had backed his own instincts against Parker's; and the gamble had paid off. It sounds strange to say that the special could give a star as narcissistic as Elvis his confidence back, but those who played on it were in no doubt that behind his triumphant display lay genuine nerves. As he said to DJ Fontana just before the first performance, 'What do you think, guys? Do you think they'll like me?' It was, after all, his first live appearance since a benefit concert in 1961.

Having emerged from his cocoon with such devastating effect, Elvis made another unprecedented move in January 1969. He decided to cut his next album back in Memphis, in Chips Moman's American Studios. This was his first return to record in his hometown since leaving Sun in 1955, and the prolific sessions are generally seen as being every bit as remarkable and as unprecedented.

While Moman provided the focus, the craft and some fine songs, Presley made the sessions work both with his single-minded devotion to the work in hand and by intervening in the publishing disputes that threatened to engulf them, insisting according to friend George Klein that 'from now on I don't care who owns it or what the deal is, I don't care about publishing, I don't care about writers, I just want some great material.'

He got it. The sessions produced four million-selling singles – In The Ghetto, which soared to number three on the US charts; Suspicious Minds, his first *Billboard* number one for seven years; Don't Cry Daddy; and Kentucky Rain – plus the tracks for his best

118

RCA album, *From Elvis In Memphis*, and one pretty good album, *Back In Memphis*. For reasons that remain unexplained, however, Presley never returned to American. The Memphis sessions were indeed, in RCA's slogan, 'Elvis as you've never heard him before!' but they were also, sadly, Elvis as we never heard him again.

Some say that Elvis himself didn't like working with Moman, who pushed him harder than any producer since Sam Phillips; while others suggest that the Colonel drove a wedge between them, using the publishing squabbles as a pretext. According to Moman himself, 'When it was just him and me, one-on-one, he was just one of the easiest people to work with and he was one of the hardest working artists I've ever been in the studio with'. Putnam says, 'A few off the guys were playing on Elvis's fears of losing face, saying things like "Are you going to let Chips push you around?"'

All in all, the Memphis sessions were not an easy experience for a man as averse to confrontation as Elvis. Curiously, it was easier for him to make movie-soundtrack pap than to put himself on the line to make the kind of significant music he recorded at American. 'In the long run it was self-destructive,' says Jerry Schilling, 'because what happened to Elvis later was what happened to any creative artist who isn't faced with a challenge.'

While the music from these sessions may not have been as innovative as Elvis's Sun output, it arguably offers a greater insight into the kind of man he was, with his voice capable of power, precision, authority and sensitivity, often within the same song. As with the 1968 TV special, this seemed to be work in which he had invested his own personality; he had, for a while, stopped obeying orders.

Presley's long-overdue return to live performances in Las Vegas crowned his comeback. Some of the excitement is captured on *Elvis In Person*, his first and best live album. For Elvis and his fans, the last two years of the 1960s were as inspiring as most of the decade had been depressing. The star himself was suddenly brimming with enthusiasm, talking of making decent movies – without any songs in them – and world tours. All things seemed possible.

1960s albums

Elvis in the 1960s is probably best sampled on the two studio albums which bookmark the decade – *Elvis Is Back!* and *From Elvis In Memphis,* both essential purchases. The five-CD box set *From Nashville To Memphis* is not quite as essential as its 1950s equivalent, but does contain almost every significant secular non-movie studio recording from the decade.

Reviews, unless specified, are of the original releases (all of which have been re-released by RCA on CD, sometimes with extra tracks). For the key compilation albums, see the section beginning on p.154.

ELVIS IS BACK!; 1960

Among the 1800 or so records in Elvis's collection at Graceland is a copy of *Elvis Is Back!*, almost white from the number of times it was played. You can understand why this would be his favourite album. In the pivotal Memphis sessions of 1954–55 and 1969, he worked with producer/mentors like Sam Phillips and Chips Moman. In the Nashville sessions responsible for *Elvis Is Back!*, however, Elvis was both singer and producer. RCA's Chet Atkins was on hand mainly to find the right musicians and to handle logistics. Once the sessions started, Elvis took centre stage.

After two years in the Army, Elvis wanted to show the world that his talent was too broad and too deep to be categorised. Thus he took the teen ballad Girl Of My Best Friend and injected it with real emotion; pounded through the gospel-flavoured rock of Make Me Know It; brought sly innuendo and wit to Fever and Such A Night; and, on Like A Baby and Reconsider Baby, sang the blues with gusto and aplomb. Listening to those two closing tracks, it's hard to believe that this commitment and exhilaration was to be heard only fitfully for most of the 1960s, often on songs buried on B sides or as bonuses on dodgy soundtrack albums.

Although A Mess Of Blues, It's Now Or Never and Are You Lonesome Tonight? date from the same sessions, they were held back for a gold record

compilation, and only joined the rest on the CD reissue. On initial release, the album that Elvis felt best expressed his musical personality, in all its facets, sold a mere two to three hundred thousand copies. It was a bitter conclusion to two glorious days at Studio B Nashville, when he had, as Ernest Jorgensen said in *Elvis Presley His Life In Music*, 'laid down as many classic performances as many artists manage in their entire career'. ★★★★★

GI BLUES; 1960

After the joyous rediscovery of *Elvis Is Back!*, the songs selected for *GI Blues* shocked Elvis so much he told Parker half of them should be cut. Sadly, however, this sold more than twice as many copies as the real Elvis album that preceded it. The only track really up to standard is **Doin' The Best I Can**, a delicate doo-wop from Pomus and Shuman, though Elvis does his considerable best with **Tonight Is So Right For Love** (the fast version, as opposed to the slower alternative **Tonight's All Right For Love**). **Pocketful Of Rainbows** is pretty, while **Wooden Heart** and **Big Boots** are charming, but the rest is pleasant without being memorable. On CD, it's boosted by some alternate takes, including the dubious bonus of an acoustic version of "Big Boots". ★★

HIS HAND IN MINE; 1960

Even after the *Peace In The Valley* EP, Elvis's first full-blown **gospel** album came as a surprise to fans still adjusting to his post-Army balladeering style. His delivery at times seemed too self-effacing, devoid of the dramatics that characterised his secular singing. Even so, this was music he felt deeply, and the simple settings worked beautifully on the title track, **Known Only To Him**, **Mansion Over The Hilltop** and **He Knows Just What I Need**. In contrast, **Milky White Way**, **Swing Down Sweet Chariot** and **I'm Gonna Walk Dem Golden Stairs** all swing nicely. And then there's **If We Never Meet Again**, which he sang as a child with his parents: morbid, lyrically hackneyed and compelling. The best place to find this, and all his gospel work, is on the *Peace In The Valley* CD set or *Amazing Grace*. *******

SOMETHING FOR EVERYBODY; 1961

Whereas *Elvis Is Back!* was the genuine result of Elvis's artistic determination to master as many genres as possible on one album, *Something For Everybody* sounds more mechanical. On first release, it seemed pleasant but short of class; only when remastered in 1999, and strengthened with the inclusion of contemporary singles, did it become a must-have.

Recorded, like *Elvis Is Back!*, with the Nashville session men known (long before Mr T) as the **A-Team**, *Something For Everybody* is more conservative than its predecessor. Thus, even though Millie Kirkham's wonderful wordless wail still kicks things off, the master of **Give Me The Right** has lost the bluesiness of take four. **Put The Blame On Me** is a more memorable nod to the blues, its lyrics a rare reminder of the rebellious Elvis. The ballads are sung with conviction as if Elvis senses this is where his future lies. **Gently** is nicely understated, with some elegant guitar work by Hank Garland, while Don Robertson's **There's Always Me** builds to a dramatic climax. Elvis apparently said, 'This is my song', and you can hear how seriously he took it. Of the extra tracks on the re-release, both **I Feel So Bad** and **Little Sister** show that, given the material, Elvis could still sing the blues, while **His Latest Flame** is simply one of his greatest singles ever. The modest sales of the original album further tilted the balance towards soundtracks. ******** (re-release)

122

BLUE HAWAII; 1961

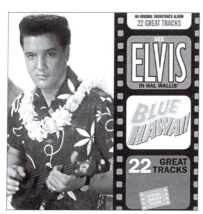

Though it's hard now to believe, only one LP – *West Side Story* – sold more copies than *Blue Hawaii* during the Swinging Sixties. Sales reached two million in the first year, and it became El's largest-selling album during his lifetime. It could almost be the soundtrack to a Bing Crosby musical, but much of it is still seductive singalong stuff. Even the slightest songs – **Ito Eats** and **Slicin' Sand** – are well sung. Don Robertson's **No More** is sweet and sincere, while as synthetic rockers go **Rock-A-Hula Baby** is daft but fun. Elvis liked **Hawaiian Wedding Song** enough to perform it on stage in the 1970s, and he delivers it magnificently, with a beautifully arranged vocal backing and virtually no errors in his painstaking Hawaiian pronunciation. The absolute stand-out, **Can't Help Falling In Love**, is in a class of its own. ★★★

FOLLOW THAT DREAM EP; 1962

While Elvis delivered a solidly professional performance of the title song – since reworked on stage by **Bruce Springsteen** – like most of the *Follow That Dream* EP the results were not that memorable. The only exceptions were **Angel**, a perennial fans' favourite, and the brisk, cheerful pop of **I'm Not The Marrying Kind**. The songs have been re-released on CD with those recorded for (or cut from) **Flaming Star** and **Wild In The Country**. ★★

123

POT LUCK; 1962

By 1962, Elvis's studio albums seemed to be minor irrelevances, selling (as this and *Something For Everybody* did) just 200,000 copies. While the absence of hot new singles virtually doomed *Pot Luck* at the time, however, its re-released, remastered version, with six extra tracks, goes some way towards re-establishing it in Elvis's canon. True, the emotional temperature was lower than ever, but then rock numbers like **Night Rider** weren't really good enough to catch fire. Elvis sounded more at ease on **Suspicion**. The considerable best of the ballads were **She's Not You, Something Blue, Just For Old Time Sake** and the wondrous **That's Someone You Never Forget**. **Fountain Of Love** and **You'll Be Gone** – originally envisaged as a rewrite of Cole Porter's **Begin The Beguine** – also reveal a definite **Latin** influence. ✱✱✱ (re-release).

KID GALAHAD EP; 1962

The pick of the six songs on the *Kid Galahad* EP – all now available on a double-feature CD with the *Girls! Girls! Girls!* soundtrack – is the ballad **Home Is Where The Heart Is**, co-written by **Hal David**. On both record and celluloid, **I Got Lucky** was also dusted with the magic that made Elvis famous, but while singer and band devoted an amazing 36 takes to **King Of The Whole Wide World**, they didn't quite manage to capture whatever they may have heard in it. ✱✱

GIRLS! GIRLS! GIRLS!; 1963

Even the producers realised there were too many songs in the film *Girls! Girls! Girls!* So they cut two of the classier ballads, **I Don't Want To** and **Where Do You Come From**, and left in fluff like **Song Of The Shrimp** and **The Walls Have Ears**. **Because Of Love** is pleasant, superficial, early 1960s pop of the kind the Beatles were soon to make obsolete, while the title track, albeit written by Leiber and Stoller, with a great Boots Randolph sax solo, never sounds more than mediocre. The one truly superior moment is **Return To Sender**. ✱✱

IT HAPPENED AT THE WORLD'S FAIR; 1963

Four of the ten songs cut for the movie *It Happened At The World's Fair* didn't even stretch to two minutes. Four good reasons why this is Elvis's shortest ever soundtrack album, with a running time of less than twenty minutes. It was also the first to sound flat, as if half the sound had simply not been recorded. As was becoming usual, both the best tracks were ballads, written by Don Robertson: I'm Falling In Love Tonight and They Remind Me Too Much Of You (which was almost canned for its initial resemblance to Chapel In The Moonlight). Elvis had a little fun with the seductive pseudo-blues of Relax, but on One Broken Heart For Sale he contented himself with a reasonable Jackie Wilson pastiche. ∗

FUN IN ACAPULCO; 1963

As can be heard on *Pot Luck* (see above) Elvis went through a mysterious and little-noticed Latin phase in the early 1960s. That may explain why he took to the soundtrack for *Fun In Acapulco* with such reckless abandon. OK, even Elvis can't rescue There's No Room To Rhumba In A Sports Car, but he delivers the Leiber and Stoller/Clovers flop Bossa Nova Baby with urgency and wit – if only they'd cut the instrumental break – and smoulders his way through Marguerita and You Can't Say No In Acapulco. Guadalajara is a real curio, sung superbly in Spanish with what sounds like the enthusiastic backing of the Jordanaires, the Amigos, the barflies of Acapulco, and every stray dog in the vicinity. ∗∗∗

KISSIN' COUSINS; 1964

Elvis is too good for his own good on most of the songs for *Kissin' Cousins*, his first low-budget movie, almost managing to convince you that ballads like One Boy Two Little Girls and Tender Feeling are better than they really are. Probably because the backing tracks were recorded in Nashville, the sound is much better than usual. The trouble was that the movies were now coming so thick and fast that even the troupe of writers hired by Elvis's publishing companies couldn't keep up. All these songs are now available on a double-feature CD with those from *Clambake* and *Stay Away Joe*. **

VIVA LAS VEGAS; 1964

It says something about the collective loss of plot in the Elvis organisation that his finest musical of the 1960s (and his top grossing movie ever) did not merit its own soundtrack album. Instead, the songs were released on singles and EPs or eked out as fillers on studio and budget albums over the years to come only finally being collected for a double-feature CD with the songs to *Roustabout*. The twelve songs recorded for the film would have comprised a 30 minute album, fifty percent more in quantity (and quality) than the *It Happened At The World's Fair* album. Elvis duetted twice with co-star and real-life lover **Ann Margret** and although **The Lady Loves Me** is fun, they are more seductive revamping the LaVern Baker/Leiber/Stoller number **You're The Boss** (cut from the film). **Viva Las Vegas** is his best movie title track since **King Creole**, almost as much fun as a weekend in Vegas. Of the uptempo numbers, **If You Think I Don't Need You** and **C'mon Everybody** are fast and painless and **Night Life** (also cut from the film) is worth playing just for the rhyme about long-legged women taking you for a trimming. The best of the ballads is Pomus and Shuman's beautiful, desolate **I Need Somebody To Lean On**. ***

ROUSTABOUT; 1964

The *Roustabout* soundtrack was number one for one week in the US – one week more than it deserved. Its highlight was **Little Egypt**, Leiber and Stoller's 1961 hit for the Coasters, while **It's A Wonderful World**, a charming frippery, was briefly considered for an Oscar nomination. The other nine songs were pleasant enough, but only **Poison Ivy** ('they give me an itch, those sons of the [pause] rich') departed from the norm. On **Hard Knocks**, a rocker from Joy Byers, Elvis sounded afraid (or too bored?) to let rip. When the title tune, written by Giant/Baum/Kaye, replaced the original version by **Otis Blackwell**, who'd penned such classics as **All Shook Up**, it marked an inglorious end to Blackwell's association with Presley. **

GIRL HAPPY; 1965

Elvis's voice sounds so speeded up on *Girl Happy* – now twinned on a dou-ble-feature CD with the *Harum Scarum* soundtrack – that you can't help imagining he and the engineers couldn't wait to get it over with. Indeed, he was so embarrassed by the title track that he asked for his vocal not to be brought up in the mix. **Do The Clam** was an ill-fated attempt to kick-start a dance craze, hardly helped by a flaccid guitar break, while **Do Not Disturb** took 36 takes before he walked out in disgust (actually it's not that bad). Even on the best track, **Puppet On A String** – not the Sandie Shaw hit – Presley sounds subdued, as though itching to get back to Memphis. ✳

ELVIS FOR EVERYONE!; 1965

The almost desperately eager-to-please title of *Elvis For Everyone!* gives the game away. By 1965, with the Beatles in their pomp, what Elvis needed above all was a proper studio album. Instead, all he and RCA could offer was this grab bag. Its highlights were a revamped unreleased Sun track, **Tomorrow Night**, and two other 1950s leftovers: **Your Cheatin' Heart** and Billy 'The Kid' Emerson's **When It Rains, It Really Pours**. The 1960s tracks varied from the brilliant, bittersweet **I Met Her Today**, and the short but touching **In My Way**, to the cheery awfulness of **Sound Advice**, from the movie *Follow That Dream*. ✳✳✳

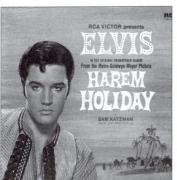

HARUM SCARUM; 1965

The one remarkable thing about *Harum Scarum* (retitled *Harem Holiday* in the UK) is that Elvis had not yet com-pletely given up the ghost. Perhaps intrigued by the chance to be a crooning Valentino, he kicks off with eerie sincerity, keeping a straight face through cod Middle Eastern rock (**Hey Little Girl** and **Shake That Tambourine**) to deliver less absurd slower numbers, like **Kismet** and **So Close, Yet So Far**. Musicians Charlie McCoy and Kenneth Buttrey had just come from Bob Dylan's *Blonde On Blonde* sessions; they must have felt they had entered a parallel universe. McCoy blames the peculiar sound quality on the absence of the echo, supposed to be added later. *

FRANKIE AND JOHNNY; 1966

Elvis threw such a tantrum when he heard the twelve songs chosen for the movie *Frankie And Johnny* that he recorded his vocals after the instrumental tracks had been laid down. Presumably it was **Petunia, The Gardener's Daughter** that sent him over the edge. Apart from the title track, on which El sounds briefly energized, and the ballads **Please Don't Stop Loving Me** and **Beginner's Luck,** when he tries out a new smooth balladeering style, the rest vary from competent hack work to … incompetent hack work. All are now available on a double-feature CD with *Paradise, Hawaiian Style*. **

PARADISE, HAWAIIAN STYLE; 1966

Only three songs on the *Paradise, Hawaiian Style* soundtrack come close to passing muster. The title number breezes along, the closing ballad **This Is My Heaven** is touchingly gentle, and the slow **Sand Castles** is so haunting, and sung with such conviction, that it was of course cut from the film. Elvis refused pointblank to sing 'Bow wow' or 'Ruff', as suggested in the original lyrics in the execrable **A Dog's Life**. It's just a shame he agreed to sing the song at all – or **Queenie Wahine's Papaya, House Of Sand** or **Scratch My Back**. *

SPINOUT; 1966

Although the Colonel asked for more fast numbers for *Spinout*, the songs coming off the conveyor belt were now so dire that they wouldn't have been fit for a Frankie Avalon beach-party movie. Only **Adam And Evil** comes close to rocking from its own momentum, and there are a couple of weighty ballads, **All That I Am** and **Am I Ready**. Elsewhere, Elvis sounds like his own impersonator. On its release, the album was mainly notable for its bonus songs: **Tomorrow Is A Long Time**, the old Clovers hit **Down In The Alley**, and the achingly beautiful **I'll Remember You**. Only the movie songs are included on the *Double Trouble* double-feature CD; the extras can be found on the 1960s box set and *Tomorrow Is A Long Time*. ★★

HOW GREAT THOU ART; 1967

Elvis's comeback started not in Burbank's TV studios in 1968, but with *How Great Thou Art*. For the first time since his initial post-Army spurt, Presley took charge of these **gospel** sessions, starting by telling RCA which gospel singers he wanted to accompany him. Failing to obtain bass singer Jimmy Jones, he drafted in his boyhood idol Jake Hess, who says, 'We sang the way he wanted it sung, he wanted that big sound.' That's the aggressive sound that sweeps **Run On** along, as though the singer really is passing judgment on those long-tongued liars. Hess's favourite was the beautiful rendition of **In The Garden**, but the whole album, even the mournful **Farther Along**, demands to be heard. On the title track and **Stand By Me**, Elvis invites the listener to share in his faith and doubt, while the tenderness as he sings 'My Jesus' on **Without Him** is incredible. Ultimately, it's that sense of commitment, of Elvis taking charge, coupled with a greater emotional and musical breadth, that makes this a more satisfying album than *His Hand In Mine*. ★★★★★

EASY COME EASY GO; 1967

Most Elvis movies, however bad, included at least one ballad of a sufficient quality to motivate the singer. Not *Easy Come Easy Go*. The 'highlight' of its seven songs – all available, with some spectacularly dull alternate takes, on a twin CD with *Speedway* – was probably the stop-start **You Gotta Stop**. It's no great shakes, but at least Elvis sounds interested. The rest are much of a muchness, apart from **Yoga Is As Yoga Does** ('How can I take this yoga serious / when all it ever gives to me's / a pain in my posterious?'). It's a pity Elvis didn't record either Ray Charles' **Leave My Woman Alone** or Lavern Baker's **Saved**; both were suggested for these sessions, though they might have jarred with fillers like **The Love Machine**. ∗

DOUBLE TROUBLE; 1967

On balance, the nine songs from *Double Trouble*, Elvis's 24th movie, were ever so slightly better than those in *Easy Come Easy Go*. The worst, a bizarre update of **Old Macdonald** complete with farmyard noises, was so bad that Elvis stormed off the soundstage – which didn't stop RCA from releasing his seventh unfinished take. Of the remainder, **Could I Fall In Love**, in which Elvis duets with himself, is pretty; **Long Legged Girl With The Short Dress On** is at least a rocker; and **City By Night** is a soft jazzy nightclub number which, despite its clichéd lyrics, is a cut above standard soundtrack fare. Heck, Elvis even sounds sophisticated. ∗∗

CLAMBAKE; 1967

By the time *Clambake* came along, Elvis's movie producers had developed an uncanny knack of spotting the one song that had an ounce of life … and cutting it. Thus **How Can You Lose What You Never Had**, a gutsy number with echoes of **Guitar Man**, was dropped, while **Confidence** (Tepper and Bennett's attempt to write a kids' novelty song like **High Hopes**) survived. It must have been hard for El to harbour high hopes for a song which included the line 'Give me a C and an O and an N and an F and an I and a D and an –ence'. Just two ballads roused Elvis from his lethargy: Eddy Arnold's country classic **You Don't Know Me**, and **The Girl I Never Loved**. Spookily, the twenty-second burst of a bluesy, acoustic version of *Clambake* on the double-CD re-release is so good it makes you forget how awful the song is. ∗

130

SPEEDWAY; 1968

Even though the ballad **Suppose** was the only song in *Speedway* that Elvis actually wanted to record, it fell victim to yet another fit of topsy-turvy 'quality control'. Of the seven other tracks, **Your Time Hasn't Come Yet Baby** has a certain childish charm and **Let Yourself Go** a dash of energy, while **He's Your Uncle Not Your Dad** is a song about income tax. This album's greatest significance is that so few people bought it that the soundtrack era came to a discreet close. ∗

ELVIS – NBC TV SPECIAL; 1968

For many fans, the *Elvis – NBC TV Special*, and the Memphis sessions that follow, represent Presley's meisterwork. Elvis is singing for his very career and, as Greil Marcus observed, the music bleeds. Thanks to the sheer quality, and quantity, of tracks recorded, RCA has released a slew of albums, though not, as yet, a definitive box set.

The best place to start remains the original *TV Special* album; marred by bursts of over-elaborate orchestration it may be, but it's still brilliant. The strongest performances show Elvis and his boys are performing live in the ring, exchanging banter, private jokes and cues. **One Night, Trying To Get To You, Baby, What Do You Want Me To Do, Lawdy Miss Clawdy, Blue Christmas**: all reveal a hunger and rawness missing from Elvis's act since "Reconsider Baby" in 1960.

Of the new songs, **Memories** is gorgeous (if soppy), **Nothingville** is an intriguing fragment, and **If I Can Dream** is simply a work of genius, from both Elvis and the show's choral director **Earl Brown**.

Recognizing the value of the 'unplugged' numbers, RCA released three further albums, *Memories*, *Tiger Man* and *Burbank 68*. All have some merit. In terms of feeling as though you're there, the best is *Burbank 68*, with its glimpse of Elvis and producer Steve Binder running through the order of the show. Many fans will want to buy them all. ∗∗∗∗

FROM ELVIS IN MEMPHIS; 1969

From Elvis In Memphis has been so analysed, eulogized and mythologized that any critical commentary seems redundant. In a sense, it's the musical antithesis of *Elvis Is Back!*, the remarkable album with which he started the decade. While exhilarating, that was also, as Elvis's conductor Joe Guercio

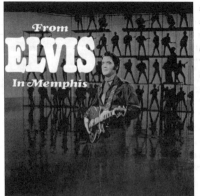

said about the man himself, like watching a marble roll down a staircase. *From Elvis In Memphis* was tightly produced, mainly by **Chips Moman**; focused on a specific musical territory, sort of country/soul with a hint of blues; and relied, crucially, not on Elvis's usual style of 'live' studio recording but on separate tracks being laid down or overdubbed later.

Without Moman's technical expertise, *From Elvis In Memphis* would not be half the album it is. According to Elvis' friend Fred Fredrick, Chips used to play all his stuff through a six-inch car speaker on his desk, asking, 'How's it gonna sound on your car radio?' His studio style was, as *Rolling Stone* described, 'to put a stirring voice in the middle of meticulous arrangements that had the sustained snaky fervour of testimonies or sermons'. Elvis does indeed sound in stirring voice – he may never have sounded better – but then no album of his had ever sounded technically as good as this. The arrangements, rich in low cello notes, were deliberately designed to echo the immense soulfulness of his singing. While American had a similar studio style to Sun, this time it was not Sam Phillips pushing Elvis but Chips Moman, pushing him for the emotion that jumps out of almost every song, and simply oozes out of him when he takes Eddy Arnold's **I'll Hold You In My Heart** past the point of no return.

Both that lament and the Della Reese/Eddy Arnold hit **After Loving You**, had been on Elvis's mind or turntable for years (as had **Stranger In My Own Home Town**) and, as they provided two of the many highlights on this album, Presley should have gone with his gut instinct more often when it came to choosing material.

Even without **Suspicious Minds**, recorded at these same sessions, *From Elvis In Memphis* is, finally, a better album than *Elvis Is Back!* because all of its tracks, if not uniformly brilliant, have their merits. There are no obvious makeweights. **Power Of My Love** allows Elvis to indulge in a little innuendo, and the modern country classic **Gentle On My Mind** gets a wonderful reading, with Elvis pouring substance into what's at heart an easy-listening number. He delivers **True Love Travels On A Gravel Road** with such soul it's no surprise Percy Sledge felt obliged to cover it.

RCA's re-release of the original album includes extra tracks like **Rubberneckin'** – why, RCA, why? – that dilute its impact. Best perhaps to treat yourself to the *Suspicious Minds* CD, which includes this whole album, plus its successor, and a bunch of other songs and outtakes that may not have made the cut but are still miles better than anything on most of Elvis's 1960s albums. ★★★★★

BACK IN MEMPHIS; 1969

Had it not followed *From Elvis In Memphis*, **Back In Memphis** would have quickly been recognised as a decent album in its own right. Having first seen the light of day as half of a double album with the best of Elvis's earliest Las Vegas performances, it was subsequently released separately (amazingly even making the US album charts) and is now available on CD, though the songs are also available on several Memphis compilations. OK, so nothing here quite reaches the emotional heights of **Long Black Limousine** or **Any Day Now**, but **Stranger In My Own Home Town** is the bluesiest, craziest thing from the entire sessions. The ballads again give Elvis the chance to sing about adult emotions: **Without Love** is simply stupendous, while **Do You Know Who I Am** is seductive and subtle. Neil Diamond's **And The Grass Won't Pay No Mind** is sensitively handled; some recompense for a writer whose sessions had been cancelled in order for Elvis to record at American. And Mort Shuman's **You'll Think Of Me** is fascinatingly different, with some of the toughest lyrics Elvis ever sang in a ballad. The weakest song, **The Fair Is Moving On**, came from El's own publishing empire. ★★★★

133

ELVIS IN PERSON; 1969

Now available as a stand-alone CD, *Elvis In Person* was the first, rawest and best of six live albums released over an eight-year period. If you only want to buy one, go for this or *On Stage*. Its highlight is usually seen as being **Suspicious Minds**, but Elvis runs through the rockers **Johnny B. Goode** and **My Babe** with panache. **I Can't Stop Loving You** and **Mystery Train/Tiger Man** are good R&B performances, while of the ballads, the Bee Gees' **Words** is delivered with real commitment, power and, for once, little sentimentality. The weakest tracks are the revamped 1950s oldies. Even the banter is a cut above average. Elvis pokes fun at his own myth, telling the audience, 'Just look at me and say, "Is that him? I thought he was bigger than that! Squirty looking guy."' and introduces himself with, 'This is my first live appearance for nine years … I've appeared dead before, but this is my first live one.' ★★★★

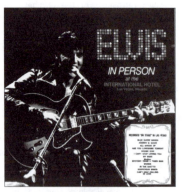

LIVE A LITTLE, LOVE A LITTLE/CHARRO/ THE TROUBLE WITH GIRLS/CHANGE OF HABIT

Confessing to liking a movie soundtrack is a bit like incriminating yourself in public, but what the heck. A handful of songs on this title (the best being **A Little Less Conversation**, **Almost** and **Clean Up Your Own Back Yard**) are worth the price of admission, and even on the dubious stuff (like the theme to **Change Of Habit**), there's a hint of social consciousness in the lyric which suggests that "In The Ghetto" was no fluke. And **Rubberneckin'**, when not stacked alongside classics like "**In The Ghetto**", has a charm all of its own. ★★★

The years of living dangerously: the 1970s

The 1970s were the most controversial and heartbreaking phase of Elvis's career. The first sign that the infinite promise of his come-back might not reach fruition came with his return to **Las Vegas** in January 1970. As W.A. Harbinson wrote in *Elvis: The Illustrated Biography*: 'Of course he can do it – no one doubts that he can do it – but then no one understands why he would want to.'

Much criticism (some unjust) has been levelled at **Colonel Parker**, but his sheer lack of imagination at this point beggars belief. His idea of managing the world's most popular singer seemed to be to find something that worked, and then keep doing until it stopped working. So, just when he was finally free from Hollywood's equivalent of the chain gang, Presley found himself stuck in another rut: Vegas twice a year, plus as many other tour dates as he could squeeze in.

King of the road

For most of the 1960s, it was the movies that kept Elvis from spending productive time in the studio; in the 1970s, it was the **endless tours**. Now the effect was even worse, because appearing live offered a fulfilment too often lacking in the studio, where sessions continued to be plagued by squabbles over publishing rights. Elvis's 'Kingship' began to weigh heavily on him, both as a person and a singer, and his simple joy in music increasingly found expression in his all-night **gospel singalongs** in Vegas with the Stamps and/or the Imperials.

The effect of the various behind-the-scenes tensions, however, did not become obvious until 1973. The decade kicked off with the feisty live album *On Stage*, from which the powerful **The Wonder Of You** reached the Top 10 in the US, and number one in the UK.

Even better were the results of a fabulously productive five-day session in June 1970 at RCA's Studio B in Nashville. Now backed by a new band, with a straighter rock/country feel, Elvis cut enough material for two decent albums (and one duff one, *Love Letters From Elvis*) and three hit singles. Perhaps not surprisingly, in light of the ongoing publishing shenanigans, many of the best moments were inspired flukes: the improvised Got My Mojo Working, the off-the-cuff bluegrass of Little Cabin On The Hill, and the sudden idea to do a country album, inspired by Elvis's reading of I Really Don't Want To Know. In fact, most of Elvis's finest 1970s music came when he threw away the script: Don't Think Twice It's All Right, I'm So Lonesome I Could Cry, Promised Land, There's A Honky Tonk Angel … all show a commitment he found hard to give to pap like This Is Our Dance and Girl Of Mine.

Filmed for the documentary *That's The Way It Is*, Elvis's Las Vegas performances in the summer of 1970 showed him focusing on ballads; indeed, all his five gold singles that year were ballads. It was apparent, as his bass player Jerry Scheff put it, that 'Elvis didn't want to be a rock'n'roll singer. He had a great voice and he wanted to be known for that voice. Rock'n'roll songs didn't do that. Anytime anybody does a medley of songs, you know they don't want to do these songs.'

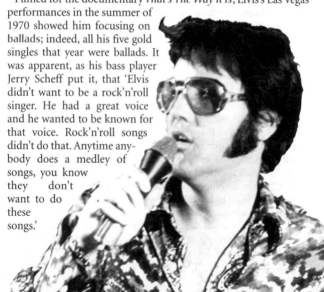

136

While he didn't have any gold singles in 1971, that failure was masked by the release of *Elvis Country*, often acclaimed as the best country-rock album of the early 1970s. It was followed by a so-so Christmas album, and a grab-bag of leftovers cunningly disguised as a new album called *Elvis Now*. This set a new standard for RCA; from hereon in, ten songs were deemed enough for a new full-price Presley album.

While the Grammy-award-winning sacred album *He Touched Me* didn't sell well, Presley did at least sound inspired. Just as Elvis, Parker and RCA seemed about to fritter away the impetus of his comeback, fans were greeted by a double whammy: a second live documentary, *Elvis On Tour*, and, in June 1972, his first appearance at Madison Square Garden. Presley, Tom Jones says, was genuinely scared by the prospect of playing New York but he triumphed. His next single Burning Love – his first genuine rock'n'roll single since 1968, and a number two hit in the US – built on that momentum.

It's a measure of how badly Presley's career was being managed that instead of putting "Burning Love" on an album of strong contemporary material, it was used to promote a budget album of old movie songs. Ed Bonja, who worked for Colonel Parker, says, 'I always felt there was a little jealousy between Elvis and the Colonel, not on Elvis's part but that the Colonel was a little jealous of him. He would invariably choose a picture for a certain project that was OK but not great and he would say, "That's good enough, the fans will buy it no matter what" … he always kept things corny – not a lot of class.' Class was certainly what *Burning Love And Hits From His Movies* conspicuously lacked, corn it had in abundance.

Madison Square Garden was followed on 14 January 1973 by an even bigger coup, *Aloha From Hawaii*. In all the talk of how many people watched it – over 1.5 billion – and how many platinum discs it earned, the most significant aspect seemed to be Elvis's heartfelt commitment to I'm So Lonesome I Could Cry.

◀ That's the way he was in 1970, rehearsing for Vegas and movie cameras

The King of pain

The success of *Aloha* made it that much harder for Elvis to moti-vate himself to go back to Vegas and criss-cross the country on tour. This, surely, was the juncture when Parker should have accepted one of the plethora of offers from overseas promoters for a world tour. Instead, within nine months, Presley and Parker were on the brink of separation. Ostensibly, the rift came when Presley scolded the Hilton on stage for firing an employee, but behind it all lay his discontent with how his career – and/or his life – was going. A world tour might have distracted Presley from the collapse of his marriage, a blow that explained his increasing attraction to such regret-laden ballads as Always On My Mind and Separate Ways. If he was feeling hollow and lonely himself, then he would sing for all the other hollow and lonely people out there.

RCA rushed out another album called *Elvis* (known to fans as the 'Fool' album) to capitalize on *Aloha*, but it sold just 200,000 copies, and they probably wished they hadn't bothered. Eager to recoup the cost of buying out Elvis's back catalogue, they set a recording session for July. But when Presley arrived at Stax Studios, the musicians (many of them veterans of the 1969 Memphis sessions) were shocked by his erratic behaviour and his appearance. The studio's technical shortcomings, and Elvis's insis-tence on kicking things off with a karate session and some gun-play, didn't improve matters much.

The album that emerged from the first Stax sessions, *Raised On Rock*, and the eponymous single, came and went with little fanfare. RCA executive Joan Deary tried to get producer Felton Jarvis sacked as a result, but Elvis wouldn't hear of it. Revenge came when Deary's pet project, the first in the *Legendary Performer* series, out-sold *Raised On Rock* by 500,000 copies. Elvis still had four years left to live, but he was already being outsold by his own ghost.

A fortnight in hospital, the finalization of his divorce, and a new relationship with beauty queen Linda Thompson combined to make Elvis's return to Stax in December 1973 much more rewarding. Two albums resulted, *Good Times* and *Promised Land*; neither is perfect, but both were a cut above the previous two studio albums. On the sixth day, he was so energized that at 4.30am, inspired by his father's presence, he jumped up to deliver a fine rendition of There's A Honky Tonk Angel.

As predictably unpredictable as ever, Presley capped this fruitful session by not returning to the studio for 15 months. Not that it was all his fault; a grand total of 158 concerts in 43 venues made 1974 even more gruelling than 1973. The very format, Top 40 radio, which had helped him in his heyday now worked against him. In the US, only country DJs played his singles heavily; thus while Got A Thing About You Baby failed to make the Top 30 in the UK or US, it was a Top 5 country hit.

By now Elvis's output was so sparse and sporadic that RCA felt compelled to release almost any new track it could get its hands on. His growing reluctance to record has never been adequately explained. Possible explanations include the usual publishing rows, which stymied plans to record two Dolly Parton songs and the Walker Brothers' The Sun Ain't Gonna Shine Anymore. In a decade of singer-songwriters, the Elvis organization's hard line on royalty sharing was self-destructive nonsense. Putnam also says, 'Whenever he asked, it would often be a case of "Oh, we couldn't get that one".'

Presley's own mood swings, exacerbated by his reliance on prescription drugs, didn't help, but Jerry Schilling says, 'He never lost his love for music, for singing, but he got tired of going into the studio, being faced with the kind of material he was faced with, he used to say he knew there was better material out there and couldn't figure out why he wasn't getting it. And he wasn't that happy with the technical side of it, even the way some of his songs sounded, they didn't sound as he heard them in his mind, so like a lot of creative people, he would rather do almost anything than face all that hassle. It got to the point that being on stage was the one place where he felt nobody could mess around with him, he was in control and could just be who he was.'

139

> In the 1970s, Elvis rarely felt as at ease in the studio as he did on stage

The thrill is gone

That summer's Vegas season was notable for two concerts. For his 19 August 1974 opening, Elvis made a brave attempt to restructure his set, both to allude to his roots and to give a more contemporary feel. On the bootleg CD, he sounds genuinely nervous, introducing himself to a mystified crowd as 'the NBC peacock' before launching into a rousing rendition of Big Boss Man. At least, it would have been rousing, if the audience had shown some enthusiasm. It was, perhaps, Elvis's final bid for freedom and relevance; had he persevered, who knows what might have followed? Sadly, however, it came before one of the least enthusiastic audiences of his career; by the next night, he was back to business as usual.

All of which puts the outbursts that followed on 2 September – the so-called 'desert storm', when Presley ranted about drugs, divorce, and the procedures for a liver biopsy – into some context. It's heart-rending stuff, but the horrible irony was that he ended by saying he'd only ever been strung out on his fans – the very group that only a fortnight before had helped condemn him to sing the same old medley of greatest hits.

For psychological, medical and musical reasons, Elvis should have stopped touring at this point. But touring was the easiest way to fund his ever more extravagant lifestyle, and almost the only revenue generator on which he and Parker could agree. After Good Times he released two live albums, one recorded in Memphis, the other, initially on Parker's own Boxcar label, a compilation of his ad-libs called Having Fun On Stage With Elvis, the most depressing aspect of which was that (reissued on RCA) it sold about two-thirds as well as his proper albums.

The professional highlights of that difficult year were two singles on either side of the Atlantic. In the US, his version of Chuck Berry's Promised Land – his best rock single of the decade – was his third Top 20 single in a row. And in the UK, My Boy – often

141

dismissed as self-pitying rubbish, but, as John Aizlewood has pointed out in Q magazine, 'so haunted it could be a Stephen King novel' – became his first Top 5 hit since 1970.

1975 kicked off with a plethora of 'Elvis – fat and forty' stories, and, more importantly, a decent album, *Promised Land*, marred by indifferent material and poor sound. In March, he made his final visit to an RCA recording studio to cut what became *Elvis Today*. While Elvis's concerts varied in quality, all were not as indifferent as legend might suggest. Reviewing a Long Island gig in July, the *New York Times* noted, 'The youthful sexuality has long gone; but in its place there is a wonderfully relaxed ironic affection that can be almost as nice. When he is putting out, reaching for the top notes and shaping phrases with the individuality that has always marked his best work, he is still king.'

By February 1976, RCA were desperate enough to send a sound truck down to Memphis so he could cut some tracks in the Jungle Room. Presley was at his most erratic, waving a gun at one point and lavishing an inordinate amount of time on Morris Albert's Feelings. He also sang as many Platters songs as he could remember, none of which, tragically, Felton Jarvis felt inclined to record. Even so, he scraped enough masters together to release *From Elvis Presley Boulevard*. Critic Dave Marsh famously said of the bellowing Hurt, 'If he felt the way it sounded, the wonder is not that he had a year left to live but that he lasted that long.' During an even less satisfactory session in November, Elvis roused himself for Way Down, and laid his emotions bare on the Lloyd Webber/Rice song It's Easy For You. Those were the last songs he ever recorded.

On tour, Elvis took to singing My Way, prompting one newspaper to remark, 'When he sang "And now the end is near" it was like witnessing a chilling prophecy.' But 1976 ended on a relatively high note: Elvis celebrated New Year's Eve, and the presence of new girlfriend Ginger Alden, with a ninety-minute *tour de force* in Pittsburgh. Bootleg CDs of the concerts on this end-of-year mini-tour show him in fine voice and varying his repertoire.

The final curtain

After Presley failed either to show up at the Nashville studios in March 1977, or to reply to enquiries about future sessions, Jarvis was reduced to following him around on tour, hoping to record enough songs to complete a ten-track album. The ensuing *Moody Blue* was released in July. However, its prospects, and that of El's final single, Way Down, were transformed by his sudden death.

Until the late 1980s, Presley's 1970s recordings were critically reviled. Such was the loathing that even the good stuff, like *Elvis Country*, was disregarded. With some justification, rock critics felt Elvis had betrayed them. The sneering has subsided, partly because rock itself seems less vibrant than it used to be, and partly out of a belated recognition that purely as a singer Presley never did quite lose his ability to conjure up his own sonic universe with a single utterance. Dave Marsh, in his essay for the 1970s box set *Walk A Mile In My Shoes*, made the point that this was a pretty iffy decade for most of rock's great acts, with the Beatles, the Stones and Dylan all failing to match their achievements of the 1960s.

What's intriguing is that many fans now listen more often to Presley's 1969–77 work than the revolutionary music of 1954–58 that we are officially supposed to prefer. As RCA once put it, 50,000,000 Elvis fans can't be wrong although the 300,000 who, like the author, bought *Paradise, Hawaiian Style* may have been a tad misguided.

1970s albums

The best starting point to enjoy Elvis in the 1970s is the *Walk A Mile In My Shoes* box set, which contains more than enough good stuff to justify the price. Of the original album releases, the glory that is *Elvis Country* (1971) is essential. But most of the individual albums have some merit; the remastered versions are usually superior, just because they sound better.

143

Except where specified, the following reviews are of the original releases (all of which have been reissued by RCA on CD, sometimes with extra tracks). For the key compilation albums, see the section beginning on p.154. Budget albums such as I Got Lucky are not reviewed separately as they are no longer available.

ON STAGE; 1970

For Elvis to release a live album of completely new songs was a first. Although the gamble paid off, *On Stage* – recently re-released with six extra tracks, and sounding better than ever – was an early indication that he was indeed 'caught in a trap'. To serve his Las Vegas audience, he had to sing either his own hits, or other songs they already knew. Here he went mostly for the latter, although he did slip in a pumped-up version of the Ma Rainey/LaVern Baker blues See See Rider. After that, the album alternates between above-average renditions of cabaret material like The Wonder Of You (which he'd been planning to record since 1966), Release Me and Let It Be Me, and faster numbers such as Runaway, Proud Mary and a stupendous rendering of Tony Joe White's Polk Salad Annie.

As Priscilla has testified, Joe South's Walk A Mile In My Shoes held considerable meaning for Elvis; at times, he'd perform it after reciting Hank Williams' Men With Broken Hearts. His faithful rendition of Yesterday suggests that, complex as his view of the Beatles might have been, they were also capable of inspiring him. ★★★★

THAT'S THE WAY IT IS; 1970

While both album and documentary share the name *That's The Way It Is*, the resemblance ends there. Far from being a high-energy souvenir of Elvis's triumphant return to Las Vegas, this is an album about falling in and out of love, filled with songs about adult emotions. Elvis sings his heart out on How The Web Was Woven, You've Lost That Lovin' Feelin', and Bridge Over Troubled Water (of which Paul Simon said, 'It was a bit dramatic but how the hell am I supposed to compete with that?'). I Just Can't Help Believing is near-perfect, while on I've Lost You Elvis sounds like a man who knows all about the point where softly, without pain, the joy of love comes to an end. A similar bittersweet mood permeates the unusual **Twenty Days And Twenty Nights**, **Just Pretend** and even **Mary In The Morning**, which isn't best served by the arrangement. Unusually for the 1970s Elvis, there are two songs that describe the happiness of love – **Stranger In The Crowd** and **The Next Step Is Love**. ★★★★

ELVIS COUNTRY; 1971

Until 1971, concept albums were not something one associated with Elvis; they smacked of an intellectual conceit that had never really been his thing. Then he surprised and delighted critics with *Elvis Country*, a collection of country songs linked by snippets of the Golden Gate Quartet's **I Was Born About Ten Thousand Years Ago**.

This being the Elvis organization, however, the album was not so much the product of a well-executed plan but of Presley's desperate search for decent material. He had done a decent cover of The Fool on 4 June 1970 in Nashville and forgot the words to **Faded Love**. Three days later, Elvis suddenly launched into a soulful reading of Don Robertson's **I Really Don't Want To Know**. Inspired, he rocked through **Faded Love**, then switched moods for the Ernest Tubb ballad **Tomorrow Never Comes** – an often-overlooked performance that perfectly illustrates the emotional vulnerability at the core of Elvis's appeal. Among his peers, only Roy Orbison sang so often and so nakedly of the damage that love could inflict. The epic session was rounded off with a brilliant (if slightly overproduced) interpretation of Willie Nelson's **Funny How Time Slips Away**, and a furious jam on **I Washed My Hands In Muddy Waters**.

The overall sense of Elvis rediscovering his roots is strengthened by the good-humoured bluegrass **Little Cabin On the Hill**, and a manic, possibly medication-fuelled attack on **Whole Lotta Shakin' Goin On**, which has to be the heaviest thing he ever recorded. Even **It's Your Baby You Rock It** is sung as though he really meant it.

Triggered perhaps by the artist's urgency, RCA responded with their best **album cover** of the 1970s – a picture of the 3-year-old Elvis that proved that lip-curling came to him naturally. Despite the level of performances, however, and a rave *Rolling Stone* review from Peter Guralnick, who wrote that Elvis 'gives us some of the very finest music since he first recorded at Sun', *Elvis Country* only sold the usual 500,000 copies on first release.
*****

LOVE LETTERS FROM ELVIS; 1971

Released without Elvis's approval, *Love Letters From Elvis* was a potpourri of leftovers from the Nashville sessions of June 1970. Its one real highlight, a five-and-a-half-minute blues jam of Muddy Waters' **Got My Mojo Working**, was typically enough taped by accident. Otherwise, only **It Ain't No Big Thing** and **I'll Never Know** rise above the general mediocrity, while **Heart Of Rome** at least shows that Elvis still dreamed of being the next Mario Lanza. Co-writer Alan Blaikley commented that it was 'a bit of a pot-boiler … I'm amazed Elvis should have decided to record it. However, he certainly made a silk purse out of a sow's ear.' As for **Cindy Cindy**, if it's indicative of the kind of rock songs Elvis was being asked to record, it's a wonder he didn't retire there and then. *

THE WONDERFUL WORLD OF CHRISTMAS; 1971

Elvis's first Christmas album being such a consistent seller, it was inevitable that RCA and Parker would suggest a follow-up. *The Wonderful World Of Christmas* isn't quite as wonderful as its predecessor, partly because Elvis obviously despises **Winter Wonderland** and can't be bothered with **Silver Bells**. Yet the tenderness with which he sings the word 'Christmas' in the title track (written by friend **Red West**) suggests that he was not, as critics usually maintain, utterly uninterested. Give him the right material and he could rouse himself: thus the groovy, soaring O Come All Ye Faithful; the bluesy reflective I'll Be Home On Christmas Day; and, best of all, Merry Christmas Baby. This album, complete with outtakes, is now best obtained on the compilation *If Every Day Was Like Christmas*. ★★

ELVIS NOW; 1972

Elvis Now is proof that the Elvis organization could no longer find enough good contemporary material for him to record. Containing a rehearsal of Hey Jude from the Memphis sessions, and I Was Born About Ten Thousand Years Ago, already released in snippet form at the end of every track on *Elvis Country*, it should have been called *Elvis Then*. The inclusion of any of Elvis's recent singles (especially I'm Leavin') could have helped matters, although even when he cut a song as strong as Help Me Make It Through The Night it was lifelessly arranged. Buffy Sainte Marie's Until It's Time For You To Go, and Gordon Lightfoot's sincere and quietly hypnotic Early Mornin' Rain were almost all that remained of an abortive plan for Elvis to record a folk album. ★★

HE TOUCHED ME; 1972

Elvis's third gospel album, *He Touched Me*, is his most critically neglected. Despite suggestions that, like his second Christmas album, this release represents the point at which a successful formula started to wear thin, he is in simply excellent voice throughout. Highlights include the Grammy-winning rendition of He Touched Me itself; the irresistible Lead Me Guide Me; and Reach Out To Jesus, a commanding performance that builds to a real blitzkrieg finish. On A Thing Called Love, his vocal is wonderfully (and, for the 1970s, rarely) understated. Elvis also drew on black gospel with I've Got Confidence and the gospel quartets of his youth with I John and Bosom Of Abraham, though his adventurous, bluesy take on Amazing Grace went unreleased at the time, and only surfaced on the 1970s box set. ★★★★

147

ELVIS AS RECORDED LIVE IN MADISON SQUARE GARDEN; 1972

Elvis's evening show at **Madison Square Garden**, on 10 June 1972, may have made a stupendous spectacle, but it didn't quite cut the mustard on record. He was clearly finding it tedious to have to run through his greatest hits, while the sound mix – much improved for the 1990s re-release – was atrocious. Only on the newer numbers – **The Impossible Dream, For The Good Times** and, best of all, the sly and sexy **Never Been To Spain** – did he appear to be stimulated by the challenge of such a high-profile gig. Since RCA released his afternoon show as *Afternoon In The Garden*, there's been much debate as to which is better; one fan on Amazon says the whole show sounds as if he knows there's a taxi waiting. ✶✶✶

ALOHA FROM HAWAII; 1973

Aloha From Hawaii was unquestionably a marketing triumph, but it was neither a musical nor a personal one. Barring the desire to have a number-one double album, there was no real need to release 23 songs from the concert, especially as ten were already available, often in better versions, on other live albums. The grandiloquence of the whole exercise affected the music – witness the dirge-like **Something** – while Elvis at his worst sounded barely involved.

It's the country material, imported to add some variety, that works best; Presley sings Hank Williams' **I'm So Lonesome I Could Cry** as though it was written just for him, treats Jimmie Rodgers' **It's Over** with similar affection, and turns up the melodrama on Marty Robbins's **You Gave Me A Mountain**. **What Now My Love** is new enough to engage both Elvis and audience, while James Taylor's **Steamroller Blues** is playful even if the lyrics are slightly gross. **American Trilogy**, of course, gets a commanding performance from the man in the American-eagle jumpsuit, while the five after-hours songs – four from *Blue Hawaii*, plus **Early Mornin' Rain** – are informal, simple and seductive. ✶✶✶

ELVIS; 1973

Elvis was not the album to capitalize on the chutzpah and commercial success of *Aloha*. RCA originally intended it to be half studio, half live, but producer **Felton Jarvis**, presumably in the interests of artistic unity, replaced all the live cuts (apart from the over-orchestrated **It's Impossible**) with ballads. Much the best were those recorded by Elvis at the piano: **I'll Take You Home Again Kathleen**, **I Will Be True** and **It's Still Here**. There's also a lovely, freewheeling jam of Bob Dylan's **Don't Think Twice, It's All Right**, available in a longer version on *Our Memories Of Elvis Volume 2*, and in a four-minute edit on the 1970s box set. ★★

RAISED ON ROCK; 1973

Raised On Rock was less interesting than the Stax Studios sessions that produced it; temporarily unhinged by his divorce, Elvis turned up with a massive entourage, did some karate and fooled around with a gun. More to the point, Leiber and Stoller had submitted some of their worst ever songs; the nadir was the senseless **Three Corn Patches**. While **Raised On Rock** itself wasn't bad, it had Elvis describing rock as a fad that wouldn't last; as a fan asked in *Elvis Monthly*, 'So who is singing this? Frank Sinatra?' Only **Just A Little Bit** of the uptempo numbers shows much life, with a glimmer of the old lip-curling arrogance. The best of the ballads, the reflective **For Ol' Times Sake**, reads as a slow, effortless, and beautifully sung look back on Elvis's fourteen-year relationship with Priscilla. ★★

GOOD TIMES; 1974

Though the world was no longer buying new Elvis albums by the time *Good Times* came out, it was actually pretty listenable, with two stand-out ballads – **Good Time Charlie's Got The Blues** and **Loving Arms** – and two good uptempo tracks – Tony Joe White's **Got A Thing About You Baby** and Jerry Reed's **Talk About The Good Times**. Elvis's voice was still in good shape, especially on the soaring **Loving Arms**, the one song, arranged, produced and performed with the sensitivity of the Memphis sessions. Sadly, many

149

of the rest sounded tinny; the eight remastered on the *Promised Land* CD now carry much more conviction and power. ✱✱✱

ELVIS RECORDED LIVE ON STAGE IN MEMPHIS; 1974

Elvis's fifth live album, *Live On Stage In Memphis*, is (most people will tell you) his worst. Don't believe them. While not in the finest voice, he sounds genuinely committed to an unusual set, tailored in honour of his first hometown appearance in thirteen years. As well as lots of early rock – Lawdy Miss Clawdy, My Baby Left Me, and a medley that included Flip, Flop And Fly – there was some stand-out gospel. Elvis told a friend, 'When I'm up there on stage, singing gospel numbers, that's my moment with God.' Listening to Kris Kristofferson's Why Me Lord, the Grammy-award-winning rendition of How Great Thou Art, and even Help Me, it's hard not to believe him. ✱✱✱

PROMISED LAND; 1975

The fact that Promised Land was Elvis's best rocker in years didn't help the reception of the *Promised Land* album; one reviewer said that if this was the best Elvis could do, he should retire. *Billboard* was more impressed, noting that he was still bothering to experiment with his voice. On Thinking About You, he even seemed to be trying out a whole new style, while both There's A Honky Tonk Angel and It's Midnight, two very different love songs, smack of real emotional commitment. The flaw was once again the material; Elvis put a lot of effort into Your Love's Been A Long Time Coming, but even the combined talent of Roy Hamilton, Clyde McPhatter and Mario Lanza couldn't bring it to life. **Mr Songman** is technically so bad that you can hear the splice between two versions. That said, it all sounds much better on the remastered CD. ★★★★

ELVIS TODAY; 1975

Unlike *Elvis Now*, *Elvis Today* almost lives up to its title; all ten songs were recorded in three days in March 1975, when RCA, desperate for new Elvis material, hurried his stage band into their Hollywood studios. Perhaps the most intriguing results came on **And I Love You So**, utterly unlike Perry Como's hit version; Elvis may have identified with it as he was singing to his then-girlfriend Sheila Ryan. **Pieces Of My Life**, a "My Way"-style retrospective on a life that failed to go as planned, also got to him; he listened to the playback thirty times before leaving the studio. **Shake A Hand**, the Faye Adams classic from 1953, marks one of the last times on record when his voice really caught fire, while **T-R-O-U-B-L-E**, a complicated, fast-paced rocker, was delivered with manic urgency. A slow bluesy jam of Rufus Thomas's **Tiger Man**, later included on the 1970s box set, suggests that raiding Elvis's prodigious memory for the blues might have been a more productive strategy. In a sense, though, this album *was* Elvis's blues, the pieces of his life. ★★★

FROM ELVIS PRESLEY BOULEVARD, MEMPHIS, TENNESSEE; 1976

Recorded at Graceland – hence the title – *From Elvis Presley Boulevard* is said by some to have been cut almost against the singer's will. Hardly surprising, then, that it proved to be his least satisfying record since *Elvis* in 1973. And yet there was always a sneaking suspicion that somewhere, buried beneath enough strings to keep Vienna's quartets happy for the next century, a better album was struggling to get out. Thanks to the fine work of Ernst Jorgensen on *The Jungle Room Sessions*, that suspicion is now confirmed. By returning to the original tapes, he has produced something far easier to listen to than its 'official' predecessor.

Not all of the blame can be laid on the arrangements. Almost all the songs are melancholy ballads, the most baffling being Roger Whittaker's **The Last Farewell** (thank god he hadn't heard Whittaker's "Durham Town"). On occasion, the wear and tear on Elvis's voice makes the melancholic sound more like colic. But for all his tardiness in turning up, his plan to nip out mid-session and wipe out the drug pushers of Memphis, and his reported threat to blow up the sound equipment, he was in fact trying bloody hard for much of the time. In particular, **Hurt**, a powerful tribute to Roy Hamilton, is delivered with conviction, while (of the ballads) **Love Coming Down** and **Bitter They Are, Harder They Fall** get a sympathetic reading, and the sentimental **Danny Boy** is movingly done. The only uptempo track **For The Heart** zips along nicely too, although it sounds better on *The Jungle Room Sessions* and the *Platinum* compilation. ✴✴

MOODY BLUE; 1977

Except for **Let Me Be There**, which had already featured on *Live On Stage In Memphis, Moody Blue* is a compilation of unreleased material, some live and some from the Graceland sessions. All of the new live stuff is in its way remarkable. The bravura **Unchained Melody** is imbued with loss and regret; it makes a far more effective anthem for these years than **My Way**, while this version is much more subtle than the heavy-breathing cut on *The Greatest Performances* CD compilation (currently unavailable) where it's hard not to be distracted by the fear that the singer won't live to finish the song. The tongue-in-cheek **Little Darlin'** is welcome light relief after such emotional desolation.

Of the studio tracks, the most effective are **Way Down** and the Tim Rice-Andrew Lloyd Webber ballad **It's Easy For You**. Elvis starts the latter as though he's in Nashville while the band are playing in Memphis, but he soon gets inside it, unable to resist the pathos of lines like 'I had a wife, I had children / I threw them all away'. A final morbid piece of musical trivia: **Pledging My Love** was the B side of "Way Down", the last single released while Elvis was still alive. In 1954, it had been the one and only hit for the Memphis R&B singer Johnny Ace, who died playing Russian roulette before it reached the charts. ✴✴✴

ELVIS IN CONCERT; 1977

It's hard to review *Elvis In Concert* calmly. By the time this TV special was filmed, Presley was clearly not so much fat as desperately ill. The fact that he was on stage at all is a scandal for which all concerned – and that includes Elvis – must share the blame. Given Guralnick's depressing account of these days, however, and the shocking video footage, the performances sound better on record than you might fear.

Presumably because of the TV cameras, Elvis plays around with his repertoire, treating us to a gospel-blues reading of I Really Don't Want To Know and a ravishing version of It's Now Or Never, on which he slightly sends himself up by over-emphasizing 'my soul surrendered'. As so often, How Great Thou Art stirs him – his astonishing cry of 'My god' seems to be summoning the Almighty to a pow-

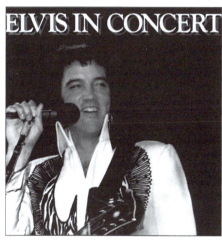

wow there and then – while the full-throated Trying To Get To You is so good that his apology for how his voice has lowered is entirely redundant. It might just be that Elvis was bored, or out of it, but there's a great sense of unpredictability, with a swamp-blues interlude in the middle of I Got A Woman/Amen, a beautiful Hawaiian Wedding Song, and a rare rendition of Little Sister that sprints along. It's true, RCA engineers had to do a certain amount of surgery on the tapes, but cut down to a single album this would have made a more than respectable record. ★★★

153

Compilations and retrospectives

The 'best of' compilation is often seen as a label's official confirmation that an artist's career is over. Not so with Elvis, whose first compilation *Elvis Gold Records Volume 1* was released less than three years after his chart debut. It eventually shifted over six million units, spawning four other volumes – the last released in 1997. The most famous is *Volume 2*, notable for the gold lamé and the subtitle *50 Million Elvis Fans Can't Be Wrong*.

RCA also released two fifty-track box sets of hits in 1970–71, chiefly notable because the second release (*The Other Sides*) included pieces of material cut from Elvis's clothes. The singer wasn't dead but RCA was already selling relics.

These compilations have been largely superseded by the posthumously released **box sets** for the 1950s (*The King Of Rock'n'Roll*), the 1960s (*From Nashville To Memphis*) and the 1970s (*Walk A Mile In My Shoes*) and various greatest hits albums.

RCA has continued to release budget albums on the Camden label. This association started in 1969. Some titles (the Christmas album, **Separate Ways**, and the 1971 gospel release *You'll Never Walk Alone*) were half-decent. Many weren't. Two successive Camden albums *Let's Be Friends* and *Almost In Love* both included the same track, **Stay Away Joe**, an error RCA later rectified.

The **strangest** Elvis album ever released has to be *Having Fun On Stage With Elvis*, the concert album with all the songs edited out. But *Burning Love And Hits From His Movies* comes a clear second. Released in 1972 on Camden, it roped together **Burning Love** and **It's A Matter Of Time**, the two sides of his hottest single for years, with eight non-hits from his movies. Anyone tempted to buy the new Elvis album on the strength of his bayou-rock smash found themselves listening to turkeys like **I Love Only One Girl** from *Double Trouble* (sample line: 'now she can cook and flirt, you can't beat her lasagne – I eat until it hurts').

Parker wanted to boost flagging sales of Elvis's budget albums. In that sense alone, it worked, reaching number 22 in the *Billboard* charts and going gold. There was a risk that new fans might have been turned off but that was the kind of cost you couldn't quantify, whereas the profits from 700,000 sales were all too visible.

In the UK, RCA's cut-priced Starcall imprint produced a rare gem, *The Sun Collection*, with sixteen performances from his most legendary sessions. A credit to artist and label – and to rock writer Roy Carr, who campaigned for its release for two years – it was finally released in the US in 1976 after a brisk trade in imports.

Camden now has a snooty younger sibling, Follow That Dream, a label designed for completists and hard-core fans which has done some fine work. FTD was set up partly to combat the plethora of bootleg albums (which are reviewed separately on p.164). FTD releases are not officially available through all the usual outlets but you can often buy them mail order from the best Elvis shops or online from some of the usual sources.

What follows is a personal selection of the best compilations and retrospectives from RCA, Camden, Follow That Dream and elsewhere available as this book went to press. In 1981, RCA released *Guitar Man*, an album re-recorded by producer Felton Jarvis with Elvis's original vocal and a new backing band. It has its advocates, but it is not listed below.

AMAZING GRACE

As essential to understanding Elvis musically as the 1950s box set, this wondrous two-CD collection of 55 of his finest sacred performances is a treat for the casual fan and collector alike. The bait for aficionados is eleven minutes of unreleased gospel singalong from *Elvis On Tour*. Even though he is relaxing with the Stamps, as his cousin Donna Presley says, 'You can hear how close gospel is to his heart from the first note.' There are almost too many highlights to pick out. The underrated classics include Run On, You'll Never Walk Alone and Lead Me Guide Me. The sound is pretty good too, although the extra aural quality can't make Put Your Hand In The Hand seem worth his effort or ours. An essential purchase. *****

ARTIST OF THE CENTURY

There are two separate *Artist Of The Century* releases. As a single CD, it's not so much a greatest hits as a 'best-of', featuring Reconsider Baby, Polk Salad Annie and Promised Land as well as the great neglected B-side ballad, It Hurts Me. The 75-track box set isn't bad either, beautifully packaged with a far more interesting selection of songs than normal. ****

THE 50 GREATEST HITS

The 50 Greatest Hits includes the two most famous Sun tracks (That's All Right and Mystery Train), Trouble (from *King Creole*) and prefers the light pop of Suspicion to El's underrated (by his own record company) version of Chuck Berry's Promised Land. That apart, this is a as close as you can get to a definitive selection. The sister album, *The Live Greatest Hits*, has a wonderful sound, a decent selection of performances but ultimately isn't quite a killer package. The fault, possibly, is in the very idea. With a few glaring exceptions (Suspicious Minds on *Elvis In Person*), many of his live versions of his hit songs don't add that much to the original. The songs which inspired him in concert were often associated with other people, numbers like Never Been To Spain and I'm So Lonesome I Could Cry which really inspired him. The omission of How Great Thou Art seems odd, too. ****

FROM NASHVILLE TO MEMPHIS

All five CDs in the *From Nashville To Memphis* box set hold something to contradict the cliché that Elvis died in the Army. Kicking off with the glory of *Elvis Is Back!*, it's crowned by the magic of *Memphis '69*. In between these twin peaks you will find ample proof that Elvis was not reduced to a completely vegetative state by the endless succession of movie sound-tracks. Indeed, you can almost hear him polishing up his craftmanship here. Rarities include a long slow version of I'll Remember You, a complete and haunting rendition of Beyond The Reef, and El's TV duet with Ol' Blue Eyes on Love Me Tender/Witchcraft. There are low points (the inclusion of Western Union, Come What May, the omission of If I Can Dream), but not many. Disc three is especially fascinating because you can almost hear, song by song, El find his way back. ★★★★

THE HOME RECORDINGS

Though criticized as overpriced, *The Home Recordings* CD offers consid-erable insight into the elusive entity that was Elvis's musical soul. While tech-nical imperfections abound, this release makes Elvis seem less remote. Consisting mainly of El and friends around the piano, it also raises the pos-sibility that, left to his own devices, he might have been more of a low-energy performer than the one we know. He gives himself over completely to old chestnuts like Tumblin' Tumbleweed and newer ballads like Dark Moon (which he relishes so much, it's a shame he didn't record it in the studio).

Another similar compilation, *Elvis In Private Moments*, has him singing the bass line to Blowin' In The Wind over a pre-recorded instrumental, then declaring – in reference to the people who made the instrumental, not Mr Zimmerman – 'These guys are sick.' Its other delights include a folky vocal version of the Bobby Bare song 500 Miles and his Ink Spots impersonation, right down to the deep monologue, on It's A Sin To Tell A Lie. ★★★★

A HUNDRED YEARS FROM NOW

A century from now, Elvis fans will still be listening to this release in the *Essential Elvis* series, a fascinating album which documents Presley's most productive sessions of the 1970s. *A Hundred From Years From Now* takes its title from the studio jam released here which, good as it is, is far from the highlight of the album. Presley's impromptu rendering of **The Lord's Prayer**, à la **Mahalia Jackson**, will either leave you stunned with the beauty of some of his phrasing or make you wonder if he's taking the mickey. This author is firmly in the first camp. This is a real alternate takefest but also includes another jam, **I Didn't Make It On Playing Guitar**, and the undubbed unedited master for El's rendition of **Got My Mojo Working**. ★★★★

THE INTERVIEWS

Buying an album of Elvis's interviews is not to be done without due care and attention. Listen to the CD if you can before buying, as on too many of these albums Elvis seems to be mumbling through a sock. This Prism release called **The Interviews**, with a clarity reminiscent of all those RCA albums called 'Elvis', is one of the best, featuring the fascinating Robert Carlton Browne interview in 1956, the **Madison Square Garden** press conference, perhaps the ultimate example of Elvis's mastery of the non-event rock press conference, and his seminal encounter with **Peter Noone** on the set of *Paradise, Hawaiian Style*. ★★★

THE JUNGLE ROOM SESSIONS

As described on p.142, *The Jungle Room Sessions* come as something of a revelation – not least because, even if it does start with him that suggesting someone shoot the phones and the yellow dog, Elvis sounds disappointingly normal and not psychotic or paranoid at all. Most of the songs improve on this release, on the Follow That Dream label. A good album to feel what it was like to be in the studio with Elvis; it's also worth buying just for the cover. ★★★★

THE KING OF ROCK'N'ROLL

In yet another adaptation of an over-familiar cliché, half a million Elvis fans can't be wrong. Yes, 500,000 punters bought *The King Of Rock'n'Roll* box set, which consists of every 1950s master plus a CD of rare and rocking songs, most of which really are either rare or rocking; some are both. Here you'll find the definitive recordings of the definitive rock'n'roller, including **My Happiness** and **That's When Your Heartaches Begin**, both sides of the first record he ever made, and loads of the famous stuff that really did change the world. There is some dross but, despite 140 tracks, not that much. Part of the joy is hearing overlooked gems like **I Got Stung, I Want To Be Free** and **Money Honey**, outstanding by any other artist's standards but overshadowed by the classic hits. ★★★★★

LIVE IN LAS VEGAS

The real rarity on the four-CD *Live In Las Vegas* set is a 1975 live version of Bobby Darin's **You're The Reason I'm Living**, sung although neither singer nor band had ever rehearsed it. There's also, finally, an official version of **When The Snow Is On The Roses**; it's not great, but it's good to have. The sound quality is pretty excellent throughout, putting RCA's earlier releases to shame, but the inclusion of three versions of **Hound Dog**, which by the 1970s Elvis usually sang as a joke, seems odd. The release also includes his four nervous performances from his first Vegas concerts in 1956. All in all, a good rebuttal to Little Richard's patronising remark about these years, 'He got what he wanted and lost what he had.' ★★★★

LOVE SONGS

This Camden release almost makes up for those 1970s budget albums of hits from his movies which either had hits which weren't from his movies or songs from his movies which weren't hits. Almost. There are almost as many permutations of Elvis ballads as there are movie soundtracks, but **Love Songs** is a decent modestly priced collection, which isn't definitive but does include such often-overlooked gems as *That's Someone You Never Forget*

159

and **Just Pretend**. Unlike the full-blown *50 Greatest Love Songs* it doesn't include **Old Shep**, surely a song about a different kind of love than most punters would expect to find on such a collection. ★★★★

THE MILLION DOLLAR QUARTET

Probably the world's most famous **gospel singalong**, though with Johnny Cash absent, Elvis, Carl perkins and Jerry Lee Lewis were not so much a *Million Dollar Quartet* as a $750,000 Trio. This is an essential release, if only for Elvis's Jackie Wilson impersonation on **Don't Be Cruel** and the spirited repeated renditions of **Brown-Eyed Handsome Man**. It's strangely relaxing to listen to, almost like taking a trip back in time to a world that had yet to be revolutionized and galvanized by the awesome talents on display here. This is now available on CD on the Charly label although you can hear other fragments, notably **Reconsider Baby**, on official Presley releases like the 1950s box set. ★★★★

PLATINUM

The four-CD *Platinum* set kicked off the **alternate takes** business. Many of Elvis's musicians are not fans of this type of release; Scotty Moore asks whether Picasso would want all his rough drafts to be made public. That said, they give you a great flavour of Elvis the studio artist, a wilder, more unpredictable and even creative beast than comes across on the official releases. Highlights include the fantastic 1970s Las Vegas rehearsals glimpsed in the *Lost Performances* video. The real problem with the set is that its sits between two stools, containing far too many official takes to really justify the 'rare and unreleased' tag. Stripped of some of the masters, this could have fitted onto one two-CD set. Still, it's a collection you'll probably find yourself listening to over and over. ★★★★

RECONSIDER BABY

As Elvis never made a **blues album** as such, *Reconsider Baby* is the closest we'll come until RCA finally releases a proper blues collection. The budget blues CD available loses points for including the fake Beach Boy Blues instead of classics like Got My Mojo Working; whereas this one holds the original 'banned' version of One Night Of Sin, I Feel So Bad, and his two greatest blues performances of all, Reconsider Baby itself and Merry Christmas Baby. ★★★★

RHYTHM AND COUNTRY

Volume 5 in the *Essential Elvis* series, and consisting of unreleased Stax performances, *Rhythm And Country* shows that Elvis's sessions at Stax probably had the potential to produce his best work of the 1970s. It's essential for anybody who can't get enough of him singing Promised Land, Good Time Charlie's Got the Blues, and Loving Arms. Some of the fooling around, too, is hilarious, especially when after some operatic warbling he says with a laugh, 'I didn't tell you I go crazy at four o'clock, you people have never seen me.' The inclusion of Girl Of Mine is a bit of a downer. ★★★

SUNRISE

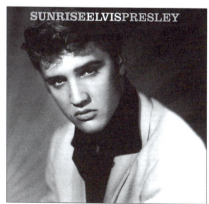

Amazingly, nobody thought to collect all of Elvis's Sun sides onto one album until 1975, a mere twenty years after he had left the building at 705 Union Avenue. RCA has since made up for lost time, however. The crowning glory of its repackaging, the two-CD compilation *Sunrise*, includes all the Sun masters, plus the two singles Elvis

161

recorded for his own pleasure, and rare live stuff such as an unreleased version of the Charms' **Heart Of Stone**.

It might be a cliché to say that the music still sounds fresh but, mysteriously, it does. At its best, it sounds utterly out of time; as if, to use Guralnick's comparison, it had like Robert Johnson's blues been unearthed and released years after it was recorded.

Even if the awful dirge-like qualities of **I Love You Because**, the politeness of **You're A Heartbreaker**, and the well-mannered sincerity of **Harbor Lights** may have dated, **Blue Moon** and **Tomorrow Night** still have a spooky charm. Initially regarded as an act of desecration by the spokesman for Tin Pan Alley, "Blue Moon", with its ghostly vocal, may just be the weirdest thing Elvis ever did. Its clip-cloppity background was the high point of what Phillips christened '**slapback**', an effect created by running the óriginal recording signal through a second Ampex machine.

Of the country sides, **Blue Moon Of Kentucky** and **I Forgot To Remember To Forget** (which Elvis initially felt was just too country for him) have lasted best. **Just Because** is belligerent and angry compared to the innocuous Shelton Brothers' original, while **I'm Left You're Right She's Gone** is a complex song well-delivered.

The wearily perfect blues that kicks off **Milkcow Blues Boogie**, the corny invocation to 'hold it', and the frenetic attack that follows, hold your attention without seeming to strive for effect. Scotty Moore says they just wanted 'to make as big a noise as we could'; ultimately, the noise they made in that barn-like studio was so big that you could almost say that we're still hearing it today. *****

SUSPICIOUS MINDS

The two-CD *Suspicious Minds* set is a must-have for any fan of the Memphis sessions, which makes it a must-have for anyone who likes Elvis. It's a perfect souvenir of those January–February 1969 days at American Studios, one of the few times in his career when El really did treat recording as if it were an art form. You get the songs, some fantastic outtakes, a gorgeous snippet of him singing 'It's the feeling that I get when I look at my brand new baby' and the feeling that you're in the studio with him as he resurrects his career and rediscovers his passion for music. For a real fan, it's hard to listen to this album and not feel very happy indeed. You might also want to track down the Follow That Dream release *The Memphis Sessions*, which has the great five-minute undubbed master of **Stranger In My Own Home Town**. ★★★★★

THAT'S THE WAY IT IS

OK, the live Las Vegas anthology *That's The Way It Is* may not be quite up there with the box sets for each decade and some of the the rehearsals on the third CD aren't actually rehearsals, but it's still a cracking memorial of Elvis in peak form as he returns to the stage. The second disc, a full show from 12 August 1970, is one of the concerts which vies for the honour of being the best Elvis show ever. The packaging is great too: unlike so many of the albums released during his lifetime, it looks as though it was actively designed. ★★★★

TOMORROW IS A LONG TIME

On a single CD, *Tomorrow Is A Long Time* collects seventeen of Elvis's best studio performances between 1966 and 1968 – and throws in **Going Home** too. True, it's all on the 1960s box set, but this is a good-value single CD, setting classic performances like the title track, **Love Letters**, **Big Boss Man**, **Hi Heel Sneakers** and **I'll Remember You** in their proper historical context. You can even forgive the macho posturing of **US Male**, and the tasteless Vietnam-related verse inserted into **Too Much Monkey Business**. ★★★★

WALK A MILE IN MY SHOES

The release of the 1970s box set, *Walk A Mile In My Shoes*, served as the first serious counterblast against those who dismissed Elvis's 1970s music as the lacklustre hackwork of an obese unreliable cabaret artist. The tantalising 48-second snippet of him singing two verses of Bob Dylan's **I Shall Be Released** almost justifies the price tag by itself; it's a crime he didn't cut the record there and then. The many other attractions include jams of **Tiger**

Man and Stranger In My Own Home Town; Twelfth Of Never; and the complete A and B sides of all his 1970s singles except Kentucky Rain but including a heart-rending take of Where Did They Go Lord? All that and a snatch of Lady Madonna. *****

The bootlegs

Literally thousands of Elvis bootlegs have appeared, with both titles and content that range from the sublime to the ridiculous. Well-known examples include Shock, Rattle And Roll, Sheikh Of The Desert and Rockin' Against The Roarin' Falls; among labels are Luxor Records, Famous Groove, Captain Marvel Jr Records and King.

The original Elvis bootleg is usually credited as the twelve-track Please Release Me, a collection of TV and soundtrack recordings on the 1st Records label that made the rounds at the Elvis Convention in Luxembourg in 1970. It included two songs from his appearance on the Frank Sinatra TV show, while side two closed with a Canadian radio tribute from 1966 by Red Robinson. Its success spawned another bootleg with additional songs, I Wanna Be A Rock N Roll Star (Viktorie NS 13026). Others that followed during Elvis's lifetime including The Hillbilly Cat Live (Spring Fever Record Club SFLP 301), The King Goes Wild (Wilde Productions PRP 207) and The Dorsey Shows (Golden Archives 56-GA-100).

At first, audience members would sneak tape machines into concert venues. As the equipment had to stay hidden from view (perhaps even wrapped in a plastic bag) most such releases featured a muffled sound, with Elvis's voice usually overpowered by the instrumentation, as well as audience conversations.

164

The situation was transformed by the emergence of soundboard recordings, taken directly from the mixing desk by sound engineers. Not originally intended for release, they too tended to feature a muted audience, because the priority was to get the sound mix right on the night. In fact, when Elvis's long speeches in 1974 used to extend his Las Vegas shows to well over an hour, the final part was often lost because the C120 cassettes were not turned over. Most Presley concerts were captured, with the exceptions of 1971 and his final Las Vegas season of December 1976; many were released on the **Fort Baxter** label's *From The Master Tapes* series.

The Dutch-based **Bilko** label, by contrast, was renowned for **studio outtakes**. Its four-volume series of twin CD sets, *There's Always Me*, was particularly outstanding. Over time, rival labels emerged, such as **Diamond Anniversary Editions** of Germany, which drew from the collection of sound engineer Bruce Jackson. *Old Times They Are Not Forgotten*, a 30 August 1976 performance from Tuscaloosa, Alabama captured in incredible sound quality, was outstanding.

Bootleg releases are not always what they seem. Thus *Opening Night '69* purports to be the first comeback concert in Las Vegas which was never recorded; it actually dates from several days into the season. Similarly, 'unreleased versions' can simply be the result of tampering by bootleggers rather than genuine alternative takes, while with the same material masquerading under different titles you have to watch out for duplication. Sound quality too can vary enormously; take a portable CD player with you to record fairs to make sure. If you exercise discrimination, however, bootleg purchases can be very worthwhile. As the law stands, it is illegal to sell bootlegs, but not illegal to purchase them.

TOP SIX LIVE CONCERT BOOTLEGS

Here I Go Again (Diamond Anniversary Editions DAE 3595-5): Las Vegas International Hotel, 23 August 1969. One of the stupendous comeback concerts. ★★★★

From Sunset Boulevard To Paradise Road (Diamond Anniversary DAE 3595-617). A rehearsal at RCA Studios Hollywood from 16 August 1974, and the opening show from the Las Vegas Hilton on 19 August 1974 (see p.141). Essential listening – it documents a strange time in Elvis's career. ★★★★★

Desert Storm (Fort Baxter 2200): Las Vegas Hilton, 2 September 1974. Double CD from Elvis's closing night, featuring the infamous 'drugs dialogue' (see p.141). **✳✳✳**

Opening Night '72 (Fort Baxter 2001/03): Las Vegas Hilton Hotel, 26 January 1972. Including the first live outings of **An American Trilogy, Never Been to Spain** and **I'll Remember You**. **✳✳✳✳**

Spanish Eyes (Fort Baxter 2099): Lake Tahoe, Nevada, 24 May 1974. Includes the title song and **Help Me**. **✳✳✳✳**

Old Times They Are Not Forgotten (Diamond Anniversary Editions DAE 3595-1): Tuscaloosa, Alabama, 30 August 1976. **✳✳✳✳**

Moody Blue And Other Great Performances (Fort Baxter 2097): Performances from 16 and 21 February 1977, including **Moody Blue, Where No One Stands Alone** and **Reconsider Baby**. **✳✳✳✳**

TOP SIX STUDIO OUTTAKES BOOTLEGS

Unsurpassed Masters Box 1 (Cool Romeo CR 008/9/10/11).
Unsurpassed Masters Box 2 (Cool Romeo CR 012/13/14).
Both these releases actually live up to the promise of the title. **✳✳✳✳**

There's Always Me, Volume I (Bilko 1898/99). Simply magnificent set of studio outtakes. **✳✳✳**

Whole Lotta Shakin' Goin' On (Circle CG 1000). A fantastic companion to *A Hundred Years From Now*. **✳✳✳✳**

As Recorded In Stereo '57, Volume 2 (Sound Advice). Decent souvenir of a great year in the studio. **✳✳✳✳**

The Other Side Of Memphis (Bilko). If you just can't get enough of the 1969 Memphis sessions, this is worth the investment. **✳✳✳✳**

166

Influences

The folk who Elvis loved,
and those who loved the King

' He had all these people inside of him.'
Charlie Hodge

Elvis was a singer of many styles and even more influences. As his bassist Norbert Putnam put it, 'Elvis could do everything, from a very quiet sensual moan and groan to a high-panic scream and was willing to do it within the context of a three-minute song, with no inhibitions whatsoever. He had a greater arsenal of sounds than anyone else. Sinatra would sing very straight and hardly ever get on the dynamic scale going anywhere. Crosby the same. He was far and away the greatest purveyor of emotion in a song ... and I have worked with 2000 singers.' And that, if anything, is what unites the best of his work in whatever genre.

In this chapter we look at Elvis as a stylist in the major genres, discuss the controversial question of his relationship to black music and check out the artists who have influenced him. We also explore, in detail, the King's own record collection, and his relationship with his great rivals: Frank Sinatra, The Beatles and Bob Dylan. Because part of Presley's contradictory appeal is that he could sound like nobody else and yet, as his friend Charlie Hodge said, 'You can [also] hear the different characters in his voice. He would be Billy Eckstine, he would be Bill Kenny of the Ink Spots, he would be Hank Snow – all these people became Elvis Presley by the time he started touring. He had all these people inside of him.'

Gospel

While even his most committed adherents might struggle to make a case for Elvis Presley as a **godly** man, he was certainly **God-fearing**, even by the standards of ill-educated, poor white Southerners. Although he adored blues and rock'n'roll, and was prepared to give almost anything a fair hearing, **gospel** was the music Presley truly loved, a rare constant in his life.

Elvis was reared upon gospel thanks to his family's membership of the **First Assembly Of God**, first in east Tupelo and then in south Memphis. Flamboyant and vaguely Pentecostal, the church embraced music as one more way to serve and proselytize about Christ. In Memphis, Elvis befriended the **Blackwood Brothers**, the city's most popular gospel quartet, who were members of the same congregation, and it was into this white vocal tradition that he tapped. He saw Blackwoods shows whenever he could, and by 1955 was often appearing on the same bill. When Gladys died, the brothers sang at her funeral, and in later years they would often pop over to Graceland to sing along with Elvis as he played the piano. Fronting his **Stamps Quartet**, deep-voiced erstwhile Blackwood brother **JD Sumner** was in Presley's band until the end.

Balm for Elvis's troubled soul, gospel was not just a private passion: he always had a gospel section in his shows. Dressed in the world's loudest sports jacket, he performed **Peace In The Valley** on his third *Ed Sullivan* appearance, and his regular, if sporadic, gospel recordings displayed a level of quality control sadly absent from his secular oeuvre. According to JD Sumner, in 1976 Elvis even considered restricting himself solely to gospel, but was told by preacher Rex Humbard that 'he was tilling the soil for others to sow the seed'.

Elvis's first exclusively gospel album was 1961's *His Hand In Mine*. Surprisingly, he won his only **Grammies** for his gospel recordings. The 1967 *How Great Thou Art* album won Best Sacred Performance, while 1972's *He Touched Me*, featuring new songs rather than old standbys, secured Best Inspirational Performance,

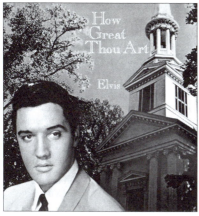

as did a live version of the title track of **How Great Thou Art** in 1974. Sideline it may have been, but Presley was such a genuinely great gospel singer that he was inducted into the Gospel Hall Of Fame in 2001, thus becoming the first person to enter the gospel, country and rock halls of fame. With his typical mix of hubris and humility, he knew how good he was: after all, as he told *True Story* in 1956, 'My voice is God's will, not mine.'

Farther Along

A spinechilling traditional song arranged by Presley himself. Remembering Gladys as he sings 'when death has come and taken our loved ones', his voice cracks with pain. It's his most vulnerable moment on record.

His Hand In Mine

Elvis is at his most reverential on this slight tune, with the Jordanaires in fine form behind him, crooning as though backing vocals were the sole criterion for ascension into heaven.

Mansion Over The Hilltop

An extraordinarily spiritual performance. Initially, Ira Stanphill's lyric seems to be an everyday morality tale about the perils of greed. Of course, the mansion turns out to be heaven; hence 'over' the hilltop not 'on' it. That might sound trite but, such is Presley's conviction, you simply don't notice.

171

Sometimes I Feel Like A Motherless Child/Where Could I Go But To The Lord?/Up Above My Head/Saved

A nine-minute medley which exudes revivalist fervour, starting slowly with The Blossoms on "Motherless Child" and building towards the call-and-response climax of Leiber and Stoller's "Saved", taking in every vocal trick in the good book. Exhausting but worth the effort.

Stand By Me

Not the Ben E King number, but a desperately moving piano-led plea for divine staying power. 'When I'm growing old and feeble. Stand by me,' he begs; what's scary is that he doesn't seem convinced the Lord will hang around.

(There'll Be) Peace In The Valley (For Me)

Presley recorded this luscious Thomas A Dorsey song several times, but his January 1957 version drew screams from the *Ed Sullivan* crowd. It was as though he was coming out of the gospel closet – and how he revelled.

Country

Though never a straight country artist, Elvis dipped freely into the genre throughout his career. When he started out, he cited Roy Acuff, Hank Snow and Ernest Tubb as influences, and it was to RCA Victor's country division that he was originally signed from Sun. The song he sang at the Mississippi–Alabama Fair and Dairy Show, when he was just 10, was country stalwart Red Foley's Old Shep, and when he sat down at the Graceland piano for the last time, Willie Nelson's Blue Eyes Crying In The Rain was among the material he performed.

In the immediate aftermath of Presley's arrival, his pop hits topped *Billboard*'s country chart. Some country disc jockeys refused to play his records. As straight country performances became commercial suicide, many country stars learned to rock. Others, such as Jim Reeves, Don Gibson and Patsy Cline, fused country and pop, stripping away the usual country instrumentation, to spawn 'crossover' hits. Elvis himself dabbled with this new 'Nashville Sound' in the early 1960s, prompting Reeves' remark that Elvis used the same microphone and musicians but sold better.

Among the numbers Elvis, Scotty and Bill tried out before their first, monumental Sun session were Hank Snow's I Don't Hurt Anymore and Eddy Arnold's recent number one, I Really Don't Want to Know (which he finally recorded in 1970). Country standards that Elvis did lay down at Sun included I Love You Because, You're A Heartbreaker and I'll Never Let You Go (Little Darlin').

Elvis could change the inflection of his voice to create a 'country feel', and yet still stamp songs with his own style. In 1956, he told Wanda Jackson that he sang country with a beat, and suggested she should do the same; she took his advice to heart, to become the 'Queen of

Rockabilly'. When he was asked in the early 1970s whether he was now a country act, his diplomatic response was that he liked 'all types' of music, including country. Privately, he loathed corny country material and pointedly refused to cut Country Bumpkin. While his record collection is largely bereft of country albums, it does include such singles as Jim Reeves' posthumous hit Distant

173

Drums. At the end of Elvis's life, his radio was tuned into gospel and country rather than pop or rock.

Country material like **Guitar Man** helped to drag Elvis out of his late 1960s doldrums, while 1971's landmark album *Elvis Country* – in its way, as important to him as the Memphis sessions – was decisive proof of the genre's personal relevance. His country spanned a broad range from Ann Murray's **Snowbird** to Jerry Lee Lewis's **Whole Lotta Shakin' Goin' On** and Bob Wills' **Faded Love**.

During the final years, Elvis's increasingly spasmodic studio visits resulted in a raft of country titles. Though associated with R&B, Memphis's Stax studios in December 1973 might just as well have been Studio B in Nashville, with heart-rending country ballads like Danny O'Keefe's **Good Time Charlie's Got The Blues** reflecting Elvis's mood. As JD Sumner put it, this period was dominated by 'lost woman' songs, and country proved the richest source.

Today's Nashville treats Elvis with a mixture of reverence and gentle mockery of his lifestyle. There have been several noteworthy covers of his tunes – Dwight Yoakam with **Little Sister**, Travis Tritt with **T-R-O-U-B-L-E**, Trisha Yearwood with **Trying To Get To You**. 'Every kid thinks about being a rock star,' **Tim McGraw**, a new generation star, said in 2002. 'I used to dress up like Elvis and imitate Elvis all over the house.'

Funny How Time Slips Away

Composed by struggling singer-songwriter Willie Nelson on his way to work, this song provided a *Billboard* country hit for Billy Walker in October 1961. Elvis gave it a blues feel at his June 1970 Nashville sessions, and it became a core part of his live act. The tender melancholy of the last verse on the studio cut (especially as he sings 'don't know when though') is simply wondrous.

Help Me

Written by Larry Gatlin, whose "Bitter They Are, Harder They Fall" Elvis also cut, "Help Me" was the last of four songs recorded on 12 December 1973 at Stax. So heartfelt was Elvis's performance that he knelt down. Originally the B side of "If You Talk in Your Sleep", it was flipped by country DJs and reached number six in *Billboard*'s country charts. It's best heard on the reissued, remastered *Promised Land* album.

It Keeps Right On A Hurtin

On *From Elvis In Memphis*, Elvis sings this underrated gem with a naturalness that makes it all sound too easy. Johnny Tillotson wrote it not about a love affair gone wrong, but about his dying father, and it's not too far-fetched to imagine Elvis is singing to his mum. The arrangement sounds almost as effortless as Elvis's vocal, with some fine country piano. Tillotson was thrilled: 'He did this in a very simple kind of country-based way, which I could really relate to.'

She Thinks I Still Care

This Dickey Lee and Steve Duffy number topped the country charts in 1962 for George Jones. Lee took quite a while to warm to Elvis's powerful reading, recorded during the Jungle Room sessions, which differed greatly from the original. An alternative take was released posthumously in overdubbed form on the *Guitar Man* album, while a faster version appeared on *Walk A Mile In My Shoes*, the 1970s box set. Both show that Elvis and Felton Jarvis were striving for something more than parody; in the end, they succeeded magnificently.

Susan When She Tried

Recorded in March 1975 for *Elvis Today*, this is one of Elvis's strongest country performances: totally committed, he flows with the song's natural strength rather than attempting to transform it into another idiom. Originally a number fifteen hit for the Statler Brothers in 1974, it brought out the King's innate ability to read a song and milk it for all it was worth.

You Asked Me To

A top ten hit for Waylon Jennings in October 1973, written by Billy Joe Shaver. 'He told me he imitated me on that song,' Jennings recalled. 'The people at RCA talked to me about seeing if I could get him interested in music again. But I have a strange feeling that if

I'd found out back then that he was a drug addict, me and him might have got more interested in drugs together! Music was something else. He'd lost interest in that along the way, but he got it back on that album. If they'd got him a country band and let him loose, he'd have been happy.' Elvis's version paid homage to the original, while brilliantly reinterpreting it, his voice complemented by James Burton's sterling guitar work. The purer second take, minus backing vocals, which was released in 1998 on *Essential Elvis Volume 5: Rhythm And Country*, includes Elvis's comment: 'Wait a minute fellas. Don't go without me … Damn, I don't know what we're doing.'

Blues

In the mid-1960s, **Muddy Waters** said of Elvis, 'That boy **made his pull from the blues**, if he's stopped, he's stopped, but he made his pull from there.' **BB King**, years later, summed up the missed opportunities both for the blues and Presley: 'Elvis, he was unique. And he loved the blues, it was a pity he didn't do more.'

As Elvis often chose to remind the media, the blues, as sung by **Arthur Crudup**, **Sonny Boy Williamson** and **Howlin' Wolf**, had been his inspiration. At Graceland, he had records by **Ruth Brown**, Atlantic's 1950s blues queen, **LaVern Baker**, the **Clovers**, **Lowell Fulson** and **Lightnin' Hopkins**, **Arthur Gunter**, as well as BB King. According to Memphis bluesman **Rufus Thomas**, who played Elvis's early records, against the management's wishes, on black radio station WDIA, 'Elvis did far more for the resurgence of rhythm and blues, which white people called rock'n'roll, than anyone else has ever done.'

To accuse Elvis's work for RCA of lacking direction is to miss the point that he wanted to unite genres. But he did so at the expense of forsaking the blues. His last R&B hit was **Bossa Nova Baby**, in

1963. By the 1970s, apart from the odd classic like **Merry Christmas Baby**, the blues had become something to inject into songs from other genres, such as Michael Jarrett's **I'll Be Home On Christmas Day**. Some of his concert rehearsals had a free bluesy feel, but as he turned to material that reflected his emotional state, his repertoire became increasingly country. Sadly he never covered B B King's melancholy **The Thrill Is Gone**. In his final concerts, however, he was still bringing dirty swampy blues into **I Got A Woman**. It's just a pity that, inspired by the triumph of *Elvis Country*, he didn't record *Elvis Blues*. Even so, he did record enough first-class blues for Joe Cocker to say, 'He was one of the greatest blues singers in the world. Give Presley a good blues number and he just sold it right'.

Baby What Do You Want Me To Do

Jimmy Reed's standard runs like a gutsy refrain through the 1968 TV special. Elvis had sung it at home in the mid-1960s, and turns to it whenever the temperature drops, singing as if in a trance. One of his down-and-dirtiest blues performances.

Down In The Alley

Elvis's rousing 1966 version of the Clovers classic is almost as much to fun to listen to as it must have been to record, at the *How Great Thou Art* sessions. You can almost hear Elvis coming back to life.

Got My Mojo Working

Elvis sounds so inspired, so enthused, jamming on Muddy Waters' classic (which segues into 'Hands off it' that it's something of a shock to learn that he described it as 'mediocre shit – not good or bad'. Such 'mediocrity' inspired all concerned to deliver the only truly outstanding performance on *Love Letters From Elvis*.

Like A Baby

178 Jesse Stone's accusatory blues fitted Elvis as perfectly as a Cadillac. He was the perfect manchild to sing this number, about a lover who cries like a baby because he can't break free of his deceitful partner.

Milkcow Blues Boogie
An often-overlooked gem from the Sun years, a fine frenetic performance – once past the ponderous intro – of Kokomo Arnold's blues, which had lately been covered and renamed by Bob Wills and his Texas Playboys. Elvis's version is fast and furious, as though he's arguuing with the listener.

Tomorrow Night
Elvis already sounds like a ghost on Lonnie Johnson's delicate classic, twenty or more years before he actually became one. This is an unusual track for Elvis at Sun, because he doesn't speed things up, just recreates the lilting melancholy beauty of Johnson's original.

Rock

Though Elvis laboured under the nickname of the 'King Of Rock'n'Roll', by the end of his career he was more likely to have his listeners sobbing than rocking. While he never lost his affection for **Fats Domino**, **Chuck Berry**, and the pioneers of 1950s rock-'n'roll, few of the rock acts that followed, barring perhaps the **Animals**, the **Dave Clark Five**, **Tony Joe White** and **Creedence Clearwater Revival**, particularly appealed to him. During the 1970s, he found it increasingly hard to find new rock songs that he liked, and seemed reluctant just to revisit rock's generous back catalogue from the 1950s. Nonetheless, as **Way Down** proved, he was still capable of cutting a rock classic when he was in the mood.

As the great English singer/songwriter Kevin Coyne said, 'To me, he invented rock and roll and that's it. I don't care whether they say he was influenced by Joe Williams and Blind Willie Whatever; basically he did it himself. Countryboy, and he invented a style of singing we're all indebted to. Like it or not, we're all singing this curious thing called rock'n'roll-style singing. He started that, really. It's not really blues singing; it's something else, really, isn't it?'

179

Elvis, stalking the mike and starting 'that thing called rock'n'roll singing'

Baby I Don't Care

Anyone else would have felt obliged to release this mumbling masterpiece as a single. For Elvis, it was merely one of the stellar attractions on the *Jailhouse Rock* EP. The performance is even more remarkable because, for once, that bubbling bass at the beginning is played not by Bill Black but by Elvis. 'Blackie' was so wound up by his failure to get the part right on his new electric bass that he threw it across the room.

Blue Suede Shoes

It took a little encouragement for Carl Perkins to create his one indisputably immortal contribution to rock'n'roll. Johnny Cash suggested he write a song featuring blue suede shoes, and Perkins finally took the hint after he heard a dancer telling someone not to step on his fancy footwear. Though Presley himself preferred the original, his own faster version is now more famous than Perkins'.

I Got Stung

One of Elvis's last great pre-Army rockers, and one of his most underrated, possibly because it was on the flip of "One Night". Its sizzling pace, and Presley's delightful playing with his mannerisms, made it a fitting sequel to "All Shook Up".

One-Sided Love Affair

In anyone else's hands, this might have been just another country number. But with Shorty Long on piano and Elvis (in his second full session at RCA) singing as though the woman he's telling off is in the studio, it became very special indeed.

T-R-O-U-B-L-E

An undeservedly neglected late rocker, from the pen of Jerry Chesnut, which gets the *Elvis Today* album off to a fine flurrying start. Presley's verve as he tears through the complex lyric is matched by the pounding piano from Glen D Hardin and David Briggs, and Ronnie Tutt's furious drumming.

Whole Lotta Shakin' Goin On

Jerry Lee Lewis maintains he still hasn't heard El's mean, almost sinister, rendition of his hit. Which is just as well: one play might send him back to the gates of Graceland, with a bottle of vodka in one hand and a pistol in the other.

Ballads

'As far as my own listening pleasure goes, I'd just as soon listen to someone else sing a **ballad**,' Elvis said in March 1956. He couldn't, he told his interviewer, sing a ballad as well as Pat Boone. This was one inferiority complex he took a while to shake off, possibly because Sam Phillips had seemed so unimpressed by his crooning.

Even as Elvis laid waste to the charts with rock music, he often cited ballads like **I Was The One** and **Don't** as his own favourite performances. Asked to pick his favourite song at the Madison Square Garden press conference in 1972, he immediately picked **It's Now Or Never**. While the key to his success as a ballad singer was his utter believability, he also applied himself to the craft, especially during the 1960s, to distract himself from the abysmal movie soundtracks.

Though Elvis's fondness for ballads wasn't always well served by his choice of material, he retained the ability to cover someone else's song in such a way that it became his. He preferred big numbers like **Hurt** in his final years, but never strayed too far, and left the catalogues of messrs Martin and Sinatra, with a few famous exceptions, largely untouched. Neither was he a sucker for show tunes unless they'd been recorded by a singer he admired, as with Roy Hamilton and **You'll Never Walk Alone**. That his home performances, released since his death, mostly reveal him singing ballads, suggests that, left to his own devices, he might have been a much lower-energy performer.

182

Blue Moon
If Elvis is haunting America, then this is the song his ghost will be crooning as he hitchhikes down some long lonely highway.

I'll Hold You In My Heart
Elvis gives himself so completely to Eddy Arnold's song that he doesn't want to stop. The repetition, and the simplicity, add to the power, as the suspicion grows that his darling might not wait for him after all.

I Need Somebody To Lean On
One of the more unusual Elvis ballads, an exercise in gentle late-night melancholy that Presley croons without mannerisms or melodrama. It's a work of subtle genius that deserves to be better known.

There's A Honky Tonk Angel
If Vernon Presley hadn't turned up at Stax Studios late one night in December 1973, Elvis might never have recorded this passionate rendition of Conway Twitty's recent hit. Presley is in pleasing, indignant form; he warmed up by telling himself to 'Get mad at it,' then did just that. It works.

Where Did They Go Lord?
Dallas Frazier never wrote a bad song for Elvis, who belts out this ballad of lost love as if there's much more at stake than a failed relationship. The line about his heart not being bitter, just empty, sounds especially poignant.

It was rock that made Elvis but ballads were probably his first (and last) musical love

183

The Wonder Of You

It's probably just as well that the 1967 session at which Elvis was due to record this former Ray Peterson hit was cancelled. Instead, he delivered it with great power and conviction live in Las Vegas, with James Burton offering able support.

Folk

The sleeve notes on Elvis Presley's first RCA album identified him as a maker of 'commercial folk music'. This is usually seen as proof that RCA didn't really know what they had just spent $40,000 on. Folk probably influenced Elvis less than any of the major genres with which he was familiar. And yet, following the success of *Elvis Country*, there was talk of him doing a folk concept album.

Though the idea sounds bizarre, Elvis did like some folk acts. He owned several Peter, Paul and Mary records, including their *In Concert* album. The trio's voices made the songs listenable; without them, he might have completely missed out on the 1960s folk boom. His friend Charlie Hodge also intrigued him with an album of Dylan covers by the black blues/folk singer Odetta, which inspired him to record Tomorrow Is A Long Time.

The *In A Private Moment* and *Platinum* albums show Elvis at home in the mid-1960s, fooling around with Peter, Paul and Mary songs such as 500 Miles. He also sang Blowin' In the Wind several times. Nobody quite sounds at ease on the version on *Platinum*, but there's a funnier rendition on *In A Private Moment*. Singing it as a traditional folk ballad over a pre-recorded instrumental track, Elvis indulges his ambition to be a proper bass singer.

Had Elvis recorded a folk album, it would probably have been country/folk, much as *From Elvis In Memphis* was country/soul. The original plan, to include a Dolly Parton track – either Coat Of Many Colors or I Will Always Love You – was scuppered by a row over royalties. In the end, what folkish performances he did record in 1971 were dribbled out on B sides of singles, one gospel album, and a couple of indifferent secular studio albums.

Although Presley's music contained precious little pure folk, Roger McGuinn of the Byrds says he was inspired to become a musician by Elvis's Heartbreak Hotel, while Phil Ochs was among the celebrities who watched the 1969 comeback concerts in Las Vegas. The experience transformed Ochs' career for the worse; see p.395.

Early Mornin' Rain
The version of the Gordon Lightfoot classic on *Elvis Now* isn't quite as warm as the cover Elvis performed winding down after the *Aloha From Hawaii* concert. This was the closest Elvis came to sounding like Peter, Paul and Mary on a commercial release.

500 Miles
As El and the boys harmonize on the old folk ballad at Graceland, Presley tries his best to sound like a genuine bass singer.

The First Time Ever I Saw Your Face
Scottish folk singer Ewan MacColl and his daughter Kirsty used to play Elvis's cover of MacColl's haunting ballad when they needed a laugh. Presley had initially tried to record it as a duet. Where Roberta Flack's version was beautifully slow, Elvis speeded up the tempo for no apparent gain. He performed a beautiful slower version in Birmingham, Alabama in December 1976, complete with the third verse, marred only by a Vegas-style dramatic ending.

I Shall Be Released
Perhaps the most tantalizing 48 seconds of Elvis in the studio. Two verses of the Dylan classic, sung while he waited to start on the vastly inferior "It's Only Love".

Loving Arms
Tom Jans cites this cover of his song as one of the highlights of his career. The power and clarity as Elvis's voice soars on the second verse is astonishing.

Until It's Time For You To Go
Reviewing El's Buffy Sainte Marie cover for the *New Musical Express*, Charles Shaar Murray uncharitably suggested he should have been strangled with the strings used. Yet Elvis superbly conveys both romanticism and fatalism, in a manner reminiscent of "Can't Help Falling In Love".

Elvis and black music

The relationship of rock'n'roll in general, and Elvis in particular, to black music is complex enough for Michael Bertrand, of the University of Mississippi, to have written an entire book about it, *Race Rock And Elvis* (University of Illinois Press).

Elvis's attitude to race as such is dealt with elsewhere in this book; see p.26. His relationship to black music, however, goes to the core of his music and his myth. As is shown by the story of how he 'ripped off' Hound Dog from Big Mama Thornton – presented fictionally in Alice Walker's *Nineteen Fifty Five* – it can be a very tangled tale indeed. After all, two of Presley's greatest covers of black music from the Sun era, Mystery Train and Baby Let's Play House, owe more than a little to white country songs.

The charges against Elvis are threefold: that he ripped off or copied what black musicians were doing, and profited financially because of the racial divide in America; that his crowning as 'king' of rock'n'roll was a racist rejection of the part played by black musicians; and that his very popularity helped to make the blues bland, and took control of the genre away from black artists.

The last charge, made by George Nelson in *The Death Of Rhythm And Blues*, is probably true, assuming you accept that rhythm and blues is dead. The sheer commercial clout of Elvis and other white singers inevitably altered the course of rhythm and blues, though it's harder to assert that Elvis or any other artist saw where this would lead. It would be similarly hard to blame Elvis for the rapidity with which easy-listening pop disappeared from the charts.

Elvis with pianist Dudley Brooks, who testified to the King's lack of racism

BB King feels that the process began with the creation of the term **'rock'n'roll'**, as if it was the media's coded way of saying that the music wasn't black. But in interviews, and the 1968 TV special, Elvis repeatedly made clear that rock'n'roll was not something he or anybody else had created in 1954: 'Rock'n'roll is basically rhythm and blues and gospel, all right, it sprang from that.' He was

187

probably the first major white entertainer to acknowledge a debt to black music. As he told one visitor in Las Vegas, 'If I had any ambition, it was to be as good as **Arthur Crudup**.'

While Elvis may have watered down the blues, he also, as contemporaries like **Little Richard** have been quick to testify, opened the way for black artists. 'When Elvis came out, a lot of black groups would say, "Elvis cannot do so and so and so." And I'd say "Shut up." Let me tell you this – when I came out they wasn't playing no black artists on no top 40 stations. I was the first … but it took people like Elvis and Pat Boone and Gene Vincent to open the door. And I thank God for Elvis Presley, I thank the Lord for sending Elvis to open the door so I could walk down the road, you understand?' Typically, Little Richard went on to claim that he was the founding father of rock'n'roll, and that if he'd been white, he'd have been even bigger than Elvis. However, you only have to compare the success of **Motown** in the 1960s with that of **Atlantic** in the 1950s to see that a door had indeed been opened, and Elvis's hand was one of those on the handle.

Memphis's own **Rufus Thomas** drew a distinction between Presley the man, and his cultural effect: 'It wasn't Elvis who denied black musicians credit, that was white society and white culture.' Presley himself made a point of being seen with, and praising, black musicians like **BB King** and **Bobby Bland**. In the context of American, let alone Southern, society in the 1950s, that was a significant statement. Of Presley's black contemporaries, **Ray Charles** seems the least impressed, although he has more downplayed Presley's significance as a pioneer than explicitly accused him of ripping off black musicians. Elvis's friend **Jackie Wilson** said that the influences went both ways: 'A lot of people have accused Elvis of stealing the black man's music, when in fact almost every black solo entertainer copied his stage mannerisms from Elvis'. BB King insisted, 'Elvis never stole anybody's music, I always respected him as an artist.'

Only one of Elvis's black-music covers, Chuck Willis's **I Feel So Bad**, is a downright copy, note for note, fluffed line for fluffed line,

188

of the original. His early Sun recording of **Tomorrow Night** is close to Lonnie Johnson's, but not an attempt to duplicate it, while his version of Lowell Fulson's **Reconsider Baby**, often cited as a direct copy, is in fact significantly different.

The picture is further confused by the business of Elvis being **The King**. Though he neither aspired to, nor accepted, the title, telling a fan who gave him a crown, 'There is only one king, Jesus Christ', it has loomed larger in his myth since his death. At the same time, much of the marketing of Elvis, while paying lip service to multi-culturalism, has seemed to whiten him out, emphasizing the Las Vegas Elvis or the country-singing Elvis at the expense of the more challenging pre-Army Elvis. Things were exacerbated by the frankly racist reaction of a vocal minority of fans to Lisa Marie's marriage to Michael Jackson.

As Gil Rodman put it, in his *Elvis After Elvis*, 'Elvis's coronation implicitly helps to reinforce the resegregation of the musical world into neat (and supposedly) mutually exclusive racial categories.' Or as funk bassist **Me'Shell Ndegé Ocello** said in 1994, 'If Elvis is King, then who the fuck is James Brown – God?' To gauge the range of opinion, you only have to juxtapose that remark with the observation by **Clearance Giddens**, an African-American Elvis impersonator, that 'Elvis was a Martin Luther King Jr in the music field. He did not see music divided by colour.'

The divide may reflect the death of another King's dream. Martin Luther King's hopes for integration seemed to die with him in Memphis in April 1968, and Elvis's own tacit commitment to the same ideals now seems as old-fashioned as the concept of 'integration'. His image has become polarized, his face superimposed on a Confederate flag and his artistic credibility disputed by those who feel the contribution of black artists has been undervalued.

Michael Bertrand says you can see the schism in the South today. 'By his generation, he is still held in esteem. For younger white Southerners, he is perhaps a curiosity. African Americans of his generation feel somewhat ambivalent, although there are more

African Americans who visit Graceland and Tupelo than the media lets on. For younger blacks, he is probably seen as a ripoff racist.'

After Loving You

Elvis brought this song to the Memphis sessions, having loved both Eddy Arnold's version and Della Reese's cover. His own reading falls somewhere between the two, but it's no compromise. SInging with a glimmer of the intensity he'd brought to "One Night", he almost spits out the line about 'just another woman'.

I Feel So Bad

By 1961, Elvis's blues performances were even rarer than his good rocking ones. But it's all here on this Chuck Willis cover, an obvious homage to the original, right down to screwing up the same line, but driven by a shared passion with El so inspired he walked over to cheer Boots Randolph's solo.

I've Got Confidence

On *He Touched Me* – as close as Presley came to a gospel album fuelled by the Memphis sound – he rattles through black gospel singer Andrea Crouch's finger-clicking stand-out as if hell-bent on proving that, hey, the Lord has the funk too. On this evidence, he was right.

One Night Of Sin

The original banned version of the Smiley Lewis hit, with Elvis at his rawest, and bluesiest. A more low-key performance than the classic single, but still effective.

Tiger Man

Rufus Thomas's Sun number served as a definitive statement of intent from Elvis in his 1968 TV special, that he planned to become king of the jungle again. Presley is still rumoured to have recorded it himself at Sun; he once introduced it by saying, 'This was my second record but not too many people got to hear it.' As that lost take will probably surface about the same time as the lost gold of the Incas, we have to content ourselves with the 1968 version.

Without Love
Elvis in self-accusatory mode, aspiring to the majesty of Clyde McPhatter on a pull-out-all-the-stops ballad that combines power and soul.

Singers and idols

The singers whom Elvis admired were not necessarily those who influenced him the most. In fact, it was probably because he felt that Roy Orbison 'had the greatest voice' – it worried him enough to call home from the Army to ask, 'What's Orbison doing?' – that he never tried to cover any of his songs. The only real mark of his respect for the Big O on record is Tomorrow Never Comes, a technically demanding performance of melancholic grandeur on *Elvis Country*.

Similarly, Presley's record collection proves that when he hailed Fats Domino as the real king of rock'n'roll, in his 1969 Las Vegas press conference, it was more than just PR. Domino played Las Vegas before Elvis, at the *Flamingo Club*, and Presley often came to watch. After one gig, Domino asked Elvis to buy his tie pin and cufflinks for $5000. During the 1968 TV special, Elvis and his band endlessly parroted one of Domino's catchphrases, 'Mah boy, mah boy', whenever it went quiet. However, the only Domino record he ever covered outright was Blueberry Hill.

Elvis doesn't seem to have been deeply influenced by anyone who rose to fame after him. Bizarrely, the 1960s band that made the biggest impression on him was not the Beatles but Peter, Paul and Mary, who turned him onto folk music, while during the late 1970s he returned to his boyhood idols such as Roy Hamilton.

Elvis's penchant for Italian quasi-operatic singers like Enrico Caruso and Mario Lanza, was matched only by his love for gospel and black blues artists. His country influences are harder to detect, but as a boy he virtually stalked Mississippi Slim into letting him play on his radio show, and he covered several great country songs associated with Eddy Arnold.

LAVERN BAKER

Singing the blues in a powerful gospel-tinged voice, LaVern Baker was almost bound to catch the ear of the young Elvis Presley. He recorded both her first hit, Tweedle Dee – until her version was released, he hoped it would be a single for him on Sun singles – and her last, CC Rider, which was a regular opener for his post-come-back concerts.

Having soaked up gospel in a Chicago church choir, Baker, like many of Elvis's favourites, signed for Atlantic Records in the early 1950s. Not given to showbiz bull, she said after Presley's death, 'he was fantastic …

When he danced, the people danced, the girls would actually faint because of what he was doing. The people didn't care if he was white or black, he was a good artist and they felt his music.'

Some of her admiration can be put down to pride that 'He said, just after that first record, "I give it all to LaVern."' On 28 August 1954, when Elvis's first Sun single had just hit the regional country charts, Baker appeared at an R&B show at Memphis's *Hippodrome*. There's no proof that Elvis was there, but given that Baker, Roy Hamilton and the Drifters were all on the bill, it's hard to imagine him missing it.

Presley cut several significant covers of Baker's tunes. **You're The Boss**, a smoky duet with Ann-Margret that was sadly cut from *Viva Las Vegas*, had been a minor hit for Baker and Jimmy Ricks in 1961. Seven years later, he celebrated his comeback with a rousing version of another of her Leiber and Stoller songs, **Saved**, a revival number he had listened to at Graceland in 1966. As so often, he overcame the duo's irony through sheer conviction.

The choice of "CC Rider" was a tribute, of a kind, to both Baker and Ma Rainey. Five years later, he paid her another joint tribute, with a fervent rendition of **Shake A Hand**, a hit for LaVern in 1960 and for Faye Adams in 1953. Both LaVern and Elvis also recorded **Harbor Lights** and **Tomorrow Night**, and in 1961 she cut an answer record to his **Little Sister**. Baker's last R&B chart hit came in 1966 with **Think Twice**, a duet with another Presley favourite, Jackie Wilson.

So what did Elvis hear in Baker that he should say he owed it all to her? Ultimately, it may just be as simple as the way she seemed to feel every song that she sang.

RECOMMENDED ALBUM: *LAVERN BAKER/LAVERN* (COLLECTABLES), INCLUDING "HARBOR LIGHTS" AND "TWEEDLE DEE".

◀ LaVern Baker belted out the blues with a fervour Elvis found irresistible

INFLUENCES

THE CLOVERS

Changety-changety-chang-chang. Those eight nonsense syllables, used
to imitate Elmore James' slide guitar on **Down In The Alley**, are often
held to be the **Clovers'** finest moment on vinyl. Elvis must have
thought so; he covered the song in 1966, asking his friend Charlie
Hodge to help the gospel vocalists the Imperials pay homage to that
immortal opening.

With an eight-year spell on *Billboard*'s R&B charts, the Clovers were
among the most durable black vocal groups. Written and arranged by
Jesse Stone, whose **Money Honey** and **Like A Baby** Elvis also
recorded, "Down In The Alley" wasn't actually one of their bigger hits,
though its B side, **There's No Tomorrow**, was the version of **O'Sole
Mio** made famous by Tony Martin.

Elvis's own "It's Now Or Never" had more to do with opera than R&B,
but that was typical of the Clovers' behind-the-scenes influence on his
music. Thus in 1957 he cut **Tell Me Why**, written by Titus Turner,
whose main claim to fame until then had been to write the Clovers' **Hey
Doll Baby**. Elvis also sang the Clovers' **Fool, Fool, Fool**, on local radio
in Lubbock, Texas, in early 1955, a performance only released on the
King Of Rock'n'Roll box set in 1992. Leiber and Stoller wrote and produced one Clovers classic, **Love Potion Number 9**, in 1959, and one
flop, four years later – **Bossa Nova Baby** – which later became a hit
for Elvis.

The influence of vocal groups on the Presley sound tends to be under-
estimated, or discussed mainly in connection with gospel quartets. But
just listen to the deep voice at the end of the Clovers' smoky version of
Blue Velvet, and you'll hear why Elvis wanted JD Sumner as a backing
vocalist.

RECOMMENDED ALBUM: *THE VERY BEST OF THE CLOVERS* (RHINO), INCLUDING
"DOWN IN THE ALLEY".

194

Arthur 'Big Boy' Crudup, the blues singer Elvis most aspired to be ▶

ARTHUR CRUDUP

The most obvious thing you can say about **Arthur 'Big Boy' Crudup**
is that, like the white teenager he inspired, he didn't sound like nobody
else. The Mississippi bluesman shared something else with Presley:
nobody wrote home about his guitar playing either. At least Crudup
could point out that he didn't pick up the instrument until he was 30.

Crudup's 'official' status as Elvis Presley's favourite bluesman is in
danger of reducing the rest of his career to a footnote. When he was

36, he tired of the meagre rewards he got for 'banging a box' in Mississippi, and moved to Chicago in 1941. After a spell busking, he was invited to play in front of such luminaries as Lonnie Johnson, and earned a recording contract at Bluebird, part of RCA. Having cut **That's All Right** in 1946, he became disgruntled over money, and left RCA just as Elvis was startling Sam Phillips with his own version.

Presley's rise to fame, his regular namechecking of Crudup, even his two subsequent RCA covers of his mentor's songs; none of this seemed to help the bluesman himself. He didn't return to regular recording until the 1960s, with sessions at Fire that Presley helped finance. His finest studio work was to follow, with Willie Dixon on the Delmark label, and he finally made some decent money before his death in 1974.

RECOMMENDED ALBUM: *MEAN OL' FRISCO* (COLLECTABLES), FEATURING "THAT'S ALL RIGHT" AND "SO GLAD YOU'RE MINE".

ROY HAMILTON

For Elvis, the highlight of his 1969 Memphis sessions was probably not cutting **Suspicious Minds**, but meeting the singer he revered above all others, **Roy Hamilton**. Elvis had always loved both Hamilton's voice and his repertoire, which encompassed gospel, ballads and blues, and arrived at American Studios early to hear Hamilton sing. He gave Hamilton a song he was himself due to record, **Angelica**, but the gift failed to lift the black singer him back onto the charts – even if Elvis dutifully bought it – and he died of a stroke later that summer, aged just 40.

Hamilton's heyday had been the 1950s. His first R&B chart hit, in 1954, backed **You'll Never Walk Alone** with **I'm Gonna Sit Right Down And Cry Over You**; Elvis covered the A side in 1967, and the B side on his first RCA album.

After Hamilton's death, and as his own death approached, Elvis returned to his idol's material. Two big Hamilton hits, **Hurt** and **Unchained Melody**, entered his concert repertoire in 1975, and seemed to be the new songs that moved him most. He also cut **Pledging My Love** at Graceland.

Along with Dino, Hamilton was probably the biggest influence on El's balladeering style. Elvis first attempted to emulate his trademark approach to big-voiced soulful ballads on **I Believe** in 1957. If his debt to Hamilton was obvious on covers like **You'll Never Walk Alone**, it was also present in his predilection for such power ballads as **Without Love**.

RECOMMENDED ALBUM: *ANTHOLOGY* (COLLECTABLES), FEATURING "UNCHAINED MELODY" AND "YOU'LL NEVER WALK ALONE".

JAKE HESS

While the young Elvis Presley may have tried to join the Blackwoods, the gospel quartet he and his father truly idolized were the **Statesmen**, led by **Jake Hess**. Gladys preferred the Blackwoods, which is why they sang at her funeral. Nineteen years later, Hess and two members of his next group, the **Imperials,** sang **Known Only To Him** at Elvis's own funeral.

Elvis first met Hess in the early 1950s in Tupelo; Hess remembered him as 'a bright-eyed boy asking all kinds of questions, and asking in a way that you would really want to tell him. You know, he just looked important even as a kid.' Fifteen years later, Hess was Presley's talisman during the *How Great Thou Art* sessions. El was so glad to have him in the studio that he embarrassed him by bringing him too far forward in the mix on **If The Lord Wasn't Walking By My Side**.

According to James Blackwood, leader of the eponymous quartet, Presley modelled his gospel/ballad style on Hess. At the very least, he certainly aspired to match the gospel singer's tenor and vibrato. Of his protégé, Hess said, 'Elvis was one of those individuals, when he sang a song, he just seemed to live every word of it. There's other people that have a voice that may be as great or greater than Presley's but he had that certain something.'

197

RECOMMENDED ALBUM: *ALL OF ME* (CATHEDRAL), FEATURING "SOMEBODY BIGGER THAN YOU AND I".

THE INK SPOTS

One of the biggest musical influences on Elvis Presley was his own mother, **Gladys Presley**. Nowhere was her gravitational pull more apparent than in his unlikely admiration for the smooth black vocal group, the **Ink Spots**. The standard Ink Spots performance consisted of three unvarying elements: a gently lurching intro, **Bill Kenny's** pure tenor, and a recitation delivered in such a deep, serious voice it made JD Sumner sound like a baritone.

The Ink Spots had cut both sides of the first record Elvis ever made: **My Happiness**, on which you can hear traces of Kenny's pure tenor, and **That's When Your Heartaches Begin**, with its trademark spoken bridge. He recorded the latter song again at RCA in 1957, and also sang it at the Million Dollar Quartet session, while the bridge device reappeared on **Are You Lonesome Tonight?** Elvis bought the Ink Spots' own *Live In Vegas* album in 1964, and, fooling around at home, collapsing into laughter because he couldn't find the necessary solemnity for the spoken bridge on their **It's A Sin To Tell A Lie**. In 1971 he recorded **There Is No God But God**, written by Bill Kenny, for *He Touched Me*.

Presley's friend **Faron Young** wrote **Is It So Strange?** for him, with its line 'If you tell me a lie you know that I'll forgive you', because he knew he liked the Ink Spots so much. Finally released on *A Date With Elvis*, Elvis's version, moody but with detectable Ink Spots influences, has over the years made Young $60,000.

RECOMMENDED ALBUM: *ANTHOLOGY* (UNI/MCA), INCLUDING "THAT'S WHEN YOUR HEARTACHES BEGIN".

MARIO LANZA

El's early 1960s conversion into an American **Mario Lanza** is often cited as evidence that he had lost his musical roots. In fact, Presley had

The original super Mario was one of Elvis's early idols ▶

made no secret of being a fan of the Italian semi-operatic singer, admiring his star turn in *The Great Caruso*, and his soaring voice in *The Student Prince* (in which Lanza was too fat to appear on screen). When he needed a soprano for Las Vegas, he hired **Kathy Westmoreland**, whose father worked with Lanza on both films.

By the time Presley became famous, Lanza was already in decline, a moody recluse with a weight problem. Lanza's daughter Colleen, however, swears that the two RCA stars talked on the phone, while his manager Terry Robinson told Jeff Rense of the Mario Lanza Web site that Elvis and A&R man Steve Sholes visited the Italian singer at his Beverly Hills home: 'He was so polite ... We played some of Mario's records and he sat there ... you know, dumbfounded.'

In any case, Elvis didn't need to meet his idol to be inspired by him. Witness his desperate need to sing the semi-operatic dramatic end to **It's Now Or Never**, and the way, in his last tours, that he'd ask Sherrill Nielsen to sing the Italian words to **O Sole Mio**. Lanza can also be heard in **Surrender** – the Italian original of which the tenor also recorded – and even on the final crescendos of **Rags To Riches**, **Hurt** and **I'll Never Fall In Love Again**. Whether you think his influence on Elvis was entirely healthy probably depends on what you think of *The Student Prince*.

RECOMMENDED ALBUM: *O SOLE MIO* (SUCCESS), INCLUDING "O SOLE MIO", "SANTA LUCIA" AND "TORNA A SURRIENTO".

DEAN MARTIN

Arguably, **Dean Martin** influenced almost every ballad Elvis ever recorded. When Sam Phillips asked Elvis just what he could sing, to Phillips' consternation it was to Dino's repertoire that Presley turned. The one early manifestation of this lifelong reverence, however, was **I Don't Care If The Sun Don't Shine**, as sung by Ol' Red Eyes in one of his movies with Jerry Lewis.

In 1958, Elvis was asked what he felt about Italian singers in general, and Martin's **Volare** in particular. If the interviewer was hoping for con-

Shirley Maclaine and Elvis celebrate Dino's birthday; Hal Wallis looks on

troversy he was disappointed: Presley replied, 'I think it's great, I rushed out and bought it.'

Elvis often tried to emulate the ease and intimacy of Martin's style (something not always a feature of Sinatra's). The archives are full of tapes of Elvis and the boys belting out Martin covers on the piano, such as **Write To Me From Naples** (released on *The Home Recordings*). When the two were neighbours in Palm Springs, Elvis used to ride his motorbike past Martin's house, trying to pluck up the courage to knock on the door. Marty Lacker says Elvis used to see Martin and Sinatra in Las Vegas in the 1960s: 'They liked to hang around Elvis because he attracted so many girls.'

Dino discovered **country** before Elvis rediscovered it – both covered **Gentle On My Mind**, to very different effect. Their paths crossed when Dino went to see Elvis in concert in Las Vegas, prompting Presley to sing a few words of **Everybody Loves Somebody**. That may not have been a first: there are unconfirmed rumours that Elvis performed **That's Amore** at the *Eagle's Nest* in Memphis in 1954. While Presley liked the songs, he was more interested in the crooner's vocal techniques. You can hear Dino most clearly in such early 1960s numbers as **Just For Old Time Sake** and **Easy Question**, though Norbert Putnam says that 'in the 1970s, towards the end, he almost started sounding like Dean Martin'.

RECOMMENDED ALBUMS: *GREATEST HITS* (EMI), INCLUDING "GENTLE ON MY MIND", AND *MAKING SPIRITS BRIGHT* (CAPITOL), A FESTIVE ALBUM THAT FEATURES "BLUE CHRISTMAS", "WHITE CHRISTMAS" AND "I'LL BE HOME FOR CHRISTMAS".

CLYDE MCPHATTER

Though the creator and most famous lead singer of the **Drifters** was not such a direct influence on Elvis as Roy Hamilton, in his ability to switch between R&B and ballads **Clyde McPhatter** set a precedent that Presley and Sam Cooke would follow.

Elvis once told Sam Phillips, 'You know if I could sing like that man I'd never want for another thing.' Ironically, as the King got older and McPhatter's solo career ran aground, his voice probably surpassed his former idol's. But in the early 1950s, it was McPhatter whose sinuous voice was creating a buzz around **Billy Ward and the Dominoes**. Even after he quit to form the Drifters in 1953, the Domino effect for Elvis continued when **Jackie Wilson** took over the singing chores.

McPhatter's effect on Elvis is at its most obvious in Presley's versions of **Money Honey** and **White Christmas**, cut during his first year at RCA. But his muse never entirely vanished. Elvis's cover of **Such A Night**, for *Elvis Is Back*, was more of a nod to McPhatter than to Johnnie Ray, while Presley again emulated his idol in the 1969 Memphis sessions, with a powerful rendition of **Without Love**.

Like Elvis, McPhatter interrupted his career to do military service and, like Elvis, his latter years were marred by his unreliability as a concert performer. One final tragic resemblance: both died prematurely, Presley at 42 and McPhatter at 40, with heart problems mentioned as a cause of death.

RECOMMENDED ALBUM: *GREATEST HITS* (CURB), FEATURING "MONEY HONEY" AND "WITHOUT LOVE".

MISSISSIPPI SLIM

Mississippi Slim was the first and most enigmatic of Elvis's singing idols and, despite Sam Phillips' claims on the position, probably the first musical mentor Presley ever had. Yet **Carvel Lee Ausborn**, to use his real name, isn't widely known today even in country music circles. Born in east Tupelo, he was a regular on Tupelo's WELO radio station, which started up when Elvis was 6. At the age of 8, Elvis used to go down to the station and follow Slim around as if he were the singer's pet dog. El's cousin recalls that Slim and Jimmie Rodgers were the boy's favourite country singers, and Slim's brother James later became a school friend.

Although Slim's records sound hillbilly, he employed a female jazz pianist, and he's praised for the subtlety of his timing and phrasing. Ironically, given what musicians like Scotty Moore were to say about El's natural sense of rhythm, despite being impressed by the boy's persistence and voice Slim kept telling him that he didn't know how to keep time. His influence on Elvis is hard to fathom, because Presley seldom talked about his boyhood hero. WELO announcer Charlie Boren feels that Slim helped give Elvis his unusual take on country. 'Slim didn't sing straight country, he sang a little boogie-type stuff.' Elvis didn't sing straight country either, and he took the boogie-type stuff a whole lot further.

203

THERE ARE NO MISSISSIPPI SLIM ALBUMS CURRENTLY AVAILABLE ON CD.

JACKIE WILSON

Although **Jackie Wilson** was known, with the reductive reasoning so familiar in showbiz, as 'the **black Elvis**', that didn't seem to harm his relationship with the white Elvis. Presley first saw him singing **Don't Be Cruel** in Las Vegas in 1956 – not that he knew his name – and was impressed enough to imitate Wilson, doing him for Jerry Lee Lewis and Carl Perkins at Sun Studios in December 1956.

Echoes of Wilson are apparent in Elvis's work from then on, notably in the 1957 Ed Sullivan version of "Don't Be Cruel" and in **Such A Night**. The most compelling evidence that Elvis was inspired by Wilson is the footage of him singing **Return To Sender** in *Girls! Girls! Girls!*, a tribute made even more significant because, according to Priscilla Presley, Wilson was on set watching. Wilson's pompadour may also have inspired some of Elvis's hairiest personal-styling moments of the 1960s. Elvis's cover of **Rags To Riches** was another tribute to Wilson, whose version had hit the R&B charts in 1953.

The two definitely met in June 1966, while El was filming *Double Trouble* and Wilson was performing on Sunset Boulevard. Presley was curious to know how Wilson sweated so much, envying the effect the excessive perspiration had on women in the audience. The salt tablets that Wilson was using had long-term side effects, and may have contributed to his mid-1970s stroke; Elvis is said to have donated as much as $30,000 towards his hospital bills. The admiration was mutual: when asked in 1973 whose records he would play if he was a DJ for an hour, Wilson replied simply, 'Elvis Presley, he's a great friend of mine.' He died seven years after Elvis.

RECOMMENDED ALBUM: *MASTERS* (CLEOPATRA), FEATURING "SHAKE A HAND" AND "DANNY BOY".

The King's rivals

ELVIS AND SINATRA

It would be an understatement to say that relations between the King and the Chairman of the Board, as is so often the case between rival potentates, got off to a rocky start. In a 1957 magazine article, **Frank Sinatra** announced that rock'n'roll was a 'rancid aphrodisiac … sung played and written for the most part by cretinous goons'. Just in case anyone still didn't know where he stood, it was 'the most brutal, ugly, desperate, vicious form of expression it has been my misfortune to hear'.

In fact, Sinatra and Presley had more in common than was obvious to either. Both idolized **Dean Martin**, who was, for all the publicity,

'To think, we did all that, and may we say not in a shy …"
the King and the Chairman at a rare summit meeting

205

the real heart of the Rat Pack, because he was the kind of man Sinatra wanted to be (a '*serenfreghista*'; literally a 'man who doesn't give a fuck'). By the simple expedient of not becoming Dino's close friend, Elvis probably had the better time out of worshipping the laid-back crooner.

Both travelled with **entourages**, the difference being that Sinatra didn't need to have his dubbed a mafia. Joe Esposito's *Good Rocking Tonight* reports Lamar Fike as complaining to Elvis about Sinatra's arrogance: 'When Mr Sinatra sits down nobody is allowed to do anything until Mr Sinatra snaps his fingers.' Presley replies: 'You'd never see me do any of that crap.' The King's own entourage were to become so adroit at anticipating his whims that he didn't need to snap his fingers.

Both men liked **Nancy Sinatra**, one as a father and one not as a father. Both co-starred with **Juliet Prowse**, who broke off her engagement with Sinatra to date Elvis; and both became synonymous with **Las Vegas**. And if that heap of coincidences isn't enough, they both recorded an 'updated' version of **Old Macdonald**; Frank, again, had the worst of the deal, because his was actually released as a single. The most painful difference between them, as far as Elvis was concerned, that Sinatra won an **Oscar** while Presley's movies only won a Golden Turkey.

Although Sinatra's most indiscreet biographer, Kitty Kelley, says that the Rat Pack privately referred to Elvis as 'Clyde' – their term for a loser – relations thawed when Sinatra, desperate to make it big on TV, paid Elvis $125,0000 (plus the cost of tuxedos for the King and the King's men) to make his first post-Army appearance as a guest on his show. Rehearsals went reasonably well, probably because Elvis was too polite to object to Sinatra referring to him as 'Sergeant Presley', and possibly because he struck up a genuine friendship with **Sammy Davis Jr**.

The show was both entertaining and anti-climactic, with Elvis injecting **Witchcraft** with more fun than Sinatra brought to **Love Me Tender**. Thereafter, the two camps circled each other in Las Vegas, where even Sinatra was stunned by the number of girls who surrounded Presley. When Elvis and Priscilla flew to Las Vegas in 1967 to get married, it was on Sinatra's own jet.

Elvis's Las Vegas heyday coincided with Sinatra's retirement, a changeover that became almost official when Presley adopted Sinatra's anthem **My Way**. By now, the two were close enough for Elvis to call Sinatra when he was trying to stop the publication of *Elvis: What Happened*. Sinatra initially offered to replace Presley's errant body-guards, then, when Elvis said, 'I could kill them', he probably jokingly said, 'I'll sort it.' Presley backed off, Sinatra telling him to call him any-time if he needed anything. They last talked just before Elvis died, Sinatra's words of encouragement putting Presley in an expansive mood.

This was a decent, generous, way to behave to a man he'd once dis-missed as a cretinous goon. When Sinatra heard that Elvis had died, he interrupted a concert to sing several Presley numbers, and told the audience, 'We have lost a dear friend tonight.' Perhaps it was the usual showbiz PR sincerity, but it may have been a genuine tribute from a man who had tried to help someone he had come to see not as a rival but as a friend in need.

ELVIS AND DYLAN

Although **Bob Dylan** said that hearing Elvis's voice for the first time was like busting out of jail, when biographers discuss Dylan's influ-ences they tend to mention Presley in passing, and concentrate on **Woody Guthrie**. What follows is not an attempt to downplay Guthrie's obvious and profound significance, but to suggest that Dylan's links to Presley are deeper and more numerous than is often realized.

Before Robert Zimmerman reinvented himself as a folk singer called Bob Dylan, he liked to listen to rock'n'roll. The usual artists: Presley – he bought **Heartbreak Hotel** and **Blue Suede Shoes** – Little Richard, Buddy Holly. In a 1966 interview, accused of abandoning folk music, he put things into perspective by saying that part of the reason he had sung folk in the early 1960s was because rock'n'roll had been 'taken over into milk – Frankie Avalon and Fabian'.

While Dylan was 'romantically turned on by Guthrie' in 1961 and 1962, he confessed to biographer Robert Shelton that, as he wrote the songs for his first folk albums, 'when nobody was around' he was listening to 'all those Elvis Presley records'. He even told interviewers that he had played piano on Elvis's early records; a put-on for the press, perhaps, but also a fantasy he half wished was true.

Elvis, on the other hand, never learned to appreciate Dylan's voice. On stage in Las Vegas he'd say, 'Give me some water Charlie, my mouth feels like Bob Dylan slept in it', or, if his voice was off, joke that he sounded like Bob Dylan. Instead he heard Dylan through performers like **Bobby Darin, Peter, Paul and Mary**, and folk/blues singer **Odetta**.

Although Elvis is rumoured to have performed various Dylan songs in concert, he only recorded two in full. Bob called the first, **Tomorrow Is A Long Time** – released in 1966, long before Dylan's own version – 'the greatest moment in my career'. The second, **Don't Think Twice It's All Right**, was partly down to James Burton providing the cue. 'Knowing Elvis he probably felt there were just too many words in Dylan's songs,' says Ernst Jorgensen. 'He would have felt there was nowhere he could hang a note.' Presley's stepbrother David Stanley says he finally came around when he heard Dylan's country album *Nashville Skyline*, the pared-down sound of which was much closer to Presley's oeuvre than the Beatles' ambitious *Sergeant Pepper*. He followed Dylan back into country with *Elvis Country* in 1971.

Guitarist Charlie McCoy and drummer Kenneth Buttrey played on sessions for Dylan and Elvis, although Buttrey probably got more artistic satisfaction out of the *Blonde On Blonde* sessions than his contribution to the *Harum Scarum* soundtrack. McCoy says, 'The difference between the two was that Bob usually left you to do your own thing while Elvis had a much clearer idea of what he wanted.'

At the sessions for Dylan's harshly received *Self Portrait* double album (1970), which featured two of Presley's favourite musicians – bass player Bob Moore and backing vocalist Millie Kirkham – Dylan cut three songs associated with Elvis. **Blue Moon** was on *Self Portrait* itself, while **Can't Help Falling In Love** and **A Fool Such As I** were released in 1973 on *Dylan*, an album whose title was a (probably unconscious) echo of all the Elvis albums called simply 'Elvis'.

Bob Johnston, who produced many of Dylan's albums up to *New Morning*, and also wrote dodgy songs for El's movies, told another Dylan biographer, **Howard Sounes**, that when Dylan wrote a song they thought might work for Presley, he tried to arrange a meeting. 'I tried to get them to record together. I think Dylan would have done it in a second.' It's an awesome possibility, and might have been very well timed, as by early 1971 Elvis was looking for material for a folk album – the songs he chose included Gordon Lightfoot's **Early Mornin Rain**, performed by Dylan on *Self Portrait* – but nothing came of it.

By then, Presley had staged his comeback in Las Vegas, watched by thousands of fans including, the evidence suggests, Dylan. He was never introduced from stage by Elvis, but Ron Cornelius, who played on *New Morning*, recalls asking him about **Went To See A Gipsy**: 'he told me it was about going to see Elvis in Las Vegas.' The central lines of the song 'Went see a gypsy at a big hotel / He smiled when he saw me coming and said "Well, well, well"' – certainly sound like an imagined conversation with Elvis. But did Dylan actually go to see him? The key Dylan biographies gloss over the point. Clinton Heylin, in *Behind The Shades*, says that Dylan saw Elvis in 1971, after he'd written the song, but he also quotes a 1980 interview in which it's clear Dylan studied his old idol closely: 'When Elvis Presley sang **That's All Right** in 1955, it had power and sensitivity, in 1969, it was just full out power. I've fallen into that trap.'

Elvis's death sank Dylan, by his own account, into deep depression: 'I had a breakdown. I didn't talk to anyone for a week. I went over my whole life, everything. If it wasn't for Elvis and Hank Williams, I couldn't be doing what I do today.'

The parallels didn't stop with Elvis's death. In 1978, Dylan matched *Aloha From Hawaii* with his own redundant live-in-the-Pacific double album, *Live At Budokan*, which featured Elvis's old bass guitarist Jerry Scheff – though at least Dylan did get as far as Japan. Dylan then discovered **Christianity** with a fervour to equal Presley's, only for his sacred albums to be panned almost as universally as Presley's had been praised. In 1997, after Dylan had recovered from a desperate illness, he joked, 'I really thought I'd be seeing Elvis soon.'

For two performers with such disparate images, they have a surprising body of work in common. As well as the Dylan songs cut by Elvis, which also included a fragment of **I Shall Be Released**, Dylan has recorded several numbers with Presley connections: **Can't Help**

Falling In Love, A Fool Such As I, Blue Moon, Tomorrow Night, Let It Be Me, Peace In The Valley, even the children's song **Froggy Went A Courtin'**. Similarly, it's clear from songs like **Dirt Road Blues** that Dylan is still listening to Elvis, if only the Presley of the Sun sessions. Dylan has even expressed admiration for his cavalier treatment of TV sets: 'Sometimes you just have to do what Elvis did and shoot the damn thing out' (**TV Talking Song**, 1990).

Just as he once distanced himself from folk, Dylan these days disavows rock,

210

'So congressmen and senators please heed the call ...'

saying that he listens to no music from the 1960s and only a little from the 1950s. Guthrie and Hank Williams remain far safer influences to cite than Elvis. Dylan was not going to pay homage to the star who made those dopey movies in the 1960s, and may now feel that the revolution that Elvis helped to create has not, in the long term, been all that good for American music. To Dylanologists, Elvis's sheer commercial taste-lessness seems to run counter to what their man is all about; if Elvis's influence is acknowledged at all, it's normally held up as a warning, just as Dylan did in the **That's All Right** comparison.

Dylan's ambivalence is encapsulated by his reaction when **Andy Warhol**, after a tour of the Factory in 1966, gave him a silk screen of the double Elvis. As Sounes says, 'it seemed to people at the Factory that Bob had wanted Warhol to give him the silk screen and was quick enough to take it when offered. Once Bob got the artwork home he made it clear he loathed it'. He swapped it with his manager Albert Grossman for a sofa, and Grossman's wife swapped it in turn for $720,000.

Bruce Springsteen famously saluted both Dylan and Presley, saying, 'Bob freed the mind in the way that Elvis freed the body.' **Nick Tosches**, in *Country*, has a different take: 'There was more mystery, more power, in Elvis, singer of "Danny Boy" than in Bob Dylan, utterer of hermetic ironies.'

If you're wondering how the two might have got on in the studio, read **Lester Bangs**' immortal *Graceland Über Alles*, which imagines that not only did Bob see Elvis in Las Vegas, but they spent several hours ranting to each other about the state of music. Perhaps the most intriguing cultural artefact about the two is the **Sam Shepard** play *True Dylan*, based on a phone conversation with Dylan. At one point, Shepard and Dylan are discussing James Dean when the hermetic iro-nist says to Shepard: 'You know what Elvis said? He said if James Dean had sung he would have been Ricky Nelson.' That sounds more like Greil Marcus speaking than Elvis, but Dylan seemed, to Shepard, con-vinced if his source. If true, this must mark Elvis's debut as a philoso-pher of pop culture.

ELVIS AND THE BEATLES

Elvis and The Beatles had a short, but complex, relationship. The Beatles are generally reported as having been disillusioned by their one group encounter, in Hollywood in 1965; one of their entourage even described Elvis as 'a boring old fart'. This reaction, and Presley's later assertion to the FBI and to President Nixon that The Beatles were anti-American, has been used to suggest there was a feud – that Elvis felt threatened by The Beatles, and put the cops on them.

The truth is slightly more complicated. Elvis did feel threatened by The Beatles; he would have been stupid not to. Yet for a man who was a master at not facing inconvenient realities, he didn't hide from them. He rented out the local cinema to watch *A Hard Day's Night*, and he owned two well-played Beatles albums, *Rubber Soul* and *Revolver* (which was banned on many Southern radio stations, including in Memphis, after Lennon's comment about The Beatles being bigger than Jesus). He also had The Beatles' single Going Slow, backed by their cover of Carl Perkins's Matchbox, both of which he contemplated bringing into his live act. Although he always said his favourite song of theirs was I Saw Her Standing There, the only numbers he added to his concert repertoire were Yesterday and Something. He also rehearsed Hey Jude at the Memphis sessions in 1969 and sang a snippet of Lady Madonna in the studio, possibly because he had heard Fats Domino's acclaimed version.

The famous summit was arranged at The Beatles' request. In his youth, John Lennon had been obsessed with Elvis – his aunt Mimi once complained: 'Elvis Presley's all very well John, but not for breakfast, tea and dinner' – and he called him the only person he wanted to meet in America. Some see the fact that the meeting took place at El's Perugia Way home as pure ego on Elvis's part, but he told Parker, 'If I was in their country, I'd go to them, but as they're in my country, they ought to come to me.'

It's agreed that the Fab Four plus one jammed, and that Paul McCartney told his idol: 'You're coming along quite promising on the bass there, Elvis.' However, biographers Goldman and Guralnick both suggest things didn't go too well. Lennon advised Mick Jagger not to bother meeting Elvis, and told others it was like meeting Engelbert Humperdinck. Yet Lennon's reactions were seldom clear cut: he wrote an affectionate piece called 'Ze King and I' in which he said that they bonded over a shared love for Peter Sellers: 'It was Elvis's sense of humour that stuck in my mind. He liked to laugh and make others laugh. Which was why I put on a Peter Sellers voice again as we walked out of the door and said, "Tanks for ze music, Elvis – and long live ze King!"'

Only five people really know whether the meeting lived up to expectations, and three of them – Elvis, John and George – are dead. McCartney and Starr have joked about how different their own recollections are: asked at the time for his opinion of Elvis, McCartney replied simply 'Odd.' For this book, we re-interviewed Elvis's valet **Richard Davis** and **Larry Geller**, whose accounts suggest the evening was a lot more fun than some reports allege.

Davis recalls, 'Elvis is sitting on the couch, and watching TV and he's got his feet propped up on the coffee table and his yachting cap on and he's smoking a little cigar. And The Beatles come in, and nobody says anything. So they keep staring at him, and finally Elvis says, "Tell you what fellas, y'all ain't going to say anything, I'm going to get up and go to bed." Well he started to get up like he was going to bed, and that broke the ice, because they came running over and wanted to talk. So John and Paul sat down on the couch and started talking, and George and Ringo headed for the bar. And the conversation got into music and how Elvis was instrumental in their career and everything, and how much they liked Elvis's style and songs and stuff, and Elvis said, "Yes, I like some of you guys' songs and stuff too, and one day I'd like to record some of them."

'They jammed together and then Paul turned to Elvis and said, because there wasn't nobody but Colonel Parker and Brian Epstein and Elvis and The Beatles and the guys that worked for Elvis, "Where's the birds?" Elvis says, "Birds?" and Paul says, "Yeah you know, girls, man, where's the girls?" and Elvis says, "Richard, are there any girls outside?" and I said, "Yeah, there's a whole bunch of them," and he says,

"Well, let some of them in." So I go out, opened the gate and picked out about a hundred or so girls, and said, "Come on in and shut the gate," and I took them inside and we partied the rest of the night.'

According to Geller, 'Their teeth were really bad, I couldn't believe that these guys were so famous and had such bad teeth. Elvis had all these guitars on stands, and John picked one up and said, "Elvis, is it all right if I ...?", and Elvis said, "Sure, go ahead" and so they started jamming. They played "Johnny B. Goode" and other stuff. And for half an hour that was where it was at.'

'And Ringo was playing pool, and Brian Epstein and the Colonel were playing roulette and I suddenly thought, "Where's George?" So I went out to the back of Elvis's house. Elvis had a real big backyard, and I couldn't see George but I could smell him, because I could smell a reefer. And there was George by the pool smoking a joint. And he handed it to me and I took a drag as well. George just never said anything. And when we went back inside, Elvis took them on a tour of the place.'

'There were literally hundreds of girls out there screaming like this mantra – "Elvis we love you, Beatles we love you" and they said to Elvis, "Man, how do you cope with this?" and Elvis said, "Man, if you don't like it, you're in the wrong job." McCartney invited Elvis and the guys to The Beatles' place the next night and El said simply, "Well I'll see".'

The next day, Davis and several other members of Elvis's entourage took McCartney up on his invite. Elvis didn't, saying, according to Marty Lacker, 'I've done my duty, I've met them.' That sounds as if he had hated every minute and yet George Klein says, 'Elvis was very fond of John and Paul. But in later years he became closer to **Ringo** because Ringo used to come to Las Vegas to see him. But Elvis thought they were immensely talented.' Indeed, he told his stepbrother Billy Stanley, after this first meeting, 'Ringo has a good ear for country music.'

As for their subsequent relationship, Steve Ellerhoff of the University of Iowa says that Kathy Westmoreland 'remembers seeing John and George at an Elvis concert ... Elvis told her he thought The Beatles were taking music where it had to go, he just wasn't that keen on heavy drug use.' Those members of the Memphis mafia who accepted The Beatles' invitations to their parties felt the same. Lacker once saw Paul playing the piano in 1966 or 1967: 'He looked up at me and said, "Do you think Elvis would ever cut one of my songs?"' McCartney confided that he'd always dreamed of producing Elvis in the studio, a fantasy shared by Lennon who, in turn, told Phil Spector of his desire to produce Elvis.

George Harrison often attended Elvis's concerts. David Stanley once ushered him into Presley's dressing room at Madison Square Garden. Harrison recalled: 'I had my uniform – worn-out denim jacket and jeans – and I had a big beard and long hair down to my waist. He was immaculate. He seemed to be eight foot tall and his tan was perfect. I felt like a grubby little slug and he looked like Lord Siva.'

Harrison always felt that he and Elvis were on the same wavelength. And he obviously didn't stop listening to Elvis, because he quoted Presley's 1969 single **Clean Up Your Own Backyard**, saying, 'Christ said "Put your own house in order", and Elvis said "clean up your own backyard" so if everybody tries to fix themselves up rather than trying to fix everybody else up there won't be a problem.' There are even rumours that Harrison tried to get unreleased tapes from RCA or the estate for the **Travelling Wilbury** sessions.

Elvis and **Lennon** never met again, although Larry Geller insists, 'John definitely had Elvis's number – *the* number that went straight through to Elvis's private phone. I don't know how often they talked, but I do know they did talk. I see so many pictures of John with Elvis buttons.' If the two had met in the 1970s, they would have found how much they had in common. Both shared a passion for numerology (Elvis was a number 8, John was a 9), astrology, Bing Crosby, preachers (Elvis liked Rex Humbard, Lennon was briefly a Pat Robertson fan) and spiritual enlightenment. Yoko's comment that 'John's always looking for a guru' equally applies to Elvis. Both became virtual recluses; both were victims of drug abuse; and both were haunted by what they saw as their failure to hold their families together (although not haunted enough to stop their womanizing).

Lennon once dreamed that he and Presley were at a party in the kitchen of the Dakota building, the apartments where Lennon spent most of the 1970s. A friend described Lennon's memory of the dream:

'Nobody's paying any attention to him. Everybody's gathered around Elvis. John shouts "Elvis!" across the room but Presley doesn't seem to hear him. Then Elvis approaches John and motions with his head to follow him. They're in John's bedroom. Elvis is sitting on John's bed and John is fiddling with the TV'.

The prime evidence for a Beatles/Presley **feud** are the documents that show Elvis telling the Nixon White House and the FBI that he thought the Fab Four were a danger. A major difficulty facing anyone who writes about Elvis is his habit of telling people what he thought they wanted to hear. He may have put it that simply – the files are not exactly clear – or he may have meant that Beatles songs like **Lucy In The Sky With Diamonds** were dangerous because they turned young people onto drugs, a view he expressed to his stepbrothers. Jerry Schilling says Elvis would have said anything to get the agent's badge he finally obtained from Nixon. In any case, he made no effort to pursue his remarks, and it didn't stop him meeting (and liking) George or Ringo. And the FBI's investigation of Lennon wasn't, as various tabloids have alleged, prompted by Elvis but by Senator **Strom Thurmond**.

Just to confuse matters further, Geller says Lennon called Elvis when he was worried about being deported from the US, and that Presley gave him some contacts and advised him to make an anti-drugs speech. After Elvis's **death**, Lennon's public reaction was the callous, oft-quoted remark that he had really died nineteen years previously, when he went into the Army. He also told a friend, 'the difference between The Beatles and Elvis is that with Elvis the king died and the manager lived, with The Beatles the manager died and we lived'. Yet two biographers say Lennon spent the next few weeks in profound depression. And the last single he released in his lifetime – **Just Like Starting Over** – was an obvious tribute to the man who had inspired him.

When George Klein accepted Elvis's induction into the Rock and Roll Hall of Fame in 1990, he was given the prize by Lennon's sons Sean and Julian. 'Julian had an Elvis pin on,' says Klein, 'just like John used to wear'.

So the real relationship between Elvis and The Beatles is far more confusing than the conventional image of the ultimate celebrity death match.

Elvis's record collection

Elvis's taste in music was as discriminating as his taste in interior decoration was dubious. True, he had his blind spots. He never needed much excuse to clear out the Christmas albums at *Poptunes* in Memphis – which is presumably how come he had Max Bygraves' *Singalongachristmas* – but most of the records he bought were, unlike the Jungle Room, in the best possible taste.

The first thing to say about Elvis's record collection is that its eclecticism suggests not the dumb rip-off merchant depicted by Albert Goldman, but a man who seemed prepared to give everything a listen. His two thousand or so records cross every genre from pop to blues and gospel to country (although there's surprisingly little from Eddy Arnold or Hank Williams), to Broadway showtunes (the original cast recording of *The Pajama Game*), to Mario Lanza to paranoid rubbish called *Marked For Death: Can America Survive?* by the televangelist Jack van Impe. In his predilection for apocalyptic pre-millennial tosh, as in so much else, Presley was ahead of his time.

Scotty Moore has an abiding memory of Elvis buying and listening to records in the early days. 'Even when he couldn't afford them, he was buying them. And he was always playing them. He played those records to death. He bought all kinds: pop, gospel, blues. But anything like Fats Domino's stuff, real simple stuff with a beat behind it, well, he couldn't get enough of that.'

Singles formed the bulk of the Presley collection. Graceland's jukebox held up to a hundred, and music could be piped to any room in the house. He also had a record player in his bedroom; the last record he actually listened to was an acetate given to him by JD Sumner and the Stamps.

217

Elvis playing his singles 'about to death' – in the words of Scotty Moore

Accounts conflict as to how much music Elvis listened to after he became famous. **Lamar** Fike says: 'Once Elvis really got going, he didn't listen to much other music. Elvis told me, "If I listen to everybody else, it'll take the edge off me." Against this is the story, in Jorgensen's *A Life In Music*, of Elvis sending the boys out in 1967, when his own career was in the doldrums, to buy the entire Top 100 singles. He'd also record songs that he listened to at home or heard on the radio.

Inevitably, he missed a lot of stuff. He knew who **Led Zeppelin** were before he met them, but mainly because his stepbrother liked them. **Eric Clapton** may have been God to many, but when he met Elvis, Presley offered to get James Burton to give him a few lessons. He wasn't being offensive: when Clapton said he was a guitar player, Presley assumed he was just starting out. He later told one of his entourage that he didn't know why Clapton wanted to meet him but he was 'a hell of a nice guy'. He once shocked a stepbrother by talking about how great **Jim Morrison** was, once you forgot all that 'political bullshit'.

The best insight into his musical mind is simply to run through a few of the records. So here are thirty of the singles in his collection, listed not in order of merit but chronologically, plus ten albums he liked to listen to. These records are not necessarily listed because they were his favourites but because they give some idea of the diversity of his record collection.

30 SINGLES

1 WHITE CHRISTMAS ★ BING CROSBY (1942). When Elvis covered this standard, fifteen years after Bing, his version owed more to Clyde McPhatter than to Crosby, but that was no disrespect to the crooner. Elvis had liked his musicals as a kid, and later sang "Blue Hawaii", which Crosby crooned in *Waikiki Wedding*. Elvis fiddled around with another song from the same film, "Sweet Leilani", but only in rehearsals or jam sessions. Crosby took some of the heat off Presley in 1956 when he told *Hollywood Reporter*, 'Don't underestimate this boy, the boy's here to stay, he's got talent and he can sing.'

2 SHAKE A HAND ★ FAYE ADAMS (1953). Faye Adams' first hit, and her first number one on the *Billboard* R&B charts, was getting a lot of airplay the summer that Elvis first walked into Sun Studios.

Elvis eventually recorded this gospel-tinged blues 22 years later.

3 JUST WALKING IN THE RAIN ★ THE PRISONAIRES (1953). The vocal group who recorded this soulful ballad (covered by Johnnie Ray in 1956) were, as their name suggests, doing time in the Tennessee State Penitentiary. One of the fifty thousand people who bought it, according to Guralnick, was Elvis, who read about both group and Sun Studios in the Memphis press in June 1953, days before he turned up to record "My Happiness" for his mum. And yet Prisonaires' lead singer Johnny Bragg insists that a shy white kid called Elvis who was hanging around Sun helped him to rehearse this song. That story may sound ridiculous, but it's supported by Sam Phillips' brother Judd, so who knows? Elvis visited Bragg in Tennessee State in March 1961.

4 MALAGUENA ★ ANDRE KOSTELANETZ (1954). A *malaguena*, in case you didn't know, is a flamenco dance from Malaga. And an 'Andre Kostelanetz' is a Russian choirleader who arranged classical music to make it easier to listen to and, not entirely intentionally, created the monster that was easy listening. His music was all the rage in the 1930s and 1940s. Connie Francis had a hit with the vocal version of "Malaguena" in 1960.

5 PLEDGING MY LOVE ★ JOHNNY ACE (1955). The A side of the last single released by Memphis blues crooner Johnny Ace, who died at the age of 25 on Christmas Eve 1954, after playing Russian roulette backstage in Houston. Roy Hamilton also recorded the song, without any fatal consequences.

6 UNCHAINED MELODY ★ ROY HAMILTON (1955). A number one on the R&B charts for El's idol Roy Hamilton. Scotty Moore recalls, 'He kept playing that one over and over,' and the King sang it over and over in concert in his final years.

7 BLUE VELVET ★ THE CLOVERS (1955). The Clovers had a minor R&B hit with this soulful rendition of "Blue Velvet" long before Bobby Vinton (one of a pack of Bobbys who chased Elvis in the late 1950s and early 1960s) cut his white-bread cover.

8 WITCHCRAFT ★ THE SPIDERS (1955). Led by the brothers Hayward and Leonard Carbo, this New Orleans vocal group, enjoyed fleeting success on *Billboard*'s R&B charts. "Witchcraft", the last of their five hits, was recorded by Elvis in 1963. You can hear the relief – that this isn't a soundtrack filler – in his voice.

9 I WALK THE LINE ★ JOHNNY CASH (1956). An inevitable presence in Elvis's record collection. Written and performed by a personal friend (who toured with Presley in the early days), a US Top 20 hit on the King's old label, and a classic slice of country music. Elvis sang this in concert in 1970 but, sadly, only after the MGM cameras filming for *That's The Way It Is* had gone home.

10 PEGGY SUE ★ BUDDY HOLLY (1957). Buddy Holly appeared on the same bill as Elvis at least twice before either achieved national fame. There is some mesmerizing footage of Presley looking wild, like he's already world-famous, with his arms draped over the shoulders of the diffident Holly, who looks like he's about to rush off to finish his homework. "Peggy Sue", a number three hit for Holly, was renamed for the woman who became his wife.

11 SKINNY MINNIE ★ BILL HALEY (1958). When Elvis supported Haley at the tail end of 1955, he went back to his dressing room half in tears, feeling that he'd failed to win over Haley's fans. Haley found him and reassured him, 'You've got a lot of talent, just go with the rhythm numbers'. "Skinny Minnie" was the last of Haley's own rhythm numbers to reach *Billboard*'s Top 30.

12 FEVER ★ PEGGY LEE (1958). Little Willie John had had a US R&B number one with "Fever", written by Otis Blackwell under a pseudonym, but it was Lee's version that influenced Presley's own reading, released on *Elvis Is Back*. In the 1970s, he changed the lyrics on the Pocahontas verse, singing, 'Myrna Smith and JD Sumner had a very mad affair / when their wives and husbands caught them / saw nothing but teeth and hair'.

13 GOOD ROCKING TONIGHT ★ PAT BOONE (1959). The only real evidence of the Elvis–Pat Boone 'feud' is that the King kept this incriminating evidence of his rival's ineffectual cover of the Roy Brown/Wynonie Harris song.

14 CHAIN GANG ★ SAM COOKE (1960). Elvis was among the many who didn't buy the 'official' version of Sam Cooke's death, after the RCA singer was shot by a hotel manageress who claimed he'd accosted her. According to Larry Geller, Elvis told him, 'I got it from the horse's mouth, he was murdered because he was shooting his mouth off, because he got out of line.' Elvis is rumoured to have sung "Chain Gang", one of Cooke's biggest hits, in concert in the 1970s.

15 STARDUST ★ FRANK SINATRA (1962). David Stanley says, 'Elvis liked Frank Sinatra's voice, he just didn't like his material.' This is one of three of Ol' Blue Eyes singles Elvis owned. The others were the inevitable "My Way" and the less obvious "Close To You".

16 GONNA MISS YOU ROUND HERE ★ BB KING (1963). Elvis never tired of music made by people in or from Memphis. And he certainly never tired of BB King's brand of the blues: there were two of the blues king's singles in the king of rock's collection.

17 20-75 ★ WILLIE MITCHELL (1964). In the 1950s, black trumpet player Willie Mitchell led the house band at *Danny's*, a club in West Memphis that was a mecca to young Memphians. Presley's classmate Fred Fredrick says, 'Elvis went to *Danny's* because of Willie. It was different. It wasn't white hillbilly and it wasn't black blues but it was danceable.' In the 1960s, Mitchell had several national R&B hits on the Memphis-based Hi label, of which this was the first – the title refers to its release number. He was also responsible for crafting the sound of Memphis soulster Al Green.

18 SHARE YOUR LOVE WITH ME ★ BOBBY BLAND (1964). The music of Bobby 'Blue' Bland and Junior Parker, Elvis told the *Memphis Press Scimitar*, was 'the real thing, right from the heart'. Bland had similar musical roots to Presley: he had sung in a gospel group, the Miniatures, and was a member of the legendary Beale Streeters with BB King and Johnny Ace. Bland had 63 R&B hits, of which "Share Your Love With Me" was one of the smaller, and is still going strong.

19 HOUSE OF THE RISING SUN ★ THE ANIMALS (1964). This is a real curio. In his 1968 TV special Elvis declared his fondness for The Beatles and the Byrds (or 'Beards', as he pronounced it), but from the evidence of his three Animals singles

221

he should have mentioned the Animals. Elvis would have known the folk original of this song but would also have been struck by Eric Burdon's vocal performance: a bluesier, grittier, variation on the Righteous Brothers' singles he loved. The other group in the 'British beat invasion' he rather liked was the Dave Clark Five.

20 MR PITIFUL ★ OTIS REDDING (1965). The Georgia soul singer had a voice that Presley had no choice but to love and he shared some of the King's musical tastes, aping Little Richard's rasping delivery and covering Clyde McPhatter's "A Lover's Question" and the Clovers' "Lovey Dovey". The flip, "That's How Strong My Love Is", is the kind of song Elvis could have recorded in the 1970s if he'd kept working with Chips Moman.

21 YOU'VE LOST THAT LOVIN' FEELIN' ★ THE RIGHTEOUS BROTHERS (1965). Like many of his contemporaries, when Elvis first heard the Righteous Brothers he assumed they were black because they had such soulful voices. This was the second successive single of theirs that he bought, the first being "My Babe", which only reached number 75 on the *Billboard* charts. Later, he incorporated the song into his own live act. After one show, he found himself with his entourage in the hotel lounge where Bill Medley, one of the Brothers, was performing. Elvis walked right in front of him and said, 'Hey Bill, how are you doing?' Medley fell to his knees in laughter.

22 IT'S A MAN'S MAN'S WORLD ★ JAMES BROWN (1966). Brown was the first celebrity to fly to Memphis for Elvis's funeral, announcing that 'I've come to see him' and spending time alone with the body. Although some of Presley's friends felt that Brown liked to make them look

small, Elvis was a genuine fan of the soul legend, as the presence of both this and "I Can't Stand Myself" in his collection proves.

23 SPANISH FLEA ★ HERB ALPERT (1966). One of the very few records Elvis owned that reflect his early 1960s Latin phase, even though by the time it was released he had moved on to country and gospel. Maybe he was just hedging his bets in case they ever asked him to make *Fun In Acapulco 2*.

24 ODE TO BILLY JOE ★ BOBBY GENTRY (1967). Elvis sang a few bars of this US number one in the studio during the "Guitar Man" sessions in 1968, after friends started teasing his publisher Freddie Bienstock for not snapping up the rights. Gentry incorporated an impersonation of Elvis into her Las Vegas act, and tabloid rumour had them romantically linked for a while in the mid-1970s.

25 BABY I LOVE YOU ★ ARETHA FRANKLIN (1967). In his search for new vocal challenges, Elvis began listening to the Queen of Soul in 1966, along with such diverse acts as Hank Williams and Judy Garland. He liked the sound so much he hired her backing group, the Sweet Inspirations, to go on tour in the 1970s.

26 LIGHT MY FIRE ★ JOSE FELICIANO (1968). Feliciano's Latin/folk remake of the Jim Morrison song was a number three hit in the US in July 1968, as Elvis was staging his own musical rebirth. Usually if Elvis bought a single by a male vocalist, it was because he thought he might cover it someday; that makes this a missed opportunity both for Elvis and for the estate of Jim Morrison. Feliciano also wrote to Elvis asking the singer to cover one of his songs.

27 EVERYBODY'S TALKIN ★ NILSSON (1969). An intriguing single to find in the collection, because it was chosen (over Bob Dylan's 'Lay Lady Lay') as the theme for *Midnight Cowboy*, in which Elvis might have played the gigolo instead of Jon Voight.

28 I HEAR YOU KNOCKING ★ DAVE EDMUNDS (1970). This was the Welsh rocker's only top ten US hit – Elvis would have known the song already, from covers by (among others) Fats Domino and Smiley Lewis.

29 YOU DON'T MESS AROUND WITH JIM ★ JIM CROCE (1972). This singer-songwriter's catalogue might have suited a King whose own publishing kingdom was unearthing precious few decent songs for him to record. Then again, Elvis might just have liked the reference to Superman's cape, as by now he was seldom seen in public without one. This was Croce's first US hit, but Elvis also knew and liked Croce's "Operator", which the Sweet Inspirations performed on stage.

30 YOU'RE A LADY ★ PETER SKELLERN (1972). It's probably just as well that the King never got around to recording this very British weepie, although it might have been preferable to his take on Roger Whittaker's "Last Farewell".

10 ALBUMS

1 *EVERY TIME I FEEL THE SPIRIT* ★ MAHALIA JACKSON (1960). The Queen of Gospel was always one of the King's favourite singers, although the musical monarchs met just once, on the set of Elvis's last feature film, *Change Of Habit*. While recording his last gospel album in 1971, Presley cut "An Evening Prayer" in tribute to Jackson, and also tried to recapture the emotional fervour of her reading of "The Lord's Prayer". *Every Time I Feel The Spirit* earned both singer, and the whole gospel genre, a first Grammy for Best Vocal Performance. Elvis was already a fan when it came out, having sung Jackson's "I Asked The Lord" to Priscilla at the piano in Germany.

2 *DINO'S ITALIAN LOVE SONGS* ★ DEAN MARTIN (1961). The timing of this purchase, just as Elvis was about to unleash his long-concealed Italian side on a barely suspecting world, seems more than coincidental. Presumably El was checking out the opposition. By the end of the decade, despite having sung his way through some of the worst material known to man, he was as accomplished a balladeer as his idol. One track here, "Return To Me", was a perennial favourite for Elvis and the boys around the piano; another is Dino's version of "There's No Tomorrow".

3 *PIANO IN THE FOREGROUND* ★ DUKE ELLINGTON (1961). Though Elvis admitted in 1957 that 'I don't really understand jazz', this underrated gem suggests that he did occasionally make the effort. On a rare trio session, the Duke is joined by bassist Aaron Bell and drummer Sam Woodward for fine interpretations of songs like "Body And Soul" and "Summertime". Its sparer instrumental setting may have attracted Presley.

223

4 THE FIRST FAMILY ★ VAUGHN MEADER (1962). The career of impersonator Vaughn Meader died at pretty much the same time as the subject of his greatest impression, on 22 November 1963 in Dallas. Before that, this satirical album about the Kennedys enjoyed twelve weeks at number one. Presley, although better known for his encounter with Nixon, liked Kennedy and was obsessed by his assassination. He owned the Warren Commission report, and became one of thousands of Americans who obsessively studied the Zapruder home movie of the killing for clues.

5 GREATEST HITS ★ CHUCK BERRY (1964). Chuck Berry mentions Elvis just once in his autobiography – in a list. The King returned the compliment, only mentioning him once, in a half-joking way, while introducing James Burton. However, Jerry Schilling recalls seeing Berry perform in Las Vegas with Elvis and Sammy Davis Jr. 'It must have been about two in the morning and Sammy and his wife were coming back to the *Hilton* with us, and there was Chuck Berry playing in the lounge. Elvis sat down and watched, hollering and clapping as Chuck played.' Presley certainly dug Berry's music, covering four of the songs on this compilation live or in the studio, and almost covering another, "Brown Eyed Handsome Man".

6 THE GREATEST LIVE SHOWS ON EARTH ★ JERRY LEE LEWIS (1964). The Killer's acclaimed live album includes his reading of "Green Green Grass Of Home". Red West loved this version but Elvis remained singularly unimpressed until Tom Jones sang it and he realized he could have had a hit with it himself. The

album contains four songs Elvis had already covered ("Hound Dog", "Memphis Tennessee", "What'd I Say" and "Mean Woman Blues"); three he would cover later ("Green Green Grass Of Home", "Johnny B. Goode" and "Hi Heel Sneakers"); and one ("Crying Time") he sang to relax on tour in the 1970s. Little could El have known when he bought this that, twelve years later, Lewis's drunken, pistol-waving form would appear on the Graceland TV monitors.

7 WHERE DID OUR LOVE GO? ★ CHARLES BOYER (1965). On this curious slice of vinyl, the French actor talks through lushly orchestrated love songs in such heavily accented English that he almost sounds like Peter Sellers' Inspector Clouseau. Elvis bought it in 1966 and played consistently thereafter, even giving a copy to a girlfriend, although his friends hated this tinkling-piano-in-the-next-apartment music. He introduced two of the songs into his concert repertoire: "What Now My Love" and "Softly As I Leave You". On the latter, a cheery little ditty El insisted was about a dying man's love for his wife, he'd talk through the lyrics à la Boyer, while Sherrill Nielsen sang them mournfully.

8 CRYING TIME ★ RAY CHARLES (1966). From the number of times Elvis sang Ray Charles's "I Got A Woman", the black singer's influence on Elvis is obvious. He owned at least two Charles albums, the other being *Ray Charles: A Man And His Soul*. This one won a Grammy for best vocal performance. Elvis adopted Charles' "I Can't Stop Loving You" as a showstopper in 1969, and can be seen singing a chorus of "Crying Time" in the limo in *Elvis On Tour*. In the 1950s, Charles worked with two of Elvis's favourite blues singers, Ruth Brown and Lowell Fulson. Much as Elvis helped blend country and blues to create rock'n'roll, Charles led the fusion of R&B, gospel, jazz and country that produced soul. Like Presley, Charles was later criticized for abandoning the earthy sound that typified his most pioneering work.

9 *LIVE IN LAS VEGAS* ★ TOM JONES **(1969).** There's no doubt that Tom Jones influenced Elvis. The debate is whether, as Goldman suggests, Presley took his entire Las Vegas stage act from Jones, or simply incorporated some of Jones's moves into his own performances. The success of Jones (who admits he based some of his stage act on Elvis's) certainly encouraged Presley, who by the late 1960s feared that record buyers were interested only in

groups. The two singers had five of the tracks here in common, and both paid their debt to The Beatles by singing "Hey Jude" and "Yesterday". At Graceland in 1976 Presley cut "I'll Never Fall In Love Again" (an inferior version to Jones's) and a morose but moving "Danny Boy".

10 *CHERISH* ★ DAVID CASSIDY **(1972).** Elvis's daughter Lisa Marie is responsible for the slightly disconcerting number of Cassidy/Partridge Family records in the Presley collection. Apart from *Cherish*, Cassidy's first solo effort, Elvis also owned a couple of Partridge Family singles (including "I Think I Love You"). The Graceland archives hold a tape of the 4-year-old Lisa giving an almost word-perfect rendition of "How Can I Be Sure?"

The Canon

50 Essential Elvis Songs
and the stories behind them

Compiling a list of Elvis's **50 most essential recordings** is a bit like naming Shakespeare's top five plays; both Elvis and the Bard were, sometimes, too prolific for their own good. That said, Will's laziest doggerel has to be preferred to Elvis's rendition of **Old Macdonald Had A Farm**, on the soundtrack to his 24th movie, *Double Trouble*.

To help with this selection, hundreds of Elvis fans from all over the world – from Chile to Australia and the US to Denmark – were asked to select the twelve Elvis songs they could not live without. After debate worthy of a Vatican conclave, the resultant list of 109 songs was whittled down to the fifty in the following pages.

Such a list cannot help but be subjective. No scientific formula, alas, can prove that **All Shook Up** is better than, say, **Petunia The Gardener's Daughter** (from *Frankie And Johnny*). Yet no fan chose the latter – the line about 'how I dance when she plants her two lips on me' must have counted against it.

So what we have is a list that tries to reconcile several different criteria. All the performances should stand in their own right; they should mean something to Elvis (did he, for example, return to the song throughout his career?); and they should illustrate some facet of his talent. You may not like some of them, and you may like others that aren't included here. But, then, Elvis probably didn't like all of them – he was never a great fan of **Burning Love**, for example. Finally, one notable absentee deserves explanation: **Blue Suede Shoes** is not included because Elvis felt that **Carl Perkins** had sung it better.

Note: All the songs here are listed in the chronological order they were recorded. To simplify matters – and to save you money – we have listed the major albums or boxed sets on which they are included, rather than comprehensively citing every occasion on which they have been released. Although RCA is currently reorganizing Elvis's catalogue, all the albums mentioned are available as this book went to press.

1 My Happiness

June 1953, Memphis Recording Studios, Memphis

Available on *Sunrise* and *The King Of Rock'n'Roll* box set.

The guitar sounds, Elvis said later, like 'somebody beating on a bucket lid'. The voice, as we listen today, is both familiar and strange, sounding less like the Elvis we came to know than someone auditioning to join the Ink Spots.

Elvis was 18 when he paid $3.98 plus tax to the Memphis Recording Service, part of Sun Studios, to record My Happiness in the summer of 1953. He maintained that the record was intended as a gift for his mother, although it wasn't in fact Gladys's birthday. Before that first visit, Sun owner Sam Phillips had seen the young Elvis pull up outside the studios and sit in the cab of his truck, trying to find the nerve to walk in. It was probably June when he finally did so, a month after he'd taken his first steps on the road to fame, by hitch-hiking 240 miles to enter the Jimmie Rodgers Country Festival.

"My Happiness" had been a pop hit for (among others) Jon and Sandra Steele in 1948. Elvis is known to have sung it incessantly to two high-school sweethearts. Indeed, this performance may be as close as any fan can come to hearing the non-famous Elvis, persistent to the verge of being irritating, as he sang at high school or around his home. His voice is yearning and plaintive, yet in its way

230

oddly calm, though he does manage to mix up 'reminisce' to become 'riminesce', much as he did seven years later when cutting "Such A Night" for *Elvis Is Back!*.

Elvis didn't sound like nobody, just as he told Sun's office manager Marion Keisker before he sang. She, of course, thought, 'Oh yeah.' But he was right. Childlike in his arrogance, but right. Something in his voice – 'soul', she called it later – persuaded her to tape him, something she had heard either in black music or in the emoting of Johnnie Ray. When she took his details, she wrote down a nickname to remember who he was: Timothy Sideburns.

2 *That's All Right*

5 July 1954, Sun Studios, Memphis
Available on *Sunrise* and *The King Of Rock'n'Roll* box set.

By all accounts, That's All Right – the recording that marked the birth of rock's most influential singer – was pure, unpremeditated serendipity. Together with Scotty Moore on guitar and Bill Black on bass, Elvis had been trying Sam Phillips' patience with an amateurish reading of "I Love You Because". Then, as they drank their Cokes, Elvis started joking around on his guitar, doing an impression of bluesman Arthur Crudup singing "That's All Right".

For this accident to happen at all, however, Elvis had to know singer and song. To Phillips, 'It was just amazing … that he even knew a Crudup song.' At the time, he asked Elvis directly: 'What in the hell have you been holding up on me?' The original had been recorded by Crudup in Chicago and released in 1946 on the Bluebird label. Elvis later recalled that 'Down in Tupelo I used to hear old Arthur Crudup bang on his box and I always said if I ever got to the place where I could feel all old Arthur felt, I'd be a music man like nobody ever saw.'

Not that the feel of his version of "That's All Right" is like old Arthur's. Elvis's voice, as *New Yorker* magazine put it in his obituary, 'was like a high sharp shiver. There isn't any part of the song not covered by a thrilling energy.' It differed from conventional white country records of the time in part because Phillips pulled Elvis's vocals back into the mix, so they fused with the music. And it was Elvis's own rhythm guitar that propelled the song into life, even before Bill Black's slapped bass made its appearance. 'I never heard that guitar on any of his records after Sun,' Johnny Cash was to complain, 'but just him and that guitar alone, that was enough for me.'

Scotty Moore is still a bit mystified by it all: 'We went in for Sam to hear his voice. We were just jamming, not doing it for Sam or for anyone but ourselves. You listen to "That's All Right" … he had a feel for rhythm that's very hard for anybody to do the same way. He had rhythm in his voice. He could hear a song and he knew what he could do with a song. And nobody else could do it.'

Elvis substituted some scat singing for a couple of verses – the 'dee dee dee dee' may have been an in-joke, lifted from Crudup's vocal on My Baby Left Me, which Elvis was to cover at RCA – to leave a song that, at under two minutes, was perfect for radio play. The single sold 20,000 copies, mostly in the South. Not bad, considering that when they played it back in the studio, Scotty and Bill thought, 'That's fine but good God they'll run us out of town.'

3 Blue Moon Of Kentucky

6 July 1954, Sun Studios, Memphis
Available on *Sunrise* and *The King Of Rock'n'Roll* box set.

As Greil Marcus so rightly said, Elvis could not have recorded his version of Bill Monroe's bluegrass standard Blue Moon Of Kentucky if he hadn't just cut "That's All Right". Having broken one barrier, by giving the blues a country tinge, it was easier to commit another act of sacrilege.

If anything, the impudence was in this case even more serious. Although bluegrass had only been invented in the 1940s – largely by Monroe himself – it was among the most traditionalist of genres, relying on a limited range of acoustic string instruments, and featuring wistful lyrics that harked back to a pre-industrial age.

This time Bill Black was the inspirational fool; his falsetto spoof of Monroe was so infectious that Elvis and Scotty felt obliged to join in. Elvis had known and loved "Blue Moon Of Kentucky" since hearing it on the radio in Tupelo. His lack of professional experience worked to their advantage as they proceeded, with Phillips' encouragement, to speed it up from a waltz to 4/4 time. Elvis's bluesy vocal, refined through various takes, retains an eerie quality, presaging the mysterious nocturnal creature that he later became.

The audacity of what they had done struck Elvis when he made his only appearance on the Grand Ole Opry, to find that Monroe was on the same bill. That he introduced himself and apologised for doing the song like this suggests he may have heard of Monroe's alleged complaint that 'He ruined my song!' Monroe was diplomatic, telling the young singer, 'If it helps you get started I'm for you one hundred percent'. He subsequently paid Presley the compliment of recording it in the same style, admitting, 'Later I got to where I liked it.' In turn, Elvis's 1970 cut of Monroe's Little Cabin On The Hill allows no doubt as to his affection both for bluegrass and for its founding father.

233

4 *Good Rocking Tonight*

September 1954, Sun Studios, Memphis
Available on *Sunrise* and *The King Of Rock'n'Roll* box set.

If there was ever any doubt about the hidden slang meaning of the word 'rock', Good Rocking Tonight removed it. Elvis's speeded-up version of Wynonie Harris's speeded-up version of Roy Brown's R&B classic has an authority and arrogance astonishing for a singer's second single. Inspired by the familiar wartime announcement, 'Good evening America, there's good news tonight', the song had served as something of a trademark for Harris – even though he had initially turned it down, perhaps because the only lyrics were written by Brown on a paper bag.

Harris's manager later claimed that Elvis derived his entire performing style – especially his pelvic thrust and curling lip – from taming down the black singer's mannerisms. On record, however, Elvis sounds as though he's hamming it up, not calming anything down. It's not so much a cover as an act of musical annexation, which also, bizarrely enough, stands as a sincere homage to the power of black music. In Presley's hands, said Nick Tosches, "Good Rocking Tonight" was more like an invitation to a holocaust than to a party. His repeated cries of 'Let's rock' leave no room for debate about what was likely to be going on for those brave enough to meet behind the barn. Elvis seems to be deliberately echoing the anarchic energy with which Harris would announce, before a gig, 'Here comes the blues!'

Meanwhile, Scotty Moore played his guitar as if Sam Phillips' repeated admonition – 'We don't want none of that soft bullshit, we want some of that biting bullshit' – had finally gotten through. Out went Chet Atkins-style finger-picking, and in came a new style where even the instinctive, spontaneous, solos emphasized the beat. With Bill Black's frenzied bass slapping, this was rock-'n'roll at full throttle. Even today, you can still hear why, in the years before Elvis incorporated "Hound Dog" into his live act, he'd use "Good Rocking Tonight" to incite the crowd to a frenzy.

5 Baby Let's Play House

February 1955, Sun Studios, Memphis
Available on *Sunrise* and *The King Of Rock'n'Roll* box set.

Implicit in the charge that Elvis and other white rock'n'rollers ripped off black singers are the twin notions that they either copied the originals note for note, or emasculated them to make them more commercial. Bluesman Arthur Gunter wrote and recorded Baby Let's Play House in late 1954, drawing in turn on Eddy Arnold's 1951 country smash "I Want To Play House With You". Play Gunter's original and Elvis's cover back to back, however, and while you may still prefer Gunter it's simply not possible to argue that Elvis copied him or watered his song down.

From the very first hiccup, Elvis's adrenaline, enthusiasm and sly humour are infectious. Though he runs through enough vocal tricks and gimmicks in two minutes and 23 seconds to inspire a million clones, he never sounds mannered. After warning his girl that he'd rather see her dead than with another man, he backs off and, in place of Gunter's 'You may get religion', sings 'You may have a pink Cadillac but don't you be nobody's fool.'

That flash of inspiration troubles those who insist it was the pink Cadillac and all it entailed that proved Presley's undoing. Should the boy have heeded his own advice? Possibly; or perhaps Elvis was simply tapping into the frustrations of his own generation, supplying an image to which they could relate. As the song fades out, he can't restrain himself, and the outgoing chorus of 'Oh baby, baby, baby' is interrupted by a giggle.

As Bill Black proves beyond all doubt that he is the best slapper

235

of a bass there ever was or will be, Scotty's rhythm guitar drives Elvis to greater heights. This was triumphant vindication of Sam's theory that the interplay of bass, guitars and voice could create a sound that was neither country nor blues but had a completely new rhythm and feel. John Lennon's Quarrymen tried to recapture that feel on their own version of the song, while this was the performance that inspired Eric Clapton and Jimmy Page to play guitar.

Fifteen years on, rehearsing for Las Vegas, Elvis sang a slower, bluesy rendition of "Baby Let's Play House". That time around he sang the line about getting religion first, as a nod to Gunter, before returning to the Cadillac. A mesmerizing performance, available on *The Lost Performances* video and the *Platinum* CD, it leaves you wishing that he'd cut a blues album after his return to splendour.

6 Mystery Train

11 July 1955, Sun Studios, Memphis
Available on *Sunrise* and *The King Of Rock'n'Roll* box set.

'Train I ride sixteen coaches long.' Mystery Train's most famous line might not have been quite as effective with the 'fifty coaches' of Little Junior Parker's original draft. When Parker recorded the song at Sun Studios in the autumn of 1953, Sam Phillips pointed out in his common-sense way that it would have to be a big city to have a train with fifty coaches pulling out of it. So sixteen it was, making it, according to Phillips, a song of universal feeling: 'It's a big thing to put a loved one on a train; maybe they'll never come back'.

Junior Parker's version, inspired by the Carter Family's "Worried Man Blues", was mournful, even ghostly. Although Elvis speeds the song up, welding it to the beat from Parker's B side, Love My

Baby, his rendition retains a supernatural power comparable to Robert Johnson's blues. Except that, although Elvis's baby has just left on a long black train, by the time the song draws to a close he has convinced himself – and us – that she's coming back.

"Mystery Train" is a superb amalgam of innocence and craft. The fire in Elvis's voice is backed up by a marvellous shuffling rhythm. They throw in an extra bar at one point, something that Scotty said only worked when he did it with Elvis. Scotty's late **guitar solo** is a thing of rare restraint and ambiguity, perfectly supporting the way Elvis transforms the sense of the song. As **Keith Richards** put it, 'Everyone else wanted to be Elvis. After hearing [Mystery Train], I wanted to be Scotty Moore.'

Elvis's closing **chuckle** has been interpreted as a cry of triumph either at his recovery of his baby, or at the realisation that he has created a musical masterpiece. Phillips' explanation, that Elvis was laughing because he thought he had screwed it up, does nothing to diminish the glory of the moment.

7 Trying To Get To You

11 July 1955, Sun Studios, Memphis
Available on *Sunrise* and *The King Of Rock'n'Roll* box set.

Had RCA had not bought his contract, **Trying To Get To You** would probably have been Elvis's sixth Sun single. By the time it was recorded, Phillips had transformed Elvis, Scotty and Bill in the studio, and you can hear the difference. They'd already tried and failed to cut a decent version of the song, originally recorded by an obscure band called the Eagles, that February. This time, Phillips brought in **Johnny Bernero** to play drums. Still buzzing from their reworking of "Mystery Train", they nailed it.

What's intriguing about Elvis's vocal is that he has audibly

237

238

"Heartbreak Hotel" – a 'morbid mess' which RCA released only reluctantly

grown in confidence, happy to raise the roof when he talks of his girl's loving letter, and yet lost little of the innocence that made "My Happiness" so appealing. The sheer, satisfying completeness of the sound can only beg the question: If Sam hadn't sold Elvis, where would they have gone from here?

Elvis's father, **Vernon**, always liked "Trying To Get To You", which may explain why it runs through Elvis's career like a refrain. Thus he reclaimed it for the 1968 TV special, in a stunning performance that recalled the power of the original without really topping it. And in one of his final concerts, in June 1977, he sang it as a favour to his dad. Starting by joking about the title – 'Trying to get you all according to which part of the country you're from' – he went on to sing the hell out of it, in a spellbinding performance that served as a fantastic adios from an artist about to leave the building.

8 Heartbreak Hotel

10 January 1956, RCA Studios, Nashville
Available on *Elvis Presley* and *The King Of Rock'n'Roll* box set.

After **Heartbreak Hotel** was recorded, RCA A&R man **Steve Sholes** was almost as heartbroken as its narrator. His bosses in New York told him to get back down to Nashville and cut it again. Better still – came the not-so-subtle implication – record something else.

Their confusion was understandable. The song was unlike anything Elvis had recorded at Sun; a 'morbid mess', Sam Phillips called it. But then it wasn't like anything else either, except perhaps the hysterical outbursts of **Johnnie Ray** on ballads such as "Cry". Some suits told Sholes he should have signed Carl Perkins instead. They pointed out, with justification, that the Sun sound had been crisp, vibrant and rhythmic, whereas this was almost drowned in

239

echo – a consequence of having to use the studio's stairwell as an echo chamber.

Mae Axton had written the song after reading a newspaper story about a businessman who committed suicide, and left a note that read simply, 'I walk a lonely street'. She decided to put a heartbreak hotel at the end of the lonely street. Glenn Reeves, the singer who cut the demo, was not impressed, saying it was the silliest title he had ever heard, and insisted his name was kept off the demo.

Elvis, on the other hand, saw something in it. Thank God. He created the decade's definitive musical statement of adolescent alienation, expressing in two minutes and eight seconds what JD Salinger had taken a novel to convey in *The Catcher In The Rye*. The sobbing bellhop and the desk clerk dressed in black seemed like characters from Edgar Allan Poe, but the crux was the singer, who sounded as if he had lost the will to live, let alone the will to enunciate the lyrics properly. The musicianship – DJ Fontana's rim shots, Scotty's savage guitar breaks, Floyd Cramer's piano – added to the air of desolation. It's easy to understand why Nick Cave speculated, on *The First Born Is Dead*, that Elvis was the product of a voodoo Southern subculture.

As only Elvis may have grasped at the time, "Heartbreak Hotel" was more than just a marvellous song, more even than one of the handful of greatest rock singles of all time. It was a musical manifesto. Among the millions who were captivated were folk singer Phil Ochs and the young George Harrison, who had his first rock-'n'roll epiphany when he heard this song blaring out of a window while riding his bike.

9 *Money Honey*

10 January 1956, RCA Studios, Nashville

Available on *Elvis Presley* and *The King Of Rock'n'Roll* box set.

Elvis may have had one of the greatest voices in popular music, but that never stopped him from worshipping other vocalists. One of his eternal favourites was Clyde McPhatter, who sang with the Drifters before pursuing a long, intermittently successful, solo career. Hearing his voice on the car radio, Elvis commented, 'If I could sing like that man, I would never want for anything again'.

Money Honey, a Drifters hit from 1953, was the first of Elvis's many tributes to McPhatter. The band had just cut "Heartbreak Hotel" and, even though nobody else seemed much impressed, they were still buzzing. Although they had regularly played the song (written by Jesse Stone), recording it took a whole three-hour session. In fact, they never did get it quite right, and ended up splicing two takes together. Elvis, however, was in fine voice: cheeky and innocent, but sexy, and shrewd enough not to be surprised when a richer man took his place in his sweetheart's affections. The band give the song a hint of "Heartbreak Hotel"'s otherworldly sultriness, to produce one of their most unusual performances.

On 4 May 1956, Gene Vincent used the same style to establish a new career. Vincent was so convincing that the first time Gladys Presley heard Be Bop A Lula on the radio, she thought it was her son. As Elvis laughingly recalled, when he met up with Vincent, 'Before I even said anything, he came up to me and said straight out, "I wasn't copying you, man." Elvis merely congratulated Vincent, predicting the record would be a smash. Twelve years later, he returned the compliment, appropriating the black leather look that Gene had made his own for his comeback TV special.

10 *My Baby Left Me*

30 January 1956, RCA Studios, New York
Available on *Elvis Presley* and *The King Of Rock'n'Roll* box set.

It was Elvis's idea to record My Baby Left Me, although A&R man Steve Sholes had previously worked at Victor's Bluebird label with its author, bluesman **Arthur Crudup**. For his own version, Elvis stuck closer to Crudup's 1950 original than he had with his cover of Crudup's "That's Alright Mama", down to duplicating the emphatic drums at the start. Elvis's performance, however, rocks to a harder rhythm, and he sings with an abandon extraordinary for any singer of the time, black or white. When he wails about wringing his hands and moaning, the slight melodrama of the image is absolutely convincing. It is, in that respect, almost a frenetic rocking companion to the desolate "Heartbreak Hotel".

Perhaps for the first time since the addition of DJ **Fontana** as a regular drummer, the band really gel in the studio. Having kicked off with the momentum of DJ's drumming and Bill Black's bass, the pace never relents. "My Baby Left Me" is as free and as fierce as anything Elvis ever cut at RCA, and ranks among a handful of his finest performances ever. Which makes its fate all the more disturbing. Released as the B side to the iffy ballad "I Want You I Need You I Love You" – allegedly because Presley had mispronounced the title – it was not released on album until 1959's *For LP Fans Only*. This was an early sign that Sam's (and Elvis's) insistence on feel would increasingly take a back seat to more commercial considerations.

Sadly, Elvis only recorded one more Arthur Crudup song after "My Baby Left Me" - "So Glad You're Mine". Their paths crossed just once more, when Elvis paid for Crudup's recording sessions at Fire Records in the 1960s. While the gesture may have been inspired by Elvis's guilty recognition that the blues singer hadn't got all his royalties, it was also, as you can tell here, a mark of respect.

11 Lawdy Miss Clawdy

3 February 1956, RCA Studios, New York
Available on *Elvis Presley* and *The King Of Rock'n'Roll* box set.

Lawdy Miss Clawdy can be seen as Elvis's answer to Jack Kerouac's *On The Road*. His relationship with the elusive Miss Clawdy scraping the bottom of a very bitter barrel, he cheerfully insists he's going to tell everyone how miserable she's made him; then ends, with a happy flourish, saying 'Bye bye baby', and hits the road.

Lloyd Price first recorded the song in New Orleans for Specialty, in 1952. One apocryphal story has Price finally delivering the goods after bursting into tears in shock at being accused of wasting studio time. What's not in doubt is the presence of Elvis's idol **Fats Domino** on piano, in a performance which, though more sedate than what followed, served as a blueprint for the kind of storming rock'n'roll popularized by **Little Richard**.

From the very first take (released on the *Platinum* box set), Elvis nailed the vocal immediately, but it took the band a while to catch up. **Shorty Long**'s piano is more aggressive than Domino's, and drives the song faster, but it's perfectly in keeping with Elvis's glee. He sings like a man who is convinced that America, and quite possibly the world, is at his mercy.

This remained one of **Scotty Moore**'s own favourite Elvis performances. Reunited for the 1968 TV special, he made a rare request for his old buddy to sing it one more time. Elvis was highly amused by the interjection, but then sang a harder-edged, bluesier, version that was a highlight of the show. In his last dramatic movie, *Change Of Habit*, he even played it on the piano, jamming with Mary Tyler Moore. And he performed it in 1974, at his first concert in Memphis for thirteen years. Never again, however, did he recapture the freedom and the verve of his very first cover.

12 Shake, Rattle And Roll

3 February 1956, RCA Studios, New York

Available on *Elvis Presley* and *The King Of Rock'n'Roll* box set.

When Bill Haley recorded Shake, Rattle and Roll, he made it sound like a novelty song. Elvis's approach was far more direct, redolent of the feel that had led Atlantic boss Ahmet Ertegun – one of black music's most passionate advocates in the 1950s music industry – to try to buy his contract from Sun.

Although Elvis performed the song live shortly after Joe Turner's original climbed the R&B charts, he only came to record it when he found himself a couple of tracks short for his all-important first album. Where Haley had cleaned up the lyrics, Elvis went full steam ahead – at least until A&R man Steve Sholes pointed out that the verse about the sun shining through his lover's low-cut dress might be a bit strong. Though leaving it out meant cutting Shorty Long's piano solo, Elvis had adjusted to the change by the next take, and managed to hang on to whatever sexual innuendo – like the 'one-eyed cat, peeping in a seafood store' (!) – that Sholes wasn't hip enough to catch. Scotty Moore's phenomenal guitar solo also survived, although he was never quite able to play it again, while those happy shouts of 'Shake, rattle and roll!' on the chorus are from Elvis, Scotty, Bill and DJ, dubbed in later.

When Elvis first appeared on national television, on the Dorsey Brothers' *Stage Show*, he sang not his first single but "Shake, Rattle And Roll", segueing into a verse from another Turner number, Flip Flop And Fly. It was his gentle way of reminding viewers that the song had originated neither with himself nor with Haley, but with a black blues singer from Kansas.

13 Hound Dog

2 July 1956, RCA Studios, New York
Available on *The 50 Greatest Hits* and *The King Of Rock'n'Roll* box set.

Despite the fact that it was written by two white Jewish songwriters, Jerry Leiber and Mike Stoller, Hound Dog is regularly cited as Exhibit A in the prosecution case that Elvis ripped off black music. Leiber and Stoller wrote the song, about a woman's relationship with her gigolo, for Big Mama Thornton, who topped the R&B charts for seven weeks with it in 1953.

Though Elvis knew Thornton's hit, his version was based on a semi-serious performance by Freddie Bell and The Bell Boys that he caught in Las Vegas, while bombing at the New Frontier hotel. Bell had upped the tempo, rewritten the lyrics (throwing in the bit about catching rabbits), and turned it into a nonsense song.

Elvis got the joke, and performed "Hound Dog" live on the Milton Berle show on 5 June 1956, to almost universal condemnation from everyone over the age of thirty. The next month, on the Steve Allen show, Elvis was forced to take things further, singing it to a basset hound. Note how he wipes his hand on his jacket, as if to wipe away the indignity. Later he commented, 'That was just Steve Allen's sense of humour; me, I thought it was about as funny as a crutch.'

The very next day, he recorded "Hound Dog" in RCA's New York studio. He didn't want to, feeling it was just a novelty for his live act, but Sholes and the Colonel convinced him. It took 31 takes before he was satisfied, dropping his idea of using an 'I got a woman'-style ending (as it became known in the trade, 'the Elvis ending'). DJ drove things along with his drums, the Jordanaires supplied 'ahs' and handclaps, and Scotty played one of his inimitable guitar solos. Dominating it all was Elvis's rasping, indignant, vocal.

To Jerry Leiber, who liked neither the joke nor the rendition, 'it was just a lot of noise'. The noise sold seven million copies, reaching number one on the pop, country and R&B charts. Blues fans prefer Thornton's version, arguing that Elvis made the lyrics incomprehensible. But listen to the way Elvis spits out, 'Well they said you was high class,' and it's obvious he's singing to the likes of Steve Allen. In Elvis's hands, the song becomes an expression of righteous anger by a working-class hero against the people who have judged and patronized him.

THE SONGWRITERS
Leiber and Stoller

Almost as hip as they thought they were, Jerry Leiber (below, left) and Mike Stoller (right) wrote some of the 1950s best songs, including such immortals as "Love Potion Number 9", "Yakety Yak" and "Poison Ivy". It was their peculiar curse to get bored with almost all their artists very quickly indeed and they had a leaner time in the 1960s, before returning to favour for a while in the 1970s with "Pearl's A Singer".

Top of their game: Jailhouse Rock.

Bottom of their barrel: Three Corn Patches. 'I said ay' indeed.

◀ Elvis kicks off an 'emotional revolution' with "Hound Dog" on Milton Berle

14 Don't Be Cruel

2 July 1956, RCA Studios, New York
Available on The 50 Greatest Hits.

Sam Phillips was in the car when Don't Be Cruel came on the radio. The Sun king was so entranced that he pulled off the road in order to listen properly. Finally, Elvis and RCA had found the groove.

It took Elvis, drained perhaps by his exertions on "Hound Dog", more than two dozen takes to find that groove. Written by black singer Otis Blackwell, "Don't Be Cruel" went on to become an R&B number one. Intriguingly, although R&B singer Wynonie Harris called this his favourite Elvis song, the biggest influence

The Jordanaires give it some doo-wop on "Don't Be Cruel"

lowed-by-guitar-chord ending sounds as though borrowed from Dino's 1955 hit Memories Are Made Of This, as does the relationship between Elvis's lead vocal and the Jordanaires' backing.

In Las Vegas that November, Elvis was surprised to hear "Don't Be Cruel" performed live by Jackie Wilson, then singing with Billy Ward and his Dominoes. When he dropped into Sun on 4 December 1956 for the 'million dollar' sessions, he reported that 'there was a guy out there doing a take-off of me doing "Don't Be Cruel" … he tried so hard he got much better boy, much better than that record of mine.'" Elvis then slowed the song down, trying to duplicate Wilson's 'Yankee' accents on words like 'tellyphone', and the way he howled the last part, about not wanting another love.

THE SONGWRITERS

Otis Blackwell

The singer and songwriting genius who wrote "Fever" and "Great Balls Of Fire", also supplied three of Presley's finest, "Don't Be Cruel", "All Shook Up" and "Return To Sender". Stopped writing for Elvis in 1964 after his title song for Roustabout was rejected. Also sang his own demos, originating some of the mannerisms Elvis made famous.

Top of his game: All Shook Up.

Bottom of his barrel: We're Coming In Loaded is as bad as Otis got for Elvis.

On the Ed Sullivan show on 4 January 1957 – the legendary time the cameras panned away as Elvis started to sway – he sang "Don't Be Cruel" just as he had described Wilson doing it. By the time he reached the final howl, the studio audience were, to use a technical term much in use in the 1950s, gone. From then on, whether in the 1968 TV special or on stage in the 1970s, there was always a hint of Wilson in Elvis's "Don't Be Cruel". Nonetheless, his own version also influenced others. Critic Dave Marsh says that the Big Bopper, of "Chantilly Lace" fame, made an entire career out of the 'hmmmm' that Elvis used to change the song's gear.

15 *Love Me*

1 September 1956, Radio Recorders, Hollywood

Available on *The 50 Greatest Love Songs* and *The King Of Rock'n'Roll* box set.

After Elvis's version of "Hound Dog" had transformed what was originally a serious song into something of a joke, Jerry Leiber and Mike Stoller attempted to turn the tables by giving him Love Me, which they'd written as a spoof country-and-western number. Elvis, however, out-trumped them. He sang it completely straight, with such obvious sincerity, that Leiber and Stoller were ultimately forced to acknowledge it as one of their favourite Elvis recordings. Later, in a classic Presley irony, he took the song back to parody again, using it in his 1970s live performances to give away as many scarves and kisses as possible.

Elvis cut "Love Me" just a week after recording the better-known ballad Love Me Tender. Though it was the latter that became a million-seller, he sounds more confident – more, well, like Elvis – on "Love Me". He couldn't match the world-weary sophistication of Dean Martin, but he succeeded brilliantly in recreating the intimacy between singer and listener that was part of Dino's charm.

Three other 1950s ballads bear comparison with "Love Me": Anyway You Want Me, the urgent and passionate flip side of "Love Me Tender"; Don't, another Leiber and Stoller ballad, on which Elvis pledges eternal love with the stop-start rhythm of so many back-seat romantic encounters; and Young And Beautiful, sung with an adolescent emotional purity and downright naivety that's astonishing coming from the larynx of a 22-year-old multi-millionaire.

16 *All Shook Up*

12 January 1957, Radio Recorders, Hollywood
Available on *The 50 Greatest Hits* and *The King Of Rock'n'Roll* box set.

Were it not for a fizzy bottle of Coke, **All Shook Up** would never have existed. A friend of black singer **Otis Blackwell** fizzed up a bottle of the real thing, then challenged him to include the words 'all shook up' in a song. Blackwell duly obliged, combining some of his finest lyrics with a shuffling rhythm that seemed certain to produce a massive hit.

Even so, two 1956 versions of "All Shook Up", by Dave Hill and Vicki Young, had met with little success by the time Elvis heard the demo. He swiftly recognized its potential, in part because 'all shook up' was already becoming a catchphrase. Settling for a perfect tenth take, he made sure it was released as his next single.

Although "All Shook Up" was much more obvious **classic commercial pop** than anything Elvis recorded at Sun, it shared something of the air of those early Sun sides. The sense of freedom in the vocal, the absence of DJ Fontana's pounding drums, the simplicity of the instrumental backing (partly owing to the slightness of the melody), even Elvis slapping the back of his guitar for percussive effect, all hark back to more innocent days. Above all, Elvis was at his most **playful**, messing around with the pauses after 'I'm in love' and sprinkling 'ooh ooh's and 'yeah yeah's throughout.

"All Shook Up" was one of the few oldies of which Elvis never seemed to tire; there's a more aggressive live version, for example, on the *Elvis In Person* album. If **Teddy Bear**, as featured in the film *Loving You*, was a synthetic, almost self-parodying, example of Presley's pop mastery, "All Shook Up" is very clearly the real thing. The Beatles recognized as much, adding 'yeah, yeah, yeah!' to **She Loves You** in conscious tribute.

251

17 One Night

23 February 1957, Radio Recorders, Hollywood
Available on *The King Of Rock'n'Roll* box set.

On 18 January 1957, Elvis Presley covered **Smiley Lewis's One Night Of Sin**, a song co-written by **Dave Barthomolew**, Fats Domino's longtime collaborator. On that version, first released in 1980, he sounded at his very bluesiest; he could be black. In the moral climate of the 1950s, however, a man recently denounced by a minister as a 'whirling dervish of sex' could clearly not release a regretful reminiscence about a night of sin. A month later, therefore, Elvis recorded his more familiar version, **One Night**, cleaning up the lyrics but, if anything, adding even more vocal intensity. It became a top ten hit on *Billboard*'s R&B chart.

It's often assumed that the first version is the 'real' one, which Elvis would have preferred to release. Even without the precedent set by "One Night Of Sin", however, "One Night" is a suggestive masterpiece. Second time around there's no regret, just anticipation of a night of infinite promise – a sense of lust, love and excitement so intense that Elvis can barely contain himself. You don't need explicit lyrics to know what exactly he's 'now praying for'.

Elvis sang "One Night" again in 1968, at a moment of triumphant personal rediscovery, in the Burbank TV studios. After initially losing his way on the climax of 'too lonely, too long', he perseveres, to create a performance with the same edge as those from eleven years earlier. The fact that he dropped in Smiley Lewis's line about making the earth stand still was seen at the time as a memory lapse, but it was surely a genuflection to the song's original roots.

18 Jailhouse Rock

30 April 1957, Radio Recorders, Hollywood
Available on *The 50 Greatest Hits* and *The King Of Rock'n'Roll* box set.

For all but those purists who think Elvis was at his best before they put drums on his records, Jailhouse Rock is impossible to resist, right from the moment the most distinctive intro in rock music history slams into life. That opening, devised by drummer DJ Fontana with Scotty Moore, was taken from a 1940s swing version of Verdi's The Anvil Chorus.

Elvis hasn't got a partner. but bravely refuses to use a wooden chair

253

DJ says he tried to think of people breaking rocks on a chain gang as he played. Just what writers Jerry Leiber and Mike Stoller were thinking of, on the other hand, is far from clear. The lyrics that Elvis howls are at best satirical, and at worst positively sub-versive – witness the lines about number 47 and number 3, hint-ing at what really happens when too many jailbirds of the same sex are cooped up together. Mind you, the verse where Bugsy turns down Henry's plan for a quick breakout, so he can stick around while he gets his kicks, ranks among the finest in the Leiber/Stoller canon.

Elvis doesn't seem to care, delivering the intricate, exuberant words with a sincere hollering conviction that he never quite matched again. A minute or so in, he cries, 'Let's rock, rock, rock', and lets the musicians take over. Perhaps he's pausing for breath; perhaps he just thinks that Dudley Brooks' piano, Scotty's power chords, Bill Black's walking bass and DJ's dramatic drumming deserve their moment of glory.

No matter, "Jailhouse Rock" is a *tour de force*, with the power to set feet tapping independent of the owner's will. As country singer Garth Brooks tells it, 'I'm sitting in the drive-through and I've got my three girls in the back and this station comes on and it's play-ing "Jailhouse Rock", and my girls are jumping up and down, going nuts. I'm looking around at them and they've heard Dad's music all the time and I don't see that out of them.' Though it has been covered many times since, only the Blues Brothers have emerged with any credit – appropriately enough, given Leiber and Stoller's satirical intent.

19 Trouble

15 January 1958, Radio Recorders, Hollywood
Available on *King Creole* and *The King Of Rock'n'Roll* box set.

Trouble may be the most aggressive song that Elvis ever per-formed. Leiber and Stoller, who wrote it for him, thought it was too hard for Elvis to handle convincingly. Muddy Waters might be able to carry off heavy stuff like 'If you're looking for trouble, you came to the right place', but Elvis? As a couple of self-appointed hipsters, they found it all a bit comical; the mass market, however, failed to share their reservations.

In truth, Leiber and Stoller – who had already grown bored with their role in the Elvis organization, though not with Elvis himself – had created a frankly weird amalgam of Chicago blues, Dixieland jazz, and rock. In anyone else's hands, things could have gone badly wrong. Elvis, however, sang "Trouble" with unrestrained ferocity, doing his very damnedest to sound like the bad-tempered offspring of a green-eyed mountain jack it proclaimed him to be.

"Trouble" became something of an anthem for Elvis. By the time he returned to it as the running theme for his 1968 TV special, the rough edges on his more mature voice gave the lyrics added menace. Watching that show at Graceland, stepbrother Rock Stanley recalled, 'Everybody laughed when he said that, and Daddy just smiled and slapped his knee and shouted, "Mah boy!"'

The ultimate irony, which even the masters of irony who wrote it failed to notice, was that the song was sung by a singer of such great passivity, especially in the 1960s, that record producer Phil Spector was convinced that he had been hypnotised. In Alan Bleasdale's musical biography of Elvis, *Are You Lonesome Tonight?*, it's Elvis's twin Jesse who sings "Trouble". His death, Bleasdale suggests, had left the surviving brother psychologically incomplete.

20 It's Now Or Never

3 April 1960, RCA Studio B, Nashville
Available on *The 50 Greatest Hits* and *From Nashville To Memphis* box set.

For rock critic Charlie Gillett, author of *The Sound And The City*, It's Now Or Never marked the point when Elvis's decline became 'official'. Presley didn't see it like that. 'When I was in the Army I called home and I said "Write lyrics to 'O Sole Mio'" and they thought I was nuts, you know, they thought, "He's from the south, he can't even sing"'. The Enrico Caruso version of the Italian song "O Sole Mio" was one of Gladys's absolute favourites, while Elvis himself was a great fan of Mario Lanza (the two RCA stars may have met in LA), who had died in Italy in 1959. As the first Elvis performance to show Lanza's influence, "It's Now Or Never" may well have been intended as a memorial.

Tony Martin had already had a hit with an English adaptation of "O Sole Mio" in 1949, with "There's No Tomorrow". Martin's version was covered by the R&B group The Clovers, and Elvis can be heard singing it in Germany on *In A Private Moment*. While Elvis loved the new lyrics for "It's Now Or Never", provided by Aaron Schroeder and Wally Gold, he admitted to Schroeder that 'I don't know if I can do this song justice.'

It was the final dramatic flourish, worthy of Lanza himself, that troubled him. He wanted, he said, to sing the notes he could hear in his mind. Trying to help, the engineer Bill Porter said they could splice on the ending separately. Elvis replied: 'Bill, I'm going to do it all the way through or I'm not going to do it.'

In a rare public reference to a specific song, Elvis commented, 'It wasn't rock'n'roll but it had a beat behind it. I thought it turned out pretty good.' With its pizzicato-picked mandolin in the background, Floyd Cramer's overdubbed castanets, and that operatic cadence, it was indeed a long way from rock'n'roll. Sixteen years later, when Elvis's voice (and weight) had grown closer to Lanza's, he returned the song to its roots in concert, asking Sherrill Nielsen to sing Caruso's "O Sole Mio" before he sang the heart out of "It's Now Or Never".

21 Are You Lonesome Tonight?

4 April 1960, RCA Studio B, Nashville
Available on *The 50 Greatest Hits* and *From Nashville To Memphis* box set.

Bill Porter, the sound engineer when **Are You Lonesome Tonight?** was cut, insists: 'Listen on a high-quality playback system, and you'll hear Elvis bumping into a microphone stand.' To create the right mood, Elvis had chased everyone out of the studio, and insisted the lights be turned down. Though that set the tone beautifully, it also meant that he couldn't see where he was going.

Even coming after "It's Now Or Never", the day before, "Are You Lonesome Tonight?" was an unusual song for Elvis to record. It was the Colonel's idea; the song was a favourite of his wife, and had featured in the repertoire of **Gene Austin**, one of Parker's first acts. Originally a hit for **Al Jolson** in 1927, it was probably familiar to Presley from a 1959 version by the **Blue Barron Orchestra**.

257

Elvis was always unfashionably fond of the Ink Spots, whose records invariably included a deep-voiced recitation of incredible gravity. "Are You Lonesome Tonight?" enabled him to give just such a speech, and he delivered his riff on the, 'all the world's a stage' theme from As You Like It with a sincerity worthy of the Ink Spots themselves. He was not, however, enamoured of his performance of the rest of the song, and even rejected it altogether, saying at one point, 'Throw that one out. I can't do it justice.' It went on to hold the number one spot in the US for six weeks.

In his later years, Elvis had to drop "Are You Lonesome Tonight?" from his Las Vegas repertoire, after being sent into hysterics by Cissy Houston's soprano obligato; the so-called 'laughing version' was a Top 30 hit in the UK in 1982. He rarely regained his old sincerity, preferring to change the lyrics to things like 'You seemed to change! You got fat!' If the song now seems over-familiar as a result, just go back and listen to the simplicity of the original.

22 Reconsider Baby

4 April 1960, RCA Studio B, Nashville
Available on *Elvis Is Back* and *From Nashville To Memphis* box set.

Elvis Presley first heard blues singer Lowell Fulson perform Reconsider Baby on Memphis's Beale Street in 1954. He was so impressed that he'd sung it to his then-sweetheart, Dixie Locke. Scotty Moore also remembers jamming with Elvis and Fulson in a black club in Houston, at some point before they became really famous. Two years after the sighting on Beale, sitting around the piano in Sun Studios with Jerry Lee Lewis and Carl Perkins, he sang it again.

Elvis finally chose to record the song at the tail end of his first post-Army sessions, playing rhythm guitar just as he used to at

Sun. While Scotty Moore and DJ Fontana offer superb support, "Reconsider Baby" only erupts into splendour with **Boots Randolph**'s steamy **saxophone solo**. This is the first (and the best) sax solo on an Elvis record, and it's so good that Elvis makes Randolph do it again, mumbling, "'Yeah… one more time,' and urging Boots on with the occasional, admiring 'yeah!'"

Though obviously inspired by Fulson, Elvis's vocal is not a note-for-note copy. Where Fulson pleaded with the girl to reconsider, Elvis sounds as though he's threatening her. If anything, he sounds more like fellow Sun artist **Little Junior Parker**. He wouldn't get this bluesy again in the studio until he cut **Stranger In My Own Home Town,** nine years later.

Elvis returned to the song at New York's Madison Square Garden in 1972. As **Robert Plant** recalls, 'He was singing some pap and then in the middle of it he stopped and began to sing "Reconsider Baby", and straight away the hairs shot up on the back of my neck.' Although this later version is more sedate, James Burton's guitar licks and Glenn D Hardin's tinkling piano still go to prove how well his 1970s stage band knew the blues.

23 Can't Help Falling In Love

23 March 1961, Radio Recorders, Hollywood
Available on *Blue Hawaii* and *The 50 Greatest Hits.*

Hugo Peretti and **Luigi Creatore**, the RCA staffers best known for crafting Sam Cooke's studio sound, linked up with **George Weiss** to turn the eighteenth-century French melody **Plaisir d'Amour** into the fatalistic love song **Can't Help Falling In Love**. Now recognized as one of the best songs to come off the Hill & Range assembly line, it was heading for the reject pile until Elvis heard it, rescued it and suggested it might be good for the movie *Blue Hawaii*.

259

The song's substance made a welcome change for Elvis, who had just done his best to make "Moonlight Swim" into something more than a soundtrack filler. He was so taken with "Can't Help Falling In Love", in fact, that he persevered for 29 takes. In the film version, he sings the first lines backed only by Dudley Brooks' celeste, which makes the song feel more genuinely Polynesian. On record, the celeste is used for accenting, with the piano arpeggios taking centre stage and Alvino Rey's steel guitar chipping in.

So what if the arrangement is a bit corny, the steel guitar is slightly intrusive, and the Jordanaires are much too far up in the mix, almost fighting with Elvis instead of supporting his vocal? Elvis rises above it all with a superbly phrased vocal performance, full of that mysterious yearning heard by Sam Phillips all those years ago. The movie version, now released on the extended *Blues Hawaii* CD, is shorter, but it's almost as charming.

Today, the sweet power of Elvis's original tends to be overshadowed by the slightly ironic, speeded-up, renditions with which he closed almost all his concerts from 1969 onwards. He often seemed to turn the song into an oblique commentary on the reactions of his fans. The most enigmatic version of all came in concert on 30 March 1977, when he forgot the words and sang, 'Wise men know, When it's time to go . . .' Accidental or deliberate? Who knows?

24 (Marie's The Name) His Latest Flame

26 June 1961, RCA Studio B, Nashville
Available on *The 50 Greatest Hits* and *From Nashville To Memphis* box set.

It took a hell of a lot of work to make (Marie's The Name) His Latest Flame sound so effortless. Written by Doc Pomus and Mort

Shuman, the song had previously been turned down by Bobby Vee, who presumably felt it wasn't up to the standards he'd set for himself with hits like "Rubber Ball". Elvis, however, warmed to it straight away, saying, 'It's a good song, I like it even if it takes us 32 hours.' It almost did, but in the end they came up with a masterful Latin-tinged slice of pop, driven by a Bo Diddley beat, starring Elvis on top form.

The early takes were a mess. Drummer Buddy Harman started off on congas, with saxophonist Boots Randolph on shakers; Floyd Cramer unleashed the very organ that had just destroyed "I'm Yours"; and Hank Garland floundered with varying levels of tic-tac guitar. Finally, someone called Shuman himself, who, although he had studied music at the New York Conservatory, was a passionate exponent of R&B piano, and asked him how he had played the piano part on the demo. Only when he listened to the song later did Shuman realize that his attention-grabbing intro was only three bars long, rather than the usual four.

While "His Latest Flame" may not be out-and-out rock, neither is it as smooth as most of Elvis's early 1960s ballads. Released as a single with Little Sister, it sold slightly less than "Surrender". Following on from the relative failure of the bluesy I Feel So Bad, that seemed to confirm that in pure commercial terms, the softer and more romantic Elvis sounded, the better. But "His Latest Flame" ranks among the best pop singles of the era, and has developed a cult following, with covers by The Smiths, among others.

THE SONGWRITERS

Pomus and Shuman

Doc (Pomus) and Mort (Shuman) are second only to Leiber and Stoller for supplying Elvis's best material. The early 1960s would have been a lot duller without their "Little Sister", "I Need Somebody To Lean On", "A Mess Of Blues" and "Viva Las Vegas". Their finest non-El moment is probably the Drifters' "Save The Last Dance For Me".

Top of their game: His Latest Flame.

Bottom of their barrel: Never Say Yes: 'Always keep the girlies guessing'. Enough already?

25 Little Sister

26 June 1961, RCA Studio B, Nashville
Available on *Elvis Gold Records vol 3* and *From Nashville To Memphis* box set.

Doc Pomus and **Mort Shuman** originally intended **Little Sister** for Bobby Darin. It wasn't Bobby's cup of tea, however, so they submitted it to Elvis. Doc felt it was just the kind of nasty blues that Elvis ought to record.

Though Elvis agreed, Shuman says that he didn't follow his demo to the letter. Instead, he 'cut the tempo in half and slowed it down'. Several **unreleased takes** can be heard on the *Such A Night* CD in the *Essential Elvis* series. Even before the first one, the engineer Bill Porter declared they were making a classic. As the third gathers steam, Elvis is so enthused he tells the musicians to 'burn'. It was the fourth that became the master, but Elvis and everyone in Studio B liked the song so much they just played it over and over until 7.30am.

Hank Garland was so worried about the electric guitar part that he borrowed a Fender he felt was funkier; in the event, his solo runs set the song alight. "Little Sister" proved to be Garland's last work with Elvis before a car accident wrecked his career, but his playing here makes a perfect memorial.

Elvis must have been flattered (and amused) when blues singer **Lavern Baker**, a key influence, recorded an answer song "Hey Memphis" on the Atlantic label. He later returned the compliment, opening many a Las Vegas show with her hit **See See Rider**.

Elvis never forgot "Little Sister", singing it both in rehearsals for the Las Vegas 1970 engagement immortalized in *That's The Way It Is*, and live, running it into the Beatles' **Get Back**. He also returned to it for his last ill-fated TV special for CBS in 1977; he sang it faithfully enough, but what little life that version holds was down to **James Burton**'s guitar.

26 Return To Sender

27 March 1962, Radio Recorders, Hollywood
Available on *Elvis Gold Records vol 3* and *The 50 Greatest Hits*.

Colonel Parker gets so much bad press for condemning Elvis to interminable movie soundtracks, it seems only right to note that without him Elvis might never have sold a million with **Return To Sender**.

Otis Blackwell, who wrote the song with **Winfield Scott** but hadn't submitted it for the film *Girls! Girls! Girls!*, mentioned it when he met the Colonel at publisher Hill & Range's New York offices. Parker pressed him to play it, then told Blackwell: 'Don't worry, that will go into the movie, because it's a great song.'

For Elvis, "Return To Sender" almost compensated for the indignity of having to sing **Song Of The Shrimp**. In fact, he was so proud of it he took it back to his home in Bel Air. Fan and friend Arlene Cogan recalls, 'He told us all, "You've got to hear this. Listen to the words. I just love this song". And he played it over and over.'

"Return To Sender" was not just Elvis's last million-seller for three years, but the last great rock/pop single from a King who was on the point of losing his throne. It was also his last classic Blackwell recording; best to forget **One Broken Heart For Sale**, created by the same team, but to much less effect.

Presley had either just seen **Jackie Wilson** in concert, or, as Priscilla remembers it, Wilson was present on set when he performed it. Either way, this is, as Guralnick says, a 'witty, almost flawless interpretation of Wilson's act … the hand gestures, the boxer's shuffle, the self-amused little shoulder shrugs all suggest Wilson.' As well as being a great record, therefore, it was also an in-joke for a singer Elvis had respected since he'd seen Wilson outdo him with "Don't Be Cruel" seven years before.

27 *It Hurts Me*

12 January 1964, RCA Studio B, Nashville
Available on *Elvis Gold Records vol 4* and *From Nashville To Memphis* box set.

In the whole of 1964, Elvis only recorded three songs that weren't written for his movies. It Hurts Me, a fine ballad of small-town love and life, was one. Confined, to a supporting role on the Kissin' Cousins single, it was arguably his greatest ever B side.

Officially written by Joy Byers and Charlie Daniels (who went on to write The Devil Went Down To Georgia), "It Hurts Me" was actually half-written by Byers' husband Bob Johnston, the Columbia records producer responsible for taking Bob Dylan to Nashville. The raw material was a cut above anything else Elvis was being given to work with at the time, and he seized on the lyrics, injecting them with the same fire and indignation that he brought, five years later, to Long Black Limousine. Indeed, he comes close to pulling off the same trick, belting out a ballad of unrequited love with such anger it almost feels like a protest song.

A few more mid-1960s performances with this kind of passion and this kind of material, and Elvis might have managed to resist the British beat invasion. Instead, it took two years before Love Letters came close to matching this performance, by which time many singles buyers had stopped listening to Elvis.

Presumably by mistake, the Italian single release of "It Hurts Me" lacked both the orchestra and the Jordanaires' vocal backing. Though some aficionados prefer it, it sounds bare in comparison. By contrast, when Elvis returned to the song during rehearsals for the 1968 TV special – a version included on the *TV Special* CD – Billy Goldenberg's orchestral arrangement threatened to drown him out, and his beefier vocal lacked the delicacy of the original. Part of what makes the first performance so powerful is the way Elvis's voice switches so effortlessly between tenderness, scorn and indignation.

28 How Great Thou Art

25 May 1966, RCA Studio B, Nashville

Available on *How Great Thou Art* and *Amazing Grace*.

In a rare burst of braggadocio, Elvis once claimed he knew every gospel song in existence. That may sound like hollow youthful boasting, but it was a point which Presley was always happy to prove at the piano.

His recording of How Great Thou Art, which was written in Sweden in the 1880s, can be seen as an attempt to console himself for never breaking into a gospel quartet as a teenager. Although Felton Jarvis was nominally in charge of the session, Elvis arranged the song in the studio, structuring it so that he could take every part of the four-part vocal, starting deep and hitting a marvellous top F right at the end. He sang it slower than the Statesmen recording he loved, because he felt it sounded more spiritual that way.

James Blackwood, a member of one of the quartets that hadn't been able to find room for Elvis, saw him perform "How Great Thou Art" as far back as 1956, in Fort Worth; he 'really belted out a top A'. More recently, Elvis and Charlie Hodge had been singing it at home in the spring of 1966.

The atmosphere in the studio that night was astonishing. Jerry Schilling, not normally a man given to hyperbole even where Elvis was concerned, remembers: 'Something almost frightening happened on that song – he turned white and almost fainted. The only way I can describe it is that it's as if his inner being was leaving his body. Something definitely happened on that song. At the end, I thought he was going to pass out.'

Something invariably happened whenever Elvis sang "How Great Thou Art" thereafter, especially in Memphis in 1974 – a powerful Grammy-winning version featured on *Live On Stage In Memphis* – and in one of his last concerts, on 19 June 1977 in

265

Omaha, when he daringly injected a hint of the blues. However out of it he might have been, the song always seemed to call him back to the task in hand, even if some renditions were almost too emotional for secular fans.

29 Tomorrow Is A Long Time

26 May 1966, RCA Studio B, Nashville
Available on *Tomorrow Is A Long Time* and *From Nashville To Memphis* box set.

Elvis had never sung a **Bob Dylan** song in the studio before **Tomorrow Is A Long Time**. He probably wouldn't have recorded this one were it not for the black Alabamian folk/blues singer **Odetta**, who performed it on *Odetta Sings Dylan*. Like Elvis's favourite folkies **Peter, Paul and Mary**, she made Dylan's songs more accessible to Elvis than Dylan himself ever could.

Inspired by a session in which he had already cut four classic gospel performances, it only took Elvis three takes to feel that he had the song in the bag. His haunting vocal performance was entirely free of histrionics or melodrama; just redolent with the delicacy and purity he could no longer bring to the endless movie songs. Together with Chip Young and Scotty Moore, **Charlie McCoy**, who had played on Dylan's *Blonde On Blonde*, provided a hypnotic, lilting **acoustic guitar** accompaniment.

Elvis may have lacked Odetta's edge, but he showed just as much soul. He sounded perfectly at ease, something he failed to repeat when, some time that year, fooling around with the boys over an instrumental version of **Blowin' In The Wind**.

Although "Tomorrow Is A Long Time" was not an especially commercial performance, it might, if released as a single, have startled those who now saw Elvis as an archeological relic. It says something about how out of touch the Elvis machine had become that this fine performance ended up instead as a bonus track on the soundtrack to Spinout. At least Dylan himself heard it, and declared it to be his favourite cover version: 'It was very simple; just this guy and these guitars.' It's one of a handful of Presley recordings that leaves you contemplating musical roads not taken.

30 I'll Remember You

12 June 1966, RCA Studio B, Nashville
Available on *Tomorrow Is A Long Time* and *From Nashville To Memphis* box set.

Elvis was only due in the studio for the sessions that resulted in I'll Remember You because RCA wanted a Christmas single. Just to show that he wouldn't be pushed around, he failed to turn up for the first night, citing a sore throat. He sent Red West along instead, armed with amphetamines and accompanied by his 'Memphis Mafia' colleagues Lamar Fike and Charlie Hodge; they dubbed vocals to three songs while the musicians laid down the tracks.

Although producer Felton Jarvis had those first acetates delivered to Elvis's hotel room, another day went by before Elvis finally made it to the studio. It took him just thirty minutes, and seven takes, to record all three songs. That might sound lackadaisical, but it's clear from the start of "I'll Remember You" that Elvis was completely captivated by the aching romance of the song.

On his best version, the unedited master on the 1960s box set, Elvis's vocal is as pure and clear as ever, but the extra time makes the song even more heartbreakingly beautiful by slowing the tempo down almost to a stop. Chip Young is on gut-string guitar, while the beautifully played backing sounds so full thanks to the contributions of two saxophonists, two drummers and two pianists. Sadly, however, "I'll Remember You" ended up buried as a bonus song on the *Spinout* album.

267

"I'll Remember You" may just be the only Elvis ballad to have been written by a former sword dancer. Hawaiian singer-songwriter **Kui Lee** died of throat cancer just six months after Presley recorded it, and the most affecting of his many subsequent live performances of the song came at the *Aloha From Hawaii* concert, which was a fundraiser for the Kui Lee Cancer Fund. Even then, singing it slightly faster but with almost as much feeling, he didn't quite manage to recapture either the precision, or the haunting melancholy, that he achieved in the studio in June 1966.

31 *Guitar Man*

10 September 1967, RCA Studio B, Nashville
Available on *Tomorrow Is A Long Time* and *From Nashville To Memphis* box set.

When Elvis heard **Guitar Man** on the radio, he immediately decided that this first-person fable of life in the music business was perfect for him. When it came to recording it, however, nobody could duplicate the guitar sound of its author, **Jerry Reed**. Eventually, producer Felton Jarvis decided that the best way to match the original was to find Reed himself.

Summoned from a fishing trip, the country singer-songwriter was whisked to the studio, where he famously observed that 'Elvis looked so good I wished I was a woman'. Reed soon took over the session, explaining that they would kill themselves trying to do all the guitar work at once.

Elvis hadn't worked with anybody this inspirational, and just plain different, since the Leiber and Stoller days. You can hear the enthusiasm in his voice as he invites Reed to 'Show 'em, son.' The 1960s box set reveals, for the first time, that he segued into a burst of **What'd I Say**, so keen was he to keep the momentum going. Reed took charge of the next song too, helping to mix country and

R&B funkiness on Jimmy Reed's blues standard Big Boss Man, one of Elvis's grittiest performances for years.

"Guitar Man" became even more firmly associated with Elvis when, along with Trouble and rewritten to make it even more relevant to Elvis's life, it became the theme for the 1968 TV special. Strangely, however, he's not known to have sung it when he returned to live performance, possibly because he decided no one could match Reed's guitar work.

Four years after Elvis's death, RCA released a remixed "Guitar Man", with Elvis's vocals backed by a new band, produced by Felton Jarvis. All that can be said in its favour is that it knocked the Bellamy Brothers off the number one spot in the country charts.

32 If I Can Dream

23 June 1968, Western Recorders, Burbank
Available on *Elvis NBC TV Special* and *The 50 Greatest Hits*.

When Elvis first heard the demo of If I Can Dream, which closed his 1968 comeback TV special, he turned to the show's producer Steve Binder and said: 'I'm never going to sing another song I don't believe in, I'm never going to make another motion picture I don't believe in.' Of all the 'if only' moments in the Presley story, that has to be the most poignant.

The TV special was originally scheduled to end with I'll Be Home For Christmas. Binder, however, desperately wanted a mind-blowing finale. He told Earl Brown, who was in charge of the vocal arrangements, to 'write me the greatest song you ever wrote'. Binder had been struck by Presley's despair when Robert Kennedy was shot in Los Angeles that June, and said, 'I wanted to let the world know that here was a guy who was not prejudiced, who was raised in the heart of prejudice, but who was really above all that.'

269

Binder's phone rang at 7am the next day; Brown announced jubilantly, 'I've got it.'

Binder agreed. So did Elvis. And so, after some fulminating, did the Colonel. Elvis sang "If I Can Dream" as if he were on trial, his voice acquiring rough edges long unheard on an Elvis ballad. Critics said that was because he couldn't master the song, but no one who has sung it since, smoother, has come close to matching his performance. Binder recalled Elvis 'in the darkened studio … writhing on the cement floor in an almost foetal position'. After he had recorded it, he sat listening to endless playbacks, as if he couldn't quite believe what he'd done.

No matter how fuzzy it might be, there was a message in "If I Can Dream", with its obvious references to Martin Luther King's 'I have a dream' speech. It was, after all, recorded less than three months after King had been assassinated in Elvis's hometown. It also had a clinching line – 'as long as a man has the strength to dream, he can redeem his soul' – that seemed to echo Elvis's most deeply held beliefs, a line his very life story seemed to support.

33 *Love Me Tender*

29 June 1968, NBC Studios, Burbank
Available on *Elvis – NBC TV Special*.

To most fans, the classic version of Love Me Tender – a ballad based on the gorgeous folk air Aura Lee – will always be the one Elvis cut on 24 August 1956, on the soundstage of Twentieth Century Fox. That would probably have soared to number one even without the aid of the eponymous movie, despite the complaints of conservative critics that you could hear Elvis's breathing, as if that were yet more proof of his indecency.

In June 1968, however, the 33-year-old singer found himself trying to resurrect his career, in front of glaring TV cameras and a hand-picked audience that included his new wife, Priscilla. After rushing through Blue Suede Shoes, he wanted to slow things down, partly, as he complained, because he was almost melting in his black leather suit. He starts off "Love Me Tender" with a joke, 'You have made my life – a wreck – complete', then adds a parody of his own singing before he changes gears to deliver a heartfelt reading.

Sung in a richer, deeper, voice than he had possessed twelve years previously, and aided by slightly over-the-top orchestration, the song acquired an emotional depth that wasn't quite there in the more naive, romantic original. Was Elvis remembering how he sang it over the phone all those years ago, to his first fiancée June Juanico? No matter – as he draws to a masterful conclusion, it's impossible not to believe in his love. He seduces the audience, the cameras, his listeners, maybe even himself, just as, in the emotional sense, he seduced June, Anita, Priscilla, Ann, Linda, Ginger and countless others.

271

◀ 'As long as a man has the strength to dream' – Elvis reclaims his destiny

34 Long Black Limousine

13 January 1969, American Studios, Memphis
Available on *From Elvis In Memphis* and *From Nashville To Memphis* box set.

In Memphis in the summer of 1955, Elvis warned his baby about the perils of pink Cadillacs. Fourteen years later, in the first recording of his legendary Memphis sessions, he rebuked his beloved with a very different vehicle: a Long Black Limousine.

This dark tale of a lover who left for the big city, promising to come back in a fancy car but only to return in a hearse, had been a minor country hit for Jody Miller the year before. Though in many ways Elvis was that small-town boy who fell for the bright lights, that didn't prevent a performance that, as Greil Marcus argued, smashed gloriously through the contradictions of his own myth.

From the moment the bells toll with funereal foreboding, "Long Black Limousine" is clearly Elvis's darkest record since Heartbreak Hotel. The ominous guitar chords from Tommy Coghill as he ends the first verse augment the general air of menace. Producer Chips Moman added horns and strings, as well as the backing singers, who chorus 'You're riding in a long black limousine' with such soulful, dismissive self-righteousness.

Thanks in part to a cold, Elvis's voice has a rough edge that makes the song more than just a maudlin country ballad. Peter Guralnick, in his original *Rolling Stone* review, spoke of 'a fierce, almost shocked indignation … the passionate intensity of Elvis's voice transforms a fairly ordinary song into a vehicle for savage social protest'. Almost as shocking is how, having attacked his love for her reckless ways, Elvis finally and painfully admits that his heart and his dreams will go with her to the grave.

35 In The Ghetto

20 January 1969, American Studios, Memphis

Available on *From Elvis In Memphis* and *From Nashville To Memphis* box set.

In a decade as politically hypersensitive as the 1960s, most white multi-millionaires singing about cold grey mornings in Chicago ghettos would have sounded, at best, patronising and, at worst, like a bad joke. Songwriter Mac Davis, who wrote his first song after seeing Elvis in Lubbock, Texas, in 1954, was so nervous when asked to perform In The Ghetto for his hero that he was truly shaking like a leaf. Elvis tried to put him at ease, assuring the writer 'That's a smash'. The question was, would it be a smash for Elvis ?

Martin Luther King had been shot in Memphis less than a year before, and, as horn player Wayne Jackson recalled, 'It was tense, specially in the parts of town that were mainly black, where Stax and American Sound were.' The studio was guarded by dogs, and there was a man on the roof with a gun minding the parking lot.

Though friends advised Elvis not to record "In The Ghetto", Presley himself seemed convinced about the song until just before the session. Only when producer Chips Moman asked if he could give it to someone else did he finally make up his mind.

According to Jackson, the doubts disappeared as soon as Elvis started to sing: 'we were actually in the ghetto, and here was Elvis singing a pertinent song about the South and the social climate of the day … chills went all over me.'

Elvis's commitment to both song and subject is obvious in the sensitivity and strength of his voice. His immaculate phrasing gently underlines the double meaning of 'well the world turns', while when the boy dies at the end, he sings not with sloppy sentimentality but with compassion. It is a consummate performance, accentuated by the grim drum rolls and the backing singers, who sound for all the world as though they are accusing the audience.

273

36 *Suspicious Minds*

23 January 1969, American Studios, Memphis
Available on *From Elvis In Memphis* and *From Nashville To Memphis* box set.

Suspicious Minds represents a triumph both of Elvis's will, and of **Chip Moman**'s. They stood their ground when the Hill & Range company, and Colonel Parker, pressured Moman to part with some of his publishing rights to the song. The producer countered by offering to refund his entire fee, and forget the whole session. When Parker's assistant Tom Diskin complained to Elvis, Presley told him to leave things to him and the producers.

The row almost sabotaged what would be the most glorious moment of a glorious session. Elvis did finally cut "Suspicious Minds", however, as the last song of his first full Memphis session. The first Elvis ballad to approach relationships in a grown-up, contemporary way, Presley's version made the original, by its author **Mark James**, sound tame. Chips had no doubt what made the difference: 'We did the arrangements about the same as on Mark's record but we had that Presley voice. Presley was a great singer, man. He could sell a song.'

The sound helped sell the song, too. At RCA, **Joan Deary**, who had awaited each new movie soundtrack with mounting apprehension, was stunned by how superior it sounded. The rippling guitar work with which it opens provides one of the most effective intros to any Elvis record, while the interaction between Elvis and his backing singers is far more sophisticated than anything previously captured on his secular recordings.

Although the fade-out/fade-in ending, added by **Felton Jarvis**, bemused Moman and discomfited some DJs – one of Elvis's friends complained that 'it almost killed the song' – "Suspicious Minds" became Elvis's first US number one for seven years. It also proved to be his last.

When Elvis first returned to live performances in Las Vegas,

274

"Suspicious Minds" formed the centrepiece of his show. There's an exquisite six-and-a-half-minute version on *Elvis In Person*. In *Aloha From Hawaii*, by contrast, when he gets down on one knee and swears he'd never lie to his lover, he looks up, grins to himself, and in a wonderful moment of self-mockery says, 'No, not much'.

37 *Stranger In My Own Home Town*

17 February 1969, American Studios, Memphis
Available on *Suspicious Minds* and *From Nashville To Memphis* box set.

The musical rebirth that flowered in Memphis in 1969 was rooted in the period at Graceland in 1966 when Elvis returned with renewed intensity to listening to music. In due course, Elvis recorded most of the favourites, old and new, that flashed across his turntable during that time; drawn from blues and country, they included such songs as Della Reese's "After Loving You" and Bob Willis's Faded Love.

Two particularly bluesy numbers featured in his American Studios sessions. His version of After Loving You brilliantly recalled the swagger of One Night. Stranger In My Own Home Town, on the other hand – written by Percy Mayfield, the so-called 'poet of the blues' – sounded like nothing Elvis had ever done. This was definitely 'his thing', however. Chips Moman stood back and let Elvis relish the moment, only stepping in later to record some rather pointless overdubs.

The lyrics could apply to Elvis's place in the contemporary music scene, or to his role in Memphis society; they also provided him with a minor catchphrase: 'You can't keep a good man down.'

Whatever was on his mind, he was obviously enjoying himself, roaming around both song and sound much as he later did on Merry Christmas Baby, and urging one of the musicians as the song fades to 'Give it a clout, give it a clout!'

In rehearsals for Las Vegas in 1970, Elvis ran through a slow, blues-laden version of "Stranger In My Own Home Town" that gave him ample scope to ad-lib. Heavily edited in order to cut out the swear words, the performance appears on the *Walk A Mile In My Shoes* box set. At one point, Elvis sings that he's going back down to Memphis to start driving that truck again, concluding with a gentle dig at the Memphis Mafia, 'Old Joe, Charlie and Richard will starve to death / Yeah, and Sonny will be in the pen'.

38 Any Day Now

20 February 1969, American Studios, Memphis
Available on *From Elvis In Memphis* and *From Nashville To Memphis* box set.

Burt Bacharach has never sounded sexier than on the tender ballad Any Day Now. At his worst, Hal David's most famous songwriting partner can sound as if his ambitions reach no higher than thinking people's elevator music. "Any Day Now", on the other hand – co-written not with David but with Bob Hilliard – offers Elvis the opportunity to convey real emotional depth. There are moments here, especially when he slows the song to a complete halt, when as Greil Marcus put it, Elvis sings 'with a naked emotion I have not heard on his recordings before or since'. He gives himself to "Any Day Now" completely, just as he did to I'll Hold You In My Heart, also on the *Suspicious Minds* album – and as he failed to do to Only The Strong Survive, which despite its 29 takes remains a little constricted.

On "Any Day Now", Elvis knows that his love will desert him, and that the 'blue shadow' will fall over town, but he's still determined to leave her in no doubt as to how he feels. As it fades to an end, his cries of 'Don't fly away my beautiful bird' become more frequent, passionate and desperate, cutting through the lavish orchestral backing.

Powerful as the climax is, it doesn't quite match the beauty of the central section, when the instrumentation is stripped right back and it's just Elvis, sounding as if he's singing to you personally with a sensitivity and precision that is genuinely moving. Though he rehearsed "Any Day Now" for his Madison Square Garden performances in 1972, sadly it never entered his concert repertoire.

39 *Polk Salad Annie*

18 February 1970, The International Hotel, Las Vegas
Available on *On Stage*.

Elvis flew Tony Joe White to Las Vegas in a private jet to see him cover Polk Salad Annie, the writer's greatest exercise in swamp rock. 'Elvis was hard and mean then, man, he looked real good,' White later recalled. 'Afterwards I went backstage, and I said to him, "You know, when you get tired of all this, I've got a place up in the Ozark mountains that is so far back in the woods ain't nobody even heard of you there. We can go up and fish and relax."'

Elvis never took Tony Joe up on his offer – at least, not before 1977 – but he did record two of White's other songs, I Got A Thing About You Baby and For Ol' Times Sake. White liked all three covers, but "Polk Salad Annie", as captured on *On Stage*, is unquestionably the most dramatic, taking the funkiness of the original and ratcheting up the tension.

While the opening monologue is largely White's, Elvis manages to sound, at different moments, just like White, a bit like Dean

277

Martin, and like a knowing send-up of himself. The words 'that's polk' served as a cue for a bump of the hip, both visually startling and an affectionate reminder of controversies and hip movements gone by. Then, with a sudden cry of 'down in Louisiana', he dives into a crazed, yet soulful, five-and-a-half-minute rendition that leaves the excellent original panting in its wake.

Elvis likes the song so much he doesn't want to let go. He pauses as the chorus of 'sock a little polk salad' builds to an irresistible crescendo, and then he drives it back up again, chanting 'Ching ching a ching ching', in frenzied counterpoint to the Sweet Inspirations' refrain of 'Chic a bom, chic a bom', until neither he, the singers, the band, nor the audience can take any more.

He rarely sounded this funky again, but he rose to the challenge of singing "Polk Salad Annie" at Madison Square Garden in 1972, stepping back to make room for some fine funky guitar, and there's also a storming harder version on the 1976 bootleg *Burning In Birmingham*. As bassist Jerry Scheff remembers, 'That was a cool song … he liked doing it because it was rock, but it wasn't Fifties rock, and he wanted to move on.'

40 *I Really Don't Want To Know*

7 June 1970, RCA Studio B, Nashville
Available on *Elvis Country* and *Walk A Mile In My Shoes* box set.

While Don Robertson wrote several songs for Elvis, including some of the few gems on his movie soundtracks, he was completely captivated by Presley's rendition of I Really Don't Want To Know: 'When Elvis sang one of my songs, I never had the feeling

279

that he was throwing them away like some artists do… he did "I Really Don't Want To Know" in a different way than it had been done before, kind of bluesy, a bit like a rock waltz with a lot of feeling.'

The song was originally a hit for the Colonel's old client Eddy Arnold in 1954. His dead-straight version left ample scope for other artists – such as Solomon Burke, the so-called 'King of Rock and Soul', who covered it in 1961 – to reinterpret it. In many ways, Burke's music occupied a similar territory to Elvis's Memphis sessions, and it's Burke's soulfulness that seems to inspire Elvis here.

The edge and feeling in Elvis voice here, especially when he extends the word 'love', in his cry of 'for my darling, darling, I love you so', into at least three syllables, recalls the best of the Memphis sessions. The band, and guitarist James Burton in particular, offer excellent support.

The world should feel doubly grateful to Robertson. This performance inspired Elvis to cut the remaining sides for *Elvis Country*, which was easily his best album of the 1970s, as well as being the only concept album of his entire career. As for the song itself, Elvis returned to it in his final concerts. Even though he can't remember the lyrics, the version on *Elvis In Concert* has a bluesy charm.

41 I Just Can't Help Believin'

11 August 1970, The International Hotel, Las Vegas

Available on *That's The Way It Is* and *50 Greatest Love Songs*.

There's a wonderful intimacy about Elvis's live recording of I Just Can't Help Believin'. If you close your eyes, and ignore the intrusive applause, it's almost as though Elvis is in your living room. It's not so much his voice, as supple, soulful and believable as that is, as the way he bosses the arrangement. As the Sweet Inspirations chorus 'This time the girl is gonna stay', he urges them to sing 'one more', and then again 'Yeah one more'. And as the song closes, he hands it over to them with a lazy, drawling, 'Take it baby'.

Written by Barry Mann and Cynthia Weil in 1968, "I Just Can't Help Believin'" had already been a hit in 1970 for BJ Thomas. That explains why Elvis's version was never a single in the US, although it did reach the charts in many other countries, climbing to number six in the UK. Elvis clearly knew Thomas's record: before singing it live in Las Vegas he joked, 'BJ Thomas has got a new record out, I don't particularly like it, but hey …'

Though both singers' versions showed strong gospel influences, Elvis's arrangement was lusher and more heavily orchestrated. This represents his Las Vegas conductor Joe Guercio's finest hour; the instrumental break provides a rare chance for his musicians to shine. Holding it all together is Elvis's interaction with the backing singers, gently nudging the song away from schmaltz and injecting the touch of soul for which he had hired the Sweet Inspirations, who had previously worked with Aretha Franklin, in the first place.

At first, the excitement of his comeback obscured the fact that the new Elvis was turning to ballads for the emotional complexity, and vocal challenge, that was no longer always found in rock songs. As Jerry Scheff put it, 'He wanted to be known for his voice and wanted songs that could show the virtuosity of his voice.' If his material and performance had always matched this standard, there would have been fewer complaints about his change of direction. "I Just Can't Help Believin'", at least, was a genuinely grown-up song, with Elvis superbly cast as the hopeless romantic who can't help believing that his next relationship will be the one to last.

42 Merry Christmas Baby

16 May 1971, RCA Studio B, Nashville

Available on *If Every Day Was Like Christmas* and *Walk A Mile In My Shoes* box set.

For a man who, by his own admission, was sloppily sentimental about **Christmas**, it is typically perverse that Elvis's two finest performances of festive songs are sexily subversive.

In 1957, he had rocked to **Santa Claus Is Back In Town**, a bad-assed Leiber and Stoller ditty in which Rudolph had been made redundant by a big black Cadillac. Although it started innocuously enough, with the Jordanaires singing a tuneful 'Christmas, Christmas', it became the kind of blues-rock that would have given Irving Berlin, the self-appointed guardian of Christmas music, an aneurysm.

Merry Christmas Baby was slower, closer to the **blues** – it was originally a blues hit in 1949 – but just as devoid of the usual festive trappings. Instead of crooning about church bells and snow, Elvis was singing about diamond rings and good music on his radio.

Hill & Range had originally suggested the song as a candidate for the 1968 TV special. Even in retrospect, that's a mouthwatering possibility. Instead, he turned to it about midnight in May 1971, in a studio decked out with Christmas decorations to try and get everyone in the festive spirit. Elvis sang as if he had just heard it for the first time, ad-libbing, coaxing one guitarist ('Dig in, James'), and scolding bass player Norbert Putnam to wake up. At the end of the first, six-minute take, he lets rip, finally screaming 'Merry Christmas baby' as if his baby is either hard of hearing or on the other side of the state line.

"Merry Christmas Baby" was easily Elvis's finest blues performance of the 1970s, although that's hardly a hotly disputed title, with its only serious rivals being a slow jam of Tiger Man and a rehearsal of Stranger In My Own Home Town. On this evidence, it's just a pity that he didn't record a blues album that May in Nashville.

43 I'm Leavin'

20 May 1971, RCA Studio B, Nashville
Available on Burning Love and Walk A Mile In My Shoes box set.

'Phew, man it's tough', Elvis declared after the first run-through of I'm Leavin', 'but the thing is worth working on.' Right on both counts. While the breakdown of his marriage to Priscilla was some months away, he needed little encouragement to pour his heart into this complex, desolate, and yet beautiful ballad, written by Michael Jarrett and Sonny Charles.

As "I'm Leavin'" opens, with its lilting chorus, Elvis sounds as though he's experimenting with his voice. But as the lyrics grow ever bleaker, his emotional need, and outright loneliness, become more obvious. The key lines 'Who will I find to lie beside me ? / To ease this emptiness inside me?', are delivered with perfectly judged feeling, steering the song past mere sentimentality into something altogether sadder.

283

Presley's performance beautifully illustrates an observation made by JD Sumner in 1985: 'I always compare Elvis singing a song to squeezing the last drops out of a wet rag. He had the ability to squeeze every drop of emotion out of every word in every line of a song.' What's more, as happened so infrequently in the 1970s, his voice, the backing vocals and the band are almost as perfectly balanced as on the Memphis sessions.

When Elvis finished "I'm Leavin'", he agreed with pianist David Briggs that it should be a massive hit. Rushed out in the US as damage limitation, after the pretentious single Life had stiffed, it wasn't. Nonetheless, Elvis returned to the song in live performance, notably on the famous occasion on 19 August 1974, when he completely reworked his Las Vegas set to introduce both more blues and more emotionally blue ballads. None of the live versions yet released, however, matches the haunting intensity of the original, which remains so depressing as to be genuinely scary.

44 American Trilogy

16 February 1972, The Hilton, Las Vegas
Available on *Walk A Mile In My Shoes* box set.

It was singer-songwriter Mickey Newbury, in 1971, who created American Trilogy by combining Dixie, John Brown's Body and All My Trials into a single song. While it gave him his first US Top 40 hit, his intent remains unclear. Some people saw it as encapsulating America's loss of innocence, but with Richard Nixon in the Oval Office and the Vietnam War ending ignominiously, most assumed it was meant ironically.

"American Trilogy" entered Elvis's concert repertoire in 1972. This being the era when he expressed his admiration for FBI director J Edgar Hoover, and made a surprise visit to Nixon to obtain a genuine federal narcotics badge, it's easy to assume that

Elvis was seized by patriotic fervour, pure and simple. His occasional habit of unfurling the Stars and Stripes during performances of this song only reinforces that impression.

In addition, however, Elvis – who had grown up, and chosen to live, in the South – could not have missed the political resonance of Newbury's selection. Charles Reagan Wilson, author of *Judgement And Faith In Dixie*, suggests that the song shows Elvis returning to his Southern roots towards the end of his life: 'His 1970s concert performances of "American Trilogy" [were] a slow, reflective, melancholy performance that suggested an emotional awareness of the complex past of regional conflict and Southern trauma.'

Apart from How Great Thou Art, no other song in Elvis's live act seemed to enthral him so consistently. The key variations in his many performances are whether Elvis helps the Stamps sing 'Oh I wish I was in Dixie' – he does so on the single version, recorded in Las Vegas, with a gorgeous, tender 'take my stand' – and whether the vital solo after "All My Trials" is played by flute or, with less impact, by trumpet. The emotional heart of the piece lies in the contrast between the gentle fatalism of 'You know your daddy's bound to die', and the bam-bam-bam triumphalism with which John Brown's body returns for the finale, imbued with majesty beyond mere melodrama.

45 *Burning Love*

28 March 1972, RCA Studio C, Hollywood
Available on *Burning Love* and *Walk A Mile In My Shoes* box set.

Elvis didn't want to record Burning Love, didn't like it when he had recorded it, and sang it as rarely as possible afterwards. And yet, as its writer Dennis Linde points out, 'He didn't sing it like that, he sang it as if he liked it a lot.'

The previous day, Elvis had lavished 24 takes on Red West's sentimental ballad **Separate Ways**. It took the combined persuasive powers of his producer, Red West, Charlie Hodge, Joe Esposito and Jerry Scheff to convince him to record Linde's Creedence Clearwater Revival-style hit. Even as he starts to sing, he doesn't accelerate into "Burning Love" with the same ease with which, eighteen months later, he would 'get it on now' in Chuck Berry's **Promised Land**. By the time he's through, however, with a sensational burst of 'hunka hunka burning love' – perhaps the King's single greatest gift to his impersonators – he has truly got into the groove.

What's odd is that it doesn't really matter. By 1972, the sheer novelty of having a **rock'n'roll** record from Elvis Presley was enough to send it to number two in the US charts. It was in any case a better rock record than most of his rivals had put out in years. Its pounding energy owed much to **Ronnie Tutt's** frantic drumming, and Linde's own guitar, which was overdubbed later; Linde describes looking nervously over his shoulder in case a figure in a white jumpsuit suddenly materialized.

Some songwriters might have been offended by Elvis's approach, but Linde had been a fan ever since he had been mystified by "Mystery Train". He also had the consolation that Elvis recorded two of his other songs with more conviction: the funky religious **I Got A Feeling In My Body**, and **For The Heart**, the only foot-tapper on the *From Elvis Presley Boulevard* album. "Burning Love" may just have been a case of the right song, at the wrong time in Elvis's life.

46 Always On My Mind

29 March 1972, RCA Studio C, Hollywood
Available on *Burning Love* and *Walk A Mile In My Shoes* box set.

In March 1972, ballads are increasingly on Elvis's mind, as is his estranged wife Priscilla

The fact that Always On My Mind was, at Elvis's insistence, coupled on a single with Separate Ways was interpreted as a public message to Priscilla. If so, the message was mixed. On this pub-jukebox classic, beloved of the emotionally bereft – more so than Willie Nelson's version, a much bigger hit in the US – the singer is pleading for one more chance to keep his girl satisfied. On "Separate Ways", on the other hand, which Elvis sings just as beautifully, he admits there's nothing left to do but go their separate ways.

Besides, it didn't take a genuine

287

emotional crisis for Elvis to warm to such a consummate ballad of regret and self-recrimination. During the 1969 Memphis sessions, when his marriage was still in pretty good shape, he had wallowed in the misery and self-accusation of Without Love.

Both the writers of "Always On My Mind", Johnny Christopher and Mark James, had tugged at Elvis's heartstrings before. James had struck gold with Suspicious Minds, while Elvis had wept the first time he heard Christopher's Mama Liked The Roses, a ballad even more sentimental than its title.

Elvis is simply himself on this song. Without doing anything too theatrical, he cranks up the emotional tension. Thus when he first sings about 'little things I could have said', he pauses before concluding 'and done', as if the admission is being wrung out of him. As the song fades out, with Elvis running through the list of 'maybe I's, it's as if he doesn't want to let it go.

47 *Good Time Charlie's Got The Blues*

13 December 1973, Stax Studios, Memphis
Available on *Promised Land* and *Walk A Mile In My Shoes* box set.

It's easy to read as much into what Elvis left out of the maudlin folk ballad Good Time Charlie's Got The Blues as into what he actually sang. A key verse is missing: 'I take the pills to ease the pain / Can't find the thing to ease my brain'. Was that too close to the bone, for a man who was by now cutting ballad after ballad that seemed to relate to the collapse of his marriage? Possibly. This being Elvis, on the other hand, he may have simply forgotten a verse; he'd just done so on the previous cut, Loving Arms.

Writer Danny O'Keefe's only hit is the melancholy tale of a man who can't grow up. Although at times it verges on self-pity, the released cut (now superseded by the remastered version on the reissued *Promised Land* CD) has a bittersweet flavour matched only by Elvis's version of Tim Baty's Thinking About You, recorded at the same time. James Burton's guitar licks in particular give proceedings a certain air of wistfulness, while JD Sumner and the Stamps' vocal support creates space for Elvis to shoulder the emotional burden. He leaves the door slightly ajar, hinting that in fact all is not quite up for Charlie, and the blues may pass.

Elvis often sang "Good Time Charlie" on stage, including at the opening of his 1974 Hilton summer season. When the lyrics referred to losing his wife, he joked, with what sounds like genuine chagrin, 'I already did that.' On the next line, about losing his life, he added with a small laugh, 'I almost did that already too.'

48 Promised Land

15 December 1973, Stax Studios, Memphis
Available on *Promised Land* and *Walk A Mile In My Shoes* box set.

Promised Land has to be the ultimate example of Elvis's unpredictability as a recording artist. In December 1973, his second sessions at the legendary Stax studios were proving much more fruitful than his first, that summer. When producer Felton Jarvis turned up on the evening of the 15th, he was hoping to tape some tracks for a forthcoming gospel album.

Instead, he found Elvis and the band laying down every Chuck Berry number they could remember. Although Elvis was a big fan, he had previously recorded only two of Berry's songs in the studio, Memphis Tennessee and Too Much Monkey Business. "Promised Land" made an unusual and unexpected third.

Berry had written it in jail in 1965, with the help of a borrowed atlas. While it gelled perfectly with his customary 'riding along in my automobile' motif, it was no coincidence that the narrator's

289

journey 'turned into a struggle halfway across Alabam'. In their drive to desegregate the South, the **Freedom Riders** had run into trouble in Birmingham and Rock Hill, South Carolina, both of which are mentioned in Berry's original. The narrator seems to be enjoying his very own freedom ride, on bus, train and jet, before ending in Los Angeles with a call to spread the good news to the folks back home.

Elvis turned the song into an ode to life on the road, faster and harder-driving than Berry's version, but neither negating the original nor being negated by it. However, Elvis could not have been oblivious to Berry's original aim and, although he doesn't mention Rock Hill, he still gets stranded in downtown Birmingham on his way to the promised land of California. In addition, the idea of a 'promised land' had by now acquired an extra resonance, as the theme of **Martin Luther King**'s last speech in Memphis before he was assassinated.

During the 1970s , Elvis was often criticized, even by some of his own musicians, for settling for a mediocre first or second take. Not this time. After they have cut a decent first run-through, he points out a wrong note by guitarist Johnny Christopher. **James Burton**'s guitar and **David Briggs**' clavinet duel and drive the song forward, the echo on 'Mississippi clean' is deliciously heavy, and Elvis's enjoyment is obvious. After storming through four takes, he sings a snatch of "Columbus Stockade Blues". Then he returns to the song in hand, propelled by Briggs' piano, and records a frenetic final take. It is a genuinely inspired performance, proving that, given the will and the material, he really could still cut it. A point he proved again on the single's (UK) follow-up, the Jerry Chesnut, Jerry Lee Lewis-inspired rocker T-R-O-U-B-L-E

49 Way Down

29 October 1976, The Jungle Room, Graceland, Memphis
Available on *Moody Blue* and *Walk A Mile In My Shoes* box set.

Way Down counts as decisive, rocking proof that Elvis didn't spend every minute of his last two years on this planet speculating about his next cheeseburger or his next envelope of medication.

Writer Laying Martine Jr, who had bought Elvis's first album at high school in the 1950s, sang his demo in Elvis's style not because he was imitating him, but it was because the style he felt most comfortable with. His publisher Ray Stevens, famous/infamous for novelty hits like "The Streak", sang the low notes at the end, then they both fiddled with the tape to make the bass notes even lower.

When Elvis came to record it, he'd just finished the wrenching autobiographical ballad It's Easy For You. Chastising himself as an 'emotional son of a bitch', he may have been in the mood to lift his and everyone else's spirits. David Briggs was at the piano; Elvis, so Ernst Jorgensen tells us in *A Life In Music*, said they only knew they really had it 'when Briggs's fingers start bleeding'.

Elvis's road band had never sounded quite this funky on record. Though Briggs' flailing piano, the throbbing bassline, and JD Sumner's limelight-stealing low notes (ending on a double low C) almost overshadow Presley himself, he was up to the challenges posed by the difficult lead vocal line and the ambitious lyrics. Producer Felton Jarvis, who invited Martine to see his song being mixed, kept telling him, 'Remember we're selling excitement here.'

This was a typically perverse way for Elvis to end his recording career. The combination of 1950s rawness and 1970s technology revealed the voice to be in much better shape than anyone suspected, as proved by the new take on *The Jungle Room Sessions* album. At a time when he was on the verge of checking out for good, he managed to summon up a performance that sounded like a man trying to start his own renaissance.

291

50 *Unchained Melody*

24 April 1977, live recording, Ann Arbor, Michigan
Available on *Moody Blue*.

During Elvis's final concert tours, he would often sit at the piano to perform Unchained Melody. Although he was a big fan of the Righteous Brothers, he always associated the song with R&B artist Roy Hamilton, one of his singing idols from the early 1950s. In fact, he first experimented with the song, trying to emulate Hamilton's breathing techniques, as far back as 1958.

When the two singers met at American Recording Studios in Memphis in 1969, Elvis was so moved that he gave Hamilton a song ("Angelica") that he had been planning to cut himself. In the last two years of his life, Elvis paid tribute to his late idol in three compelling performances. On 19 July 1975, in Uniondale, New York, he suddenly treated his audience to a piano rendition of You'll Never Walk Alone, a number one for Hamilton in 1954. On 5 February 1976, he recorded an apocalyptic version of Hurt, echoing another Hamilton recording from 1954.

As Elvis's concerts became increasingly erratic, he seemed, according to Guralnick, 'to invest every fibre of his being' in "Unchained Melody". His rendition in Ann Arbor in April 1977 marked perhaps the last time his singing really caught fire on stage. Both bursting with romantic longing, and aching with loss and grief, his voice soared with a freedom by then heard all too rarely in the studio. All that mars things is the backing track, which was overdubbed later, and, set too loudly at the end, almost drowns out Shaun Nielsen's superb falsetto.

"Unchained Melody" is not the kind of recording anyone would have expected Elvis to make, when he started out in the business back in June 1954. But like so much of his best work over the 23 years since then, it was a faithful expression of his emotional state.

The Movies

Elvis on Screen: a movie,
video and dvd guide

' I'd like to make one good film before I leave,
I know this town's laughing at me'

Elvis to co-star Marlyn Mason on the set of *The Trouble With Girls*

Accepting an award as one of the 'ten outstanding young men of America' in 1971, Elvis Presley famously proclaimed that every dream he'd ever dreamed had come true a hundred times. That was not quite accurate; the one dream he never realized was to establish himself as a serious dramatic actor. 'He still talked about it even in those last few years,' remembered his cousin Donna Presley. 'He had mastered everything else he had set out to do professionally and it still rankled with him.' Both Donna and Larry Geller insist that in the summer of 1977 Elvis was seriously considering giving up touring to try to get back into acting.

Elvis's 31 feature films and two documentaries may seem, as one fan put it, 'about as significant to his accomplishment as one of those scarves he used to give to the audience'. Collectively, however, they mark the death of a dream, without which Elvis might never have made the music on which his reputation rests today.

David Halberstam, in *The Fifties*, wrote: 'What [Presley] really wanted from the start was to go to Hollywood and be a movie star like James Dean, it was almost as if the music was incidental.' In 1956, Elvis himself described acting as 'my greatest ambition, all my life I wanted to be an actor'.

295

☆ ☆ ☆ THE MOVIE STUDENT ☆ ☆ ☆

Much has been made of the young Elvis's immersion in the musics of his youth; far less of his devotion to the movies. When his father Vernon took him to see his first film in Tupelo, he recalled, 'We couldn't let the church know anything about it.' As a boy, he watched Gene Autry and Flash Gordon in Saturday matinees, and snuck in to Bing Crosby and Astaire/Rogers musicals. At 8, he entertained school friends with adventure stories based on the Tin Woodsman in *The Wizard Of Oz*.

Though stories of Elvis brandishing a guitar at Humes High School in Memphis are legion, by his own account he dreamed of being Tony Curtis. He didn't just work as a cinema usher in 1951 to earn money; as he put it, 'I saw the movie and I was the hero of that movie.' Marty Lacker remembers, 'He saw [Curtis] in *Son Of Ali Baba*… Elvis thought he had the ideal masculine look… that shiny black hair and blue eyes. Some people say Elvis copied his haircut. I don't know because he liked Rudolph Valentino too.' Millions of teenage boys fantasized that they were the next Tony Curtis; how many idolized Valentino, who died nine years before Elvis was born? Elvis confided to cousin Billy Smith that he was fascinated by the way 'Valentino projected a lot out of his eyes'.

☆ ☆ ☆ THE NEW JAMES DEAN? ☆ ☆ ☆

Elvis arrived in Hollywood convinced of three things: he was going to act, not sing in his films; he was going to be a brunette (he told George Klein that dark-haired actors lasted longer 'than blond California types'); and that, like the actors he admired, he wasn't going to smile much. At least he got to dye his hair black.

Ludicrous as it might seem now, many in Hollywood hoped Presley would become the new James Dean, who had died, at great inconvenience to himself and the studios, in September 1955. Elvis himself played down the parallel, saying, 'I would

Looking through the lens, Elvis realises that the only fireworks on set are those Red West has thrown from the star's trailer

never compare myself to James Dean in any way because James Dean was a genius.' He had, however, seen *Rebel Without A Cause* 44 times; when he first met its director, Nicholas Ray, he got on his knees to recite pages of the script. He'd memorized not just Dean's lines but the entire movie, a habit he continued, at first at any rate, on his own movies. One of Elvis's few lasting Hollywood friends, Nick Adams, was a confidante of Dean's, while his first affair with a movie star was with Natalie Wood, Dean's co-star in *Rebel*.

Hal Wallis, who was to produce nine Elvis films, drew a different comparison from Elvis's 1956 screen test: 'I hadn't a clue how he would do; he might have been quite awful. But after a few minutes, I knew he was a natural in the way Sinatra was. And with just as much personality.' Many movie veterans agreed. Director George

297

Cukor dropped in on a Presley set in the early 1960s intending to stay an hour, but was so enthralled he stayed all day. He told Elaine Dundy: 'He can do anything. He would be a dream to direct. His comedy timing is faultless.' Hal Kanter, who directed *Loving You*, recalled: 'Philip Dunne and I were comparing notes and he said Elvis had a natural ability to perform in front of a camera. He could have been an excellent movie star and not just a freak attraction ... It never happened because Tom Parker wouldn't allow it to.'

Walter Matthau, Presley's co-star in *King Creole*, said: 'I hesitate to say he was an instinctive actor because that is almost derogatory, saying, "Well you know he's just a dumb animal who does things by instinct." No, he was intelligent enough to understand what a character was and how to play the character simply by being himself through the means of the story.'

Don Siegel, who at first balked at the task of directing Presley in *Flaming Star* – in a part written for another of Elvis's heroes, Marlon Brando – said later, 'He was very good in it. His manager thought there should be more songs. He was wrong on two counts: Elvis could have become an acting, as well as a singing, star; also, he would have been much happier. You could see that he had a lot of layers, a lot going on. God, that boy had potential.'

☆ ☆ ☆ **HIS NAME IN LIGHTS** ☆ ☆ ☆

Elvis's movie debut came not, as he had hoped, alongside Katharine Hepburn and Burt Lancaster in *The Rainmaker*, but in *Love Me Tender* – a renamed Western, spiced up with a few songs, including a multi-million-selling title tune, that recovered its costs within days. The only person less impressed than the critics was Elvis himself. As he recalled, 'That first one almost finished me off in the business. They rushed me in the thing to get my name, you know, on the marquee. And the picture wasn't all that good.'

With each of Elvis's pre-Army movies, however, there was a sense of progress made, ability stretched and lessons learned.

Loving You was a cut above *Love Me Tender*, while both *Jailhouse Rock* and *King Creole* required Presley to do more than play himself. At first, his decision not to hire an acting coach did not seem a problem; he got such glowing reviews for *King Creole* – 'Cut my legs off and call me shorty! Elvis Presley can act!' – that he may not have felt he needed one. Friends say they had never seen him happier; maybe the dream was going to come true after all.

Watching those films, you can see the truth in Quentin Tarantino's assessment: 'He's the biggest tragedy of all rock stars … He could have been a truly terrific actor if he had worked with a lot of other real actors. If ever I see *Orpheus Descending*, I think Elvis would have been the best person to play that part.'

The dream turned sour when Elvis returned from the Army. Reacting perhaps to the ridiculous roles he was being asked to play, he began to isolate himself from Hollywood, and with it any potential mentors. George Sidney, who directed *Viva Las Vegas*, recalls, 'What you knew about Elvis 15 minutes after meeting him was just about all you'd ever know; he was like a piece of glass. At the end of a long day with Frank Sinatra, Dean Martin, Clark Gable, you'd sit around together and have a lot of laughs. But not with Elvis. He had his own little troupe and you couldn't get close to him.'

Presley's first post-Army film, *GI Blues*, reasserted his box-office power, but established the pattern that between 1961 and 1963 set the rest of his film career in stone. The films that had a point or a story – *Flaming Star*, *Wild In The Country*, *Follow That Dream* – were the least successful financially. Those that stuck most closely to the emerging bland formula – *Blue Hawaii*, *Girls! Girls! Girls!* – struck box-office gold. As WA Harbinson put it in *Elvis: An Illustrated Biography*, 'If Elvis stops singing, the cash registers stop ringing and there ain't another thing to discuss.'

Viva Las Vegas (1964) was formulaic but showed what could be achieved when the ingredients were right: a good director, a sexy co-star, and some half-decent songs. *Roustabout*, made the same

299

year, was a change from the usual wholesome hero he played during this era. Then the penny-pinching Colonel Parker brought in producer Sam Katzman, the 'King of the Quickies', who slashed the production costs of *Kissin' Cousins* and *Harum Scarum* to $1.5 million. The formula was never as successful again, on celluloid or on vinyl. Hal Wallis gave up on Presley when *Easy Come Easy Go* became the first Elvis picture to lose money, in 1967. United Artists followed suit after *Clambake* in 1967, and MGM made its last film with Presley as an actor a year later.

Presley's waning magnetism at least gave him licence to experiment. More unusual offerings included the raucous slapstick of *Stay Away Joe*, in which he played a womanizing Native American, and a Western, *Charro!*, in which he didn't sing a note. The best of the bunch was the underrated *The Trouble With Girls*.

By then, the game was up. The only studios Parker could interest in making an Elvis film were Universal and a minor called National General, but in any case his disgusted client had insisted he wouldn't sign another movie contract. Presley's last fictional feature, *Change Of Habit*, was the first American film to make its UK screen debut on TV. The two documentaries that followed were praised as extravagantly as his feature films had been condemned – *Elvis On Tour* even won a Golden Globe – but that was little consolation.

☆ ☆ ☆ **THE STAR SYSTEM** ☆ ☆ ☆

Elvis's defenders describe his movies as the last products of Hollywood's star system. It was Presley's misfortune to arrive just as that system began its long, slow, death. As critic Dave Marsh put it, it was Parker's peculiar genius 'to sign Elvis to a contract at the very moment every other star was breaking free from the shackles of the studio system'. Bing Crosby and Frank Sinatra had been buoyed by the system, which put the finest talents to work on their pictures; Elvis was fatally undermined by it.

One poisonous feature of the old system that remained as strong as ever was typecasting. So although Elvis received flattering offers to appear in films like The Defiant Ones, pretexts were found to reject them. Parker's insistence on top billing for his boy prevented his playing second fiddle to Liz Taylor in Cat On A Hot Tin Roof, while the Paul Newman role in Sweet Bird Of Youth simply didn't fit with Presley's respectable post-Army image. Yet directors never quite gave up: both Roman Polanski and John Schlesinger considering working with Elvis in the late 1960s. Parker's demands also lost Presley his last chance as a serious actor, to play the declining star in Barbra Streisand's 1970s remake of A Star Is Born (see p.352).

Success is known to breed success in showbiz, but Presley's movies prove that failure can breed bigger failure. By 1962, his films were held in such low esteem within Hollywood that Edward Anhalt only agreed to write the screenplay for Girls! Girls! Girls! when Hal Wallis guaranteed he could script Becket.

Sue Anne Langdon, who twice co-starred with Elvis, admitted, 'For an actress, appearing in an Elvis movie was either a step down or a "take the money and run kind of thing"'. Stella Stevens, told she would be starring in Girls! Girls! Girls!, says 'I told Paramount the script was a piece of shit … I said I'd rather starve than do this junk so they told me if I did Girls! Girls! Girls! my next film would be with Montgomery Clift.' She never did co-star with Clift.

Of 1967's Double Trouble, Peter Biskind wrote that 'as a novice [Irwin] Winkler got stuck with an Elvis Presley movie'. Even at MGM, the only major studio still committed to Presley, producing his films was something only a 'novice' would do willingly. Winkler puzzled Parker by asking to meet the director, Norman Taurog. When he did so, 'an elderly gentleman got out of the car with difficulty, tottered slowly up the steps and extended a frail hand, covered with liver spots'. Taurog told him, 'I like to drive myself but I can't see very well … I'm blind in one eye and the other eye is going real fast.' He directed two more Elvis movies, making nine in total, before the other eye did, indeed, go. Taurog's own verdict was that 'I was proud of the job we did if not of some of the material, but I don't think Elvis ever reached his peak as an actor. I always wanted to direct him as a cold-blooded killer.'

Screenwriter Allan Weiss, who wrote six of his seven screenplays for Elvis, was under standing instructions from Wallis not to make his screenplays too deep. His morale faltered as he saw how his depressed star 'just started walking through the movies. All that natural gift, that extraordinary ability he had, squandered.'

Presley's acute awareness of how Hollywood perceived him was rammed home when he read in 1964 that Wallis, interviewed on the set of *Becket*, had said, 'To do the artistic pictures, it is necessary to make the commercially successful Presley pictures.' Wallis insists Presley never complained about being typecast, but Jerry Schilling disagrees: 'Once, we were on set, and Elvis walked up to the producer and said, "Mr Wallis, when do I get to do my *Becket*?" It wasn't that he wanted to just do dramatic pictures, he didn't mind doing light musical comedies, he just didn't want to do ten of them right after the other.'

In Wallis's words, 'We did not sign him as a second Dean or second Brando. We signed him as a number one Elvis Presley.' A defence which would be more convincing if one didn't sense that Wallis regarded number one Elvis Presley as a circus manager would his favourite performing seal. The producer challenged his critics: 'I would like to see any one of them create something out of Elvis, some dramatic presence instead of letting him be natural. There was so absolutely no point in pushing him.' On that, he and Parker agreed. In 1960, Presley's manager noted that Elvis's movies 'will never win any Academy Awards, all they're good for is to make money.' Schilling says they reflected the manager not the star: 'They were the kind of films the Colonel liked as a young man … He was always more comfortable with the tamer Elvis.'

So how is it that a star Wallis had hailed as having a Sinatra-like presence was, by the time he produced *Girls! Girls! Girls!*, starring in scripts that were inferior even to the Martin and Lewis formula movies with which he had whiled away the early 1950s?

Finances didn't help. Although the total box-office revenue of Elvis's films was over $200 million, few were massive hits, and most generated less than $5 million in the US. The budgets were skewed to maximize Presley's (and Parker's) income, with $1 million fees and a hefty slice of the profits. Schilling says, 'He knew they were spending all the money on him and none on anything else, especially the co-stars … He couldn't care less about the money, he wanted to be in a good film.' The need to stick to budget made Simone Signoret too expensive for *Wild In The Country*, and priced Juliet Prowse out of *Blue Hawaii*.

When the makers of *Elvis On Tour* interviewed Elvis in 1972, he made it clear how deeply he loathed making many of his films: 'It was a job. That's how I treated it. But I cared so much I became physically ill. I didn't have final approval on the script, which means that I couldn't tell you "This is not good for me." I don't think anyone was consciously trying to harm me. It was just Hollywood's image of me was wrong and I knew it and I couldn't say anything about it, couldn't do anything about it. I was never indifferent. I was so concerned until that's all I talked about. It worried me sick so I had to change it. I had thought they would … give me a chance to show some kind of acting ability or do a very interesting story but it did not change. They couldn't have paid me no amount of money in the world to make me feel some sort of self-satisfaction inside.'

☆ ☆ ☆ THE HAND OF THE COLONEL ☆ ☆ ☆

If, as Elvis commented, 'I didn't have final approval on the script', who did? Officially, the answer seems to be nobody. Colonel Parker maintained he never read the scripts, saying, 'For the $500,000 a picture they're paying him, plus $5000 a day overtime – they're going to offer Elvis a bad script?'" When director Gene

Elvis on the *Follow That Dream* set, refusing Parker's latest cash demand

Nelson sent Parker the script for **Kissin' Cousins**, he was told an appraisal would cost $25,000 (no small fee, out of a total budget of $800,000). Yet there is ample evidence that Parker was involved. On **Roustabout**, for example, which was set in a carnival, he did receive $25,000 as an old carny for his detailed script advice.

George Kirgo, who co-wrote **Spinout**, recalls: 'We sat down and we tried to imagine what Elvis's life was like. And we wrote that.

The next thing we knew, the head of the studio called us in and said, "The Colonel read the script and said when he does Elvis Presley's life story, he'll get a hell of a lot more than a million dollars for it." 'As for the second draft, Parker came into our office, threw it on the desk and said, "This is great. Just one thing. Put a dog in it."' Later still, the studio head told the writers: 'We can't accept this script, there's no racing in it.' *Viva Las Vegas*, in which Elvis played a racing driver, had been his biggest grossing film ever. 'You could put racing in it, couldn't you?' suggested the studio head. So they put racing in it, and told Pasternak it was called 'The singing racecar driver'. The producer said, 'No satire'.

Parker was, after all, credited as technical advisor on 24 Elvis films. Maybe he did earn his crust. He suggested to Hal Wallis in 1958 that he set an Elvis film in Hawaii. He pressured MGM to tell George Sidney to give Ann-Margret fewer close-ups in *Viva Las Vegas*. After seeing the first cut of *Harum Scarum*, he suggested it be narrated by a talking camel. He came up with the title *Clambake*, even if it was originally for what became *Spinout*. He wrote to MGM in 1967 asking them for some 'good rugged stories' for future Elvis movies. And he bombarded the makers of *The Trouble With Girls* with suggestions for the scenes in the travelling show.

Presley certainly thought Parker had a hand in the scripts. When a scene poking fun at yoga was inserted into *Easy Come Easy Go*, he immediately blamed his manager, believing this was Parker's way of getting in a dig against his new interests.

☆ ☆ ☆ THE FORMULA ☆ ☆ ☆

It's over-simplifying things to say that Presley pictures were all about girls, songs and gorgeous locations. The template was actually a whole lot more detailed than that.

Presley had to have a manly occupation (he was a racing driver three times, a boxer, a rodeo rider, a soldier and an ex-frogman) or be a professional singer. His inevitable buddy could either be as dodgy as Elvis was basically good, or straight if Presley was a lovable wide boy. Where possible, cute children should be on display; but to balance things, Elvis should get into a fight, in which he was invariably the innocent party. Thanks probably to Parker, carnivals, shows and fairgrounds were never far away. And, for reasons that remain unclear, Elvis should go to jail, be put on trial, or at least be harried by a tax inspector, before finally managing to get his car, or perhaps his speedboat, ready to win the race. It would be nice if he could also find the time to sing on the back of a truck.

The movies served their primary purpose – to make money both at the box office and, via the soundtrack album, in the shops – until the mid-1960s. A subsidiary aim was to serve as a substitute for the world tour Elvis never made. As Tom Diskin admitted in *Billboard* in 1964: 'The Colonel always says that in films Elvis can reach his fans in the remotest corners of the world – something it would take the best part of his life to do in concert appearances.' That Parker was later found not to have a valid American passport does not entirely invalidate this argument. Peter Nazareth, a professor at the University of Iowa who was living in Uganda when most of Elvis's films were released, admits, 'I was disappointed if he didn't sing a lot; we had lots of actors we could go and see but there was only one Elvis.' Even as the movies flopped ever more resoundingly in America, the formula remained popular in places like Thailand, where, says Nitaya Kanchanawan of Ramkhamhaeng University in Bangkok, 'his kind of movies fit the idea of Thai entertainment … People were happy when they left the theatre.'

The bottom-of-the-barrel Presley pictures work today as camp classics. As Alf, the cuddly sitcom alien, observed, 'Elvis was a brilliant actor. He could play anything from a singing race-car driver to a singing deep sea diver.' By the late 1960s, the fact he only appeared in movies that most people refused to watch somehow added to his aura of mystery. As the films got worse, it was as though he had retired into a twilight world where he sang only of gardener's daughters, shrimps, and chambers of commerce. Critic Pauline Kael summed up the orthodox view: 'Presley made 31 films which ranged from the mediocre to the stupid – and in that order'.

The last word belongs to Elvis: 'Who is that fast-talking hillbilly son of a bitch that nobody can understand? One day he's singing to a dog, then to a car, then to a cow. They are all the same damn movie with that Southerner just singing to something different.' In truth, the number of his movies which don't fit that stereotype is in single figures.

A note: All the following films have been available on video but some have been deleted (though you can still find them if your're persistent), presumably prior to being released on DVD. The reviews which follow focus on the Hollywood movies he made and the best of the other releases that were available as this book went to press. If you're buying a DVD, remember to check which part of the world it has been made to play on.

☆ LOVE ME TENDER ☆

Twentieth Century Fox, 1956 VHS
Director Robert Webb; **co-stars** Richard Egan, Debra Paget, Robert Middleton.

For Elvis's debut, *Love Me Tender*, Hal Wallis loaned his new star out to Fox. Elvis played Clint Reno, who marries his eldest brother Vance's fiancée (Debra Paget), thinking that Vance had died in the Civil War. Matters get complicated when Vance (Richard Egan) proves to be very much alive. Clint goes off the rails briefly but comes good in the end, just before he dies; the death scene had millions of fans weeping.

Elvis's first movie is often seen as very different to all those that followed. In many ways, however, it gave the tyro actor a foretaste of

307

Elvis movies as an autobiography

Elvis always denied that the singing hillbilly he usually played had anything to do with the real him. When you watch all of his 31 feature films, however, certain real-life themes recur so often it's hard not to conclude that the similarities are deliberate.

What are the three things we all know about Elvis Presley? That he had a **manipulative manager**; that his **mother died** when he was a young man; and that he had a **stillborn twin** brother. Now think of your favourite Elvis movie and the chances are that one of those themes surfaces somewhere. Each is discussed in more detail in the pages that follow, on p.311, p.321 and p.331 respectively.

Other echoes of Presley's life resulted from what Wallis called an effort 'to parallel his own life with his screen personality'. Minor traits, like his habit of **breaking guitar strings**, are added for verisimilitude, while his **return from the Army** is worked into *Kid Galahad*, *Follow That Dream* and *Blue Hawaii*, and his

promiscuity is alluded to too often to need underlining. The Cherokee blood in Elvis's veins may explain why he twice plays a **Native American**, sympathetically in *Flaming Star* and for laughs in *Stay Away Joe*, and declares in *GI Blues*, 'My grandmother's a full Cherokee. They don't all sit around smoking corn-cob pipes, you know.'

Perhaps the most damning way the movies parallel Elvis's real life is in their cumulative presentation of an **emotionally retarded womanizer**, with no ambition deeper than finding the right girl (even if he seldom wants to marry her), winning the race, or buying a new boat. Only very rarely does he have a responsible job: he's a doctor in *Change Of Habit*, a show manager in *The Trouble With Girls*, wants to be a writer in *Wild In the Country*, and applies to join the space programme in *It Happened At The World's Fair*. That's about it, unless you count his iffy stint as a helicopter pilot in *Paradise, Hawaiian Style*.

Elvis's first film *Love Me Tender* didn't impress critics or the star himself

the future. He would often be involved with his co-stars – here, he proposed to **Debra Paget** (who has variously said she wasn't interested and that she might have wed him but her family prevented her). He found himself singing four songs in a film he had been assured would not be a musical. And when *Love Me Tender* was released, it was **lambasted**. *Time* famously compared him to a sausage and a goldfish, while the *Hollywood Reporter* called him an 'obscene child'. The *New York Times*, alone, paid him a backhanded compliment: 'He goes at it as if it were *Gone With The Wind*'.

Even with ersatz hill-billy songs, a ghostly Elvis singing the title track to his true love, and decent direction by **Robert Webb**, *Love Me Tender* cannot quite disguise its antecedents.

309

Hal Kanter says the part of Clint Reno 'was built up for Elvis … It was originally four or five lines.' Elvis's performance is never less than watchable, always sincere, at times over-passionate, at others off-key. Richard Egan was the first of many co-stars to wonder why Elvis was so underused: 'They seemed to put him in front of a backdrop and have him sing a song. He could do that easily but he had much more depth. He showed extraordinary ability to catch on.'

According to Elvis himself, 'If you play yourself you're much better off. Like Jimmy Dean, Marlon Brando… With *Love Me Tender* I couldn't play myself because this character I was portraying was so far from me it wasn't even funny.' ***

☆ LOVING YOU ☆

Paramount, 1957 VHS, DVD
Director Hal Kanter; **co-stars** Lizabeth Scott, Wendell Corey, Dolores Hart.

As nature had never intended Elvis to be a Reno brother, *Loving You* was in a sense the first proper Elvis movie. After seeing Presley's screen test, its sceptical writer/director Hal Kanter exulted, 'This man just absolutely jumps off the screen.'

To tailor the film to his star, Kanter visited Presley in Memphis and watched him perform at the Louisiana Hayride. Apart from discovering that Elvis had memorized General MacArthur's farewell speech to Congress (just to prove he could), Kanter noted the reaction of the crowds, reproducing that excitement in his concert scenes. The movie crafted a sweetened version of the Elvis story, as orphan Deke Rivers, a singer whose talent is matched only by his innocence, is manipulated to the top by press agent Miss Glenda, brilliantly played by Lizabeth Scott.

Loving You was a blueprint for 'the Elvis Presley movie,' with a plot designed (in this case, artfully) to make room for several songs. The script was passed on to Elvis's music-publishing

The Svengali figure

Probably the highest profile **manager** in rock'n'roll history, **Colonel Tom Parker** was certainly, as a percentage of his client's earnings, the highest paid. Parker gets a sex change in **Loving You**, mutating into the more pleasing form of Lizabeth Scott, whose fifty percent of Elvis sets the benchmark for Presley's fictional managers. Elvis's cellmate in **Jailhouse Rock** makes him sign a similar deal, though Vince Everett achieves what Elvis never did, and manages to pay just ten percent. In **Fun in Acapulco**, the 12-year-old Raoul gets half of Elvis's earnings for securing bookings at the hottest nightspots. Walter Matthau plays a darker version of the Parker/Svengali figure in **King Creole**, as a mobster-manager who blackmails Elvis into signing a blank sheet of paper, telling the boy not to worry because he'll fill in all the details later. It's a compelling image, informed by the sense that the real Elvis did, indeed, sign contracts as if they were blank bits of paper. Presley's more innocuous movies give us Parker-lite. Both Bill Bixby in **Speedway** and Gig Young in **Kid Galahad** can be slippery and cynical, but turn out to be decent enough. Intriguingly, Bixby loses Elvis's money **gambling** – Parker's own gambling losses are notorious.

partner Hill & Range, whose writers submitted songs for consideration. The process worked well: Elvis got first crack at rock'n' roll standard Mean Woman Blues, while Got A Lot Of Livin To Do was a fine good-time-had-by-all romp. Kanter also began the practice of dropping in allusions to Elvis's real life. When Presley turns to Scott and asks, 'That's how you're selling me, isn't it? Like a monkey in a zoo?', it's hard not to believe Kanter is alerting the star. Later, Scott and a hard-nosed colleague sack Deke's fellow acts without telling him, an obvious parallel to the fate of Scotty and Bill.

Elvis's performance in the faster numbers gave non-Americans the chance to see the style that had enslaved the youth of America. Scott and on/off boyfriend Tex (Wendell Corey) made a fine comic duo, while Dolores Hart played Deke's sweetheart Susan as though she had already joined a convent (she did so for real after co-starring in *King Creole*). And Elvis's mother got to appear – in the audience in the final scene, clapping along as her boy sings Got A Lot Of Living To Do. Her cheerful presence, one of the rare moments when her enjoyment of her son's fame was unabashed, ensured that after her death he could not bear to watch the movie again. ★★★★

☆ JAILHOUSE ROCK ☆

MGM, 1957 VHS/DVD
Director Richard Thorpe; **co-stars** Judy Tyler,
Mickey Shaughnessy, Jennifer Holden.

'A dreadful film. An unsavoury nauseating, queasy-making film, to turn even the best insulated stomachs.' And that's one of the nicer reviews for *Jailhouse Rock*, from Donald Zec in Britain's *Daily Mirror*. MGM could not have been entirely surprised. It's a cynical, hard-bitten movie full of human vermin in which good still triumphs over evil, but very late in the day, and only just.

Elvis stars as Vince Everett, an ex-con who becomes a rock star and 'a heel overnight'. In jail, Vince's cellmate Hunk Houghton – played by Mickey Shaughnessy, an odd choice given that his nightclub act was said to consist of 'taking Elvis over the coals' – gets Vince to sign away half his earnings. Wily old Hunk does this knowing that he has hidden bags of fan mail received by Vince after his appearance on a TV special. Outside, Vince teams up with beautiful, petite Peggy van Alden (Judy Tyler, who was killed in a motorbike accident just after filming was completed) to form

312

their own record company. The rest of this entertaining film reinforces the old lesson about gaining the whole world but losing your soul. Except that Elvis, after a fight with Hunk, regains his soul and his sweetheart, and doesn't have to give the world back.

All five songs are classics, though only the title song gets the visual treatment it deserves, in a famous routine choreographed

Scotty and Bill share rare quality on-screen time with Elvis and Judy Tyler

by Elvis and Alex Romero and applauded on set by **Gene Kelly**. That's the mesmerizing highlight of an intriguing performance by Elvis. While Shelley Winters says Elvis hated making *Jailhouse Rock*, this was the kind of challenging role he had come to

313

Hollywood for. In one scene, he grits his teeth as he's whipped for involvement in a prison riot, a punishment more usually associated with Marlon Brando. The flogging may also refer to the rumour (mentioned by Elvis's cousin Billy Smith) that Vernon Presley was bull-whipped in Parchman Prison.

Perhaps the most astonishing thing about the movie is the way it damns almost every character except Peggy, including Elvis's heel/hero. The retinue he acquires, and dismisses with a click of his finger; his quaint style of dating, taking a starlet for a tour of the homes of the stars and for burgers and Coke; his manipulative manager demanding half his money – all are funhouse mirror reflections of the real Elvis. In *Elvis And Gladys*, Elaine Dundy suggests this was Parker's doing, but writers Ned Young and Guy Trosper may just have been recycling real life.

Despite critical scorn, fans rioted and *Jailhouse Rock* grossed $4 million. Along with *King Creole* and *Flaming Star*, this is one of Elvis's three great movies. Fans especially cherish the moment when, after crushing Tyler in his embrace, the lip-curling Presley tells her: 'That ain't tactics honey, that's jest the beast in me.' *********

☆ KING CREOLE ☆

Paramount, 1958 VHS, DVD
Director Michael Curtiz; **co-stars** Carolyn Jones, Walter Matthau,
Dolores Hart, Liliane Montevecchi, Dean Jagger, Vic Morrow.

For Elvis's fourth movie, **King Creole**, Herbert Baker and Michael V Gazzo adapted Harold Robbins' novel **A Stone For Danny Fisher**, turning the hero from a boxer to a singer. The working title (*Sing You Sinners*) was discarded to make room for Leiber and Stoller's fine title song, while the locale was switched from New York to **New Orleans** not for the picture-postcard settings but to accommodate Elvis's Southern accent. And, apart perhaps from **Dolores**

Hart as Elvis's virginal love interest, the casting was excellent. At first, director Michael Curtiz may have confused Elvis with his character in *Jailhouse Rock*. He was so convinced his star was a 'conceited boy' that he told Elvis to shave his sideburns and lose weight, half hoping to provoke a tantrum. Presley simply assured Curtiz, 'You're the boss', and did as asked.

On paper, the plot sounds a tad melodramatic. Against his father's wishes, Elvis gives up school to become a nightclub singer on Bourbon Street. He's successful enough for mobster Maxie Fields (Walter Matthau) to try to hire him, using blackmail after a legal approach fails. What lifts the movie is that Curtiz creates a superbly realized milieu, getting top-notch performances from a fine cast and seamlessly integrating the songs into the narrative. There is some great dialogue and for once Elvis gets to say it, telling femme fatale Ronnie (Carolyn Jones), 'That's a pretty piece of material, you ought to have a dress made out of it someday.' At the end of the shoot, Elvis walked over to Curtiz and said: 'Thank you very much Mr Curtiz, now I know what a director is.'

The critics, for once, loved *King Creole*. Paul Dehn, in the British *News Chronicle*, wrote: 'The part gives him scope to stop acting like an electrocuted baboon and to act like a human being, which he does with a new skill, a new restraint and a new charm.' The *New York Times* headline on its review simply ran, 'Elvis can act'. According to Elvis's cousin Billy Smith, 'That was his best film. He thought so too. If he'd been allowed to carry on with dramatic pictures like that, the entire story might have been different.' Yet (and this was something Parker and Wallis must have noted) *King Creole* was Elvis's least commercially successful pre-Army film, grossing less than later, skimpier, movies like *Tickle Me*. ✶✶✶✶✶

☆ GI BLUES ☆

Paramount, 1960 VHS, DVD

Director Norman Taurog; **co-stars** Juliet Prowse, Robert Ivers, Leticia Roman.

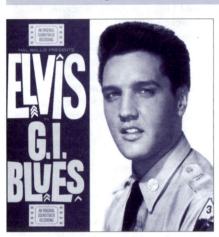

GI Blues marked the birth of Elvis as an all-round entertainer. Its flimsy plot – in which as GI Tulsa McLean he accepts a bet to spend the night with a nightclub dancer played by Juliet Prowse, then falls for her and tries to call the bet off – was really an excuse for an old-style Hollywood musical comedy. At least it was smartly done: the cast wasn't bad, it was well shot, and the script had no offensively idiotic moments, even if Elvis's limited on-screen function left Prowse, with her erotically charged nightclub act, to steal the show.

But the music had already begun to suffer; the songs weren't yet awful, and they worked reasonably well, but only Doin' The Best I Can and, arguably, Wooden Heart stand out. Colonel Parker ruled out Leiber and Stoller's songs, partly because they wouldn't share copyright and partly because they'd been urging Presley to make a movie with Elia Kazan.

Elvis, who complained about both script and songs to Priscilla and to the Colonel, consoled himself with practical jokes. He also had a fling with Prowse, even though she was engaged to Frank

Sinatra (of whom she said, 'Frank's a nice guy but he can get a bit difficult after a couple of drinks').

Presley's reservations were drowned out by box-office takings of $4.3 million, his largest since *Love Me Tender*. *GI Blues* remains a favourite with fans probably because, despite the caveats, it still offers more genuine entertainment than many of its successors. The *New York Times* said Elvis had become so wholesome he must have honey in his veins. Welcoming the new 'grown-up' Elvis, the *Times* notes: 'there are moments when the ghostly image of the youthful Bing Crosby flickers across the screen'. It was a ghost with whom star, fans and critics were to become more familiar. ★★★

☆ FLAMING STAR ☆

Twentieth Century Fox, 1960 VHS
Director Don Siegel; **co-stars** John McIntire,
Dolores Del Rio, Steve Forrest, Barbara Eden.

Though arguing as to whether the moody Western *Flaming Star* is a better film than *King Creole* is as fruitful as trying to decide whether "Suspicious Minds" is better than "Mystery Train", critic Philip French is firmly in the *Flaming Star* camp: 'this is by some way his best picture … He turns in a fine performance as a half-breed torn between two cultures.' Written originally for Brando, it's certainly Elvis's best post-Army film. He plays Pacer, a half-breed Kiowa, trapped in a civil war and unable to find peace with either side. After helping his white brother to escape his own tribe's attacks, he rides off into the distance to die.

Peter Guralnick says Elvis struggles to cope with the part, looking unsure and stiff, and is effectively just a supporting member of a fine cast that includes John McIntire (as his father), Dolores Del Rio (his mother) and Barbara Eden (the object of his unrequited love).

317

Director Don Siegel disagrees. He was at first dismayed by Presley's casting, which necessitated much rewriting: 'The studio wanted Elvis to sing at least ten songs.' Backed by producer David Weisbart, however, he whittled that down to one: the period piece A Cane And A High Starched Collar. 'Presley surprised me with his sensitivity,' Siegel admitted. Elvis's key scene comes just after Pacer's mother has died, when he angrily declares his love to a stunned Barbara Eden. 'Elvis felt he couldn't do the scene, and begged for more time to prepare. Almost childlike, he offered me the use of his brand-new Rolls Royce until we had to do the scene.' Two weeks later, the time duly came, and Siegel returned the car: 'To his amazement and mine, Elvis gave his finest performance ever.' That scene is indeed the highlight of the movie, and one of the few moments in Elvis's career when he transcends his star personality.

While not without its longueurs, *Flaming Star* is, as one critic noted, 'a well-shaped, logical, frequently convincing, occasionally moving picture'. Elvis was delighted with a script that, according to Britain's *Monthly Film Bulletin*, 'makes some cogent points about peace among men … gives Presley a good role, and he makes the most of it'.

Siegel sensed the film's impending commercial doom when studio promotion failed to mention that it was a dramatic Western (and wrongly claimed it contained 'four new songs'). For Elvis, whose great-great-great-grandmother was a Cherokee called Morning Dove, there was only the consolation of being presented with an award for his constructive portrayal of a Native American.
*****

☆ WILD IN THE COUNTRY ☆

Twentieth Century Fox, 1961 VHS
Director Philip Dunne; **co-stars** Hope Lange,
Tuesday Weld, Millie Perkins, John Ireland.

Elvis always harboured not-so-secret ambitions to be the next James Dean; he even begged David Weisbart to let him star in *The James Dean Story*. When *Wild In The Country* finally gave him the chance to play a role reminiscent of Dean, however, he did so as a rebel without applause.

As Glenn Tyler, Elvis plays a sullen young man who might realize his hidden literary talent if he can only stay out of jail and not be distracted by the women in his life: anodyne childhood sweetheart Millie Perkins, bad girl Tuesday Weld, and older woman Hope Lange.

Though the premise sounds ludicrous. what ultimately sank this film was the studio's decision to fire gifted playwright Clifford Odets two weeks before filming started. He had delivered a 300-page script, enough for two movies, but it was over-written, and some key scenes were left blank. After Fox refused to pay Odets any more money, Philip Dunne had to both write and direct. Financial restraints also meant that the sympathetic older woman Elvis was to fall for would not be played by Simone Signoret, but by Hope Lange, who was just a year older than Elvis.

Dunne declared himself astonished by 'the extraordinary talent of Elvis Presley: he took to his part as if he had been a dramatic actor all his life'. Guralnick, however, says that Presley's acting sinks the picture, suggesting that his quick-fire dialogue reveals his use of amphetamines. Repeated viewing suggests that it's the big speeches that Elvis finds most taxing, possibly because at their worst they sound like a parody of Tennessee Williams. In the simpler, more naturalistic scenes, such as when he and Lange get stranded in a motel during a storm, he is much more effective, creating a real sense of mood and emotion.

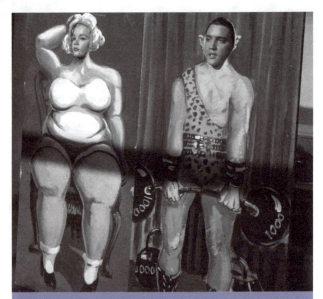

Tuesday Weld and Elvis go wild at the country showgrounds

Fox head Spyros Skouras, who had set out to promote Elvis as a dramatic star, panicked and ordered four songs to be inserted. Elvis hated singing them, and preview audiences jeered when he burst into song. The same previews determined that Lange shouldn't, after all, succeed in her suicide bid.

Dunne noted that 'Whenever the Colonel and Skouras put their heads together, I knew some disaster to the integrity of the film was being plotted'. Not all the flaws in *Wild In The Country* can be blamed on the studio, but you can see why this was almost the last of his own films that Elvis liked. His views were less relevant than the box-office returns, which were poorer than for *GI Blues*. ***

☆ BLUE HAWAII ☆

Paramount, 1961 VHS, DVD
Director Norman Taurog; **co-stars** Joan Blackman,
Angela Lansbury, Joan Blackman, Roland Winters, Iris Adrian.

Blue Hawaii is basically a Bing Crosby musical, with Crosby's former director at the helm, and featuring a theme song Bing had recorded for the same studio's 1937 comedy *Waikiki Wedding*. But

The missing mother

Asked in *Roustabout*, 'What would you know about a family?', Elvis's leather-jacketed rebel replies: 'Nothing.' In a nutshell, that's how Elvis appeared in most of his movies. When both his parents were still alive, that may have been a bid for sympathy. After Gladys' death, however, Elvis has a visible mother who is alive when the film finishes only in two movies: *Blue Hawaii* and *Kissin' Cousins*. In *Flaming Star*, his mother dies on-screen. Both Ma Kwimper in *Follow That Dream* and Ma Heywood in *Clambake* are conspicuous by their absence; Elvis is orphaned and surly in *Roustabout*; and in *Girls! Girls! Girls!* he's adopted.

A common adjunct of the absent mum is the **shiftless, ineffectual dad**, a figure seen by various biographers, associates and relatives in Vernon himself. Although in the novel on which *Wild In the Country* is based, Elvis's mother is still alive, in the movie she has died when he was a child; a death he blames on his drunken irresponsible father and brother. Dean Jagger in *King Creole* is a good but fatally weak man, who lets other men smack him in the mouth. In *Follow That Dream* Pa Kwimper is an ornery, handout-hunting patriarch, whereas *Stay Away Joe*'s Pa Lightcloud has married again, as did Vernon, but is feckless and henpecked.

321

because the star is Elvis, a synthetic coating of youthful rebellion is applied. Elvis's character Chad Gates – 'Chaaad-wick!!!', as his appalled on-screen mum Angela Lansbury pronounces it – is at odds with his folks because he doesn't want to work for Daddy's fruit company.

But it is, at least, an entertaining star vehicle that doesn't disgrace the star. Elvis is ably supported by Lansbury, a mere three years his

The Elvis film formula in one PR shot: girls, toy guitars and a smiling Elvis

senior, Roland Winters, and Joan Blackman as his Hawaiian-French love interest Maile. He and Blackman began an off-screen affair that would be revived when they were reunited in *Kid Galahad*.

The score is a cut above average, thanks to the ludicrous twisting energy of Rock A Hula Baby and the magical Can't Help Falling In

Love. And Elvis still gives his all vocally, even confronted with obvious fillers like Moonlight Swim. Yet he struggles to move naturally when singing, his finger-clicking the last resort of a man whose waist is only allowed on screen on the understanding that he doesn't move it. In fact, he's most at ease stood perfectly still.

The *New York Times*, while generally approving, concluded that 'Nothing could be prettier or emptier than *Blue Hawaii*'. As far as his manager and producer were concerned, these were Presley's finest 101 minutes on screen: a brisk comedy musical that offended no one (or no one Wallis and Parker paid any heed to), made $4.7 million, and spawned a multi-million-selling album. It's just that the star, perhaps sensing the trap that was about to close, seemed (to friends who saw him on set) genuinely disgusted by his new bland role. **★★★**

☆ FOLLOW THAT DREAM ☆

United Artists, 1962 VHS

Director Gordon Douglas; **co-stars** Anne Helm, Arthur O'Connell, Joanne Moore.

Richard Powell was not best pleased when he heard his novel *Pioneer Go Home* was to become an Elvis Presley movie: 'I was shocked. I didn't think he'd do a good job.' To producer David Weisbart and director Gordon Douglas, he confided, 'My only real fear was that Presley would say to himself that this was a funny story and that he would have to act funny. The humour in the book was character humour, which had to be played straight to bring it out … They assured me that he would play the role straight, which he did and he did a very good job.'

The title had to be changed, though; none of the tunesmiths in Elvis's publishing empire could find a rhyme for 'pioneer'. So *Follow That Dream* it became, with Elvis as Toby Kwimper, the son in a family of holy fools, who alight on a stretch of unopened

323

highway in Florida and decide, more due to the contrariness of the father (Arthur O'Connell) than anything else, to stay.

Although the music isn't great – I'm Not The Marrying Kind is the best of a mild bunch – that barely matters because the comedy actually makes you laugh. There are lapses, like O'Connell's country dancing, and Elvis looks distinctly chubby, though as he's also fairer-haired than normal that may just be the character. However, Weisbart and Douglas were the first (indeed, almost the only) team to exploit Presley's comic timing. They earned him and the film some unusually good reviews – *Films And Filming* went so far as to describe Elvis's part as 'brilliantly conceived' – but only so-so at the box office. ****

☆ KID GALAHAD ☆

United Artists, 1962 VHS
Director Phil Karlson; **co-stars** Joan Blackman, Gig Young, Charles Bronson, Lola Albright.

There was an inevitability about the way the *New York Times*' Bosley Crowther ripped into both *Kid Galahad* and Elvis himself: 'The expanses of flesh that he exposes when he gets into boxing togs are a fair indication that most of his muscles come from punching a guitar,' sniffed Bosley.

To movie buffs like Crowther, United Artists had committed celluloid blasphemy by remaking a Warner Brothers boxing classic as a musical. It didn't matter that there were only half a dozen songs; that Elvis was supported by a top-quality cast; or that Elvis himself, as in *Follow That Dream*, played the innocent fool with aplomb.

As Galahad – or Walter Gulick, an unusually ethnic name for an Elvis character – Presley turns up in Cream Valley after being demobbed, and wants a job. Inevitably, he gets two: one as a mechanic, and one as a sparring partner for a local boxer. When

324

Elvis knocks out the boxer he's sparring with, the manipulative, but decent manager Gig Young sees his potential as a fighter; he's less keen on having Elvis as a brother-in-law, and tries to discourage his sister, Joan Blackman, from falling for him.

Up-and-coming director Phil Karlson had made his name directing crime B-features. It took a string of so-so A-movies like *Kid Galahad* for Hollywood to recognize that he wasn't the next Samuel Fuller. Blending a story of corruption in the fight game with the music and romance required of an Elvis film would have taxed anyone, but Karlson seemed to give up. Apart from I Got Lucky, the songs didn't spring naturally from the action, and the boxing storyline lacked tension.

Presley is said to have asked why Michael Curtiz, who had directed the Warners original and done so well with *King Creole*, wasn't in charge. He didn't get on with Charles Bronson, who treated him with indifference, and he was unhappy that his own weight had ballooned to 200lbs, a minor disaster as he spent so much screen time topless. Although he took his boxing coaching seriously, the ring scenes weren't brilliantly shot. He wasn't helped by the strange decision to put a band aid on his head whenever his character was badly hurt. Presley was most effective in the quieter moments, especially when he floors the boxer he's sparring with and asks nervously, 'Do I still get my five dollars?' Watchable, especially if unlike Bosley Crowther you've never seen the original, *Kid Galahad* was not a box-office smash. ***

☆ GIRLS! GIRLS! GIRLS! ☆

Paramount, 1962 VHS
Director Norman Taurog; **co-stars** Laurel Goodwin, Stella Stevens, Jeremy Slate.

Though title, soundtrack, and even film all seem eminently forgettable, *Girls! Girls! Girls!* has a special place in Elvis's movie history. It is, after all, the only one in which 'little Elvis' makes an erect appearance, as he sings The Walls Have Ears. Before the scene was shot, Elvis complained that his black trousers were rubbing him the wrong way. The next day at dailies, he groaned as he saw little Elvis pointing straight at co-star Laurel Goodwin. 'Look at that,' said Elvis, 'it's sticking out like a sore thumb… well sort of like a thumb.' He was certain the scene would be reshot or edited to conceal his excited state; Taurog didn't notice and the shot stayed in.

That was probably the only time anybody got excited about *Girls! Girls! Girls!* Elvis is Ross Carpenter, a singing tuna fisherman so desperate to buy his own boat he can't even be tempted ashore by yummy Stella Stevens, an actress described in less politically correct times as 'having a figure that would look good in a sack'. When he finally does come ashore, for the finale, love interest Goodwin has to stand and watch as he sings the title track to a selection of beauties from around the world.

By this point in his movie career, Elvis has effectively become a piece of scenery, whose main ambition seems to be to get through the film without undue embarrassment. The other actors don't amount to much: Jeremy Slate is suitably sleazy as a villain, while Goodwin's movie career pretty much starts and ends here. Even in the crude terms of Hollywood star power, Elvis's romance with her makes little sense; only Stevens has the on-screen charisma to provide a real foil. But Stevens was in the cast under protest, and later claimed, 'Elvis was drunk when he did Return To Sender. He was not a very professional actor.' According to Priscilla, on the other hand, Elvis was trying to impress Jackie Wilson, who had dropped by.

Even Paramount's associate producer Paul Nathan fretted there were too many songs: 'We got the "Oh shit, not another song" feeling … I know we all love "The Shrimp Song" but honest to God, it got nothing last night.' Despite iffy previews, The Shrimp Song stayed, but four mostly decent ones were cut. In the end, *Girls!*

Girls! Girls! made $2.6 million, almost $1 million more than *Kid Galahad*, and the soundtrack sold 600,000 copies. The relationship between Elvis singing, and cash tills ringing, was more clearly established than ever. ★★

☆ IT HAPPENED AT
THE WORLD'S FAIR ☆

MGM, 1963 VHS
Director Norman Taurog; **co-stars** Joan O'Brien, Gary Lockwood, Ginny Tiu.

It Happened At The World's Fair was originally going to be called *Mister, Will You Marry Me*. The switch to the exotic locale of Seattle necessitated the change in title, presumably an allusion to the Clark Gable comedy *It Happened One Night* (coincidentally, Elvis used Gable's former dressing room during shooting).

Elvis plays Mike Edwards, a crop-dusting pilot who heads for the world's fair with his feckless pal Danny (Gary Lockwood), and finds himself responsible for the seven-year-old Ginny Tiu. Director Norman Taurog had worked with Shirley Temple, which may explain why he over-estimates Tiu's appeal; her semi-continuous on-screen presence provides the excuse for such slight numbers as Take Me To The Fair, Cotton Candy Land and How Would You Like To Be? Elvis meanwhile becomes so besotted by nurse Diane Warren (Joan O'Brien) that he abandons his wolfish bachelor ways.

Surprises are few and far between – the biggest comes when Elvis joins the space programme – though there is a classic pop-culture moment, when he's kicked in the shin by the young Kurt Russell, who'd play him in John Carpenter's TV movie. At least it's all done with reasonable efficiency. O'Brien, who had starred with Tony Curtis in *Operation Petticoat*, is a cut above the usual love interest, while Lockwood is amusing as the bantering buddy for whom life

327

is a poker game. Elvis was snappily dressed by Sy Devore, who was shocked to discover that the star never wore underpants.

By far the best song is They Remind Me Too Much Of You, sung on the monorail as Elvis reflects on his new love, even if, as he's only just met her, its inconsolable sentiments seem a trifle premature. One Broken Heart For Sale is mainly notable for the speed with which neighbours and strangers emerge from the shadows to listen, join in and sway to the beat. From now on, characters in Elvis movies will possess an uncanny ability to recognize when El is about to burst into song. Given some of the stuff he crooned, it's a wonder they didn't run to their houses and turn their TV sets up to maximum volume.

The traditional defence for Elvis's post-Army movies is that, whatever else they may have been, they were feel-good films. That holds true here, partly because MGM still brought a certain gloss to its product, and partly because Elvis's scenes with O'Brien and Lockwood are decently scripted and handled. Even the songs, though mostly mediocre, don't plumb the depths that were to follow. ***

☆ FUN IN ACAPULCO ☆

Paramount, 1963 VHS

Director Richard Thorpe; **co-stars** Ursula Andress, Elsa Cardenas, George Chakiris, Paul Lukas, Larry Domasin.

Despite the title, Elvis wasn't actually allowed to have any *Fun in Acapulco*. All his scenes were shot in Hollywood. The official, rather flimsy, excuse, as Colonel Parker explained to Hal Wallis, was that Elvis had been misquoted as making a disparaging remark about Mexican girls, so security might be a problem. An awful lot of time was therefore spent matching scenes to the Mexican backdrops.

328

Yet Elvis seems slightly more engaged in his role as a trapeze artist who has developed a fear of heights after a tragic accident than he did, say, as a singing tuna fisherman. Ultimately he overcomes his fear in spectacular fashion, diving off La Perla to win the heart of Ursula Andress. Director Richard Thorpe makes the journey to that inevitable destination more enjoyable than in many Elvis films.

The music, especially Bossa Nova Baby, helps. Perhaps inspired by the fact that at least the formula was different, Elvis does his utmost with the rest, bringing a sultry charm to the seductive Marguerita and even delivering El Toro, a song about a morose matador, with insane conviction. But even El can't make a silk purse out of There's No Room To Rhumba In A Sports Car.

Andress, who had sprung to fame with a walk on the beach in *Dr No*, loathed the limits that were imposed on her. 'They wouldn't let me wear lipstick or mascara, and they put a ribbon in my hair to please the innocent little girls who made up Elvis's audiences', she complained. 'They wouldn't even let me wear a proper bikini saying, "You can't show your navel in a Presley picture.".

If a woman looked sexy, like El's former date Elsa Cardenas here, or Yvonne Romain in *Double Trouble*, it was usually a sign that she was bad or loose. One of the many ironies of Elvis's movie career is that he found himself imprisoned by the rigid sexual morality of the Eisenhower era, the very morality that he did more than anyone, except possibly Marilyn Monroe, to break down.

Finally, for the third time in an Elvis movie, his manager demanded (and got) fifty percent of his earnings. In this case, the fact that the manager was a 12-year-old boy (played with spirit by Larry Domasin) only added to the humiliation. ***

☆ KISSIN' COUSINS ☆

MGM, 1964 VHS

Director Gene Nelson; **co-stars** Yvonne Craig, Pam Austin,
Arthur O'Connell, Glenda Farrell, Jack Albertson.

Kissin' Cousins is not the worst Elvis movie ever made. But it was probably his worst to date, and his most embarrassing. Some days, co-star Yvonne Craig recalled, he would be so ashamed he wouldn't want to leave his dressing room. At the time, this was blamed on his reluctance to don a blond wig as Jody Tatum, a distant cousin of the other character he plays, Lieutenant Josh Morgan. He also found the twin theme, a recurring motif here brought to the fore, creepy. It didn't help that the script presented this bunch of Southerners as ignorant, feckless, moonshining, tax-dodging alcoholics.

As if all that was not indignity enough, the film was at Parker's instigation produced by Sam Katzman, the 'King of the Quickies', and shot in a mere sixteen days. According to director Gene Nelson, Katzman 'knew how to make pictures, he just had lousy taste in writers and wouldn't know a story if it hit him in the face'.

As Josh, Elvis has to persuade the Tatums to lease their mountain for a missile base. As Jody, he has to wrestle every visitor into submission, eventually falling for the first to outwrestle him, a clerk played by Cynthia Pepper. With Jody distracted, Josh pursues his younger sister Azalea (Craig, in her second Elvis film). To complicate matters, a collection of 'mountain cuties' known as the Kittyhawks, long-lost relatives of Russ Meyer's Supervixens, scour the area looking for men in a desperate quest for male offspring.

That the film is less excruciating than its synopsis suggests is down to a fine cast, including Jack Albertson as Josh's superior officer, and Glenda Farrell and Arthur O'Connell as Ma and Pa Tatum. Elvis does his damnedest, though he's more successful as a lieutenant, possibly because he has something to do, whereas

330

They're everywhere: twin babies in *GI Blues* ▶

The twin brother

The motif of twinship, and Elvis as a twin, haunts many an Elvis movie. *Kissin' Cousins*, which sees him playing identical cousins **Josh**, in a blond wig close to his natural hair colour, and **Jody**, in his more familiar black-blue look, is simply the most spectacular. In *Loving You*, Wendell Corey's character comments, 'I wish I were twins: I'd have someone to blame for this.' As Elvis sings **Mean Woman Blues**, he's watched by a twin in the crowd, with the same hairstyle, apeing his gestures. A few minutes later, the camera pans to identical twin girls, slapping each other's hands to the music. Elvis's family in *Follow That Dream* adopts orphaned twins whose rhyming names, Eddy

and Teddy, echo Jesse Garon and Elvis Aron, while in *Girls! Girls! Girls!*, his adoptive father has twin teenage daughters.

As Tulsa McLean in *GI Blues*, Elvis is at one point surrounded by baby twins. When he sings **Doin' The Best I Can** in a bar, a soldier selects **Blue Suede Shoes** by Elvis Presley on the jukebox. As the new, family-friendly Elvis on celluloid competes with the old, outrageous Elvis on record, the soldier pointedly insists, 'I want to hear an original.' Finally, in a minor variation on the theme, Elvis almost kills his brother in the opening scene of *Wild In the Country*, and really does so (accidentally) in *Fun In Acapulco*.

331

Jody's only function is to reinforce Hollywood stereotypes about dumb hillbillies. Nelson noted of his star, 'Even with the kind of trivial dialogue we had, there were moments where he incorporated a great deal of thoughtfulness into his delivery.'

Kissin' Cousins made $2.8 million, not bad for a film that, excluding fees for Elvis and Parker, cost only $650,000. Lance Le Gault, Elvis's double – who's looking at the camera in the final scene, when both twins dance at the same time – says it set the dire pattern for what was to follow. 'Once they realized they could do a film that quickly, from then on we were on quick pictures.' **

☆ VIVA LAS VEGAS ☆

MGM, 1964 VHS, DVD
Director George Sidney; **co-stars** Ann-Margret, Cesare Danova, William Demarest.

Just when Elvis's movie career seemed about to plumb the depths, he starred in *Viva Las Vegas*, an above-average musical, blessed with director George Sidney, responsible for *Anchors Aweigh*, and a co-star, Ann-Margret, with whom he fell seriously in love. Its overall air of sumptuousness betrays the fact that, although released after *Kissin' Cousins* (and its financial constraints), it had been shot before.

Elvis plays Lucky Jackson, a singing racing-car driver who wants to win both the race and the girl, Rusty (Ann-Margret). The only serious obstacle is her fear that he might kill himself racing. Even if the plot is standard, the songs are classier than anything El had sung on celluloid for years. Elvis and Ann-Margret have immense on-screen chemistry – especially dancing together in the magnificent C'mon Everybody, his most successful dance routine since *Jailhouse Rock* – probably because their off-screen chemistry was so intense they discussed marriage.

To go with his usual budget worries, Parker was concerned at the number of close-ups Ann-Margret was getting. Ironically, this was the very thing Sidney felt was wrong with all of El's previous movies: 'He had all the close ups it was boy, boy, boy, when it needed to be boy, girl.' Even though Parker swung into action, killing off one duet (the sultry You're The Boss) and balancing out the close-ups, it's still as much Ann-Margret's movie as Elvis's. Parker's clout may have been diminished because producer George Cummings, as son-in-law of MGM's old boss Louis B Mayer, was used to getting his way.

El's best solo moment comes when he walks through the hotel lounge while I Need Somebody To Lean On is sung as an interior monologue. It's a reflective sequence of unparalleled sophistication, good enough to feel at home in a classic MGM musical. Even the *New York Times* gave El grudging praise: 'Not only does he sing better – at least more audibly – but the tunes continue to improve.'

The most puzzling part of the film is the end. It takes less than a minute for hero and heroine to be married, seen off on their honeymoon, and reappear for the title song. You can't help suspecting Parker had prompted MGM to stop Sidney's spending.

At $5.5 million, *Viva Las Vegas* was Presley's biggest grosser. It broke box-office records in Tokyo and Manila, and did pretty well elsewhere, although as the 1956 movie *Meet Me In Las Vegas* was known internationally as *Viva Las Vegas* it had to be retitled *Love In Las Vegas*. Only the authorities on the island of Gozo were not impressed: they banned the film after protests from local priests. ★★★★

☆ ROUSTABOUT ☆

Paramount, 1964 VHS, DVD

Director John Rich; **co-stars** Barbara Stanwyck,
Joan Freeman, Leif Erickson, Sue Anne Langdon.

Hal Wallis's first act on *Roustabout*, his seventh Elvis movie, was to fire off a letter telling Parker what he expected of his star. He insisted that as Elvis was playing a 'lean, tough, hard-hitting guy'; he

Ann-Margret and Elvis in *Viva Las Vegas*, probably his best 1960s musical

'cannot be pudgy looking … [He] must train down to get the look or the character will not be believable.' Last of all, he wanted 'all the dye and goo' taken out of Elvis's hair. It was as though Elvis's appearance, rather than any deficiencies in script or music, was the only reason not all his movies were as profitable as *Blue Hawaii*.

According to scriptwriter Allan Weiss, his original story had Elvis's character Charlie Rogers drummed out of the Army for running under fire. Once that detail disappeared – 'Wallis wanted everything kept pretty shallow' – Rogers became a drifter with a chip on each leather-jacketed shoulder, whose sense of injustice seemed to spring solely from the fact that he never knew his family.

Director John Rich clashed with his star over a song that Elvis wanted to cut with the Jordanaires. Rich argued that it was sung when Elvis was out on the road on his bike, 'so where would we put the backing singers?' Elvis thought for a second and replied, 'Same damn place you put the band.' Though you won't find that bite in any of his on-screen lines, some of Weiss's original sharpness remains, especially when Jack Albertson says that Elvis's smiling demeanour at the teahouse 'conceals the instincts of a Mau Mau'. (One of the girls drinking cokes here is Raquel Welch in her movie debut.) And Elvis's rebelliousness, even if slightly synthetic, is preferable to the by-now-obligatory blandness.

The film is immeasurably helped by the presence of Barbara Stanwyck as the owner of the carnival where Elvis works while his motorcycle is repaired. Inevitably, he falls in love with Joan Freeman, whose drunken bad-tempered father (Leif Erickson) takes violent exception to him, only to change his tune when Elvis saves the carnival. Wearing the finest blue jeans costume designer Edith Head ever produced, Stanwyck sparks well with Elvis. Stories differ as to how they got on off screen. Co-star Sue Anne Langdon says the actress was appalled Elvis didn't know who Athena was; Elvis's friends recall him being seriously impressed by Stanwyck, going out of his way to tell her how good she was in *Cattle Queen Of Montana*.

The big pity, again, is the songs: even the best, the Leiber and

335

Stoller import Little Egypt, was given the trappings of a crass novel-ty number. Though *Roustabout* wasn't as big a hit as *Viva Las Vegas*, it did make $3.3 million, which suggests that there was still profit, financial and artistic, in alluding to Elvis's early rebel image. *******

☆ GIRL HAPPY ☆

MGM, 1965 VHS
Director Boris Sagal; **co-stars** Shelley Fabares, Gary Crosby,
Harold J Stone, Mary Ann Mobley.

For once, in *Girl Happy* Elvis isn't chasing girls; he has to stop gang-ster's daughter Valerie (**Shelley Fabares**) from being chased. Which is made harder by the fact that Fabares and her pals are in Fort Lauderdale devoting their end-of-term vacation to meeting boys.

Producer **Joe Pasternak** had tried to cast Elvis in the beach movie *Gidget* in 1957. Now he got him, for another formulaic sub-genre, the **college kids movie** – a vein Pasternak had profitably mined in 1960 with *Where The Boys Are*. Like many Elvis directors in this era, **Boris Sagal** had made his name in, and would soon head back to: television. Though he brought no special distinction to the project, he was so moved by the disgust with which Elvis regarded the songs that he suggested the star give up these hackneyed pictures and learn acting at the Actor's Studio. A non-committal Elvis said he didn't have time, but assured Sagal, 'I'm looking forward to doing a picture when I can finally act and not just sing.'

Girl Happy is what it is: better than some of the college-kid movies it's modelled on, and worse than others. Fabares was prob-ably Elvis's favourite leading lady, and in the first of their three on-screen pairings, their rapport is obvious. Schilling says, 'She wouldn't go out with him, she was seeing Lou Adler at the time, but they had a real good chemistry and he adored working with her.'

Elvis had a point about the songs. In response to the threat posed

336

by the Beatles, there were some faster numbers, but where the Fab Four were singing I Feel Fine, El had to make do with Wolf Call. Choreographer David Winters clearly had a bad day at the office: he had done wonders on *Viva Las Vegas*, but for *Girl Happy* he came up with that most transient of 1960s dance crazes, the clam.

Girl Happy was another reasonable hit, making over $3 million (a good profit, as production costs were less than $1 million). It's still cherished by fans for the scene where Elvis breaks into prison to speak to Fabares, and has to break out again in drag. ★★★

☆ TICKLE ME ☆

Allied Artists, 1965 VHS
Director Norman Taurog; **co-stars** Jocelyn Lane, Julia Adams, Jack Mullaney.

Tickle Me was the third-highest-grossing film in Allied Artists' history, keeping the studio from bankruptcy for a year. It didn't impress critics; the *New York Times* called it 'the silliest, feeblest and dullest vehicle for the Memphis wonder in a long time'. That hasn't stopped it being a cult favourite, with some even detecting post-modern ironic intent in its celebration of Elvis's image.

Elvis plays Lonnie Beale, an out-of-luck rodeo rider (personal credo: 'They don't make women who aren't interested') who gets a job at a health ranch. Joy of joys, he's surrounded by beautiful women, among them haughty fitness trainer Pam (Jocelyn Lane).

The script, by Three Stooges writers Elwood Ullman and Edward Bernds, holds some Stooges-style humour, but at heart it's a Dean Martin/Jerry Lewis comedy, with Elvis as Dino and Jack Mullaney as madcap comic sidekick Jerry. It kind of works. Elvis found his co-star hilarious off screen and on, and they share a genuine rapport. And Lane is prettily arrogant as Pam, who is secretly looking for her grandfather's gold in the nearby ghost town of Silverado. She and Elvis have the inevitable falling out, but are married after he helps unmask the villains who have been trying to steal the gold. Dubbed the 'British Bardot', she was to give up movies to marry (and divorce) Prince Alfonso von Holenhoe, and design her own line of feather necklaces.

The songs are slightly stronger than usual, unlike Elvis's lip-synching, because they all came from studio albums – Allied couldn't afford to buy any new songs. On film, the merest hint that he's clearing his pipes for a spot of warbling is enough to have girls leaving the swimming pool, emerging from the sagebrush, and throwing themselves at his feet. *******

☆ HARUM SCARUM (HAREM HOLIDAY) ☆

MGM, 1965 VHS

Director Gene Nelson; **co-stars** Mary Ann Mobley, Fran Jeffries, Michael Ansara, Jay Novello, Billy Barty

In one sense at least, *Harum Scarum* (*Harem Holiday* in the UK), Elvis's first camp classic, was fiendishly well timed. Twenty years later, Elvis, Parker and Sam Katzman would have been lucky to escape a fatwa.

Presley was initially excited at the chance to emulate Rudolph Valentino, albeit in a tongue-in-cheek way. In fact, he often seems to be enjoying himself, as though the thrill of dressing up in those costumes cannot be entirely erased by abysmal music, shoddy sets and an incomprehensible plot.

Elvis is Johnny Tyrone, a singing movie star who is kidnapped by a group of assassins under the impression that he can kill with his bare hands. In return for the lives of some orphans and slave girls of whom he's grown rather fond, the villains want him to assassi-

Harum Scarum even scared the Colonel; at least Elvis liked the costume ▶

nate the king of Lunakan, while singing 'Shake that tambourine, that tambourine'. (Actually, they don't order him to sing; he just does that to keep his spirits up.) But he can't really kill the king because he's too nice, and because he realizes the slave girl he loves, Mary Ann Mobley, is the king's daughter.

Katzman gave director Gene Nelson all of fifteen days to shoot the film. The pressure was almost too much; he always remembered with gratitude Presley's offer to pretend to be sick to earn some more time. Elvis's own verdict was contained in an autographed picture he gave Nelson afterwards: 'Someday we'll do it right'. Even Parker was shocked. He wrote to MGM that 'a 55th cousin of PT Barnum' would struggle to sell the picture, and suggested that if it was narrated by a talking camel people might think it was supposed to be ridiculous. Amazingly, without the benefit of a single – the only decent song was So Close Yet So Far – it still made $2 million. What's more, the soundtrack album made it into the US top ten, though it was the last one to do so.

It might seem perverse to speak up for a film described in MGM's official history as the 'worst film of the year'. But *Harum Scarum* is weird enough to be compelling, simply less boring in its unbelievable way than guff like *Paradise, Hawaiian Style*. There's a fantastic moment when one of Elvis's thieves hits the bongos and, for an instant, you think he's going to sing "Do The Clam" again, as if choreographer David Winters can't give up on the craze he thinks is his meisterwork. Elvis rather suits a burmoose. It's just a pity he never got to play Valentino in more promising circumstances. ★★★

☆ FRANKIE AND JOHNNY ☆

United Artists, 1966 VHS, DVD
Director Frederick de Cordova; **co-stars** Audrey Christie, Donna Douglas, Harry Morgan, Sue Anne Langdon, Nancy Kovack.

Although not of course without its flaws and frustrations – some

The movies Elvis liked

Elvis's own experience in Hollywood did not put him off movies. Hiring Memphis cinemas for 'midnight movies' was a tradition; the day before he died, he asked one to get a print of Gregory Peck in *MacArthur*. According to **Alan Fortas** in 1969, 'We'd run the pictures one after the other, sometimes from eleven o'clock to six in the morning. Every night is generalizing but you'd be safe saying five nights a week. Believe me, he was a very avid movie fan.'

Elvis had a weakness for movies about generals; *Patton*, starring George C Scott, was his all-time favourite, and he memorized its opening speech. He also liked almost anything with **Peter Sellers**, watching *Dr Strangelove* six times in a row, and saw *Monty Python And The Holy Grail* five times when the cinema first had it. He was so struck by the underrated 1970s crime movie *Across 110th Street*, starring Yaphet Kotto and set in Harlem, that when Myrna Smith admitted she'd never seen it, he took her through the whole thing, reciting every character's dialogue line by line. Both *Shaft* and *Superfly* tickled his fancy – especially as a source of inspiration for his wardrobe – while he always felt that *To Kill A Mockingbird* should have swept the 1962 Oscars, instead of *Lawrence of Arabia*.

Other favourites included *Dirty Harry*, all the James Bond movies, *The Godfather*, *The Wild Bunch*, *A Streetcar Named Desire*, *One Flew Over The Cuckoo's Nest*, *The Man With The Golden Arm* – he was a big fan of Kim Novak – and *On The Waterfront*.

of the songs, the numerous scenes of drunken comedy that aren't actually funny – *Frankie And Johnny* ranks among Elvis's better 1960s vehicles. Based on the old ballad about the star-crossed sweethearts, it casts Elvis as compulsive gambler Johnny who, to

341

change his luck, steps out with a redhead called Nellie Bly (Nancy Kovack), thereby angering his beau Frankie (Donna Douglas, for whom this marked a final escape from the *Beverly Hillbillies* franchise). This being an Elvis film, Johnny was not allowed to die, let alone to be shot in the balls, as in some versions of the song. But he suits the role of a riverboat gambler and he suits the period costumes, even if he does fill some of them a little too amply.

Alex Gottlieb's script has some genuinely funny one-liners, especially in the verbal fencing between Harry Morgan as a henpecked songwriter and Audrey Christie as his wife Peg. Things

only go awry when romantic complications take over, though some of the songs are so dodgy that Elvis threw a tantrum and had to record his vocal track separately to the band.

One scene has received a level of critical analysis way beyond that normally applied to an Elvis film. After Douglas has thrown away his newly won fortune, Elvis strolls disconsolately down the street and sings a bluesy number called Hard Luck. It may be fake, Hollywood, blues, but Elvis sings it with conviction, accompanied on the harmonica (or 'Mississippi saxophone') by a black shoe-shine boy. The boy's occupation is made explicit when the camera lingers on the word 'shine', written on his box in chalk. Is this a response to the charge, by then already in circulation for a decade, that Elvis had once said that blacks were fit only to shine his shoes and buy his records? The boy here doesn't shine Elvis's shoes, but joins him as an equal. The points seems to be made so explicitly that it seems even more far-fetched to say it is just accidental. ★★★

☆ PARADISE, HAWAIIAN STYLE ☆

Paramount, 1966 VHS

Director Michael Moore; **co-stars** Suzanna Leigh, James Shigeta, Marianna Hill.

Paradise, Hawaiian Style could have been the film in which Elvis co-starred, briefly, with the Beatles. Hal Wallis gave up on the idea after contractual complications. It's probably just as well: it was in Elvis's interests that as few people saw this turkey as possible.

Superficially, the decision to return to Hawaii made sense. Elvis liked the islands, and two of his most successful films (*Blue Hawaii* and *Girls! Girls! Girls!*) had been set there. To make full use of the location, associate producer Paul Nathan advised director Michael Moore: 'As often as possible we should try to get clothes

343

◀ Elvis and favourite co-star Shelley Fabares rev their motors in *Spinout*

off our cast – in the water, on surfboards, even in the helicopter landing on the beach.' Elvis complicated matters by turning up, as Moore tactfully put it, fat, though you can see him lose weight as the film grinds on.

The star's behaviour on set was erratic enough for Hedda Hopper to scold him in her gossip column. The temptation is to seek a pharmaceutical explanation, but Elvis's discontent may have run deeper. His old friend and bass player, Bill Black, had just been diagnosed with a brain tumour, while during filming he met the Beatles and Tom Jones, both of whom seemed to be replacing him in very different ways. He was wearying of the treadmill, complaining to Priscilla that he wasn't getting a chance to play serious roles. Bitter and, for him, unusually combative, he refused to sing dog noises in A Dog's Life, though, sadly, he did not protest as 9-year-old Donna Butterworth, in a display of appalling hip-swinging precocity, murdered Bill Bailey Won't You Please Come Home?

Elvis plays Rick, a pilot who, fired for kissing a stewardess, sets up a helicopter service with James Shigeta. Then, through no fault of his own, he endangers his livelihood, as well as those of his buddy and of the office Girl Friday, played by English actress Suzanna Leigh. The one spark comes when Marianna Hill flashes her legs during Scratch My Back: like Juliet Prowse in GI Blues, she underlines how tame Elvis has become. Hill did, at least, escape the curse of the Elvis movie, appearing in the political thriller Medium Cool and Clint Eastwood's High Plains Drifter.

Sadly, only the final medley of This Is My Heaven/Drums Of The Island makes decent use of the Hawaiian scenery, and the love story is hardly developed. Elvis doesn't even get to kiss Leigh, possibly because she's styled (and acts) as if she's the rejected prototype for Lady Penelope in Thunderbirds. The best way to watch this is with your finger on the fast-forward button, stopping to watch those songs that aren't sung, wholly or in part, by Butterworth. *

☆ SPINOUT ☆

MGM, 1966 VHS

Director Norman Taurog; **co-stars** Shelley Fabares,
Diane McBain, Deborah Walley, Dodie Marshall

The shenanigans that went into the making of *Spinout* have
already been discussed, on p.304. Its fate was probably sealed
when MGM decided cars were the key to boffo box office.
Obviously the success of *Viva Las Vegas* couldn't be down to the
fact that it had a decent director, decent songs and a decent co-
star.

So Elvis is back behind the wheel as Mike McCoy, a part-time
racing-car driver and leader of a nomadic pop group (with a novel
style in erecting tents), who's trying to avoid marrying his drummer (Deborah Walley), a bestselling author (Diane McBain) and a
spoiled little rich girl (Shelley Fabares). This was second time
around for both Fabares and Jack Mullaney, who reprises his Jerry
Lewis shtick from *Tickle Me*.

The title debate almost took as long as the script: *Never Say No*
was, Parker said too suggestive (even for the Swinging Sixties) so
it became *Never Say Yes, Never At Midnight, Always At Midnight,
After Midnight, Jim Dandy, Clambake* and then *Spinout*. Even the
slogans betrayed a hint of desperation – the best MGM's legendary marketing machine could come up with was *With His Foot
On The Gas And No Brakes On The Fun*. The critics were too bored
by this 'below par pelvis' to make wisecracks. Only *Time* got
worked up, complaining of Elvis's hairdo, 'He now sports a glossy
something on his summit that adds at least five inches to his alti-
tude and looks like a swatch of hot buttered yak wool.'

Most of the songs are ersatz rock – bright enough at the time,
but they linger for about a nanosecond in your memory. The ballads, Am I Ready and All That I Am, are slightly better. That said,
the film is reasonably easy to watch as long as you suspend your
powers of reason and treat it as an extended pop video. And

345

The synthetic Elvis

The most visible proof that something very weird had happened to Elvis by the late 1960s was the way he **looked** in films like *Spinout*. As Jane and Michael Stern put it in *Elvis World*, 'He is surrealistically perfect, all his famous eccentricities reduced to formulaic elements. His skin has the texture of a nylon stocking; his hair looks like poured tar.'

Hollywood didn't just smooth off the rough edges of his music, it smoothed away the edges that made Presley so distinctive in the first place. The **sneer** became a faint echo of its former derisive self; it was hair today, gone tomorrow for his **quiff** and **sideburns**; and his **body movements** were so circumscribed that somewhere between *Girl Happy* and *Spinout* he seemed to lose his sense of rhythm.

The **clothes** get increasingly bizarre too. At the end of *Spinout*, as he rips into **I'll Be Back**, Elvis is wearing four layers of clothing on the upper half of his body: a polo-necked jumper under a jacket, waistcoat and open-necked shirt. He wears a white jacket so much in *Double Trouble* he looks like a waiter – one who eats too many leftovers. By 1965, Presley was putting off his movies for as long as possible by putting on weight; that might explain *Time*'s complaint (of *Spinout*) that 'his cheeks are now so plump that he looks like a kid blowing gum'.

This sorry state of sartorial affairs may partly be explained by the absence of **Edith Head** in the costume department and of **Sy Devore**'s outfits. His image began to improve in films like *Stay Away Joe*, even before the 1968 TV special. By the time of his last two movies, *The Trouble With Girls* and *Change Of Habit*, he was once again authentically Elvis, complete with sideburns, a hairstyle that looked vaguely contemporary and some half-decent costumes. But for a while, Elvis was the worst-dressed man in Hollywood.

346

there's no teeth-gratingly precocious child. 1966 marked Elvis's last appearance among the top ten box-office draws in the annual movie exhibitors' poll. The wonder is that his appeal lasted that long. ★★★

☆ EASY COME, EASY GO ☆

Paramount, 1967 VHS
Director John Rich; **co-stars** Dodie Marshall, Pat Priest,
Elsa Lanchester, Frank McHugh.

By 1966, producer Hal Wallis had grown tired of the musical-comedy Frankenstein he had helped create. The world was also confusing him. He couldn't understand the success of the Beatles: 'They have no sound, no rhythm.' So *Easy Come, Easy Go* proved to be his last Elvis movie, and he told director John Rich to 'just put them through their paces'. Rich complained later that all Wallis cared about was cutting costs.

This lack of interest didn't stop Wallis swiping at his star, complaining that 'the costumes get tighter and tighter and our hero looks fatter and fatter'. Not content with asking Rich to tell Presley to slim down, he had another pop at Elvis's hairstyle: 'If he comes up from underwater, takes his helmet off and discloses that perfectly combed pompadour the whole picture will be ridiculous'.

Wallis's commitment to realism in the rest of the movie is fitful, as rare in fact as a half-decent song. Elvis is a former Navy frogman who, with the help of a nightclub owner and Jo the dancer (Dodie Marshall), hopes to beat two villains to some sunken treasure. Jo is, to use the kind of dated slang that peppers the script, 'far out'. She's learning yoga and shares her house with the kind of crazy cats who think art is having a vat of spaghetti tipped over you. Elvis's car is even turned into a mobile by a street artist, something Wallis, with his grasp of 1960s youth culture, found

347

completely plausible. The cast do their best, with Pat Priest prettily effective as a blonde villainess, and Elsa Lanchester (yoga instructor) and Frank McHugh (mad sea captain) providing comic cameos.

Easy Come, Easy Go was a movie nobody really wanted to make: not the producer, not the director (it was his last film), and not the star. How fitting then, despite the cliché that all Elvis's films made money, this one failed to cover its costs, grossing just $1.9 million. The snappiest review is by Elvis himself. Asked by George Klein what it was about, he said 'Same film, different location.' ★★

☆ DOUBLE TROUBLE ☆

MGM, 1967 VHS

Director Norman Taurog; **co-stars** Annette Day, John Williams, Yvonne Romain.

It's hard to top the *British Monthly Film Bulletin*'s seven-word verdict on the comedy-thriller *Double Trouble*: 'All is brisk, painless and rather dull.' Even so, it was a slight step up from its predecessor (though in fact it was filmed earlier but released later). Without actually leaving Hollywood, Elvis sweeps through swinging London and Antwerp, pursued by two attractive women: the virtuous but irritating Jill (Annette Day, in her first and last movie), and the evil but alluring Claire (Yvonne Romain). Norman Rossington also earned a unique spot in pop culture history, as the only actor to have co-starred with Elvis and the Beatles, though presumably *A Hard Day's Night* did more for his career.

The thriller element works reasonably well; the attempted murder at a masked carnival is genuinely scary. It's Taurog's approach to comedy that lets the film down. His idea of humour is to have a variety troupe called the Wiere brothers, who hadn't made a film in twenty years, pretend to be three Belgian variations of

Inspector Clouseau. Their scenes must have been especially galling to Presley, who was a genuine fan of Peter Sellers.

Double Trouble did hold one pretty song, Could I Fall In Love, plus an astonishing slice of jazz-blues, City By Night. Even Long Legged Girl (With The Short Dress On), though the title is almost as long as the song, had an energy not heard since *Viva Las Vegas*. On the other hand, the filmmakers did their darnedest to equal things out by making Elvis sit on the back of a truck and sing Old Macdonald.

In the end, fans weren't that fascinated by Elvis taking 'mad mod Europe by song as he swings into a brand new adventure filled with dames, diamonds and discotheques', as the posters put it. *Double Trouble* grossed just $1.6 million; its working title, *You're Killing Me*, summed up what films like this were doing to Elvis's career.**

☆ CLAMBAKE ☆

United Artists, 1967 VHS, DVD
Director Arthur Nadel; **co-stars** Shelley Fabares, James Gregory, Will Hutchins.

In *Clambake*, an innocuous variation on the prince-and-pauper theme, Elvis stars as Scott Heywood, the son of an oil millionaire. He swaps places with a water-ski instructor (Will Hutchings), so he can get ahead on his own terms, and be sure the next girl who falls for him won't be a gold-digger. The script went through the usual pre-production metamorphosis: its original working title, *Too Big For Texas*, presumably had to be changed once the speed-boat motif was added. *Clambake* had been Parker's standby title for *Spinout*. Elvis balked at what he was being ask to do, openly complaining to friends and, for once, to studio executives, though officially filming was delayed because he'd suffered concussion after a nasty fall.

349

The song said you gotta have *Clambake*; the world wasn't as convinced

On screen, Elvis falls for Shelley Fabares, but he can't admit he has the money she's looking for in a man. Neither Fabares – Elvis's love interest for the third and last time – nor Bill Bixby as a rich villain can quite stave off the overall tedium. The by-numbers approach is best revealed when Fabares loses her bikini top while swimming, a fate that also befell Joan Blackman in *Blue Hawaii*. The one unexpected development is the appearance by Flipper the dolphin, whose career, like Elvis's, was waning; her last NBC TV series was shown in 1967. Properly exploited, this could have given the film a cult following, but sadly Flipper has only a cameo role. The music doesn't help, either. At least the seven songs are spaced out to fit the story, but only three are any good, all ballads: You Don't Know Me, The Girl I Never Loved and A House That Has Everything. Who Needs Money? and Confidence are truly dreadful.

If you ignore the usual absurdities and the worst of the songs, this is watchable enough. Elvis was finally making a fuss about his scripts, but at the very moment when his box-office star was waning. Grossing $1.6 million, *Clambake* made a very small profit, but hardly gave him the leverage to press for better roles.

The *New York Times* summed it up best: 'What do we see over his shoulder when the star drives Miss Fabares to the Miami airport and professes true love? Mountains, real Florida mountains.' **

☆ STAY AWAY JOE ☆

MGM, 1968 VHS

Director Peter Tewkesbury; **co-stars** Joan Blondell, Burgess Meredith, Katy Jurado, Thomas Gomez

Despite plummeting box-office returns for Elvis's assembly-line musicals – described in *Elvis Monthly* as 'animated puppet shows for not overbright children' – MGM signed him up for a new deal. Their decision to take a more adventurous approach to roles and subject matter coincided with tightening budgets, variable scriptwriting and doubts as to how far the 'new Elvis' could go.

The result was *Stay Away Joe*, in which Elvis plays a womanizing Navajo called Joe Lightcloud. Detested by critics, it earned

351

The alternative Elvis movie career

Stories abound of the roles that Elvis could have played, and the acting career he might have enjoyed. Perhaps his saddest missed opportunity was the very first, playing the emotionally disturbed Jimmy Currie, with Burt Lancaster and Katharine Hepburn, in *The Rainmaker* (1956). Although he tested successfully, the marketing machine insisted on *Love Me Tender* as his movie debut. Similarly, while rows over fees scuppered Elvis's hopes of starring with Robert Mitchum in the moonshining movie *Thunder Road* (1958), it wasn't the kind of role the Colonel had in mind.

After Elvis's return from the Army, the offers dwindled. When Leiber and Stoller had the bright idea of putting him in touch with *On The Waterfront* director Elia Kazan to star in Nelson Algren's *A Walk On The Wild Side*, Presley was intrigued, but Parker was incandescent. One of the characters was a lesbian, for heaven's sake! Elvis might have generated much-needed critical buzz by

appearing in John Cassavetes' *Too Late Blues* (1962) about a jazz musician, but Bobby Darin got the part. Post-comeback, a resurgence of interest led to rumoured offers to star as Sundance in *Butch Cassidy And The Sundance Kid*, and as the gigolo in *Midnight Cowboy*.

The most famous offer of all came in 1975, when **Barbra Streisand** walked backstage in Las Vegas to invite Elvis to play the alcoholic fading star Norman Maine in her remake of *A Star Is Born*. According to Jerry Schilling, 'He basically said he'd do it … He was incredibly excited'. Parker's insistence on $1m in advance, rather than a percentage of the gross, caused the deal to fall apart, and the role went to **Kris Kristofferson**. Other possibilities included a part in a **Paul Newman** film, and one opposite **Sammy Davis Jr** as two convicts chained together on the run. Davis said that Elvis rang him up crying to tell him that the Colonel had vetoed the role.

Elvis a Golden Turkey nomination for the worst racial impersonation in a movie (he lost out to Marlon Brando in *Teahouse Of The August Moon*). It was also accused of stereotyping Native Americans, although, in truth, they're presented no less favourably than the other characters or, indeed, the hillbillies in *Kissin' Cousins*.

Based on a bestselling novel by Dan Cushman, *Stay Away Joe* was shot on location in Arizona. Elvis looks great, slimmer than for years, enjoys himself hugely, and is well supported by veterans like Burgess Meredith, Joan Blondell, Thomas Gomez and Katy Jurado. But the plot, in which he persuades a congressman to give his family some cattle, soon takes second place to parties and fights, as director Peter Tewkesbury (fresh from the acclaimed comedy *Sunday In New York*) opts to play for farce. Elvis manages to save the day, just, while avoiding a shotgun marriage and irate boyfriends. The rodeo scenes are particularly shoddy, littered with bloopers and continuity errors, while the songs include Stay Away, sung with feeling over the credits, a decent light-blues All I Needed Was The Rain, and a tribute to his bull, Dominic, that he insisted he didn't want released even if he died.

The studio clearly didn't know what to make of *Stay Away Joe*, promoting it with the slogan 'Elvis is kissin' cousins again – and also friends, and even some perfect strangers', and it only made number 65 on *Variety*'s list of the year's top-grossing films. ★★

☆ SPEEDWAY ☆

MGM, 1968 VHS

Director Norman Taurog; **co-stars** Nancy Sinatra, Bill Bixby.

After the commercial and critical failure of the offbeat *Stay Away Joe*, it was back to the formula for *Speedway*, with Elvis as a successful stock-car driver. As his well-meaning but inept manager

(Bill Bixby) hasn't been paying his taxes, he's pursued by the mysterious Susan Jacks (Nancy Sinatra, in a part turned down by Petula Clark), who proves to be an Internal Revenue agent. Sinatra took second billing, although her kitsch classic Those Boots Are Made For Walking had been a US number one in 1966. Her presence – she even gets a solo number, Your Groovy Self – may explain why *Speedway* bucked the trend, and raked in $3 million.

Speedway zips along quite brightly, with Presley, Sinatra and Bixby making a genuinely likable threesome. Director Norman Taurog put a bit of effort into the car scenes, drafting in seven professional drivers and using ten cameras. Sadly, the races are so predictable that ten times as many wouldn't have made any difference.

As for the music, Elvis's seduction number Let Yourself Go was good enough to use in his forthcoming TV special. None of the other songs match it, though Your Time Hasn't Come Yet Baby, sung to a child, is as charming as *Clambake*'s Confidence was charmless. By now, the fans had stopped buying the soundtracks; this one, his last, rose no higher than number 82 on the US charts. *Speedway* did at least register with the young Quentin Tarantino: *Jack Rabbit Slim's*, the bar in Pulp Fiction, is clearly a homage to *Speedway*'s groovy car-themed *Hangout*. *****

☆ LIVE A LITTLE, LOVE A LITTLE ☆

MGM, 1968 VHS
Director Norman Taurog; **co-stars** Michelle Carey, Celese Yarnall, Rudy Vallee, Don Porter, Dick Sargent.

354

Based on Dan Greenburg's novel *Kiss My Firm But Pliant Lips*, Live A Little, Love A Little was intended to be an updated screwball sex comedy. Norman Taurog, directing his ninth and last Elvis picture, even recalled the 'wall of Jericho' device that separates Clark

Gable and Claudette Colbert in *It Happened One Night*. Sadly, that's the only Capra-esque touch. While the classic screwball comedies were full of implausibilities, they had an inner logic that kept you watching. This one doesn't; instead, its strongest card is probably Elvis's image. No longer the pudgy eunuch of yore, he's slimmed down, well styled, and snappily dressed.

It opens with Greg Nolan (Elvis) driving his Jeep in ever-decreasing circles on a beach, then being confined to the sea by a ferocious Great Dane. In real life, Albert was Elvis's own dog, Brutus; here he belongs to Bernice (Michelle Carey). She nurses Greg through the resultant fever, but not quickly enough to prevent him getting sacked as a newspaper photographer. He then finds two jobs, one working for a posh ad agency run by crooner Rudy Vallee, and one on the *Playboy* clone *Classic Cat*, under the amusing rogue Don Porter, who was later to excel in Robert Redford's *The Candidate*. Meanwhile, unbeknown to Greg, Bernice has moved all his possessions into her house. Add to this confusion the fact that everyone seems to call Bernice something different, and you have enough permutations to keep the comedic wheels in motion.

While Michelle Carey interacts well with Elvis, who seems to relish the change of emphasis, the character of Bernice is so confusing that even Katharine Hepburn couldn't pull it off. She does get to enjoy a unique distinction, however: this is the one Elvis film in which, even if we don't see it, he clearly goes all the way with his heroine. The lucky Bernice is so shocked she runs away, after writing a thank-you note in lipstick on the bedroom mirror.

The script, written by Michael Hoey, isn't brilliant, but has the odd neat flourish. Asked 'Aren't you cold?', a scantily clad receptionist replies, 'Only from nine to five' – for an Elvis film, that's positively Wildean. And the songs are better than average. Edge Of Reality may be the best song ever performed with a talking dog; though the lyrics don't quite make sense, Elvis rises manfully to the challenge. Neither A Little Less Conversation nor the ballad

355

Almost In Love is going to change the world, but they're mature and listenable. **★★★**

☆ CHARRO! ☆

National General, 1969 VHS, DVD
Director Charles Warren; **co-stars** Victor French, Ina Balin, Solomon Sturges.

Elvis must have thought he was dreaming when he saw the script for *Charro!*, his first completely non-musical role. Yes, the opening scene really did feature several bare-breasted ladies of the night, and nowhere was he expected to sing about a shrimp or to a precocious brat. So he arrived on set, sporting a beard and hoping the resemblance to a Clint Eastwood movie would run deeper than having a score by Hugo Montenegro. He was soon dismayed to find producer/director/writer **Charles Marquis Warren** had ditched the opening in favour of a bar brawl right out of his own TV series, *Gunsmoke*.

As reformed gunslinger **Jess Wade**, Elvis has been framed by gang leader Vince Hackett (**Victor French**), for murder and for stealing a cannon that fired the vital shot in Mexico's struggle for independence. The two men are also rivals for the affections of saloon girl Tracy Winters (**Ina Balin**). The build-up is reasonably intriguing, but Warren – who had not directed a film in a decade – fails to keep a taut enough grip, and both cast and sets are unconvincing. That said, one scene, in which the newly deputized Wade bumps a prisoner's head against the bars, belongs in a much better movie.

Presumably Warren came cheap. As Elvis films were now making less than $2 million each, there wasn't the budget or belief to get a top-notch director like Don Siegel (of *Flaming Star* fame) or

357

◀ Elvis and his star-crossed lover Celese Yarnall in *Live A Little, Love A Little*

Sam Peckinpah. A shame: Westerns suited Elvis, and he's at ease in his beard and greasy leather pants as he never really was as a singing racing-car driver. In different hands this movie might have worked. As it is, critics blasted it, with *Variety* saying, 'Elvis strolls through a role that would have driven any other actor up the wall.' Note that the DVD release of this film is not of the highest technical quality. **

☆ THE TROUBLE WITH GIRLS ☆

MGM, 1969 VHS
Director Peter Tewkesbury; **co-stars** Marlyn Mason, Sheree North, Edward Andrews, Vincent Price, John Carradine.

By 1969, the world had written off Elvis the film actor. That's a pity, because, while MGM's decision to give Elvis a nine-year-old screenplay about a travelling show (*chautaqua*) might smack of desperation, the gamble pays off. Despite its ridiculous subtitle, *The Trouble With Girls (And How To Get Into It)* is probably his most successful film since *Viva Las Vegas*, and all the better for representing a considerable change of pace.

Elvis is Walter Hale, the anachronistically white-suited manager of a troupe whose visit to a small Iowa town coincides with a murder. When his cardsharp is accused, Elvis has to solve the mystery to save the show and his job. Marlyn Mason plays a shop steward, whose approach to industrial relations is complicated by the fact that she's half in love with her boss, Elvis. The naturalness of their rapport disproves the cliché that Elvis can't react to his co-stars, as does his easy banter with Edward Andrews, his right-hand man. The supporting cast is excellent, with John Carradine greasily effective as the womanizing murder victim; Sheree North almost perfect as the bitter blonde murderess; and Vincent Price in an amusing cameo.

All the songs fit into the story – most are performed on stage – and director Peter Tewksbury doesn't feel the need to exaggerate the audience's response. Even the worst material – Signs Of The Zodiac, a duet with Mason – is acceptable in context, while Clean Up Your Own Backyard, odd as it is, is a rare venture into social comment.

The Trouble With Girls is not without flaws. There are some silly anachronistic slip-ups, and the scene where Sheree North has to be forcibly sobered up goes on far too long. Worst of all, as far as the Colonel was concerned, Elvis wasn't always on screen. Instead, Tewkesbury focused on the milieu and his characters in a way that later critics might have called Altman-esque. At the time, it was panned, although one writer called it 'a good deal of unpretentious fun'. But a few more brave attempts like this might have lengthened the King's reign in Hollywood. ★★★★

☆ CHANGE OF HABIT ☆

Universal, 1969 VHS

Director William Graham; **co-stars** Mary Tyler Moore, Barbara McNair. Jane Elliot.

You might expect Elvis's last feature film, *Change Of Habit*, to mark his career low as an actor. In fact, as John Carpenter MD, a New York slum doctor, he seems so at ease it's almost as though he's playing an idealized version of himself – which of course he did do, in the two MGM documentaries on his revived musical career that were to follow.

That the movie made its UK debut on TV is oddly appropriate. It's not that bad – not that it's brilliant either – it just feels like a pleasant way to while away a wet Wednesday afternoon, an impression reinforced by the fact that two of its stars, Mary Tyler Moore and Ed Asner, remain far more associated with the small screen.

Tyler Moore and her fellow nuns take off their habits and go undercover as nurses at Elvis's surgery, as part of an experiment by the local Catholic church. Assuming that Tyler Moore merely *looks* virginal, Elvis is soon hung up on her. Cue some good touch-football scenes, a fair bit of sugar-coated social commentary – and a shocking hint of blasphemy in the final scene, when the troubled Tyler Moore returns to church to see Elvis perform Let Us Pray. As the camera pans from Elvis to the statue of Christ, she seems to be faced with a straight choice: Elvis or God? Most viewers believe she will choose Elvis. Was the film saying that Elvis was bigger than Jesus? Hard to believe – surely that was John Lennon's thing.

The set was not without its tensions. Although Elvis named William Graham – later responsible for the TV movie *Elvis And The Colonel* – as one of his favourite directors, he hid himself behind the impenetrable wall of his Memphis mafia. In addition, says stepbrother David Stanley, Elvis didn't much like Tyler Moore. Being a Southern gentleman, he hid his dislike so well that she has never stopped saying how gorgeous and downright nice he was. *******

☆ ELVIS: THAT'S THE WAY IT IS ☆

MGM, 1970 VHS, DVD (new version)
Director Denis Sanders; **director of photography** Lucien Ballard.

Good as *Elvis: That's The Way It Is* may be, it doesn't quite live up to the title. This documentary about Elvis in Las Vegas in 1970 falls roughly into two parts: *Elvis: That's The Way He Rehearses*, and *Elvis: That's The Way He Performs*. Director Denis Sanders tries to dig deeper, but his interviews with fans and hotel personnel are predictable and unenlightening, while the backstage footage seems to have been edited as much to avoid offending anyone as to let us watch Elvis in action. The best example is the shot of Elvis reading good-luck telegrams. A clip not used here, which surfaced in *This Is Elvis*, shows him reading one that says, 'Dear Elvis, after

360

fourteen years we have finally learned to understand what you say on record, yours sincerely RCA.' That's funnier than anything that stayed in, and gives a flavour of the sharp humour his friends recollect, but was apparently just too darned controversial.

Colonel Parker suggested other cuts, some because he felt that they demeaned Elvis or his fans. Yet the nastiest implication was left in: a shot of Elvis rehearsing while, on the other half of the screen, steaks are hauled into the hotel kitchens; the not-so-subliminal message being that, in Vegas at least Elvis is just another piece of meat.

361

The *That's The Way It Is* rehearsals were more revelatory than the shows

The concert footage is a must for all fans. Elvis is in fine form and humour. Even lesser songs like Patch It Up come across with such excitement that it's easy to see why Sammy Davis Jr is jumping around the showroom. And Suspicious Minds is tremendous, with Elvis still deeply in love with the song. Good as all that is, the rehearsals are even more of a revelation: Elvis chats with the Sweet Inspirations, quips, 'If the songs don't go over, we can always do a medley of costumes', and looks so downright nervous you think he's going to faint before he walks out on stage.

The recent recut version of *That's The Way It Is* strips away all Sanders' pretensions to documentary making to add more footage of both rehearsal and concert. Bizarrely, "I Just Can't Help Believing" has been cut, even though he still refers to his fear he'll forget the words. As a straight concert video, it is superb (although the song selection ignores some fine ballads from the period), but the original, in its ham-fisted way, said more about the mania that surrounded Elvis. ***** (for recut)

☆ ELVIS ON TOUR ☆

MGM, 1972 VHS
Producers/directors Pierre Adidge, Robert Abel.

Elvis's last film, *Elvis On Tour*, was his first to win a major award, a Golden Globe for best documentary. Perhaps documentary was in the doldrums in 1972, but Pierre Adidge and Robert Abel deserve their glory for creating a movie that says something about the man, and what the 1970s had in store for him.

As a record of Elvis the concert performer, this is significantly inferior to both versions of *That's The Way It Is*. That's not the filmmakers' fault, though thanks possibly to the young Martin Scorsese, who worked on the montages, they overdo the split screen. The main problem is that Elvis is paler and pudgier, already perhaps suspecting that in swapping movies for concerts he may have just exchanged one rut for another. At times, especially early on when wearing a red jumpsuit, big jewellery and even bigger sunglasses, he looks like one of his own impersonators. The light visible in his eyes in those 1970 Las Vegas performances only flickers here.

Elvis is professional yet slightly detached, amused by the madness of it all. There's a marvellous bit when, on his knees for the slow verse of Suspicious Minds, he looks down, spots the camera beneath him, and gives an astonished grin. Moments of genuine fervour are rarer: a rousing Never Been To Spain, a great American Trilogy, and, most intriguing of all, when he stands like a boy in church to listen to JD Sumner and the Stamps sing Sweet Sweet Spirit.

Some of the behind-the-scenes stuff seems inconsequential, but collectively it works. You get a glimpse of what a very strange trip it was to be Elvis, perpetually on tour for seven years, greeted in every strangely familiar city by a high-pitched chorus from dimly seen fans. Elvis seems closest when he's watching his backing singers sing For The Lighthouse around the piano. The movie closes, however, with an enigmatic shot of Elvis staring out the window of a limo, utterly alone even though the car is full.

Perhaps the best thing about *Elvis On Tour* is that, unlike many of the movies that preceded it, it gave Elvis some genuine satisfaction. He was watching the Golden Globe ceremony on TV in his bathroom at the Las Vegas Hilton when his entourage heard a sudden yell: 'My God! Sonofabitch! We've won! We've won the Golden Globe.' ★★★★

☆ THIS IS ELVIS ☆

Warner Brothers, 1981 VHS
Directors Malcolm Leo, Andrew Solt, Gil Hubbs.

Put together after Elvis's death, and linking genuine footage with unconvincing reconstructions, *This Is Elvis* is to be prized for its concert highlights, clips from TV shows and home movies – even if most of them are available elsewhere. Its script, with presumably unconscious irony, is about as sophisticated as those of the movies in which Elvis had once starred. He said enough sharp, intelligent things in his life to come across as a far more complex individual than he does in the filler scenes here.

So long as you fast-forward past soundalike Ral Donner puffing 'I wish I coulda seen what was happenin to me', *This Is Elvis* is very watchable. The appalling spectacle of Elvis singing Are You Lonesome Tonight? in his final concerts has genuine dramatic power. Why was a man so desperately ill allowed to perform rather than being tucked up in hospital? ****

☆ ☆ ☆ THE CONCERT PERFORMANCES ☆ ☆ ☆

A handful of 'Elvis in concert' videos/DVDs are essential purchases. Any collection should start with both MGM tour documentaries, the Virgin video *Elvis 56 In The Beginning*, either the official *1968 TV Special* or its sister release *One Night With You*, and *Aloha From Hawaii* or *The Lost Performances*. For reference purposes, we have reviewed the 1977 CBS TV special *Elvis In Concert* even though it is not available as an official release and probably never will be. Otherwise, we have focused on the best of the available material, reviewing it in chronological order of the performances. For a retrospective of his career as a whole, *Elvis Presley The Great*

Performances is available on video (if you can't find it, Elvis Presley Enterprises it is still selling it) and is recommended.

☆ Elvis 56 In The Beginning ☆

Virgin, 1988 VHS, DVD

All the clichés about the documentary *Elvis 56* – 'words can't praise it highly enough', and so on – are absolutely true. Drawing on stunning black-and-white stills by Alfred Wertheimer as well as fantastic TV footage from the *Milton Berle* and *Ed Sullivan* shows, it immortalizes the most controversial and dramatic year of Elvis's life. Elvis himself transforms from the innocent blond-looking boy at the start to become a confident, black-haired, Tony Curtis lookalike, whose charisma is even louder than the Jordanaires' jackets.

Presley is also put into context, as American society struggles to get a grip on the changes unleashed by this softly spoken monster. One droll snippet shows Perry Como singing "Hot Diggity" with what seems to be an oversized toilet roll. And you see Elvis jam with Liberace. If you can't remember 1956, this is the next best thing. *****

☆ 1968 TV Special/One Night With You ☆

Warner/HBO both releases available on VHS, DVD

Even today, well over three decades since it was filmed, Elvis's *1968 TV Special* has lost little of its original fascination. The format may be familiar from countless copycat *MTV Unplugged*s, but this is not some neophyte, desperate to show off his music smarts: it's the mysterious, unknowable figure that is Elvis.

There are three very good reasons why the special still feels like a revelation. First, it contains the finest live performances Elvis

365

The 'steamy' bordello sequence, cut from the *1968 TV Special*

ever committed to film; second, his stories and gags are as close to a proper interview with the man at the eye of all the hype as we ever got (and, friends insist, as close as he ever came on screen to his manner in everyday life); and third, because to anyone raised on Goldman's cartoon version, the Elvis on display here comes as quite a shock. He's not dumb, but intelligent, engaged and amused – and, at times, extremely amusing.

Fans also cherish it as one of the few moments when Presley bucked Colonel Parker. Instead of singing a stack of Christmas songs, as his manager had envisaged, he assembled a body of songs that works as a musical autobiography. He even wound Parker up by singing a rewritten version of It Hurts Me at the Colonel's birthday party, with the final line 'Is it too much to ask for one lousy, tired ol' Christmas song?' In the event, Blue Christmas was indeed inserted into the show, after an irate Parker threatened to postpone it until the summer, and record a separate Christmas special.

Credit must go to producer Steve Binder, who gave Presley the encouragement needed to shape the show. Even so, some of his wackier conceits do seem downright weird. The video release includes a sequence in which dancers prance around to a honky-tonk tune while the image flickers like a silent movie. If any of you are lucky enough to meet Mr Binder, maybe you'd ask him what that was all about. Those fans who prefer their Elvis straight prefer One Night With You, a tidy compilation of the best on-stage moments. But the full version remains an essential purchase: some of Binder's ideas, like the gospel medley, pay off big time.

The two elements that completely outshine the rest are Elvis performing in black leather on that small stage, and the superlative finale of If I Can Dream. The ad libs fly thick and fast, from a man who has seldom said more than 'Yes, Sir' and 'No, Mam' in public before. In one marvellous moment early on, for no apparent reason, he interrupts his act to pick up the microphone, brandish it like a spear and shout 'Moby Dick'.

367

Presley may have resurrected his career with this show, but not everyone was impressed. The *LA Times* complained snootily, 'I don't think many viewers care to see singers sweat on TV', while showbiz bible *Variety*, to its eternal shame, sniffed, 'He still can't sing'. Thankfully, most agreed with Bruce Springsteen's future manager Jon Landau, who wrote in *Eye* magazine, 'He sang with the kind of power people no longer expect from rock and roll singers. He moved his body with a lack of pretension and effort which must have made Jim Morrison green with envy.'

Binder's last remark to his star has a particular poignancy. When Elvis asked him what he thought lay ahead now, Binder replied: 'Elvis, my real, real feeling is that I don't know if you'll do any great things you want to do. Maybe the bed has been made already, maybe this'll just be a little fresh air you'll experience for a month.' Though the 'fresh air' lasted a little longer than Binder feared, in the end he was absolutely spot-on. *****

☆ The Lost Performances ☆

Warner, 1992 VHS

Although presumably that's not the idea, *The Lost Performances*, which combines rediscovered outtakes from both *That's The Way It is* and *Elvis On Tour*, enables viewers to pinpoint the moment when Elvis's euphoria at his return to splendour began to evaporate. That he's so charismatic, good-humoured and inspirational in the Las Vegas segments makes the takes from *On Tour* all the more depressing. Elvis was too committed a performer just to go through the motions, but he has gained weight, doesn't look well and sings with less passion. What's astonishing about the ensuing decline is not that his performances grew increasingly erratic, but that he stayed on the treadmill for another five years. ****

✩ Aloha From Hawaii ✩

Warner 1973, VHS, DVD

Ultimately, the most impressive aspect of 1973's *Aloha From Hawaii* TV special was its 1.1 billion global audience, which proved that for much of the world, Elvis Aron Presley was still America's most potent export. No one really talks about the music; Greil Marcus certainly didn't repeat his praise of the 1968 special, that this was 'the finest music of his life'. And, for Elvis himself, *Aloha* may have seemed the bitterest of ironies. Even as he gained the attention of the whole world, he had lost, if not his soul, then his wife and child.

The concert took place for good business and personal reasons. Colonel Parker clearly hoped it would distract Elvis from the breakdown of his marriage, put him back in the headlines, and stimulate record sales, especially in the Far East, which saw the show live. (In the event, *Aloha* won the highest ever share of the TV audience in Japan, and an amazing 92 percent in the Philippines.) In addition, it might have stoped people asking Parker when Elvis was going to tour the world.

Initially, the idea seemed to work. Presley went on a crash diet and lost 25 pounds, as requested by producer Marty Pasetta. He got heavily involved in the design of his jumpsuit, telling Bill Belew he wanted something to symbolize America – hence the eagle. In rehearsals, the first cape was so heavy that Elvis fell over and lay laughing on the stage.

As the hour of the concert approached, however, Elvis seemed depressed. His friend Bill Burk was struck by his eyes: 'I may be on my own on this, but whenever I think of *Aloha* I think of his eyes. Those are real sad, heartbroken eyes.' No surprise, then, that Elvis seems most moved by Hank Williams's I'm So Lonesome I Could Cry (introduced as 'the saddest song I ever heard'), It's Over, You Gave Me A Mountain and What Now My Love.

Movies influenced by Elvis

Although Presley's ghost has, as far as filmmakers are concerned, often been a pernicious influence, there are enough Elvis-related movies to programme a film festival.

You don't have to delve far into most **Quentin Tarantino** movies to find an Elvis allusion. In *Pulp Fiction*, Uma Thurman's character makes the (largely true) observation that you're either an Elvis person or a Beatles person, which may explain why she ends up in a club that bears a striking resemblance to the one in *Speedway*. Some fans speculate that Marsellus's mysterious briefcase contains Elvis's gold suit, as worn when Val Kilmer plays Elvis's ghost in the Tarantino-scripted *True Romance* – a film in which the spectral Presley performs the same advisory role as Humphrey Bogart in Woody Allen's *Play It Again Sam*.

Probably the finest film to star the ghost of Elvis, Jim Jarmusch's *Mystery Train* (1989), tells three initially unrelated stories in which a pair of Japanese tourists, an Italian widow and a gang of criminals all have a miserable time in Memphis. Elvis's version of the title song kicks things off; the bellhop and the clerk (Screaming Jay Hawkins) trade Elvis trivia at the *Arcade Hotel*; Elvis's eerie version of "Blue Moon" plays constantly on the radio; and he appears to the Italian widow who has met someone who tells of giving his ghost a lift to the gates of Graceland. Also in the cast is Beale Street legend **Rufus Thomas**, who sang "Bear Cat", a homage to/rip-off of Willie Mae Thornton's "Hound Dog".

An earlier, jaundiced, look at Elvis was *A Face In The Crowd*, Elia Kazan's overwrought parable about a hillbilly singer who becomes, by a process too complex to detail here, a demagogue. The legend gets a more sympathetic reading in Sidney Lumet's *The Fugitive Kind* (1961), based on Tennessee Williams' *Orpheus Descending*. Even though the hero is a young guitar player who plies his trade in small-town Mississippi, and is doomed by his own sexual magnetism, Brando got the role – not Elvis. Lumet says, 'Years later, I suddenly thought of Presley. What would it have been like if Val had had Presley's simplicity, lyricism, and rather strange otherwordly quality?' That same year, future Elvis co-star **Ann-Margret** starred in *Bye Bye Birdie*, a lightweight musical spoof about Elvis being drafted, directed by George Sidney, who later helmed *Viva Las Vegas*.

Elvis as a motif then largely disappeared from movies until after his death. In 1980, **Paul Simon**, made *One Trick Pony*, a movie about a failing folk musician who is told by his wife, 'You have wanted to be Elvis Presley since you were thirteen. Now that's a goal you're not likely to achieve. He didn't do so well with it himself.' *Touched By Love*, also from 1980, tells the true story of a handicapped girl's devotion to Elvis, while the equally sentimental *Eat The Peach*, from 1986, was a charming Irish comedy in

which Vinnie and Arthur distract themselves from their problems by building a replica of the 'wall of death' from *Roustabout*.

Nicolas Cage was astonished to find himself sharing the screen with the ghost of Elvis in two successive movies. Elvis was used strictly for laughs in *Honeymoon in Vegas*, although its 34 flying Elvises prompted the *Las Vegas Sun* reviewer to ask: 'If Sinatra has had as big an influence on our culture as Elvis, where are all the flying Sinatras?' David Lynch's strange road movie *Wild At Heart* is piled high with Presley references; its most famous scene, when Cage beats someone up and then croons "Love Me Tender", is almost the posthumous realization of Taurog's dream of Elvis as a cold-blooded killer. Nonetheless, the wackiest piece of posthumous Presleyana has to be Finnish director Aki Kaurismäki's *Leningrad Cowboys Go America* (1989), in which the struggling quiff-laden rock band cross America, stopping to buy a Cadillac off Jim Jarmusch, to tour Sun Studios and sing "That's All

371

Right Mama". In a nice touch, they also rebel against their tyrant of a manager, as Elvis never did on celluloid and only rarely did in real life.

Finding Graceland (1998), in which **Harvey Keitel** gets to play a King-like figure (and Priscilla Presley is executive producer) is not quite as memorable but works thanks mainly to Keitel, **Jonathan Schaech** (as the bereaved motorist who gives Keitel a lift), and **Bridget Fonda** (as a Marilyn Monroe lookalike).

While Elvis is consummately professional, it's a strangely impersonal performance, lacking the sense of fun of the 1968 TV special. What we get instead, as the *New York Times* put it, is 'shameless old-fangled showmanship'. This is Elvis at his most iconic, the Elvis his impersonators would aspire to become. He walks out on the stage, he strikes poses – but doesn't actually move that much – runs through most of his usual repertoire, has a few laughs with Fever, flings his cape into the audience, and he is gone. Whereas the 1968 special had brought the world closer to Elvis, *Aloha* made him seem more remote. In the last four years of his life, he was to become remoter still. The official concert performance is available on video and DVD, as is the dress rehearsal billed as The Alternate Aloha. Collectors and completists will want to have both. ★★★

☆ Elvis In Concert ☆

CBS, 1977

Some revisionists argue that *Elvis In Concert* – the 1977 CBS TV special – is not as bad as everyone says it is. That theory gets some support from the double album, which finds Presley in great voice on several numbers (mainly from the Rapid City show). For most of us, however, watching this is like watching footage of a relative dying. Officially, Presley's estate has only licensed fragments to be included in other films or videos, though you can track down some footage on the Internet. Despite the odd moment of magic, it's a shocking, galling experience.

☆ ☆ ☆ OTHER VIDEOS ☆ ☆ ☆

The range of Elvis videos varies from stuff which pokes affection-ate fun at fans (*Mondo Elvis*) to Joe Tunzi's collections of rare footage on releases like *Welcome Home Elvis*. This is only a small selection of the material on offer because the quality varies almost as widely as the subject matter.

☆ All The King's Men ☆

E-Realbiz.Com, 1997 VHS

All The King's Men is not for anyone who doesn't want to hear about Elvis's darker side, but if you want to really understand what happened and why, this isn't a bad place to start. You might have heard some of the stories before, and the material is padded out a bit to stretch over two videos, but it's intriguing just to hear Marty Lacker, Billy Smith, Red and Sonny West tell them. There are also some rare and unseen home movies and clips. ★★★

☆ Classic Albums ☆

Pioneer, 2002 VHS, DVD

Featuring insight from Sam Phillips, Dixie Locke, Scotty Moore, BB King and Keith Richards, *Classic Albums*, a TV documentary about Elvis's first self-titled album, is essential viewing even though it doesn't have much footage of the man himself. ★★★★

373

☆ Elvis In Hollywood ☆

BMG, 1993 VHS, DVD

The *Elvis In Hollywood* video ranks as a must-have for the footage of Elvis's original screen test for Hal Wallis. It should really have been called *Elvis In Hollywood 1956–58*, however: the rest of his film career is largely ignored. The interviews – with Scotty Moore, George Klein and Leiber and Stoller – are not that illuminating. *******

☆ Elvis Presley's Graceland ☆

Congress Entertainment, 1988 VHS, DVD

Like a lot of products from the Presley estate, the official *Elvis Presley's Graceland* video is professionally made, decently narrated, and just a little bland. Even if it can't compare to being there, however, it's not a bad substitute or souvenir. Most fans will have seen both the home movies and the concert clips before, but it's still a compulsory purchase, if only because El's ideas on home decoration were as individual as his approach to music. *******

☆ Elvis Private Moments ☆

Telstar, 1997 VHS

The video of June Juanico's book *Elvis In The Twilight Of Memory*, *Elvis Private Moments* is an affectionate retelling of an intriguing story, with the occasional pointless interpolation from Elvis's buddy George Klein. The footage of Elvis out fishing with his folks in Biloxi, Mississippi, in the summer of 1956 is the highlight, but the whole documentary gives a flavour of what it was like to be the young Elvis, in that fleeting interval after he became a household name and before the fame became so massive it imprisoned him. ********

374

☆ Elvis The Missing Years ☆

Music Video Distribution, 2002 VHS, DVD

Rare footage of Elvis in Germany, on leave in Paris and singing at his mate Eddie Fadal's home. A must for collectors. The DVD release includes a 55-minute audio documentary and a CD. ★★★★

☆ He Touched Me ☆

EMD/Chordant, 1999 VHS, DVD

The two volumes of **He Touched Me** may depict Elvis as a cardboard saint who was kind to animals, generous to the poor, and helped little old ladies across the road, but it's one of the better examples of the genre, and focuses on one of the least explored parts of his life, his love for gospel music. It makes up for minimal footage of Elvis performing gospel with a wealth of anecdote and interviews. ★★★★

☆ Welcome Home Elvis ☆

JAT, 2001 DVD

The teaming of Elvis and Sinatra, on Sinatra's 1960 TV special, is available in its entirety on this limited-edition collectors' DVD from Joe Tunzi. Although Elvis looks distinctly nervous, he carries off neat versions of Fame And Fortune and Stuck On You. On the duet he seems even more lost, but still cool, and makes a better stab at Witchcraft than Ol' Blue Eyes does at Love Me Tender. The DVD also contains El's first post-Army interview, some of Tunzi's private photos and clippings from *TV Guide*. ★★★★

375

The TV movies

Some of the Elvis-related TV movies are about as essential as El's version of "Old Macdonald". *Elvis And The Beauty Queen* (1981), the story of Presley and Linda Thompson, is chiefly remembered among aficionados of trash TV for **Don Johnson**'s awesomely bad portrayal of Elvis. In contrast, **Beau Bridges**' turn as Colonel Parker is the main redeeming feature of *Elvis And The Colonel* (1993). *Elvis And Me*, the 1988 TV movie of Priscilla's book, is worth changing channels to avoid. Only **John Carpenter**'s 1979 TVM *Elvis* stands out as the best-known, and the best, fictionalization of Elvis's life. **Kurt Russell** plays the King believably, somehow acquiring the charisma he so often lacks, and was deservedly nominated for an Emmy. As everybody from Felton Jarvis to Larry Geller and Sam Phillips helped out, it's a pity the songs are sung not by Elvis but by **Ronnie McDowell**.

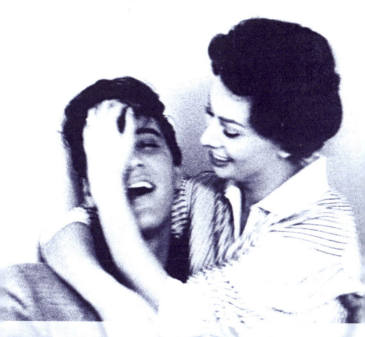

The Icon

'Without Elvis you're nothing'
Madonna

◀ previous page: Sophia Loren smooths the Presley brow

*'It's like he whispered the
same dream in all our ears'*

Bruce Springsteen

Elvis Presley has been an icon for so long and in so many ways it's easy to underestimate the power of his image and the breadth and depth of his appeal. This is, let us remember, a man who has united in admiration such disparate individuals and groups as BB King and The Beatles, Morrissey and Jim Morrison, Cher and Nick Cave, Bob Dylan and Robbie Williams, Eddie Murphy and Alice Cooper, Bill Clinton and Imelda Marcos, Jimmy Carter and Boris Yeltsin, among an almost endless cast ...

In this chapter the focus is on Elvis as icon: the image, the clothes, the hair, the make-up, and, most interesting, the personas that he took on – the rebel who in many ways created the so-called generation gap, and the rock'n'roll culture that we live in today; the romantic hero, successor to Rudolph Valentino and (as Camille Paglia maintains) Lord Byron; the sexual liberator, whose libidinous performances changed the whole sexual climate of postwar America; the regal Elvis, the Vegas institution, furled in $65,000-jumpsuits, aping the comic book heros of his childhood and finally the absurd Elvis, dead but still to inspire punk bands, assorted anarchists and a global host of impersonators.

♪♪♪ 'What's an Elvis?' ♪♪♪

To understand Elvis's iconic power, you need to look back to the point in his (and our) history when he became newly famous. His advent was peculiarly well timed, as his family friend Janelle McComb explained: 'He burst onto the scene when everybody needed a sunrise. We'd come through depression and war. Everybody was ready to give vent to their emotions.' And in 1956 the average American teenager had $10.55 a week to spend, a sum, historian David Halberstam reckoned, 'close to what the average American family had in disposable income fifteen years earlier'. Presley would inspire them to spend both their money and their emotions.

The very name 'Elvis' was weird – 'like something out of a sci-fi comic', Scotty Moore said when he first heard it. Bill Burk, the Memphis reporter who would later befriend Presley, vividly recalls first hearing "Mystery Train" on a jukebox in Memphis in 1955. 'What's that? he asked his friend. 'That's Elvis,' said his friend. Burk, none the wiser, asked: 'What's an Elvis?' Mac Davis, who would later write "In The Ghetto" for the King, spent the day after he first heard "That's All Right" on the radio scouring record stores for the new record by Alvan Parsley. While in New York, the young Paul Simon recalled, 'His name was about the weirdest I'd heard. I thought for sure he was a black guy. My grandmother thought he was Jewish, she thought he was called Alvin.'

If the name was unprecedented (especially as it was a stage name) – it comes from the Norse name 'Alwiss', meaning 'All-wise' – it was consistent with the act and the look. Elvis's voice, of course, was hugely distinctive, but the look was equal to it and inspired immediate devotion. Paul Simon noted: 'I grew my hair

The artist formerly known as Alvan Parsley, Alvin Presley ... ▶

like Elvis, imitated his stage act – once I went all over New York looking for a lavender shirt like the one he wore on one of his albums.' Alice Cooper heard "Hound Dog" as a boy, and 'as soon as I heard that song, I got myself a quiff. I guess I must have looked a pretty strange six-year-old kid.'

Elvis's hair had always been different – different enough for him to seem, as he famously said, 'like a squirrel just come down from the trees' to his more conventionally coiffed contemporaries. He combed it continually, checking it in the mirror, out of narcissism and determination. In 1956 the hair was increasingly jet black – in imitation of Rudolph Valentino and Tony Curtis – and a perfect contrast with what one journalist (female) called his 'heavy lidded boudoir eyes'. The crowning glory was the sneer, the most famous lip curl in history. Here was, as comedian Jackie Gleason put it, 'Marlon Brando with a guitar'.

Yet the Brando comparison was not entirely apt. In the 1950s, Brando was the archetypal leather-jacketed, T-shirted macho male. Elvis, by contrast, liked to mix black with pink (the latter was the female colour of the 1950s) in his stage clothes, while his use of make-up – mascara and royal-blue eye shadow – so shocked Chet Atkins at the Grand Ole Opry in 1954 that he remarked, 'It was like seein' a couple of guys kissin' in Key West.' Elvis was renowned for giving his girlfriends make-up and styling tips – strange behaviour indeed for the 1950s. k.d. lang, who practised being Elvis in front of the mirror when she was 12 years old, says, 'He was the total androgynous beauty.'

The clothes, right from the start, were provocative – clothes that previously only black musicians would wear. In a 1956 interview, Elvis claimed: 'On the streets, out in public, I like real conservative clothes. But on stage I like em as flashy as you can get.' However, his idea of 'real conservative' was, as Bill Burk put it, 'trousers with a stripe down the side of them ... They weren't bought at *Lansky's* [Beale Street store], where the black musicians bought theirs but looked just like they had been.' As for the stage gear, his very first pink-and-black outfit stunned even his relatives, with Billy Smith recalling, 'My family thought, "Why doesn't he just go down on Beale Street and live with em?"'

The Liberator

'You handsome thing you!'

Elvis – mid-tantrum – to a mirror at Graceland

The sexuality of Elvis's stage performances in the 1950s was truly revolutionary. The hip-swinging, the leg-twitching, the pelvic gyrations – these were gestures that had been employed by black performers like Wynonie Harris and Bo Diddley, but never before in the American mainstream, and by a white singer who looked, in the eloquent words of a girl who attended one of his first concerts, like a 'great big hunk of forbidden fruit'. And the effect was sensational: as one woman fan put it, 'Kinsey [author of the famous 1950s report on American sexual mores] told women it was unusual for them to be easily or rapidly sexually aroused. Presley showed us it wasn't. Presley and the Pill brought about women's liberation.'

Indeed, so potent and subversive was Presley's sexuality deemed to be that after his one controversial appearance on *Ed Sullivan* in 1956, the American TV networks decided he should be shown only from the waist up. Jack Good, the *New York Times* TV critic, actually suggested that Presley's success could actually be cured by better sex education, while the *Miami Herald*, reviewing one of Elvis's concerts, suggested that the best remedy for the 14,000 screaming girls in the audience was a 'solid slap across the mouth'.

And it wasn't just sex that enraged conservative America. Elvis may have been a God-fearing Southerner but there were those

383

who saw his style as a threat to white supremacy. His movements seemed, in their very abandon, to cross racial boundaries, and, as such, brought condemnation by the White Citizens Council, and even in Congress, where Congressman Emmanuel Celler asserted, 'Rock and roll has its place, among the coloured people.' Even in liberal New York, the *Daily News*, reviewing a 1956 Presley concert, complained about the 'primitive jungle beat rhythm'. And

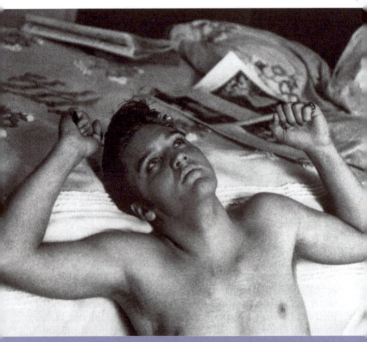

Elvis, looking – to his critics – disturbingly post-coital

Valentino and Byron

Rudolph Valentino was one of Elvis's earliest and most influential idols. He studied the movie star's style, looks and gestures, and in the film *Harum Scarum* he even brandished the star's sword. In the 1920s, Rudolph Valentino brought sex (as opposed to romantic love) to Hollywood movies. Elvis did the same for music thirty years later, topping Tin Pan Alley's romantic clichés of moon and June with an invitation to meet behind the barn.

Valentino, like Elvis, was both adored and reviled for his sexuality and for encouraging women to express feelings that they weren't 'officially' supposed to have. The American press ridiculed the Latin lover's following, and poured scorn on the 'collective hysteria' that greeted his early death, in 1926. And the critics worried about race as well as sex. While Elvis brought black culture to the American mainstream, Valentino had thrust a Latin sensuality into the nation's movie houses.

One figure even Elvis might have been surprised to be compared to is the English Romantic poet **Lord Byron**. Camille Paglia, in her book *Sexual Personae*, drew some intriguing parallels between Byron and Presley. The personality and looks of poet and singer often struck friends as feminine, and a friend's list of Byron's traits – 'caprices, fits of weeping, sudden affections and dislikes' – fits Elvis to a T. Byron was even noted for the contemptuous curl of his upper lip.

Oddly, Byron shared Elvis's struggle against obesity, died prematurely (at 36), and also, according to his autopsy report, suffered from an enlarged heart and damaged liver.

The first teen idol?

these attitudes were not limited to politicans and media bigots. Many men felt so threatened by Elvis they waited around to punch him after gigs.

The sexual liberator, or predator, was an image that Colonel Parker did his best to rein in, keen to present the other side of Elvis – the church-going, God-fearing teetotaller, who was painfully polite to his elders. He must have purred when Ed Sullivan

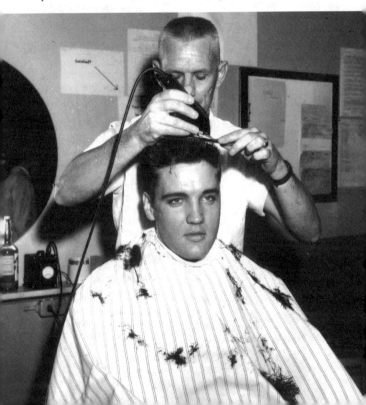

famously introduced Presley in 1957: 'I wanted to say to Elvis Presley and the country that this is a real decent, fine boy.' But the Colonel was not always helped by his charge. Elvis, asked about marriage, once famously observed, 'Why buy a cow when you can get milk under a fence?'

Those responsible for public welfare breathed a sigh of relief when in 1958, joining the US Army, Elvis had the most famous haircut since Samson's. The cut was, his cousin Gene Smith says, hyped 'like it was being announced to one and all that it was a kind of castration'. Mick Farren, author of *Elvis The Complete Illustrated Record*, recalled: 'Even with the limited symbolic appreciation of young boys we knew what the highly-publicized haircut meant, why every cheap-shot comedian was putting so much emphasis on it, We lived through the haircut bullshit at school.'

Camille Paglia asserts that 'Presley, a myth maker, understood the essence of his own archetypal beauty'. And his bass player Norbert Putnam recalled: 'He wasn't highly educated but he was a very quick study and I always felt that he was responsible for every detail, every nuance, of his image.' Elvis may not have had much idea of the long-term impact he would make on American and popular culture – but then who could have? – but he certainly had a precise and intuitive grasp of what worked for him and what didn't. The dyed hair, the make-up, even the eternally turned-up collars (to hide a neck which, he told a friend, was too long), were parts of a very conscious makeover by a man whose look represented almost as challenging a synthesis as his music.

This was, after all, a man who could, in the middle of a rage, catch sight of himself in a Graceland mirror and say, 'You handsome thing you!' before resuming his tantrum.

Collectively, the impact this package had on the world in the 1950s was enormous. As the American composer and conductor Leonard Bernstein put it, 'Elvis Presley is the greatest cultural

387

◀ The most famous haircut since Samson's

force of the 20th century. He introduced the beat to everything, and he changed everything – music, language, clothes ... A whole social revolution – the Sixties comes from it.'

♪♪♪ King and Super-Hero ♪♪♪

'I read comic books and I was the hero'

Elvis Presley, 1971

However much he might have created the decade, the 1960s were not, for the most part, vintage Elvis – as Bob Dylan and The Beatles took over his mantles as rebel and pop idol, Yet, after a period of uncertainty over his role and image, Elvis came back magnificently with the *1968 TV Special*. This wasn't just about a man reclaiming his music; it was about a man reclaiming his style. The hair was blacker than ever – blue-black, the sideburns were an outrage on their own, and the black leather was a happy inspiration by costume designer Bill Belew.

Elvis had been dubbed 'the King' in the 1950s, but it was between 1968 and 1970 that he really began to accumulate regal trappings. The scene for this was, of course, Las Vegas. (Whilst Elvis had worn black for the TV special, for the first high-collared jumpsuit, and for the karate suit he wore in most Vegas concerts in the summer of 1969, the following year he switched to white). It was a new style Elvis: more Liberace than James Dean, with its extravagant jumpsuits and comic-book capes, and stylized shows ('the essence of kabuki drama', as *Variety* observed). It was commemorated in all its glory on the movie *That's The Way It Is*, and in *Aloha From Hawaii* in 1973, which was watched by more people than saw Neil Armstrong walk on the moon.

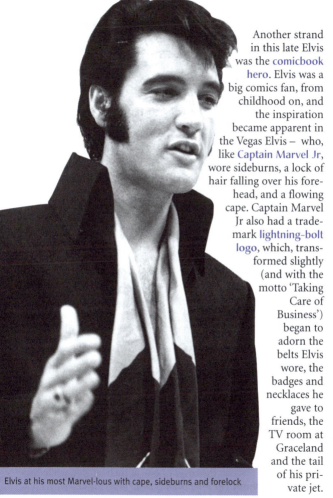

Another strand in this late Elvis was the comicbook hero. Elvis was a big comics fan, from childhood on, and the inspiration became apparent in the Vegas Elvis – who, like Captain Marvel Jr, wore sideburns, a lock of hair falling over his forehead, and a flowing cape. Captain Marvel Jr also had a trademark lightning-bolt logo, which, transformed slightly (and with the motto 'Taking Care of Business') began to adorn the belts Elvis wore, the badges and necklaces he gave to friends, the TV room at Graceland and the tail of his private jet.

Elvis at his most Marvel-lous with cape, sideburns and forelock

389

The TCB Business

The logo of a lightning flash and the words 'Taking Care of Business' – or TCB – are a constant in late-period Elvis. The TCB phrase was a black expression – Aretha Franklin uses the initials on her performance of "Respect" and it was the title of a TV special by Diana Ross and the Supremes in 1968.

The logo has rather more varied explanations, but Elvis's cousin Billy Smith and his childhood biographer Elaine Dundy trace it to the lightning bolt Captain Marvel Jr used to defeat Captain Nazi in the comics Elvis read as a child. Kathy Westmoreland says in her autobiography that Elvis decided on the logo after a statue in Graceland's Meditation Gardens had been struck by lightning. Priscilla insists that she and Elvis came up with it after a plane they were on flew through a thunderstorm. Marty Lacker, meanwhile, claimed the bolt was the symbol of the West Coast mafia (and that the logo and words meant 'Whatever you've got to do, do it quick').

Whatever the source, the depth of Presley's attraction became clear when he commissioned jewellers (first Sol Schwartz's partner Lee Albeseron in Hollywood, then Lowell Hays in Memphis) to produce necklaces incorporating the TCB lightning design as well as TLC (Tender Loving Care) equivalents for a number of women friends. Receiving either of these necklaces was dramatic and expensive proof that you had entered Elvis's inner circle. As Lowell Hays, who made most of them, said, 'When Elvis gave me my necklace, it was like being knighted.'

More than a quarter of a century later, another modified lightning bolt became the distinguishing mark on the forehead of the young Harry Potter, a permanent reminder that JK Rowling's hero had triumphed over evil. Or maybe she, too, had Elvis in mind?

In Presley's final years, the media, which had fixated on his pelvis in the 1950s, saw only his paunch. The manner and location of his death seemed a final triumph for such critics. His death was cheered by some punks, but his image inspired others: the Smiths put the acned Elvis on the cover of one of their singles, while Nick Cave, whose album *The First Born Is Dead* is permeated with Elvis, said, 'On those late concerts, just before he died you see a man who fought an incredible struggle with life. It is one of the most brutal things ever captured on film. In those pictures it has a unique glow of heroism.'

And so began Presley's second comeback – all the more astonishing since the man himself was dead. At the onset of the new millennium, as cultural commentators looked to the key figures of the twentieth century, Elvis's

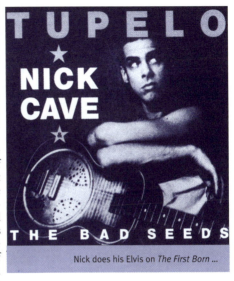

Nick does his Elvis on *The First Born* ...

place was pretty much assured. *Time*, never great Elvis enthusiasts, produced a list of the great artists and entertainers which excluded Presley on the grounds that he didn't write his own material, a criterion which somehow failed to exclude Bart Simpson. But Elvis appeared almost everywhere else, in trumps. *Las Vegas Sun* columnist Scott Dickensheet put it most neatly, in discussing the relative cultural influence of Elvis and Sinatra: 'The rock'n'roll aesthetic underpins our culture, from music to fashion to movies to consumerism – it sells us everything from sneakers to software. This is Elvis's world, all right, we just buy stuff in it.'

391

The King's robes

Elvis's dress sense was always a source of consternation, with early photos showing a taste for see-through white shirts which, even today, would be deemed immodest. But the costumes which he is most associated are the jumpsuits, which became almost a uniform for the most regal phase of his career.

The jumpsuit, previously the preserve of car mechanics and astronauts, was an intriguing solution to the dilemma which faced Elvis when he returned to live performances in Las Vegas.

As designer Bill Belew told *Country Rhythm* magazine: 'I spoke to Elvis and he said, "I want something different. I don't want to go up there in a tuxedo, I don't want to wear a suit." So, the first thing we did was a jumpsuit. It was comfortable and he liked that. The public just sort of identified with it. We tried new stuff, but whenever he went back to Vegas, it never quite worked.'

Although the patterns of the suits would become more elaborate, the basic design never changed. The Napoleonic stand-

'If the songs don't go over, we can do a medley of costumes...'

up collars, pointed sleeves, bell-bottomed cuffs, scarves and belts were constant fixtures. Capes weren't – he seldom used them after 1974 because fans tried to grab them while he was still wearing them. The collars were Belew's idea; the belt was Presley's suggestion.

Belew devised most of the costumes, although Presley OKed them. The two Elvis specifically requested were, famously, the American eagle jumpsuit for Aloha and a leopard design where two leopard heads met on the shoulder, which he wore rarely. Elvis liked black but wore white more often because it was easier to light and because it galvanized the fans more.

The jumpsuits were not cheap: the Aloha one, Belew says, cost $65,000 and would cost four times that today. Most of the suits were made from 100 percent Italian wool gabardine (most ice skaters' costumes were made from the same material) and it usually took eight to ten people four days to make one, although in emergencies, they could work faster.

Just such an emergency occurred in the build-up to Aloha. Elvis gave his white-eagle-bejewelled belt to his actor friend Jack Lord (chiefly famous for his use of hair lacquer as Steve McGarrett in *Hawaii Five-O*) and threw his cape into the audience after a rehearsal. But Belew managed to get belt and cape on a first-class flight to Oahu in time.

The jumpsuits may have been comfortable but they weren't light: the first suits weighed 25lb, while some of the latter ones weighed in at 75lb (including the cape). Elvis had, Belew said, 'a great build … He was one of the few men could carry them off … But he was very hard to buy clothes for because he had a 42in chest, a 30in waist and stood 5ft 11½in tall.' As Presley put on weight, the suits would be altered. (He could throw a tantrum if one didn't fit.) The jumpsuits on display in Graceland, especially the sundial one he wore often in his last year, look smaller than they ought, given all the stories about his weight. Are the nice folks at Graceland indulging in some posthumous spin-doctoring? We'll never know.

The names of the designs have a certain resonance: American eagle, blue Aztec, Mexican sundial, blue prehistoric bird, white prehistoric bird, peacock and mad tiger. These garments have been seen as coronation robes for a king, as priest-like vestments and even, by Camille Paglia, as alluding to Mithras (the Persian sun king and god of light) and the later, more florid costumes of the emperor Napoleon.

♪♪♪ The 'new' Elvises ♪♪♪

' They called Elvis the king, why not me?'

Michael Jackson, before he married Lisa Marie

Ever since Elvis made it big, anybody with a quiff has been dubbed the 'new Elvis', and since the King's death an eclectic army of imitators have stalked the planet. But the lot of new Elvises has not often been a happy one, with heart attacks, car crashes and living death in Vegas all too common fates.

Historically, the first 'new Elvis' tag goes to Carl Perkins. There wasn't, really, any similarity between the two, but as 1956 opened panicky RCA executives rushed out Perkins' version of "Blue Suede Shoes". Gene Vincent was more of a contender. He actually sounded like Elvis. Indeed, the resemblance was so uncanny that Scotty and Bill initially assumed Elvis was working on a solo project behind their backs. Like Elvis, Vincent went on to sing with the Jordanaires and to appear on the *Ed Sullivan Show*, while his own black leather stage costume influenced the style of Elvis's 1968 comeback. Travelling in Britain with the Anglo-American Beat Show, Vincent was a passenger in the cab that crashed and killed Eddie Cochran, whose own ersatz Elvis schtick was at its finest on the chorus of his hit "Summertime Blues". Vincent himself died in 1971, victim of career fade-out and hard living.

Next up in the 'new Elvis' stakes were Conway Twitty, whose Elvis soundalike smash "It's Only Make Believe" was covered by Presley session musician and impersonator, Glen Campbell – and a trio of Bobbies – Vee, Darin and Vinton. Bobby Vee was a hit machine, for a while, after being asked to play with the Winter Dance Party after the plane crash that killed Buddy Holly. Bobby Vinton, following a promising bid for Elvis status with "Blue Velvet", enjoyed his greatest critical success with "My Melody Of Love", which enjoys the rare distinction of being adopted by Polish Americans as an unofficial national anthem. The best of the Bobbies was Bobby Darin, who modelled himself on Sinatra, but had a physical style much closer to Elvis. Like Elvis, he survived a poor childhood, only to be dogged by health problems in later life; he went on to play Vegas in the twilight of his short career, and died in 1973 aged 37.

Another side of Elvis was carried by Rick Nelson, child star of *The Adventures Of Ozzie And Harriet*, in which he appeared in one episode dressed up as Elvis. He launched his own recording career by covering Fats Domino's "I'm Walkin", and recorded with the young James Burton, Elvis's longtime guitarist. However, his career gave out in the early 1970s, and – it's getting spooky – he was killed in a plane crash in 1985.

Phil Ochs' bid for musical monarchy

Perhaps the oddest contender of all was Phil Ochs – a folk singer who, in the 1960s, threatened Dylan's pre-eminence. On 27 March 1970, Ochs startled fans at Carnegie Hall in New York by appearing on stage in gold lamé, singing the old Presley hit "A Fool Such As I" and declaring, 'If there's any hope for America, it lies in a revolution, and if there's any hope for a revolution in America, it lies in getting Elvis Presley to become Che Guevara.' Ochs had been a fan of Elvis's since he first heard

"Heartbreak Hotel". But the reaction to his lamé reincarnation was so hostile he never made another album. Six years later, plagued by writer's block, alcoholism and mental illness, he took his own life.

Cliff Richard became the first serious non-American new Elvis in 1958, with a curled lip, four litres of Brylcreem on his quiff and the debut single "Move It". However, Cliff got Jesus and went bland as a curate. The baton of Elvisdom was taken up across the Channel by the French Elvis, rocker Johnny Hallyday. Born in Belgium as Jean-Phillippe Smet, Monsieur Hallyday launched his career in 1960 looking like Elvis, moving like Elvis and singing forgettable rock'n'roll. In French. Hallyday became a huge star in France, and went on to duet with Million Dollar Quartet veteran Carl Perkins and, with grim inevitability, to play Vegas.

Elvis's naked sexuality, allied to the inadvertent high camp of the Vegas years, opened the way for more sexually ambivalent new Elvises. After seeing k.d.lang in concert, Madonna was moved to say 'Elvis is back – and she's beautiful'. And, of course, there was David Bowie (see box), who really did try and be Elvis in his androgynous creation, Ziggy Stardust.

Elvis and Bowie

'Elvis was a major hero of mine. I was probably stupid enough to believe that having the same birthday as him actually meant something,' David Bowie recalled in 1996. The 'major hero' echoes throughout Bowie's career. He had played "Hound Dog" hundreds of times as a kid, and his first live appearance was doing an Elvis impersonation before an audience of Bromley cubs when he was 11. When he joined RCA in 1971, he called home excitedly to say, 'Mum, I'm going to be bigger than Elvis.'

Bowie's creation of Ziggy Stardust was inspired by American rocker Vince Taylor, who worked in France as an Elvis impersonator before bringing his career to an end when he

Bowie as 'Elvis' Stardust

appeared on stage in white robes and announcing he was Jesus Christ. Ziggy Stardust concerts usually ended with the song "Rock'n'Roll Suicide" for which Bowie often changed into a white jumpsuit, copied from one of Elvis's by designer Fred Buretti. Bowie's manager Tony De Fries even used the announcement 'David Bowie has left the building' at concerts.

Bowie admitted to having been inspired by Elvis at Madison Square Garden in 1972, a concert Ziggy Stardust's alter ego had overcome his fear of flying to attend. Bowie recalled, 'I walked in on a Saturday evening in full Ziggy garb to see Elvis and he nearly crucified me. I felt such a fool and I was way down in the front. I sat down there and he looked at me and if looks could kill! Ziggy changed on the Monday night. It was probably Elvis Stardust [laugh] for about a week.' It didn't traumatize Bowie, though. He took the Elvis lightning-bolt logo and painted it on his face for the cover of his album *Aladdin Sane*, the following year.

Bowie's video of "Young Americans" was a further borrowing of the Elvis style – with its deliberate emulation of Elvis's appearance on the *Ed Sullivan Show* – and the song itself employed Elvis vocal tricks. But perhaps the most Elvis moment of Bowie's career was his song "Golden Years", which he is rumoured to have written hoping Elvis would record it, and which he recorded in Elvis's style.

For straightforwardly bizarre, though, it's hard to beat El Vez, a diminutive Mexican Elvis impersonator who struts his camp stuff in rhinestone jumpsuits with pictures of saints in place of the American eagles. El Vez, real name Robert Lopez, has carved out a lonely but profitable niche as the foremost exponent of Latin-themed covers of Elvis tracks given a political bent. His classics include "Mexican American Trilogy" and "Misery Tren" – both on the album *G.I. Ay Ay Blues.* His version of "In The Ghetto" (renamed "In The Barrio") is actually a far more interesting reading of an Elvis song than most covers.

But even El Vez's story pales into ordinariness when contrasted with that of Dean Reed, the American who became the semi-official Elvis Presley of the Soviet Union. Reed's story (rumoured to be a film starring Tom Hanks) has certain similarities with Elvis's. Like the original, Reed lived a stellar multi-million-selling existence and died a mysterious, premature death. He was just 48 when he was found dead in a lake in East Germany, an enigmatic end to a peripatetic existence which had begun on a Colorado chicken farm in 1938.

Reed had gone to Hollywood to make his fortune, made a record which went gold in Latin America, became a superstar in Chile and, appalled by the misery in which many Chileans lived, flown to the Soviet Union. He never actually defected (he filed tax forms annually with the IRS and kept his American passport) but toured the Communist bloc, wowing crowds in the biggest arenas, settling finally in East Berlin, where he married a film star and died four years before the Berlin Wall was breached. Opinions differ on how fine a singer he was. One Russian official complained he wasn't even as good as Pat Boone. Yet his friend Phil Everly maintained, 'You can't fool crowds that size anywhere.'

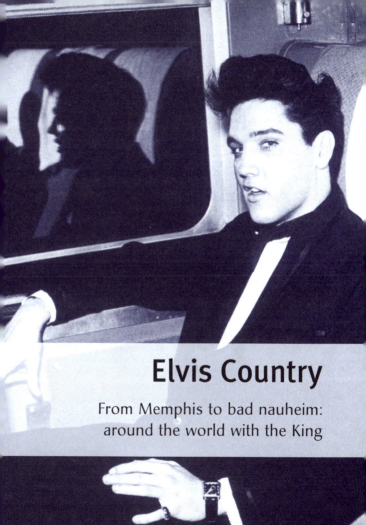

Elvis Country

From Memphis to bad nauheim:
around the world with the King

' I only really feel at home in Memphis, at my own Graceland mansion. A man gets lonesome for the things that are familiar to him. I know I do.'

Elvis, 1960s interview

Elvis Presley had 25 homes and one ranch during his lifetime, spread through Mississippi, Tennessee, Hollywood and Germany, but the emotional heart of Elvis country will always be Memphis. This was the city where he arrived with his parents, flat broke, in 1948, with the family belongings stuffed on the back of the truck. And this was the city where, despite the allure of America's twin showbiz metropolises, New York and LA, he spent most of the remaining 29 years of his life.

This chapter begins, logically enough, with a look at the city Elvis called home, and the Southern-style mansion on Elvis Presley Boulevard which he called home for almost half his life, from 1957 to 1977. But Elvis country has two other key shrines: Tupelo, the Mississippi town he was born in and where he spent the first eventful thirteen years of his life, and Las Vegas, the gaudy, glitzy city where Presley reigned supreme from 1969 until his death.

Elvis country is dotted with smaller shrines: Nashville is worth a visit if you're in the area, and Bad Nauheim in Germany has belatedly begun to recognize the kudos to be had by celebrating the short-term residence of the local Army base's most famous GI.

Memphis, Tennessee

General James Winchester gave Egyptian names to two new Southern cities in the early nineteenth century. Cairo, close to his own plantation and intended as a future Tennessee state capital, lasted for a century before it became a ghost town. Memphis, which he helped to found in 1819, has become not a ghost town, but a city overshadowed by the ghost of its most famous resident.

At times, especially on a midweek mid-afternoon, the liveliest thing in Memphis seems to be the ghost of Elvis Presley. Sun Studios, where he made the music that changed the world, still stands on Union Avenue. Over a burger at what used to be *Taylor's Café* next door, you can imagine that Elvis, Carl Perkins and Jerry Lee Lewis are swapping gossip at a nearby table. Elvis's statue stands at one end of Beale Street, done in appropriately gaudy gold but still feeling too stiff and formal, more like a statesman than a rock singer. Nearby, the *Elvis Presley Restaurant* serves appropriate Southern cooking, though it doesn't go so far as to offer only meatloaf for several weeks, as El once requested from his cook at Graceland. That site was recently vacated by Presley's favourite clothier, *Lanskys*, which now has a berth in the *Peabody Hotel*, the basement of which used to host radio station *WREC* and a young DJ called Sam Phillips. Elvis himself attended his own high-school prom at the *Peabody*.

For Elvis fans, of course, neither the *Peabody*'s famous ducks nor Memphis's grandiose riverfront pyramid are reasons to delay heading straight to Graceland, hidden away on the city's southern outskirts. Locals account for less than one percent of the 650,000 visitors who troop through the house each year. According to journalist Bill Burk, a friend of Elvis, 'If a Memphian comes up to me and says, "I went to Graceland for the first time today," I always say, "Let me guess, someone came in from out of town and want-ed you to take them" and that's always how it is.'" Mike Freeman, co-author of *Memphis Elvis Style*, puts the city's relationship with

The most famous gates in this world, even better known than Bill or David

403

Presley in context: 'To Memphians Elvis was and is the local boy who made good. There are a million stories about Elvis in this town. He lived his life in a very theatrical way, was somewhat accessible to the people, and most important, he started in life so poor. Elvis is the ultimate rags-to-riches story. I think a lot of older Memphians are still amazed that he succeeded at all. Still a lot of people don't like to dwell upon him. It's the hometown syndrome, the hero is least appreciated in his own town.'

★ ★ ★ Graceland ★ ★ ★

The King's castle came into being in 1939, when Ruth Brown Moore and Dr Thomas Moore commissioned a Southern colonial mansion to be built on 13.8 acres of what had been a 500-acre farm. The house kept the name of the farm, Graceland, in honour of Mrs Moore's great-aunt Grace. Nobody was living there when Elvis bought it. According to his uncle Vester, when the Presleys first saw it, a religious service was taking place. Vernon was impressed by the house but, typically, worried about the price.

While Graceland looked like a traditional Southern mansion, it was virtually new – an important consideration for a young rock star just starting to enjoy his wealth – and was in keeping with what Karal Ann Marling, author of *Graceland: Going Home With Elvis*, called 'the prevailing architectural fantasy of 1930s and 1940s Hollywood'. Elvis proclaimed that 'This is going to be a lot nicer than Red Skelton's house when I get it like I want it.' As the comedian's house contained a shocking-pink piano, a stuffed gorilla in the pool shower room, circus relics on the lawn and a driveway that lit up at night like a landing strip, this was quite a statement. Clearly, however, Elvis's aspirations were directed more towards the Hollywood model than anything closer to home. As architect Charles Jenks noted, Graceland possesses 'many features which define the archetypal movie star house: gates, guards and long drives, blockbuster facades which demand to be ogled and, as you progress into the house, an informality which flatters guests that they have been admitted into the star's inner sanctum'.

Elvis bought Graceland in 1957 for $100,000, fulfilling his promise to buy his parents a nice big house. Back then, it was out in the country, not engulfed by car lots and budget hotels. Gladys kept chickens out back, a reminder of simpler days in Tupelo. But she died in 1958, having barely enjoyed her son's present. Vernon didn't live at Graceland for long either: he moved into another house on the estate in 1960 with his second wife, Dee Stanley.

Elvis casually dressed to match the walls of his new $100,000 mansion

In *Elvis And Me*, Priscilla says that there were times at Graceland when she felt an almost oppressive sorrow in the atmosphere, as if it were haunted by Gladys's spirit. When it was open house, it could seem like the liveliest place in the world; at quieter moments, the absolute stillness could be disconcerting. For all the commotion and commerce that surrounded Graceland, to live inside the house was almost like living in a separate kingdom.

Obviously, a major reason for the ongoing popularity of what is, after the White House, America's most famous home, is the apparently limitless fascination of the man himself. But

Graceland details

Graceland stands ten miles south of downtown Memphis at 3734 Elvis Presley Boulevard (☎901/332-3322, ⊛www.elvis-presley.com). A $20 cab ride from downtown, it can also be reached on bus #13 from Third and Union.

The **ticket office** is open March–Oct Mon–Sat 8.30am–5pm, Sun 9.30am–4.30pm, and Nov–Feb daily 9.30am–4pm. **Tickets** cost $16 for the mansion tour (10 percent off for students and OAPs), children aged 7–12 pay $6, and under-7s go free. All-inclusive admission, also covering the aeroplane and other attractions, costs $25 for adults, with similar discounts. The day's first tour starts thirty minutes after the ticket office opens; the last tour starts as it closes.

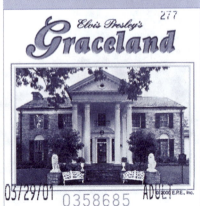

there's also the fact that, whatever your expectations, you're unlikely to leave disappointed. At other historic homes, it can be all but impossible to conjure up the spirits of their bygone inhabitants. As soon as your bus takes you through Graceland's legendary musical-note gates, on the other hand, you enter Elvis's world. By the time you emerge from the Meditation Gardens, an hour or more later, you will have been completely immersed in Elvisness.

Graceland is a monument both to Presley's taste, whatever you may think of it, and to his supreme self-confidence. Some of its more Baroque excesses, perpetrated in the 1970s when he was bored and trying to please his new girlfriend Linda Thompson, have been removed. But there are still rooms that are unlike anything you have ever seen. And in two of them, the TV room and the controversial Jungle Room, El feels so close you wouldn't be totally astonished if he offered you a blast of Gatorade. Because, finally, even if you're not a fan, his home is as gaudy, humorous and impossible to ignore as the very best of his Las Vegas concerts.

The tour

Be sure to buy a ticket for the house as soon as you arrive at Graceland Plaza; at busy times, it may be quite a while before the first available tour. Once your tour is announced, you'll have your photo taken as you wait in line; as Joan Freeman put it in *Roustabout*, 'You don't know how you look until you've got your picture took.' In due course you'll be ferried across Elvis Presley Boulevard in a blue-and-white minibus, taken through the famous gates, and deposited in front of the house itself.

Visitors are only allowed downstairs in Graceland: Elvis's bedroom and the master suite are off limits. However, you can see the marvellous staircase down which he'd make his entrances – and at the foot of which, on one occasion, he found Lisa Marie prostrating herself and shouting, 'Ailvis! Ailvis!'

407

★ **THE LIVING ROOM** ★ Graceland's living room is, in terms of sheer size, one of the few rooms in the house that's fit for a king. On Priscilla's instructions, it has been revamped to look more as it did in the early 1960s, when its owner was still mindful enough of his dead mum's wishes not to give free rein to his wackier decorating ideas. The sunburst clock above the fireplace, for example, is a classic American piece of the late 1950s/early 1960s. Elvis's Great Danes used to lie on the white leather sofa; judging by the size of Brutus, who co-starred with Elvis in *Live A Little, Love A Little*, they needed every inch of its 15ft length. At the other end of the room, peacock stained-glass windows frame the entrance to the music room, where Elvis and James Brown sang gospel songs together in a jam session in Presley's last year. Peacocks are a symbol of eternal life, but, unbeknown to El, they bring bad luck if displayed indoors.

★ **THE DINING ROOM** ★ Given El's eating habits, you'd expect his dining room to reflect his personality, or at least his diet. Perhaps it did during the 1970s, when Elvis and Linda Thompson decorated it in a colour that one visitor referred to as 'whorehouse red'; now, however, it's gone back to the original, rather stilted, look it had for most of the 1960s. When Elvis was at home, meals were served no earlier than 9pm. Elvis always sat at the head of the table, and every December the Christmas tree was put up just behind his chair. Although the guidebooks talk of wild stories and laughter around the table, you get little sense of that today. It's pretty to look at but about as expressive of Elvis's personality as *Clambake*.

★ **THE KITCHEN** ★ Elvis's kitchen was where cook Mary Jenkins used to whip up those peanut butter and banana sandwiches, fried in butter. Just one, the dieticians say, contains 92 percent of the maximum healthy daily fat intake for an adult male.

★ **THE TV ROOM** ★ Go down the mirrored, slightly unsettling, staircase and you come upon Graceland's *pièce de résistance*, a dazzling blue and yellow masterpiece with a mirrored ceiling. Although designer Bill Eubanks takes

Hundreds of yards of fabric make the pool room feel smaller than it is ▶

the credit for the look of the TV room, the lightning-bolt TCB motif on the wall is basically Presley's seal of approval. This was one of the happier fruits of his 1970s redecoration with Linda Thompson, although the bank of three TV sets, which meant he could watch a football game and two less interesting programmes (with the sound off) at once, it seems more his than hers. From the TVs, to the bar, where a fabric panel can be lifted to accommodate a movie projector, to the jukebox stocked with a hundred singles, the room is like an adolescent fantasy of bachelorhood. Mere photographs cannot do it justice. Like Elvis in concert, you just have to be there.

★ **THE POOL ROOM** ★ Although it's the Jungle Room that's normally cited as proof that Elvis knew as much about interior decoration as Pat Boone does about hip-hop, his pool room is much weirder. It took three workmen ten days to hang the four hundred or so square yards of fabric that

cover its sofas, walls and ceiling, a hell of an effort and expense for a room whose centrepiece is an old pool table. The oddest part of all is that it all just goes to make an already small room feel even more claustrophobic.

★ **THE JUNGLE ROOM** ★ Had Elvis not died, the Jungle Room might just be a memory. After he recorded his last studio songs here in 1976, Presley decided that he rather liked the room the way it was, with all its Hawaiian furniture removed. Fate intervened, and the Jungle Room now stands as Exhibit A when critics charge El with a lack of taste. Conflicting theories explain why Elvis wanted it to look like this. One story has it that Vernon came home one day in 1974 saying that he'd just seen the ugliest furniture he'd ever laid eyes on in the local store, Donalds. Either in jest or because he genuinely liked the sound of it, his son ran out and bought the lot; certainly it's known that it took him just thirty minutes to pick it all out. Bill Burk, on the other hand, says that every poor boy in Memphis vowed to buy his furniture from Donalds when he got a little money, and that the whole set was on sale. According to stepbrother David Stanley, El hated shopping for furniture, and he just bought the first thing that Linda liked. Yet others suggest it reflects El's love of Hawaii and Hawaiian culture. As Elvis could buy furniture as swiftly and as casually as the rest of us might buy a soft drink, we'll probably never know. Best just to soak it all up, and maybe imagine the young Lisa Marie curling up for a nap on the enormous monkey chair. Don't hurry this room, as the joy really is in the detail – take a peek, for example, at the feathered mirror frame, or try and count the different species of wildlife on show.

★ **THE OFFICE** ★ Vernon Presley's office serves to show just how frugal the old man was. Once you've seen the video of Elvis's post-Army press conference, held right here, you're probably best off following the advice of Vernon's sign on the door: 'No loafing in office'.

410

★ **THE SMOKE ROOM** ★ Although Graceland's previous owners used the 'smoke room' to smoke meat, the smoke in question for Elvis and his pals was gunsmoke; they used it for target practice for a while in 1964. Somewhere around here, Elvis's aunt Delta Mae buried one of her old wigs in a fit of pique, after she found two maids arguing over who was going to wear it.

★ **THE STABLES** ★ Elvis really got into horses during the mid-1960s, and named one of his horses 'Mare Ingram' after Memphis's Mayor Ingram. His favourite was a palomino called Rising Sun; naturally, its stables were called The House Of The Rising Sun, in a tongue-in-cheek tribute to the Animals single. The puns never end: when Rising Sun died, it was buried facing the rising sun. Priscilla has vowed that, as long as Graceland is owned by the Presleys, there'll be a palomino on the estate.

★ **THE HALL OF GOLD** ★ The corridor known as the 'Hall of Gold', lined with gold and platinum records, is simply overwhelming. All those figures about the squillions of records Elvis sold suddenly seem real. No matter which part of the world you're from, you'll probably find an award from your country either here or in the overflow area in the racquetball court.

★ **THE BIG ROOM** ★ Perverse as it sounds, the only real drawback about the 'Big Room' is that there's almost too much to take in, especially on a busy day. The glimpses of the private Elvis are intriguing, with his arsenal of guns, and a collection of police badges that stunned fellow collector Dan Aykroyd. The movie posters, assorted paperwork and outfits, however, good as they are to see, only serve to reinforce what you already know about Elvis.

★ **THE RACQUETBALL COURT** ★ Elvis spent the last night of his life in his racquetball court, before returning to the master suite upstairs. After a joke game of racquetball with his cousin Billy Smith, he sat down at the piano to play "Unchained Melody" and "Blue Eyes Crying In The Rain". Built in 1975, the court is the only visible evidence of Elvis's obsession with the sport; his investment in a scheme to build loads of centres almost triggered a financial crisis which was used by his dad as an excuse to fire the West brothers and Dave Hebler. What's most funky about Elvis's own racquetball court is the blue-and-white-tiled bathroom upstairs, which is too small for visitors to squeeze into.

411

★ **THE MEDITATION GARDENS** ★ If you're a fan with tears to shed, prepare to shed them now. If you'd rather keep a grip, it's probably best not to read the inscription that Vernon dictated for Elvis's gravestone; it's long, awkward, and has the mawkish sincerity of one of Elvis's own sentimental ballads. If you're tempted to read significance into the four nineteenth-century Spanish stained-glass windows, or the combination of Christian and pagan icons, don't bother. Even Larry Geller, who's inclined to find spiritual significance in the way Elvis blew his nose, says that he, Elvis and Marty Lacker just sketched this area out roughly in the mid-1960s. They chose the furnishings to fit El's desire to create a space like the Lake Shrine gardens of the Self-Realization Fellowship in California, where he could flee from his public self and simply meditate. Lacker's brother-in-law Bernie made it for Elvis for $22,000; Vernon thought that was an almighty sum, but Elvis didn't care. When it was finished, he went to see it for himself and came back crying, saying how beautiful it was. That seems appropriate somehow, given the tears that have fallen here since.

★ **GRACELAND PLAZA** ★ If your spirits need lifting after the Meditation Gardens, Graceland Plaza is the ideal place for a spot of Elvis-related retail therapy, whether you want books, posters, CDs, or an Action-Man-style doll of Elvis as a GI or in the American eagle jumpsuit for *Aloha From Hawaii*. You can also find slightly different merchandise at, dare one say it, slightly more reasonable prices in the shops nearby: walk a few hundred yards along the road, as though you were going back into Memphis.

★ **THE AUTOMOBILE MUSEUM** ★ Elvis loved cars, which is one reason he gave so many of them away. He never haggled with car dealers, even though given the quantities in which he bought cars he could have had some hefty discounts. But he got mad if he felt he'd been sold a dud. In 1960, he was so incensed by a faulty Ford Thunderbird that, after getting no satisfaction from his dealer, he called Edsel Ford, then head of the Ford Motor Company, to get his money back. While the pink Cadillac he bought for his mum – who couldn't drive – may be the most famous car purchase in the world, the museum shows his taste in cars to have been almost as catholic as his taste in music. Apart from Cadillacs, you can also

413

Elvis in *Spinout*, with one car he didn't shoot for mechanical failure

see his Stutz Blackhawk, originally earmarked for Frank Sinatra but snapped up by Elvis after he charmed the salesman into letting him have it. Sadly, it was almost wrecked in an accident soon afterwards, while on its way to be washed. He had a habit of shooting cars that stalled on him, but, the Ferrari on show is not the one that made him draw his gun to teach it a lesson after it stalled. The motorcycles and golf karts are pretty cool, too, especially the 1957 Harley Hydro-Glide.

★ SINCERELY ELVIS ★ Sincerely Elvis holds yet more enjoyable bric-a-brac, including objects that he desired, both obscure and not so obscure. Be sure to watch the video, *Walk A Mile In My Shoes*, though you won't really get to walk in El's size twelve shoes, either real or metaphorical.

★ LISA MARIE AND HOUND DOG TWO ★ In 1975, Elvis bought two planes – a Convair 880, which he named after his daughter, and a Lockheed Jetstar, christened Hound Dog Two – in which to tour the world, at a total cost, including remodelling, of $1 million. The most adventurous journey the Lisa Marie ever took turned out to be a famous flight to Denver to buy El's favourite peanut butter sandwiches. And there, you might say, you have the tragedy of his later life in a nutshell. To see where the money went, just follow the gold theme on the belt buckles and the washbasins. Lisa Marie celebrated her ninth birthday, her last with her dad, in the conference room on the jet. Owning your own jet was the ultimate rock-star perk in the 1970s: when Elvis met Led Zeppelin, he couldn't understand why they leased theirs.

Heartbreak Hotel

3677 Elvis Presley Blvd; ☎901/332-1000

For the estate to open its very own hotel was not a bad idea; previously, fans were faced with the unenviable choice of budget motels along the Boulevard, or staying downtown ten miles away. And you can't fault the attention to detail: the hotel is indeed on Lonely Street, and the desk clerk really is dressed in black. Only the absence of constantly weeping bellhops lets the side down slightly. The rates are reasonable, at $80–100 per night, and include free piped-in Elvis movies, although fans have noted the alarming frequency with which the movie seems to be *Clambake*. The suites, especially the one inspired by Elvis's TV room, have to be seen to be believed. You can also get married here, in the Chapel In The Woods, and if the weather's right you can have your pictures taken in front of Graceland. But would you want to honeymoon in a place called Heartbreak Hotel?

★ ★ Other Memphis sights ★ ★

Sadly, much of the Memphis that Elvis knew has disappeared; his first home in the city, on Poplar Avenue, was for example demolished long ago. Many other historic sites have fallen victim to the 'white flight' from downtown Memphis, and the razing of entire neighbourhoods in the name of progress. Other noteworthy casualties include American Studios, where Elvis made the finest music of his later career, which is now beyond restoration, and Stax Studios, where he had two contrasting recording sessions, which although it has been destroyed was being considered for reconstruction as this book went to press.

There's still a tremendous amount to see in Memphis beyond Graceland, however, including Sun Studios, where the story began, and Beale Street, long the epicentre of black culture across the region. For anyone who plans to spend days tracking every Elvis-related site in the city, *Memphis Elvis Style*, by Cindy Hazen and Mike Freeman, makes essential reading. For that matter, given its wealth of stories about Elvis from Memphians who knew him, it's probably essential reading anyway.

1034 Audobon Drive

Mike Freeman and Cindy Hazen now own the first house that Elvis bought with the fruits of his success, and are returning it to its 1956 appearance. They may not go as far as hanging the washing out to dry, as Gladys did, to the neighbours' outrage. Elvis moved to Graceland after a year, following constant complaints about the crowds of fans who hung around hoping for a glimpse of him.

Beale Street

Although Beale Street has changed a lot since the teenage Elvis used to stroll down it, it remains an essential stop for any fan. The pick of its blues clubs has to be *BB King's*, even if some find it too too commercial. Nearby, in the former premises of Lansky's the tailors (see p.402), the *Elvis Presley Restaurant*, belonging to Elvis Presley Enterprises, also features live entertainment, as likely to be rockabilly as the blues. *A.Schwabs* store must have looked pretty much like this when it opened in 1876, let alone in 1956, though its extraordinary range of merchandise now includes some very cheap Elvis souvenirs alongside blues accoutrements like the legendary John The Conqueror root.

Humes High School

Humes, a mile or so from Poplar Avenue, was the school where, when the music teacher Mrs Morman told Elvis he couldn't sing, Presley replied, 'You just don't like my kind of singing.' Her disapproval was countered by the applause of his peers at the annual variety show – quite possibly the moment when he realized his ambitions weren't quite so ridiculous after all. In 1956, Elvis returned to Humes, with his friend Nick Adams, to meet the pupils and answer questions. He gave his favourite teacher, Mrs Scrivener, a peck on the cheek as he left. What impresses most about the school today is its very ordinariness.

Elvis on Beale

WC Handy, author of "Memphis Blues", used to say, '**If Beale Street could talk ...**' If the most famous street in blues history ever did acquire the power of speech, it might finally tell us what the young Elvis Presley was doing on its pavements, and when.

Did Elvis, as local lore suggests, haunt Beale as a teenager, absorbing the blues? Or, as Goldman says, is the idea that a white mother's boy would be allowed onto a street where locals boasted about the murder rate just too absurd to contemplate?

So many memories conflict that it's best to tread carefully. As Mike Freeman puts it, 'There are black musicians still alive who claim Elvis used to sit in their shows in Beale Street nightclubs. Who am I to say that they are wrong?' On the other hand, Elvis's most authoritative biographer, Peter Guralnick, argues that if he did sample the nightlife on Beale, it was probably after July 1954, in the company of **Dewey Phillips**, the DJ who gave him his first break on local radio.

The Goldman scenario, of a timid mama's boy, is easily disposed of. Clothier **Bernard Lansky** recalls seeing the young Elvis hanging outside his shop for the first time in 1951. Presley was

also spotted browsing at Nat Epstein's pawnshop, by **BB King** among others. Elvis's favourite reporter **Bill Burk** says it was not uncommon for white youths like himself and Elvis to go down to Beale in this period; '*Lanskys* and those shops were like a show, we'd just stand around and watch what was going on.' He also notes that Loew State Theater, where Elvis worked in 1951, was just a few blocks from Beale.

According to Burk, a dancer at the ***Club Handy*** saw Elvis standing on the pavement outside the club sometime in 1951, 'presumably because he was too young to be let in'. There's clearly some merit to Guralnick's objection – how did they know it was Elvis? Even so, by 1953, Elvis was, as Sun's Marion Keisker noted, so conspicuous in Memphis that he was known as 'the kid with the sideburns'.

The *Club Handy* is a recurring motif in Elvis's early life. It was there, writes Michael Bane in ***White Boy Singing The Blues***, that Elvis entertained a black audience when it was still illegal for a white person to enter a black entertainment venue. The fact that he won the initially sceptical crowd over with a version of **Milkcow Blues Boogie** suggests this probably occurred after the summer of 1954, at roughly the same time and place as he saw Lowell Fulson perform **Reconsider Baby**.

The **Home Of The Blues** record shop, at Main and Beale, was another of Elvis's haunts. Rockabilly singer **Johnny Burnette**, whom Elvis briefly idolized, remembers going in there after school to flick through the records and seeing Elvis.

It seems probable that Presley, from around 1951 onwards, did roam around Beale, often with his high-school friends, soaking up the atmosphere and dreaming of the day when he could afford a suit from Lanskys, or a decent car. **Johnny Black**, Bill's brother, remembers meeting Elvis in another record shop, and Elvis suddenly turning to him and saying, 'Some day I'm going to be driving Cadillacs'. It struck Black as an odd thing to say, given that they didn't even have enough money to buy Cokes.

Whether Elvis snuck into clubs, however, remains unproven.

Certainly he'd listened to the blues in Tupelo, so we know he loved the music. But in Memphis he may have listened to it on the radio and in the record shops. Blues guitarist **Calvin Newborn** remembers Elvis sitting in with his band and breaking his guitar strings, but band member Herman Green says that happened at the *Plantation Inn* in West Memphis, where the musicians were all black and the customers were all white. And he can't pinpoint it any more precisely than to say it was after 1952.

When and why Elvis was on Beale is one mystery which will finally be solved only after they decide whether there really was a gunman firing from behind the grassy knoll in Dealey Plaza.

Lanskys

The young Elvis Presley used to stop to stare through the window of the Lansky Bros clothing store on Beale Street, which started life as an army surplus store in the late 1940s. One day, when Bernard Lansky invited him in to look around, Elvis came out with the immortal words: 'Mr Lansky, when I'm rich I'm gonna buy you out.' Lansky responded: 'Don't buy me out, buy from me.' Elvis did just that for twenty years. Lansky knew that Elvis needed to look different from the other singers who bought their clothes at his store, like Carl Perkins, BB King and Roy Orbison. He dressed Elvis in black pants, hi-boy collars and pink shirts; he also wore patent leather boots, and black jackets with pink piping. In his later years, Lansky ran him up a pimp-like baby-pink leather three-quarter-length coat with fur trim, which hangs on the shop wall today. Elvis had torn the lining and sent it back for repair. 'He never picked it up,' says Lansky. 'He must have forgot. He had so many clothes, see.' In 1956 Elvis bought a black-and-red Messerschmitt car. When Lansky spotted it, he told Elvis he'd like it when he'd tired of it. A few days later, the car was his. If Elvis was visiting when other customers were buying clothes, he'd pay. 'He was a most generous man,' remembers Lansky. For those who insist the King still lives, he adds, 'It makes me angry. Them folk are livin' in a dream world. I dressed him in his first suit, and I dressed him in his last.' The brothers' store moved to the *Peabody Hotel* in 1981, where it continues to draws tourists from across the world.

Lauderdale Courts

Apartment 328 on 185 Winchester Avenue, Lauderdale Courts, was Elvis's second home in Memphis. Unlike his first, it has been spared from demolition. When the Presleys arrived in 1954, this

419

◀ Elvis's statue – his one undisputed appearance on Beale Street

was public housing, limited to families who earned less than $3000 per year. Elvis used to rehearse his singing in the laundry room in the basement, where no one could see him. He was so embarrassed when two girls crept in to watch that he fled. He wasn't always so shy, though: at other times he'd stroll around strumming his guitar and crooning for anyone to listen.

Libertyland

Elvis's favourite amusement park, Libertyland, is still there at 940 Early Maxwell Boulevard, and his favourite rides – the dodgems and the Zippin Pippin roller coaster – are still running today. He last rented it out a week before he died, on 8 August 1977, for Lisa Marie.

Sun Studios

As Mike Freeman points out, it's unusual for a building to be clearly identifiable as the birthplace of a musical genre. Few could dispute, however, the claim that rock'n'roll was invented at Sun Studios, ten minutes' walk east from Beale Street at 706 Union Avenue. And it's a distinction guarded jealously: Sun's founder Sam Phillips still hasn't quite recovered from the decision to locate the Rock'n'Roll Hall of Fame in Cleveland. You only have to come on the 'tour' here , and step into the 30ft by 18ft room that's the main attraction, to picture Elvis, Scotty, Bill and Sam setting out on their amazing journey. The outtakes from those historic sessions, played over the studio speakers, are every bit as evocative as the room itself. It's amazing to think that this shrine later became an (unsuccessful) scuba-diving shop. Afterwards, drop in to the adjoining café, in which, when it was *Taylor's Café*, Elvis would hang around sipping Coke and trying to catch Sam Phillips' eye.

Tupelo, Mississippi

Elvis spent the first thirteen years of his life in Tupelo, Mississippi. They were thirteen event-packed years, in which he lost a twin brother even before he was born; just escaped a tornado that swept through town; saw his dad carted off to Parchman Fram prison; and entered the Alabama–Mississippi Fair singing "Old Shep". By the end, the boy Elvis had watched his family's fortunes slide so far that they felt they had to leave, because whatever else they found couldn't be any worse. After all, Gladys finally ordered Vernon to move after one of their neighbours in the Shakerag quarter had been decapitated.

How often Elvis returned to Tupelo is hotly debated. Though some of the Memphis mafia say he never did, gospel singer Jake Hess insists that he first met Elvis in Tupelo, not Memphis. Plenty of anecdotal evidence suggests that he didn't, as myth would have it, turn his back on his birthplace as soon as the truck pulled out of town.

Even so, not all that much tangible evidence of Elvis survives in modern Tupelo. At least the city is trying to catch up, having erected a statue of the 13-year-old guitar-wielding Elvis and organizing what it hopes will be an annual festival in his honour. The local visitor centre, at 399 E Main St (☎601/841-1245), hands out details of a four-mile driving tour of Elvis-related sites.

The most obvious shrine in town is the tiny Elvis Presley Birthplace, at 306 Elvis Presley Drive (Mon–Sat 9am–5pm, Sun 1–5pm; $1 for the house, $4 for museum). This two-room shack, built by Vernon for $180 in 1934, has been prettified, but it's still small enough to fit into Graceland's dining room. Despite its size, it proved too expensive for the Presley family to keep, and they moved out in 1938. The adult Elvis is said to have driven down here, as a rule at night, to show his girlfriends where he came from. The shack now forms part of the Elvis Presley Center, which also includes a museum, memorial chapel and park.

The two-room shack Elvis was born in, one frosty morn, in January 1935

Another crucial stop on Elvis's journey to fame was the Tupelo Hardware Store, at 114 West Main Street. That was where a man with the unlikely name of Forrest L. Bobo sold Elvis his very first guitar. According to Bobo, Elvis didn't, as legend has it, want a $50 bike, he wanted a rifle. The rifle was too expensive, however, and in any case Bobo would hardly have sold a .22 calibre bolt-action rifle to a boy who wasn't even 10. The guitar was Bobo's desperate attempt to placate the disappointed mite. He even told him, 'If you play that you might be famous someday.' It cost $7.75, plus two percent sales tax. Elvis didn't have that much money, but his mum made up the difference.

Finally, Elvis's stillborn twin Jesse Garon is probably buried somewhere in the Priceville Cemetery on Priceville Road, in an unmarked grave. The only doubt is cast by Billy Smith, El's cousin, who reckons it was in another cemetery near the Old Saltillo Road.

On your way back to Memphis, it's worth calling in on the market town of Holly Springs, in northeastern Mississippi, where Graceland Too, at 200 East Golson Avenue, is a fabulously weird Elvis museum. Created by the self-proclaimed number-one Elvis fans, father and son Paul and Elvis Aaron Presley MacLeod, it holds a simply stupefying quantity of memorabilia. The MacLeods were outside the gates at Graceland on the night that Elvis died, when MacLeod Junior was just 4, and have what may be the last ninety seconds of film footage ever taken of Elvis. Tours can take three hours or more, and *it's usually open between noon and 8pm but times can vary*. OK, there's no Jungle Room, but you can buy infinitesimal snippets of rug taken from the one at Graceland.

Las Vegas, Nevada

Too busy dreaming up new money-making schemes to indulge in nostalgia, Las Vegas, Nevada, is not a city to wax sentimental about its past, and the returning Elvis would find little to remind him of his twenty-year reign as King. He himself, however, is if anything more popular than ever; in fact he's probably more of an icon in Las Vegas than anywhere else.

The *New Frontier* casino, where Elvis made his first unhappy appearance in Las Vegas in 1956, is still there on the Strip, though it's scheduled to be replaced in the near future by a recreation of San Francisco. A little way north, the *Sahara* was a favourite hangout when Elvis was shooting *Viva Las Vegas*; it's now dominated by a couple of car-racing themed rides, which would surely appeal to Presley and the boys. Elvis married Priscilla at the *Aladdin* on 1 May 1967, nine months to the day before the birth of Lisa Marie, and eight years before Michael Jackson first clapped eyes on Lisa Marie, at a Jackson Five gig in Las Vegas. That incarnation of the

423

Greetings from Las Vegas

International Hotel

Aladdin was demolished in 1998, but it's since been replaced by a new, and so far unsuccessful, namesake.

The venue that will be forever associated with Elvis, however, is the *Las Vegas Hilton*, half a mile east of the Strip. The hotel opened, as the *International*, in 1969. Elvis wisely allowed Barbra Streisand to inaugurate its showroom, and profited from her less-than-happy experience when he took over a month later. When *Hilton* bought the property a year later, they made it a condition of the sale that they took over Elvis's contract as well. Elvis went on to sell out 837 consecutive shows, appearing in front of 2.5 million people. The *Hilton* people remain grateful: a statue of Elvis in the main lobby commemorates the King's achievement, while a memorial service was held here for Colonel Parker in 1998.

Less than a mile west of the Strip, at 3401 Industrial Rd, you'll find the city's largest Elvis shrine, Elvis-A-Rama (daily 10am–7pm; $15; ☏309-7200, ⓦwww.elvisarama.com). Memorabilia here includes his 1955 concert limo, bought with his $5000 bonus for signing with RCA, and now worth an estimated $340,000; a 1962 Glastron Bayflite speedboat; and his application for an American Express card. The stiff admission fee is justified by hourly live impersonator shows on a small stage, featuring Elvises both young and old. The same performers also make regular appearances at the *New Frontier*.

Quite apart from the lookalikes to be spotted in any self-respecting bar or wedding chapel, there are currently estimated to be *eleven* singing, sweating Elvises still putting the 'Viva' into Las Vegas. The King is also top of the bill in *Legends In Concert*, at the *Imperial Palace*, and *American Superstars*, at the *Stratosphere*; he's getting all shook up in his own shows at the *Riviera*, *Fitzgeralds* and the *Fiesta Rancho*; and he can frequently be found shedding hunks of his burning love in the huge domed lounge at the front of the *MGM Grand*.

425

Elvis impersonator shook up by lack of action at Las Vegas's Elvis-A-Rama

If you're looking to get married while you're in Las Vegas, most of the city's wedding chapels can persuade Elvis to arrive in a pink Cadillac and sing Love Me Tender. Perhaps the best bet is the *Graceland Wedding Chapel*, 619 Las Vegas Blvd S (☏382-0091 or 1-800/824-5732, Ⓦwww.gracelandchapel.com). Elvis prefers not to conduct actual weddings – although he will renew vows – but he makes a great best man, and sings six songs.

Nashville, Tennessee

Although Nashville may be the capital both of Tennessee and of country music, it's hardly overflowing with mementoes of the most famous artist who ever came here to cut a record. Visitors can at least see Elvis's gold Cadillac in the Country Music Hall Of Fame, at Fifth and Demonbreun; its forty coats of paint contain crushed diamonds and Oriental fish scales. RCA's Studio B, too, on Music Row, is worth a look. Elvis used it to make some of his finest records, including the *How Great Thou Art* album and *Elvis Country*. The fact that it has recently been handed over to a non-profit organization for redevelopment may, however, affect its future availability to tourists.

Outside America

Not surprisingly, the world beyond the United States holds few sites associated with the memory of Elvis Presley, with the obvious exception of Germany.

★★★ Elvis in Germany ★★★

When Private Presley, USS53310761, arrived in what was then West Germany on 1 October 1958, the influence of American youth culture was dreaded by much of society, and he was portrayed as a madman who cashed in on primitive instincts. In fact, during his entire career, Elvis only had one number one record in Germany, In The Ghetto.

Elvis spent seventeen months on German soil, stationed in Friedberg and living in Bad Nauheim. In 1978, Helmut Radermacher founded the Elvis Presley Society of Germany, which pleaded with both cities to commemorate the King's European sojourn. It took seventeen more years before Bad Nauheim unveiled a memorial in June 1995, consisting of a granite column and a marble bust. Months later, Friedberg christened a public square Elvis-Presley-Platz, while its American barracks renamed a place Elvis-Presley-Park.

The tourist office of Bad Nauheim now offers Elvis Presley Stop Overs, guided two- or three-day tours of the most interesting places. Visitors can stay at the Hotel Grunewald and sleep in the very bed where Elvis slept – Room 10 is in its original state – or take a day-trip to a wine store in the Pfalz (Palatinate) that's run by the Pressler family, who claim to be descendants of Elvis's German ancestors. Stop Overs also include visits to the archive of the Bad Nauheim Elvis Club, and a stay at their pub, where you

427

HEADQUARTERS
1ST BATTALION

32ND ARMOR

Elvis as a GI in Germany, the look later inspired an Action Man-style doll

can sample an Elvis cocktail. For Elvis's seventieth birthday, in 2005, Bad Nauheim will host a general meeting of fan clubs from across Europe. For further info about the festival and tours, contact Bad Nauheim Stadtmarketing und Tourismus GmbH (☎00 49 6032 929920).

While Elvis was stationed in Germany, he also went on three much-publicized weekend sprees to Paris, staying at the *Prince de Galles* hotel and making regular visits to the *Lido*.

★★★ Elvis in Britain ★★★

Elvis's one and only appearance on British soil was a brief stopover at Prestwick airport in Scotland, on his way back to the US from Germany on 3 March 1960. A plaque marks the spot, and a few years ago the airport opened a bar called Graceland. The whole experience, short as it was, has left a deep impression on the Scottish psyche, inspiring among other things a tribute band called Elvis Prestwick and the Ryanaires.

★★ Elvis Museum, Denmark ★★

Europe's one Elvis Presley Museum can be found in Sondervig, Denmark (tel 45 9733 9383). Its fifty displays hold more than two thousand items, including Elvis's bible, TCB necklace and sunglasses, as well as *Janis & Elvis From South Africa*, which is said to be the rarest record in the world. It also features the 1950s-style *Heartbreak Café*.

429

Kingology

Lists, Books, Web sites

'How much does it cost if it's free?'

Colonel Parker's provisional title for his autobiography

How much of your disposable income are you prepared to devote to the accumulation of objects connected with Elvis Presley? This is a question every fan has to confront, and it is one that can leave significant others suspecting, not unjustifiably, that a dead rock star means more to you than your plans for the future. After all, even the understandable (and not that obsessive) goal of buying every album Elvis ever made would cost you a four-figure sum. And buying his music is only the first step on a long lonely highway which can, if you're not careful, lead to bankruptcy and/or divorce. Only a tiny minority of fans can be as lucky as father and son Paul and Elvis McLeod, owners of *Graceland Too*, and turn their obsession and collection into a museum.

Still, once you've had a stern word with yourself, and vowed to limit yourself to one Elvis-related spending binge a year (topped up, of course, with a few essential purchases made on a monthly basis), you can safely enjoy the many-splendoured world of Elvis shopping.

That's what most of this chapter is about: buying Elvis records, buying books about the King, buying memorabilia. That – and a few of those obsessions we fans like to indulge in: the weirdest songs, the songs Elvis never sung, and the top Web sites to discuss such matters.

Records

The ultimate Elvis records ought to be those first five Sun singles, both because of their historic import and their relative rarity. And they do fetch reasonable prices at auction if in good nick: the final Sun single, "Mystery Train" recently went for $1668 (though you can find Sun singles in reasonable condition for as little as $500). But in record collecting, rarity ultimately wins out, so you can find, on sites like *www.elvisspecialties.com*, a promotional eight-LP box set of Elvis's greatest hits in mint condition at $700, while a mint, unplayed, RCA US single of My Boy/Loving Arms, with a rare grey label, will cost you only $100 less.

If you want to check prices, Jerry Osborne's book *Elvis Presley Records And Memorabilia* – and *Record Collector's Price Guide* – give good ballpark figures, but this is a highly complex area. Perhaps the best example of the different values which dominate the collectors' world is that, while the most you can reasonably pay for any version of Elvis's first RCA album is $350, you might have to splash out $5000 for a copy of Aloha From Hawaii which includes the "Chicken Of The Sea" sticker from the show's sponsors, the right cover and the inner sleeves.

Of Elvis's straight RCA singles, the 78s of Heartbreak Hotel and Hound Dog will fetch $60–100 depending on their condition. Extended players are often more expensive because of their scarcity and the near death of the format, so even Elvis's last foray into this world, Easy Come, Easy Go, could change hands for anything from $25 to $80. A rare maroon-labelled A Touch Of Gold Vol 2 EP recently fetched $1600.

The rarest albums are often bizarre permutations of official releases produced overseas. The rarest is usually cited as Elvis and Janis, a nine-track album on which Elvis sings four songs, and Janis Martin (aka The Female Elvis) the rest. Rumoured to have been released for just one day by RCA South Africa in 1956/7, this album has a seriously groovy cover and could cost $3500 or more.

Martin was so impressed with Elvis that she also recorded the single My Boy Elvis. Parker wasn't so impressed, though, allegedly ordering RCA South Africa to cease and desist.

As a generalization, Japanese Elvis product is either worth more than the standard album releases, or is at least better-looking. Elvis wasn't marketed brilliantly anywhere when he was alive, especially in terms of sleeve design and packaging, but many of the releases in Japan were a cut above average.

Some goodies

Here are a few examples of choice Elvis record product, along with country of origin and approximate prices. Bear in mind that prices can vary by almost as much as 100 percent depending on the condition, state of the market, etc.

Stay Away Joe LP ★ This is a neat story: one copy of this album was pressed for one radio station in Arizona to broadcast once – to coincide with the end of shooting of the *Stay Away Joe* movie. Confusingly, none of the songs on the disc are from the film but are gospel numbers. The Colonel got this album back after it was played and it was part of his estate. For the full story, see *www.jerryosborne.com*. Possibly the world's rarest Elvis record.

His Latest Flame/Little Sister ★ This compact 33 single with picture sleeve sells for anything from $400 to $12,000.

Elvis Christmas Album ★ RCA, 1957. Depending on the state this is in, it can set you back $275, if it's got all the pictures.

Too Much/Playing For Keeps ★ RCA single with picture sleeve, $85.

Elvis Sings Flaming Star German Club ★ A CD rarity – one of several CDs issued in editions of 1000 for the German fan clubs by BMG. Yours for $75.

Perfect For Parties ★ A US promo record on which Elvis sings "Love Me" and introduces songs by other artists of deep obscurity. $75.

From Memphis To The World ★ One of Elvis's finest albums – but the one you want is the RCA Uruguay LP with gatefold sleeve. $50.

The 10 weirdest songs

Say what you like about the claims of Dylan or Morrissey, when it comes down to it, you can't beat the King for weird songs – songs about seafood, tax departments, dancing in sports cars. And who but Elvis could try and reconcile Darwinism and Christianity on one A side? If released on an album, the tracks that follow would make the *Having Fun On Stage With Elvis* album look downright normal.

Fort Lauderdale Chamber Of Commerce
On the one hand, it's hard not to admire the ease with which Sid Tepper and Roy Bennett make a hook out of the unpromising words "Fort Lauderdale Chamber Of Commerce"; on the other, it's hard not to think: Why did they bother? And why, more importantly, did Elvis?

Froggy Went A Courtin'
A hilarious stop-start assault on this old standard, which slows down, at one point, to a macho blues where Elvis sings the words 'froggy went a courtin' and he did ride, uh-huh' as if this was sinister news of great import.

He's Your Uncle Not Your Dad
The uncle in question being Uncle

Sam, this is a song about tax – something else to blame on the Internal Revenue Service.

Ito Eats
The title begs two questions: who is Ito and what's so special about his eating habits? To which the answers are: Ito is a blubbery Hawaiian buddy of Elvis in *Blue Hawaii* and he eats like teeth are out of style. Mercifully, these revelations soon tail off into a Harry Belafonte-style 'day oh' ending.

Life
An heroic attempt to reconcile Darwinism and Christianity in three minutes and six seconds in which matter forms and breaks the curse of nothingness, nature reaches its highest goal and love is life and life is love. Elvis said it best, in the studio: 'This damned thing is as long as life itself.'

Queen Wahine's Papaya
Thoroughly silly number with alliterative, but nonsensical lyrics. When RCA executive Joan Deary heard this, her only thought was how Elvis managed to sing it without laughing. Yup.

Smorgasbord
In *Spinout*, Elvis is wild about

smorgasbord – and he's not talking about Scandinavian food. He will, he promises, a little anachronistically, 'take the dish I please and please the dish I take'. Safe to say this isn't Camille Paglia's favourite Elvis track.

Song Of The Shrimp

From the film *Girls! Girls! Girls!,* this is the tragic tale of a shrimp, misled by an offer in the shrimp newspaper to get a free ride to New Orleans, who meets a grisly end. All sung and played with an alarming sincerity.

There's No Room To Rhumba In A Sports Car

The lack of space for rhumba-ing in your average sports car obviously came as shock to messrs Wise and Manning, who wrote this little ditty. And, sadly, they don't advise which vehicles the serious rhumba enthusiast should buy.

Yoga Is As Yoga Does

Elvis's hairdresser Larry Geller says this song was inserted into *Easy Come, Easy Go* just to make fun of his (and Elvis's) foray into alternative religion. Could be. Hard to think of any other reason why anyone would have wanted to write or record it.

Elvis rouses himself for the vocal challenge presented by "Queenie Wahine's Papaya"

Janis And Elvis ★ Belgian fan-club release of the South African album mentioned above. $30.

Jailhouse Rock/Heartbreak Hotel ★ RCA Japan single 977, issued with marvellous pseudo-Pop Art sleeve. $15.

In The Ghetto/Any Day Now ★ This RCA US single is probably the top Elvis bargain – an original copy in mint condition sells for only 50 cents or so on most US sites. And the music is magic ... Strange, that.

Books

There are vast numbers of books about Elvis – including more than one hundred biographies, alone – so the reviews below are selective, focusing mostly on the best, but with a few nods to the most wacko and wrong-headed. Completists may want to check out Infinite Elvis: An Annotated Bibliography by **Mary Hancock Hinds** (A Cappella), which covers all of the literature on Elvis in commendably dispassionate fashion.

Biographies

★★★ THE MAIN BIOGRAPHIES ★★★

Down At The End Of Lonely Street Peter Brown and Pat Boeske *Arrow* ★ This is not a bad starter on Elvis: a lighter read than the definitive Guralnick and almost as salacious as Goldman (see below), but worth buying, especially for the light it sheds on Elvis's drug taking and the cause of his death. ★★★

Elvis Albert Goldman *McGraw-Hill* ★ Goldman's Elvis is infamous: the book that did the dirt on the King. Goldman's version of Elvis has been hugely influential on all subsequent accounts, and yet this is a very poor book, packed with exaggerations, misinterpretations and errors – errors, apparently minor in isolation, which pile up to justify his presentation of Elvis as rock'n'roll's answer to the bearded lady, a freak. It's hard also to know what to make of a book about the king of rock'n'roll which, along the way, dismisses James Brown as 'an African witch doctor'. Or what to make of any book which includes the sentence 'They's many a crazy, likah drinkin' pill-poppin'countrah boy that kin get hissef jes' as racked up n' ragged as the craziest coon on Beale Street.' Actually, it's not. For it is Goldman's bigotry that really undoes his book. Had Elvis been black or Jewish, Goldman would not have been able to make fun of the shape of his 'pecker'. If Elvis had been from any ethnic minority, Goldman would not have been allowed to portray his family as members of 'a deracinated and restless race'. He should not be able to get away with his prejudices, and it is hard not to conclude that all his disgust (Vernon Presley is a 'hard, mean, nasty redneck … with deadened dick' – that about a man whose wife's health could not risk bearing another child) must really be self-disgust. Poor Albert Goldman – by his own estimation the leading intellectual in the western hemisphere – having to earn a crust by stamping on the graves of morons like Elvis, Lenny Bruce and John Lennon, all of whom, to his chagrin, are unaccountably more famous than he is. ★

Last Train To Memphis and **Careless Love** Peter Guralnick
Little, Brown ★ These two books are close to definitive biographies of Elvis: at least, they tell the story of what happened better than any others. Guralnick is not so strong on the question 'why', and his attempts to get inside Presley's head, delivering a kind of interior monologue, are less convincing. What he's best on is the music: the recreation of the Sun sessions in the *Last Train*, and of the 1969 Memphis sessions in *Careless Love* are thrilling. What mars the books, and this applies most to the second volume, is that, as the life unfolds, Guralnick seems to call more and more of the debates against Elvis. Perhaps the most

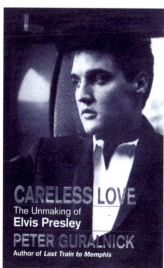

CARELESS LOVE
The Unmaking of
Elvis Presley
PETER GURALNICK
Author of *Last Train to Memphis*

439

blatant example is the account of the March 1972 recording sessions where he notes: 'Felton continued to have faith that Elvis could cut a hit record anytime he wanted. The trouble was, he wasn't interested in cutting a hit record.' This was three months after Priscilla had left Elvis (and a month after she had told him she was seeing Mike Stone) and it is not hard to understand why, at that time, songs like "Separate Ways" appealed to him. Still, these two books remain a fine achievement. **★★★★**

Elvis Dave Marsh *Thunder's Mouth Press* ★ As you would expect from a rock writer of Marsh's stature, this inexplicably out-of-print 1984 biography is very good indeed. It's a fan's perspective, as well as a critic's, and features some of the finest, most passionate, prose ever written about Elvis. **★★★★★**

Elvis And The Final Years Jerry Hopkins *Simon & Schuster/Warner* ★ Hopkins pioneered the Elvis biography and every author who has followed in his wake has had to acknowledge the debt. Although some of his stories (notably whether Elvis made his first record for his mum's birthday and who was in the studio at the time) have been amended or challenged in time, these still form a good basic biography of the man. **★★★★★**

Elvis And Gladys Elaine Dundy *Futura* ★ A fine biography of the young Elvis and the most important person in his life – his mum. At times, Dundy achieves an astonishing empathy with Elvis and this is one of the few books which genuinely has new things to say about him, detailing his boyish passion for Captain Marvel Junior, his Jewish and Cherokee blood, and his 200-mile hitchhike to enter a country music festival when he was just 18. One star off, though, for a very weird chapter on El's fluencies, and for Dundy's obsession with Parker, which leads her to suggest some labyrinthine plots. For all that, a must-read. **★★★★**

★★★ REFERENCE TOMES ★★★

Elvis Day By Day Peter Guralnick and Ernst Jorgensen *Ballantine* ★ Guralnick and Jorgensen do exactly what their title says. And they do it very well indeed. **★★★**

Elvis: His Life From A To Z Fred L Worth and Steve D Tamerius *Corgi* ★ A creditable and credible reference book. **★★★**

Elvis Word For Word Jerry Osborne *Harmony* ★ It may not quite live up to its hype as a virtual oral autobiography, but this collection of Elvis press conferences, statements, speeches and rambles is still an essential purchase. Maybe in the next edition Osborne could delete a few of the times Elvis introduces himself in concert as Wayne Newton. ★★★

★★★ INDIVIDUAL MEMOIRES ★★★

Early Elvis Bill E. Burk *Propwash* ★ Not everyone likes Burk's style: essentially a collection of interviews and memories. But he has done some valuable work, correcting many of the myths which surrounded Elvis's early years. This trilogy (focusing on the Tupelo years, the Humes High school days and the Sun years) is a worthwhile addition to any fan's collection. ★★★★

A Presley Speaks Vester Presley *Wimmer Brothers* ★ Vester's reminiscences, even in big type, don't stretch far. But he does tell a very funny story about how he used to threaten to steal Elvis's peanut butter and crackers. Elvis was so worried by his uncle's threat that, every time he came around, the young Elvis would shout to his mum, 'Hide them, Uncle Vester is going to steal them.' ★★★

Elvis Aaron Presley: Revelations From The Memphis Mafia Alanna Nash *Harper* ★ Somehow, this oral biography told by messrs Lacker, Fike and Smith (Billy not Gene) to Nash makes the tragedy sadder than even Guralnick's biography. And the tellers have a gift for metaphor: Smith says Priscilla is as 'cold and hard as the highway out there'. The added bonus is the sense you get of them being in the same room, arguing with each other. As essential to understanding Elvis as *From Elvis In Memphis*. ★★★★★

Elvis And Me Priscilla Presley with Sandra Harmony *Random House* ★ Hardly a tell-all, Priscilla's account of her life and marriage with Elvis is still an intriguing read. The best line ('While my classmates were deciding which college to attend, I was deciding which gun to wear with what sequined dress') gives you a taste of how good this could have been. ★★★

Elvis And The Colonel Dirk Vellenga with Mick Farren *Delacorte* ★ The first book to expose Parker's Dutch origins, this is well researched, and written with an indignation which never gets in the way of the facts. ★★★★

Elvis In Texas Lori Torrance with Stanley Oberst *Republic Of Texas Press* ★ A fine account recapturing the dim, distant days when the eyes of Texas were upon Elvis, Scotty and Bill – told through anecdotes, photographs and press clippings. ★★★★

Elvis In The Twilight Of Memory June Juanico *Warner* ★ Not ghostwritten, and written by someone who can write, this is an affectionate and amusing account of Juanico's romance with Elvis, especially treasured for the light it sheds on his family and that idyllic summer of 1956. ★★★★

Elvis In The Words Of Those Who Knew Him Best Rose Clayton and Mick Heard *Virgin* ★ And in the words of some who didn't know him that well at all … but this is still a worthwhile addition to any fan's bookshelf. ★★★★

Elvis Precious Memories Donna Presley Early and Edie Hand (with Lynn Edge) *The Best Of Times* ★ A quietly moving portrait of Elvis by members of Vernon's side of the family, this always looks for the good in Elvis, is often sentimental, but is no whitewash. There are some hilarious stories about Elvis's aunt Delta Mae, and less amusing tales of how the Memphis mafia deliberately isolated Elvis. ★★★

Elvis We Love You Tender Dee Presley, Billy, David and Ricky Stanley told to Martin Torghoff *NEL* ★ The first book by the Stanleys – longtime Elvis associates – pulled no punches about El's flaws, but without the contempt which blighted Goldman's book. ★★★

Good Rocking Tonight Joe Esposito *Avon* ★ Joe's memoir has, at times, all the depth of a press release. The Colonel and Elvis were the greatest team showbiz has ever seen, blah, blah, blah … but not a word about Parker's gambling habit, and Elvis is blamed for encouraging the 'rumour' (as Joe puts it) that Parker was an illegal alien. When the Colonel called this 'the most honest and truthful book ever written about Elvis', one can only assume he was indulging in a double bluff. Joe may also be the only person in the world who thinks the Memphis sessions were a triumph – for Felton Jarvis. ★★

If I Can Dream Larry Geller *Simon & Schuster* ★ Geller's book stands in relation to the rest of the Memphis mafia memoirs as the Book of John does to the synoptic gospels. Focusing on the singer's quest for spiritual comfort, this gives an altogether different view of Elvis. The key section is a diary-style account of the singer's last few months which provides a fantastic insight into a life spun out of control. ★★

442 **That's Alright Elvis** Scotty Moore *James Dickerson Music Sales* ★ Scotty waited too long to give his account of his days with the King. This never quite got the buzz it ought to have had but it's a good, honourable – indeed, almost charitable – memoir. ★★★

The music

Elvis: A Life In Music **Ernst Jorgensen** *St Martin's Press* ★ Simply irresistible: you almost feel as if you were in the studio with Elvis in this account of his recording sessions and concerts. This is one book you'll want to dip into again and again. ★★★★★

Elvis: The Complete Illustrated Record **Mick Farren and Roy Carr** *Eel Pie* ★ This long-out-of-print book is an opinionated, entertaining, quirkily illustrated guide to his life as a singer. ★★★★

Mystery Train **Greil Marcus** *Omnibus* ★ Marcus has done more than anyone to put what Elvis's music meant into words, and his essay on Elvis in this book has never really been bettered. ★★★★

The movies

Chow Time on the Movie Set

The Elvis Film Encyclopaedia **Eric Braun** *Batsford* ★ The subtitle 'an impartial guide to the films of Elvis' gives the game away. The positive spin is a pleasant change but anybody who gives "Queenie Wahine's Papaya" three stars (out of four) might be deemed to be overcompensating. ★★★

Elvis: The King And His Movies **Peter Guttmacher** *Metro* ★ Colourful, with a bonus CD, and good use of studio memos, this is probably the best history of Elvis in Hollywood. ★★★

443

Reel Elvis Pauline Bartel *Taylor* ★ This is a fun, deeply trivial, and rather nicely titled guide to Elvis and his movie career. ★★★

Photographic books

Elvis: A Celebration Mike Evans *Dorling Kindersley* ★ This new 600-page coffee-table blockbuster was prepared with the Graceland Estate on the 25th

anniversary of Elvis's death. The biography is a decent year-by-year account but it is the lavish selection of photos that are the stand-outs: a trove of rare memorabilia, lots of personal photos of his family and home life, and hundreds of images, classic and obscure, from every era of his career. ★★★★

A CELEBRATION
IMAGES OF ELVIS PRESLEY FROM THE ELVIS PRESLEY ARCHIVE AT GRACELAND®

Elvis 56: In The Beginning Alfred Wertheimer *Macmillan/Pimlico* ★ A great photographic collection of Elvis at the outset of his career in 1956 – no outsider would ever get this close again. It is especially fascinating because it documents a time when everything was new, everything extraordinary, and not even Elvis and Parker had no idea what lay ahead. ★★★★★

Elvis For The First Time Ever Joe Tunzi *JAT* ★ Tunzi, for those who don't know him, has done a remarkable job tracking down rare photos and info on Elvis life. (See ⓦwww.worldwideelvis.com/JOETUNZI.HTM for more info.) This is a 96-page book of rare photos of Elvis in concert from 1969 to 1977. But the $50 price means it's one for completists. ★★★

Elvis World Jane and Michael Stern *Bloomsbury* ★ A coffee-table book, wonderfully illustrated, and fun to read, this is a fine introductory guide to the parallel universe that is Elvis World. ★★★★★

Graceland **Chet Flippo** *Mitchell Beazley* ★ This is the authorized book about El's Memphis pad – a superbly illustrated tome, and well written by an ex-*Rolling Stone* journalist. ★★★

The King Of The Road **Robert Gordon** *Hamlyn* ★ A glossy, authorized, souvenir of Elvis's concerts, worth buying just for the pictures. ★★★★

Essays and oddities

Dead Elvis **Greil Marcus** *Viking* ★ The academic of rock's book on Elvis would be worth the cover price for the essay on Albert Goldman alone – but there's plenty more of interest in this lively, readable collection. (Don't confuse this outing with Marcus's oddly awful *Double Trouble* – a book of essays on Elvis and Bill Clinton, which is about as seminal as the Elvis film it's named after.) ★★★★★

Elvis After Elvis **Gilbert Rodman** *Routledge* ★ Well-argued, amusingly illustrated book about Elvis's career as an ex-living legend which, for all the long words, ultimately can't quite explain the phenomenon. ★★★

Elvis and The Apocalypse **Steve Werner** *Xlibris* ★ Supposedly, this is a satire of 'Armageddon predications, New Age hopes, and Elvis fanaticism' but the book in which a matron called Marie relates Elvis's life and times to the Bible and all kinds of secret signs almost ends up making the Presley story seem even more miraculous. Every paranoid fantasy about Elvis's career is alluded to here (including the rumour that the FBI paid Hollywood to tame Elvis) but strangely, by the time you finish it, you warm heartily to the King. ★★★★★

Elvis Undercover **Gail Giorgio Brewer** *Bright Books* ★ For hard-core delusionists only. ★

Graceland: Going Home With Elvis **Karal Ann Marling** *Harvard* ★ If you're tired of books that interpret the King through his diet, then try this – a book which interprets his life through the houses and places he lived in, and his skills as an interior designer. Her evocation of the flight to Memphis is wonderful, but her account of the rest of El's life not always as sure-footed. ★★★

Images Of Elvis Presley In American Culture **George Plasketes** *Haworth Press* ★ Ultimate proof of the inescapability of Elvis in America. ★★★

In Search Of Elvis Vernon Chadwick (ed) *Westview* ★ There's plenty of academic posturing in this collection of essays from the first Elvis conference at the University of Mississippi in 1997, but there are also some very good essays, especially Peter Nazareth's on Elvis as a singer who contains and alludes to other singers as diverse as Nat King Cole, Mario Lanza and Chuck Willis. ★★★★

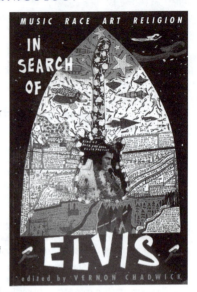

MUSIC RACE ART RELIGION

IN SEARCH OF ELVIS

edited by VERNON CHADWICK

Memphis Elvis Style Mike Freeman and Cindy Hazen *John F. Blair* ★ Essential reading if you're going to Memphis or, for that matter, if you never get further than reading this book. ★★★

Race, Rock And Elvis Michael Bertrand *University of Illinois Press* ★ This excellent book connects the cultural shifts Elvis initiated with the political change, especially on civil rights, taking place in the South in the 1950s. ★★★★

Where's Elvis? Dan Klein and Hans Teensma *Wedenfeld & Nicolson* ★ It's hard to resist an Elvis book modelled on the *Where's Wally?* children's books, in a gentle satirical take on the afterlife sightings. Spot Elvis in scenes ranging from the Pope's Easter address to the Iran–Contra hearings. ★★★

General music books

Awopbopaloobopalopbamboom Nik Cohn *Grove* ★ This classic book on the phenomenon of rock'n'roll contains a great essay on Elvis, second only in impact to Greil Marcus' in *Mystery Train*. Cohn's contrasting approach also helps. Unlike Marcus, he's not looking ffor social and intellectual connections: he happily admits that he is a sucker for a fine pop song.

Country **Nick Tosches** *De Capo* ★ Although Tosches is responsible for some of the finest writing about Elvis, he hasn't actually written a full-blown biography. He has, however, written a wondrous essay in this book about Elvis, which brilliantly encapsulates Presley's sheer contradictoriness. His *Unsung Heroes Of Rock And Roll*, although it officially ends before Elvis's rise to fame, is worth a read too.

Flowers In The Dustbin **Jim Miller** *Fireside* ★ **The Sound Of The City** **Charlie Gillett** *De Capo* ★ These two books are the definitive histories of rock'n'roll – fine accounts that place Elvis brilliantly in his musical and cultural context. Gillett is perhaps best on the music, and Miller on the culture, making clear, while never glossing over his flaws, how central Elvis was to the emotional revolution of the 1950s.

Fiction, poetry, graphic novels, etc

Elvis is, as you might expect, commemorated quite widely in fiction, and he makes some very strange appearances indeed in poetry, cartoons and graphic novels.

★★★ FICTION ★★★

Burning Elvis **John Burnside** *Vintage* ★ In this fine collection of short stories, Elvis only appears in the title story, but there's a wonderful moment where the boy remembers Elvis's movies: 'a vague recollection of contained grace, and a kind of beauty that seemed remote and aimless, like the beauty of the tigers at the zoo'. ★★★

Elvis In The Morning **William F. Buckley Jr** *Harcourt* ★ This novel by the American conservative columnist spun a tender tale of a young boy's friendship for the King, and outed the author as a fan. ★★★

Elvis Presley Calls His Mother After *The Ed Sullivan Show* **Samuel Charters** *Coffeehouse* ★ A fascinating, if at times exhausting, character sketch of the young Elvis. ★★★★

447

Kill Me Tender and **Blue Suede Clues** **Daniel Klein** *St Martin's Press/ Minotaur* ★ Elvis's dreams of becoming a cop may have got no further in real life than an immense collection of badges but in death, as a fictional entity, he has become a sleuth in Klein's *Singing Sleuth* series. In *Blue Suede Shoes* he takes a break after *Kissin' Cousins* to help a fellow GI wrongly accused of murder. This may sound ludicrous but somehow it works. ★★★

★★★ **GRAPHIC NOVELS** ★★★

Elvis Shrugged **Patrick McCray** *Revolutionary* ★ Elvis and a host of celebrity co-stars (Madonna, Sinatra, the Colonel, Sinead O'Connor) try to save the world. As McCray explains, the 1970s Elvis was an evil clone, the real Elvis snuck away to do good deeds and only Priscilla noticed.

Invasion Of The Elvis Zombies Gary Panter *Raw* ★ Elvis is the hero, of a kind, of this graphic novel: he is eaten by his adoring female fans and resurrected as a cross between Godzilla, King Kong and himself. The book comes complete with a completely irrelevant flexidisc.

★★★ POETRY ★★★

All Shook Up Will Clemens (ed) *University of Arkansas Press* ★ The best and the worst of Elvis odes are collected in this book. And Elvis has inspired some truly awful poetry – Gail Giorgio's ode to him in "Elvis Undercover" being the Marianna Trench in a book slosh-full of low points. Not all of the bad stuff is doggerel written by fans, though. Thom Gunn wrote two poems about Elvis: "Elvis Presley" (in which even he admitted there was only good line, about the singer turning 'revolt into style'), and "Painkillers", which is obsessed by the Vegas Elvis's weight. Joyce Carol Oates' "Waiting On Elvis 1956" and Fleda Brown Jackson's "Elvis At The End Of History" are the stand-outs.

Books Elvis read

If you really want to get closer to the King, here's a list of books he is known to have bought and read.

Autobiography Of A Yogi Paramahansa Yogananda

The Bible

Cheiro's Book Of Numbers

The City Of God St Augustine

The Guinness Book Of Records

The Impersonal Life Joseph Benner

Moby Dick Herman Melville

The Prophet Kahlil Gibran

The Scientific Search For The Face Of Jesus Frank Adams

The Stranger Albert Camus

Sun Signs Linda Goodman

They've Killed The President Robert Sam Anson

Magazines

For Elvis fans of a certain age, the definitive magazine about the King was (and forever will be) Elvis Monthly, the British fan-club magazine which developed a worldwide following but closed a few years ago after forty glorious years. Back issues of the monthly have now become items of memorabilia themselves. But here is a quick guide to the best publications still with us.

Elvis The Man And His Music ★ This has some of the feel of the old *Elvis Monthly* which, for this author who grew up on those mags, is a very good thing indeed. Most issues contain good interviews with people who have worked with Elvis either in the studio or on a film set, and there are good reviews of official CDs and bootlegs. A must-have. Email: ✉n.d.t@virgin.net

Elvis Today ★ Endorsed by BMG's Elvis committee, this is the replacement for the much-missed *Elvis Monthly*, edited by Todd Slaughter and Pal Granlund. Find out more on ⓦwww.elvistoday.com

Elvis Unlimited ★ Editor Arjan Deelen has done some of the best interviews with El's musicians in recent years and this is full of good stuff. You can find out about prices and availability by emailing ✉elvis@post7.tele.dk or calling ☎00 45 8646 9230.

Elvis World ★ Produced in Memphis by Bill Burk, this is a very different read to many other Elvis mags, with a mix of good contributions from overseas and Burk's own contribution from the mecca of Elvis world, Memphis. Write to Burk Enterprises, Box 16792, Memphis, TN 38186-0792, for details.

Essential Elvis ★ Editor Andrew Hearn has deliberately set out to get the big interviews, and in recent issues has been rewarded with good stories on Linda Thompson and Ginger Alden. For info: ⓦwww.essentialelvis.co.uk

◀ Elvis's dream of being a comic-book hero realized, albeit posthumously

Elvis in art

Elvis was his own finest work of art. Think of the effort which went into those hairstyles, the make-up, the street clothes which would have made even a self-confessed dandy like Tom Wolfe feel sartorially challenged, and all those entrances down the Graceland staircase. And he has inspired countless artists, from the globally famous and glamorous Andy Warhol to folk artists like Joni Mabe and Howard Finster, and those factories down Mexico way that turn out those tacky but strangely powerful velvet Elvises that Elvis Presley Enterprises objects to.

★★★ ANDY WARHOL ★★★

Andy Warhol's infatuation with Elvis as a subject runs far deeper than the famous silver-gun-toting Elvises From *Flaming Star*. In 1956, his The Golden Slipper Show included a buccaneer's boot which he identified as for Elvis Presley. In 1962, he devised the Red Elvises, the very name enough to justify an FBI file on the King. A year later, Warhol started on the Silver Elvises, playing off Presley's rare combination of macho and androgynous appeal. Artist and singer never met, although Warhol watched a lot of Elvis movies. He did, though, meet Priscilla Presley in 1979 and noted in his diary: 'God what a beauty. I wonder if she had her nose fixed.'

★★★ PETER BLAKE ★★★

Warhol wasn't the only Pop Artist to draw on Elvis. British artist Peter Blake used Elvis as a theme in his self-portrait and in his alphabet in which K Is For King (it's not, alas, one of his better works).

★★★ HOWARD FINSTER AND JONI MABE ★★★

Elvis has been a semi-continuous subject for two folk artists from the state of Georgia: Howard Finster and Joni Mabe.

Like Warhol, Finster (who died in October 2001) didn't meet Elvis – although he says the singer walked into his garden one afternoon years after his death. Finster admitted he partly used Elvis because his image was so famous, yet he also said, 'One thing in my lifetime that I heard about and looked at and listened to was Elvis Presley.' Some of Finster's finest work has been tweaking Elvis album covers (especially *Burning Love* and *He Touched Me*).

Mabe, who only became interested in Elvis when she heard of his death, is in danger of becoming more famous for owning Elvis's wart (a gesture whose irony was lost on a gullible media) than for such fine works as the Elvis prayer rug. Although she is one of the finest contemporary artists in the American South, she can't quite explain Elvis's fascination: 'There's something so mysterious about him that I can't figure out, which keeps me interested because he's such a contradiction of himself all the time.'

★★★ NAOKI MITSUSE ★★★

Naoki Mitsuse is a Japanese artist, now resident in California. She was just 11 when Elvis died, and painted her first Elvis at art school in California. She then had to return to Tokyo while her visa was sorted. It took seven months, which she passed painting pictures of Elvis. She got her visa and now says, 'I feel satisfied I did my share to create more Elvis paintings and have really no plans to paint Elvis again.' Fair enough.

Memorabilia

Colonel Parker turned Elvis into a multi-billion-dollar franchise, and mortality did the rest. Having started out selling black-and-white photographs at ten cents a time, Parker soon realized Elvis was good for everything from bubblegum to pyjamas to guitars. These have all become items on the international Elvis memorabilia market, while Elvis Presley Enterprises carries on Parker's good work issuing new souvenirs. It claims a monopoly on Elvis memorabilia, although this was successfully challenged in the UK in 1997. London trader Sid Shaw won a court case against EPE, who alleged that he was infringing their copyright by selling souvenirs under the name Elvisly Yours. The judge disagreed and Shaw still sells his Elvis memorabilia through his Web site.

But the really big money is in Elvis's belongings. Since Elvis's death, a bizarre range of his personal possessions has found its way past the gates of Graceland and opened up a whole new market. If you've got money to spare, you can drive home in his Lincoln convertible (sold at auction for $250,000), or watch Elvis's favourite tapes – including *Monty Python* and *Blazing Saddles* – on his personal VCR.

For the fans who attach a quasi-religious significance to Elvis, items worn by Elvis are revered as sacred relics – and attract top prices. A wristwatch sold for $32,500, his personal Bible sold for $25,000, and an Elvis impersonator called Anthony Ciaglia paid $8500 for one of his shirts. Ciaglia had a particularly good reason for wanting his own piece of Elvis memorabilia – Elvis's music had roused him from a coma as a teenager.

This Elvis repeat-print T-shirt from 1967 was one of a range from London designers John Dove and Molly White's Wonder Workshop label. It sold in the thousands, in London and New York, but is now a sought-after item, to be found in fashion museum collections and the occasional auction. ▶

Elvis memorabilia sites

You need a real relic? Or a few original posters, or tasteful Mexican Elvis souvenirs? Here's where to look ...

www.elvisstamps.com Of the postage not the gospel-singing variety.

www.jerryosborne.com Jerry will appraise your stuff, sell it or sell you some more memorabilia.

www.sothebys.com and **www.christies.com** These London auction houses have regular rock memorabilia sales for serious-money collectors.

www.ebay.com and **www.ebay.co.uk** and **www.qxl.com** The major Internet auction sites are always awash with Elvis items.

www.guernseys.com This New York auction house often has unique rock (and Elvis) memorabilia for sale.

www.elvis-collectors.com The danger with this excellent site, which covers collectibles and the latest news and reviews, is that you won't be able to drag yourself away.

www.elvisly-yours.com Sid Shaw is the Elvis fan who took on the might of Elvis Presley Enterprises and won the right to sell Elvis souvenirs – in the UK. A good selection of stuff but probably best to skip the poetry.

Choice items

Here, for all of us fans and obsessives, are some choice Elvis items, listed in ascending order of price and rarity. Prices quoted are mainly from Ebay and specialist Elvis memorabilia sites on the Internet (see above).

★★★ **UNDER $100** ★★★

Life-size cardboard Elvis $29.95 ★ A life-size free-standing cut-out of Elvis showing him in his famous gold lame suit. Standing over 6ft tall, it was recently advertised on Ebay as 'great for any room or party'. Also available as a talking version, apparently.

TCB walking stick $39.95 ✶ The ultimate accessory for the Elvis-fan-about-town, the TCB walking stick features a cap inexplicably modelled on a 1920s doorknob and embossed with the TCB logo. Also features a nonslip tip.

✶✶✶ $100–1000 ✶✶✶

Unused concert ticket $106 ✶ Two unused concert tickets for front-row seats issued for Elvis's planned concert in Utica, New York, and dated 19 August 1977 – three days after Elvis died.

Ceramic Graceland $150 ✶ Ideal for those unable to make the journey to Memphis' most famous landmark, this ceramic model of Graceland lights up and comes complete with a Cadillac, wrought-iron gates, lawn decoration and two Christmas-tree lawn decorations.

Piece of wood $175 ✶ Not just any piece of wood, this is a piece of wood from the fence that ran around Graceland until 1976, presented in a special presentation case and authenticated by none other than former Elvis employee Mike McGregor.

Signed record sleeve $500 ✶ Cover of the record "Pledging My Love", signed by Elvis with the words 'Best wishes, Elvis Presley' in blue ballpoint.

✶✶✶ $1000–10,000 ✶✶✶

Elvis's pipe $4000 ✶ It's not widely known Elvis smoked a pipe, but this 14 carat gold version handcrafted in Italy was one of several he kept on his desk. Others are on display in the *Elvis Presley* Memphis restaurant.

Elvis's jogging pants $4999 ✶ Preserved behind ultraviolet protective glass, these are the jogging pants Elvis wore during divorce proceedings in Santa Monica, California. Accompanied by pictures of Elvis wearing them and a letter of authenticity from Sonny West.

Elvis's TV $5300 ✶ Purchased by an Elvis fan from Florida, this extravagantly priced TV was a limited-edition set presented to Elvis by RCA, and one of three originally installed in Elvis's bedroom. Elvis shot the TV in a fit of pique and covered it with a beach towel. Discovered by Elvis's uncle, the set was later repaired and is back in working order and was sold complete with the original remote.

457

Elvis's sixth-grade report card $8000 ✶ Sold at the MGM *Grand Hotel* auction dubbed the 'Graceland garage sale', the report card revealed that Elvis scored D grades in Maths and Geography – and an A in Music.

Home movie $12,500 ★ The most expensive Elvis item ever sold by Ebay was this four-minute film taken by a fan and showing Elvis at a motel in Florida, talking to fans before leaving for the set of *Follow That Dream* on which (in a great moment of pop culture) he would meet a young fan called Tom Petty.

Letter from Elvis £14,100 ★ Written by Elvis to Anita Wood while he was serving with the US Army in Germany in 1958, the letter was sold at auction in London in 2001. In it, Elvis referred to Anita as 'Widdle Bitty', and ended, 'Please don't let anyone read this.'

Web sites

Somehow, it was inevitable that the king of the whole wide world should be king of the World Wide Web. Best to set yourself a time limit while surfing or you could end up living in the King's cyberspace. But it's all out there: news, interviews, reviews, sightings, tasteless gags ...

General

http://groups.google.com/groups?q=alt.elvis.king&hl=en ★ You will probably find this Elvis newsgroup terribly addictive.

http://groups.google.com/groups?q=alt.elvis&hl=en ★ Time just flies by on this newsgroup.

www.elvis.com ★ The official site – get an Elvis email address but don't spend too long in the online shop or you'll go bankrupt.

www.elvisfind.com ★ The Elvis search engine.

www.elvis-memories.com ★ It's all here and we do mean all; almost too much to take in.

459

◀ The wonderful world of Christmas cards, Elvis-style

www.ibiblio.org/elvis/elvishom.html ★ The original unofficial Elvis homepage.

www.biwa.ne.jp/~presley ★ This Japanese fan site is a living archive of news about Elvis Presley, a fantastic much-cherished resource.

http://elvisandyou.com/home.html ★ Good gateway site, with general info, which also promotes the book *Elvis And You*.

www.elvis.com.au ★ Run by the Australian fan club, this is one of a handful of sites which are truly essential with news, interviews and reviews.

www.elvisnews.com ★ A very good news site with decent reviews.

www.elvispresleynews.com ★ News and interviews, although sometimes the interviews aren't that easy to read.

www.elvisunlimited.com ★ This gorgeous site from the Danish fan club is full of facts, news and info. Indeed it puts the official site slightly to shame.

http://members.tripod.com/beyondthereef__1/elvis.html ★ Info on Elvis the martial artist and rare songs he performed in concert.

http://filmsgraded.savantnetworks.com/elvis/elvis.htm ★ An impressive site with stories about the songs, and a stimulating guide to his catalogue of albums, official and bootleg, and details on where you can find them.

http://girlsguidetoelvis.com ★ Fetchingly decked out in one of El's favourite colours, pink, this is an essential gateway site, even if you're not a girl.

The King's kin, men and musicians

www.lisapresley.com ★ Buttonhead's own private piece of cyberspace.

www.geocities.com/Hollywood/Bungalow/4660/index.html ★ Joe Esposito's site, $20 for an autograph.

www.bootsrandolph.com ★ The joy of sax.

www.djfontana-tcb.com ★ Pay DJ a visit.

www.chipsmoman.com ★ 'Listen easy you can hear Chips calling …'

http://cdmemphis.com/norbert.html ★ Putt's awake and he's back in business.

Ten songs that passed Elvis by

One of the enduring frustrations of being an Elvis fan, especially in the 1970s, was how despite public offers of songs from the likes of Elton John and Bruce Springsteen, Elvis ended up recording makeweights like "This Is Our Dance". While the whole business of songs Elvis could or ought to have recorded is, alas, redundant, you can while away happy hours with this Elvis parlour game – and that's one of the most popular pursuits among Elvis sites on the Internet. Here's our contribution ...

Brown-Eyed Handsome Man
A Chuck Berry song which was a UK hit for **Buddy Holly**, it was another victim of the aborted studio sessions of August 1967. Snatches of it were recorded at the famous 'Million Dollar Quartet' session.

Golden Years
David Bowie is said to have written "Golden Years' hoping that Elvis might record it, though there is no record of the song being officially submitted to Elvis or to his publishing company. Of course, Bowie sung it himself in pretty much Presley fashion.

I Saw The Light
Elvis may have sung this **Hank Williams** classic at the *How Great Thou Art* sessions. The song is not mentioned, however, in the session notes and if Elvis tried it out it was not committed to tape.

I Will Always Love You
Originally a hit for its writer, **Dolly Parton**, in 1974, "I Will Always Love You" would surely have got an emotionally charged reading from Elvis. However, Parker's insistence that his publishing company received half the song rights ensured the King never cut it. 'Elvis loved it,' Dolly recalled, 'but we ran into a problem. He was here in Nashville recording, and wanted to do it. So Felton Jarvis got in touch with me and I got so excited. But then he said, "Of course Elvis has to have half the recording on the song. Everything he records, unless it's already a standard, Elvis has to have half the publishing." Well, I had just started my own publishing company. So I said, "I'm really sorry, but I don't give my publishing to nobody. If the song is that good, he'll record it anyway." Everybody told me I was crazy to

461

turn down Elvis, but thank God I said no, because the song made me more money than all the others put together. Elvis also loved "Coat Of Many Colours", but I wouldn't give up the publishing on that either.'

Only The Lonely
Roy Orbison was so certain his composition was tailor-made for Elvis he is rumoured to have travelled to Graceland to let the King hear it in person. Unfortunately he arrived at 6am, seemingly ignorant of Elvis's nocturnal habits. It was also turned down by the Everly Brothers, forcing Orbison himself to record it.

Ramblin' Rose
A late hit for **Nat King Cole** before he died from cancer, "Ramblin' Rose" was among the titles Elvis was to record at RCA's Hollywood studio on 22–23 August 1967 but at the last minute the sessions were cancelled.

Sitting' And Thinkin'
Written by **Charlie Rich**, Elvis loved the song but was prevented from cutting it both because of his inhibiting publishing situation and the fact it was felt that the lyrics conflicted with his image.

Stirring Up Feelings
A song that was on hold for Elvis when he was due to record in Nashville in early 1977, written by **Bill Rice and Jerry Foster** (Elvis did record Bill Rice's solo composition "Girl Next Door Went A' Walking" in 1960) specifically for Elvis. Several acts have recorded the tune but none had a hit with it.

Suzie Q
Try as James Burton might (and he often improvized a few bars in the studio) he couldn't get Elvis to record the old **Dale Hawkins** hit on which, as a 17-year-old, he had played the distinctive guitar licks.

There's A Fire Down Below
Written by Elvis's bass player, **Jerry Scheff**, "There's A Fire Down Below" was selected by Felton Jarvis for Elvis to record at the second Graceland sessions in October 1976. But only a rhythm track was laid down, as Elvis did not feel like recording. Jarvis carried the backing around with him in the forlorn hope that Elvis might be persuaded to add a vocal. The uptempo backing was eventually released on *The Jungle Room Sessions*, and even from the instrumental you can hear why Jarvis liked it.

http://home2.pi.be/verbrugp ★ 'John Wilkinson on rhythm guitar'.

www.theimperials.org ★ Get into an Imperial lather online.

www.jakehess.com ★ Elvis's favourite gospel singer. Don't be put off by the hairdo or the manic smile.

www.jordanaires.net ★ By rights the site should 'ooh' and 'aah' as it downloads.

www.kathywestmoreland.com ★ 'And the little girl with the high voice …'

www.scheff.com/jerry ★ 'Play the bass, Jerry.'

www.halblaine.com ★ As the man himself says 'Happy drums'.

www.charliemccoy.com ★ Charlie has played on *Double Trouble* and *Blonde On Blonde*. Not many people can say that.

www.jdsumner.com ★ JD's sweet sweet spirit still hovers over this site.

Specialist

http://greggers.granitecity.com/elvis/women/index.html ★ Elvis female co-stars: who they were, what happened to them.

www.doghaus.com/collection.html ★ Make of this what you will.

http://home.wxs.nl/~hruyter/elvis_on_tour.htm ★ Elvis on tour. In amazing detail.

http://home.mem.net/~welk/elvisdiaries.html ★ The strange case of the lost Elvis diaries, aka a mystery novel on the Web.

http://jubal.westnet.com/hyperdiscordia/sacred_heart_elvis.html ★ The First Church of Elvis. Not to be visited if blasphemy offends you or you don't like jokes about Elvis.

www.cs.virginia.edu/oracle/elvis.html ★ The Oracle of Elvis at Virginia allows you to play the Kevin Bacon game only with someone more charismatic.

www.elvisjeweler.com/tcbtlc.htm ★ Those TCB necklaces from Lowell Hays, the man who made most of them.

http://foia.fbi.gov/presley.htm ★ The King's FBI files. The ones you can see, anyway.

www.musicman.com/mp/ep.html ★ If you've ever wondered what *Blue Hawaii* was in Serbo-Croat, this collection of foreign Elvis movie posters is the place to be.

www.geocities.com/Nashville/5826 ★ The recording sessions lovingly detailed.

www.royaturner.com/elvis.html ★ Turner was the Tupeloan who introduced Elaine Dundy to Gladys's sister Lilian, and this wonderful site (which may take a while to download) focuses on the King's early years.

www.worldwideelvis.com ★ An essential waystation in cyberspace for collectors.

www.gwu.edu/~nsarchiv/nsa/elvis/elnix.html ★ Elvis and Nixon. Richard not Mojo or David.

www.courttv.com/legaldocs/newsmakers/wills/presley.html ★ Where there's the will.

Fan clubs

General/Search Directories

The Presley Connection ★ http://members.aol.com/presleyconnect

Search ★ www.elvis-presley.ca/fanclub.htm

Search ★ http://users.pandora.be/davidneale/elvis/epfc/index.html

International

Asia ★ www.elvisworldwide.com

Australia ★ www.elvis.com.au

Austria ★ www.always-elvis.com

Brazil ★ http://www4.sul.com.br/epkingd/index.htm

Chile ★ www.geocities.com/elvischile

Czech Republic ★ www.geocities.com/elviscz/start.html

Denmark ★ http://home7.inet.tele.dk/elvis/

Eire ★ www.irishelvisfanclub.com

Finland ★ www.phnet.fi/public/elvisclub/elvis1.htm

France ★ www.elvismyhappiness.com

Germany ★ www.elvisclubberlin.de

Hong Kong ★ www.elvis.org.hk

Italy ★ http://epresley.free.fr

New Zealand ★ http://elvisnz.com

Norway ★ www.flaming-star.com

Poland ★ www.kki.pl/elvisal

Portugal ★ http://cofeburningstar.homestead.com

Spain ★ http://pagina.de/clubelvis

Sweden ★ www.tcefanclub.com_

Turkey ★ www.elvisisinistanbulnow.com

UK ★ www.elvis-presley-fan-club.com

USA

Club Elvis ★ http://club-elvis.freeyellow.com

Elvis Extraganza ★ www.elvis-extravaganza.com

Jailhouse Rockers ★ www.geocities.com/hidden_lodge/newelvis.html

Florida ★ www.geocities.com/hidden_lodge/newelvis.html

Florida ★ http://members.aol.com/Betspage/index.html

Georgia ★ http://members.tripod.com/elvisstillrockn

Illinois ★ www.freehomepages.com/ecs

Memphis ★ www.geocities.com/Hollywood/
Club/8112/ElvisMemphisStyle.html

New York ★ http://hometown.aol.com/tcb4eapfanclub/club.html

North Carolina ★ www.angelfire.com/nc2/NevadaBlue/ElvisDeb.html_

Pennsylvania ★ http://pw1.netcom.com/~rnekich/aefc.htm

Virginia ★ http://touchedbyelvis.com

Index

This index is designed to point you to the most significant mentions of songs, movies, people, and places. *Song*, *album* and *movie titles* are in italics.

c

d

e

INDEX